"This is an outstanding and needed book. Michael Goheen gives us a distinctive introduction to mission study that takes full account of both the momentous changes happening in global Christianity and recent thinking about the missional nature of the church. Rich in its biblical and theological grasp of mission, the book addresses precisely the right issues confronting the mission of God's people today. This introductory text is accessible, balanced and, at times, profoundly moving. Readers beware! This book will reshape your thinking about the nature and practice of Christian mission."

Dean Flemming, MidAmerica Nazarene University

"*Introducing Christian Mission Today* is a well-written, accessible and comprehensive survey of mission theology. Michael Goheen provides the reader with an authoritative and balanced account of the salient developments—starting with a robust biblical theology that puts the mission of God at the dynamic center— that have transformed our understanding over the past century. This work edifies and challenges."

Wilbert R. Shenk, Fuller Graduate School of Intercultural Studies

"Based on Scripture and in light of current and historical developments, *Introducing Christian Mission Today* recalibrates the church's understanding of mission. Evangelical in spirit yet ecumenical in breadth, this is an important and stimulating introduction to the foundations, challenges and issues of Christian mission today."

Craig Ott, Trinity Evangelical Divinity School

"Michael Goheen has distilled some of the best of recent Western missiological thinking into a readable and well-organized presentation. The book is current and has God's entire, comprehensive and worldwide mission in view. There are also particular examples and focused discussions on such crucial topics as urban mission. Many congregations, individuals and mission agencies will find great insight and reap much benefit here."

J. Nelson Jennings, Overseas Ministries Study Center

"Michael W. Goheen has produced here more than an introduction to mission studies. In this volume of some four hundred pages he provides a comprehensive, scholarly survey of the biblical, historical and contemporary issues in world mission that will serve to inform a generation of students and pastors. It is a remarkable achievement."

Gerald H. Anderson, Overseas Ministries Study Center

"Very few people can combine multiple areas of expertise in their own thinking, let alone in a single book. Mike Goheen is one of those few. This wide-ranging survey is the fruit of a true teacher's passion for the whole scope of his discipline. We are led steadily to understand mission from its biblical foundations, in theological reflection, through millennia of historical practice, across multiple cultural and ecclesial contexts, to the most urgent issues facing the church in mission today and tomorrow. Theologically enriching, reliably informative, and both conceptually and practically challenging."

Christopher J. H. Wright, Langham Partnership

Introducing Christian Mission Today

Scripture, History and Issues

MICHAEL W. GOHEEN

IVP Academic

An imprint of InterVarsity Press
Downers Grove, Illinois

InterVarsity Press
P.O. Box 1400, Downers Grove, IL 60515-1426
World Wide Web: www.ivpress.com
Email: email@ivpress.com

InterVarsity Press® is the book-publishing division of InterVarsity Christian Fellowship/USA®, a movement of students and faculty active on campus at hundreds of universities, colleges and schools of nursing in the United States of America, and a member movement of the International Fellowship of Evangelical Students. For information about local and regional activities, write Public Relations Dept., InterVarsity Christian Fellowship/USA, 6400 Schroeder Rd., P.O. Box 7895, Madison, WI 53707-7895, or visit the IVCF website at www.intervarsity.org.

All Scripture quotations, unless otherwise indicated, are from the THE HOLY BIBLE, NEW INTERNATIONAL VERSION® NIV®, Copyright© 1973, 1978, 1984, 2011 by Biblica, Inc.™ Used by permission. All rights reserved worldwide.

While all stories in this book are true, some names and identifying information in this book have been changed to protect the privacy of the individuals involved.

Cover design: Cindy Kiple
Interior design: Beth Hagenberg
Images: Huang Xin/Getty Images

ISBN 978-0-8308-4047-2 (print)
ISBN 978-0-8308-9543-4 (digital)

Printed in the United States of America ∞

Library of Congress Cataloging-in-Publication Data

Goheen, Michael W., 1955-
 Introducing Christian mission today : scripture, history, and issues /
 Michael W. Goheen.
    pages cm
 Includes bibliographical references and index.
 ISBN 978-0-8308-4047-2 (hardcover : alk. paper)
 1. Mission of the church. 2. Missions—Theory. I. Title.
 BV601.8.G64 2014
 266--dc23

                                                                                            2014012656

P 26 25 24 23 22 21 20 19 18 17 16 15 14 13 12 11 10 9 8 7 6 5

Y 36 35 34 33 32 31 30 29 28 27 26 25 24 23 22 21

To Lesslie Newbigin, George Vandervelde and Jan Jongeneel

Contents

Preface

ભ

THIS BOOK ARISES OUT OF A COURSE that I have taught for twenty-five years in a number of undergraduate and graduate institutions. When I first taught an introduction to mission course in 1988, I struggled to structure the course in keeping with the momentous changes taking place in the world church and mission during the twentieth century. I was acutely aware of the inadequacy of the colonialist paradigm, which had given rise to a certain way of teaching missiology. But I did not know a better way to proceed. After teaching the course a few times, I happened upon David Bosch's *Transforming Mission* days after it was released. I devoured that book. I saw a new path for mission studies and a new way to structure an introductory course. Of course, today, over two decades after the release of that book, we know its importance. It has served to help many reconfigure and restructure their way of teaching missiology in a new setting where the church is now in every part of the world.

I have used Bosch's book many times in courses but have found that its length and density are sometimes prohibitive for students. I hoped that someone would offer a more popular version that employed Bosch's basic structure that I could use as a textbook. Although many good books on mission have emerged since that time, none has tried to cover the waterfront of mission studies as his does yet in a more popular way. And as I faced the difficulty, in almost every chapter of this book, of trying to summarize enormous amounts of material in brief chapters, I understand why! Nevertheless, I have persevered, and I offer this as a more popular introduction to mission studies. It is intended as an introductory book for students and pastors.

I start with the *missio Dei* as narrated in the biblical story and place the mission of the church in that narrative context. Mission is participation in the story of God's mission. The role that the people of God are to play in that story gives them their missional identity. Thus, the church is missional by its very nature, and the whole of its mission springs from this identity. So this book roots mission in ecclesiology; it is thus a missiology that takes the church with utmost importance—something that is surprisingly rare. It is also a missiology that takes history seriously, attempting to understand and learn from the church as it has carried out its mission in various historical and cultural contexts. It is, moreover, a missiology that takes the global context seriously, formulating a missiology that understands mission to be in, from, and to all parts of the world. It is, finally, a missiology that takes the contemporary context seriously. The various tasks facing the global church today in its different settings set the agenda for mission.

No one is neutral, of course. And so my confessional and geographical location has greatly shaped this book. Considered from a global perspective, I stand in the Evangelical tradition. More specifically, the authors who have shaped me most are J. H. Bavinck, Harvie Conn, Lesslie Newbigin and David Bosch. And so it is from within the Reformed tradition that this introductory book arises. Bavinck and Conn set the structural girders for my thinking early, and that early foundational formation remains to the present. And so my approach to missiology stands more narrowly within the Dutch Neocalvinist tradition, although I hope that my appreciation for many other traditions is evident. My indebtedness to Newbigin and Bosch at many points will be obvious. I believe them to be the leading mission thinkers in the latter part of the twentieth century, and therefore I have attempted to read all of their writings. I have also benefited tremendously from many others. I think specifically of Hendrik Kraemer, Wilbert Shenk, Gerald Anderson, Darrell Guder, Chris Wright, Andrew Walls, George Vandervelde and Jan Jongeneel.

I am also a Canadian, and no doubt this will be evident as well. It is the Western context that informs my scholarship, but I have attempted to listen to brothers and sisters from outside the West. I have had many opportunities for interaction with brothers and sisters from other parts of the world. I have also taught a course in contextual theology for a number of years, most recently at Regent College, Vancouver, and this has helped me hear voices from other parts of the world. Both my reading and personal contact have contributed to a more global perspective in my own thinking, as well as enriching and correcting my thinking. No doubt I have not quoted them as much as I should, but their insight has shaped my work more than what appears in the footnotes.

I am thankful to Dean Flemming, Mark Glanville and Albert Strydhorst, who have taken the time to read earlier versions of the whole manuscript, as well as Mike Williams, Chris Gonzalez, Tim Sheridan, Wilbert Shenk and Andrew Beunk, who read certain chapters. They have offered helpful comments and critique, and as usual, I am unable to incorporate all their good suggestions, sometimes because of inability and sometimes because of time. I am also grateful for my family, who have discussed with me as well as practiced much of what is in this book. My wife, Marnie, and many of my grown "children," as well as some of their spouses, have taken the course out of which this book arises. All have taken their role in God's mission, and many of the topics of this book continue to be fodder for ongoing family discussion. I have also learned much from my brothers and sisters in the congregations where I am set. My present congregations, both New West Christian Reformed Church in Burnaby, British Columbia, and Missio Dei Communities in Tempe, Arizona, have been a source of enrichment that has contributed to my understanding of mission. The Geneva Society has given oversight to a chair in worldview studies that I have occupied over the past seven years. The Oikodome foundation and Pieter and Fran Vanderpol have funded it. Both have enabled me to carry out my scholarly calling, of which this book is a part. I have been warmly received by the Missional Training Center—Phoenix, by Calvin Theological Seminary as the Jake and Betsy Tuls Chair of Missiology, and by Newbigin House of Studies as professor of missional theology in the next stage of my academic career, but I remain deeply grateful for the sacrifice and work of the many who were involved with the funding and oversight of the Geneva Chair. Finally, my thanks go to Daniel Reid at InterVarsity Press, who has supported this project from the beginning even though many factors have prohibited me from getting the manuscript in on time.

There is a website that supports this book along with others I have written.

There are many free resources, ranging from scholarly and popular papers to PowerPoint presentations of all sorts, in the areas of biblical story, worldview and mission. Professors who use this book as a text will be able to find Powerpoint presentations for lectures and syllabi there that may be used for an introductory course in mission. That website is www.mission worldview.com.

I worked on my PhD dissertation for a decade studying Newbigin as well as the missiological developments that informed his thinking. During that time, not only the life and writings of Lesslie Newbigin, but also the expert supervision of both Jan Jongeneel and George Vandervelde, helped me refine my thinking in missiology. George and Lesslie are with the Lord, while Jan continues to be academically productive in retirement. I dedicate this book to those three men.

Introduction

A Paradigm Shift in Mission Studies Today

C03

When the words "mission" or "missions" or "missionary" or "mission field" or "missiology" are used today in many Christian circles, the traditional idea of *geographical expansion* still predominates. Mission is considered to be a unidirectional activity that proceeds from the West to other parts of the world such as Africa, Asia or Latin America. A mission organization or denominational mission arm is the agency that sends missionaries to do certain tasks. The home base where these sending institutions are located is the Christian West, and the mission field is a non-Christian area outside the West. In its traditional understanding, missiology is the discipline that studies the issues arising from the geographical expansion of Western Christianity into other cultures.

This use of the word "mission" carries resonances of the traditional practice of the modern missionary enterprise of the last two centuries. But it also points to the theological concern of taking the gospel to those who need to hear it.

> In its traditional understanding, missiology is the discipline that studies the issues arising from the geographical expansion of Western Christianity into other cultures.

During the twentieth century the word "mission" began to be used with growing frequency in Christian circles and was broadened significantly in the process. Nevertheless, the word still carries much of the theological and traditional meaning of the modern missionary movement, at least in the Evangelical tradition.

The word "mission" derives from the Latin word *mittere*, "to send," and thus assumes a sender, someone sent, a place or persons to whom the messenger is sent, and a task to fulfill. The Jesuits were first to use this word when in their fourth vow they promised obedience to the pope in regard to mission outside the church's fellowship—including Protestants—to gather them in to mother church. Given this origin, it is surprising to see how quickly Protestants employed the word to describe their task of propagating the gospel among those who had never heard. Indeed, mission had become a new orthodoxy by the end of the nineteenth century, and today for the most part, at least in the Evangelical tradition, the word continues to carry positive connotations.

At the beginning of the eighteenth century over 90 percent of Christians in the world were found in the West. Thus, an important motivation for the missionary expansion that took place over the next two hundred years was the biblical motive to take the good news of Jesus Christ to people and places where there was no witness. But at the same time this missionary activity coincided with Western colonialism. Thus, the course and the practice of Western Christianity's geographical expansion were deeply shaped by colonialist patterns.

"Colonialism and mission, as a matter of course, were interdependent; the right to have colonies carried with it the duty to Christianize the colonized."

David J. Bosch, *Transforming Mission*, p. 227

Over the course of the last half-century many factors combined to make a traditional understanding of mission unsuitable for today. This is not to say that the missionary enterprise of the nineteenth and twentieth centuries was a mistake. Indeed, a scriptural impetus drove much of the motivation and practice of mission. Nor do I want to eclipse cross-cultural missions. The concern to take good news to places where there is no witness remains a continuing aspect of the church's mission. It is rather to say that dramatic changes in the twentieth and twenty-first centuries have made a traditional paradigm of mission inadequate for our time.

CHANGING WORLD CHURCH

Over the past century a dramatic demographic shift has taken place in the world church. Until just over a quarter of a century ago the majority of Christians lived in the Western world, especially Europe and North America. However, over the past century the center of gravity has shifted southward and eastward to Africa, Asia and South America. Whereas the overwhelming majority of Christians lived in the West when the modern missionary movement began, today perhaps as many as two-thirds to three-quarters of the world's Christians live in places outside the West. As Philip Jenkins summarizes, "The era of Western Christianity has passed within our lifetimes, and the day of Southern Christianity is dawning."[1]

"A Christian Rip Van Winkle, who fell asleep under a tree midway through the twentieth century and then woke up this past week to the sound of church bells (or a synthesizer with drums) on a Sunday morning, would not recognize the shifted shape of world Christianity. It is as if the globe had been turned upside down and sideways. A few short decades ago, Christian believers were concentrated in the global north and west, but now a rapidly swelling majority lives in the global south and east. As Rip Van Winkle wiped a half-century of sleep from his eyes and tried to locate his fellow Christian believers, he would find them in surprising places, expressing their faith in surprising ways, under surprising conditions, with surprising relationships to culture and politics, and raising surprising theological questions that would not have seemed possible when he fell asleep."

Mark A. Noll, *The New Shape of World Christianity*, pp. 19-20

Numerical growth does not tell the whole story of this revolution. While there remains much need in churches of the South and the East, and while the church in those parts of the world is not always faithful to the gospel, it is also true that there is much vitality in the Southern church evidenced in

---

[1]Philip Jenkins, *The Next Christendom: The Coming of Global Christianity* (Oxford: Oxford University Press, 2002), p. 3.

worship and prayer, and in doctrinal and moral faithfulness. Moreover, the churches in the South and the East have now begun to take responsibility for the lion's share of cross-cultural missions.

The dramatic growth of the church in the South and the East has coincided with steep decline in the older churches of the West. Today Christians in Europe and European-derived cultures only make up about 15 percent of the total Christian population. David Barrett estimated almost three decades ago that the Western church was losing about 7,600 professing members every day.[2] Lamin Sanneh's estimate a decade ago, 4,300 people per day,[3] was lower; nevertheless, it is clear that the church in the West is dwindling. Moreover, the numerical decline is accompanied by deep compromise to the secular humanist worldview of Western culture. And alongside of the growing participation in cross-cultural missions of churches in the majority world, the church in the West has seen a corresponding decline.

> TODAY CHRISTIANS IN EUROPE AND EUROPEAN-DERIVED CULTURES ONLY MAKE UP ABOUT 15 PERCENT OF THE TOTAL CHRISTIAN POPULATION.

This brief sketch is not intended to simply paint a romantic and rosy picture of the church in the South and the East, nor a dark and gloomy picture of the church in the West. Indeed, there is much to be concerned about in African, Asian and Latin American Christianity, and much to be heartened by in Western Christianity. This characterization is rather to indicate a significant shift in global Christianity that makes a traditional view of mission inadequate for today. In light of these statistics it would seem absurd to divide the world into a Christian home base and a non-Christian mission field, and to classify the growing churches of the South and the East as a mission field and the declining churches of the West as the home base for Christian mission.

Beyond the growing Southern church and the declining Western church,

---

[2] David B. Barrett, ed., *World Christian Encyclopedia: A Comparative Study of Churches and Religions in the Modern World, AD 1900-2000* (Oxford: Oxford University Press, 1982), p. 7.
[3] Lamin Sanneh, *Whose Religion Is Christianity? The Gospel beyond the West* (Grand Rapids: Eerdmans, 2003), p. 15.

a third factor in the global church is transforming mission today: the explosive growth of the global Pentecostal church. The year 1980 was a watershed year in the history of Christianity because two things happened: the number of nonwhite Christians surpassed the number of white Christians for the first time, and Pentecostals surpassed all other Protestant groups to become the biggest in the world.[4] Perhaps the term "Pentecostal" is the imposition of a Western category on the growing churches of the South and the East; these churches often manifest marks that have been associated with Pentecostal churches, yet these are indigenous churches that differ significantly from each other. For the moment, there is no easy categorization, so I will continue to use the term "Pentecostal" with the hope that a more suitable way of classifying these churches will emerge.

"Already today, the largest Christian communities on the planet are to be found in Africa and Latin America. If we want to visualize a 'typical' contemporary Christian, we should think of a woman living in a village in Nigeria or in a Brazilian *favela*."

"Soon, the phrase 'a White Christian' may sound like a curious oxymoron, as mildly surprising as 'a Swedish Buddhist.' Such people can exist, but a slight eccentricity is implied."

Philip Jenkins, *The Next Christendom*, pp. 2, 3

In 1980, after less than a century of existence, Pentecostals had grown to become one of the three largest Protestant communions in the world. They joined the Anglican and Baptist churches, all with numbers around 50 million adherents. By 2000 the Anglicans had grown to 76 million, the Baptists to 110 million, and the Pentecostals to over 400 million. Today Pentecostals may number as many as 500 million. They continue to grow at the remarkable rate of 55,000 per day and 20 million each year. The large majority of Pentecostals are found in the churches of the South and the East. Perhaps it is true that because of its short history and incredible growth rates,

---

[4]Vinson Synan, *The Spirit Said "Grow": The Astounding Worldwide Expansion of Pentecostal and Charismatic Churches* (Monrovia, CA: MARC, 1992), p. 5.

"the appearance of the Pentecostal-charismatic movement may well be the single most important fact of twentieth century Christianity."[5]

For the past five centuries it has been primarily three traditions—Roman Catholic, Protestant Evangelical and Protestant Ecumenical—that have carried the mission of the church. But Pentecostals, especially those from the two-thirds world, constitute a fifth tradition beyond Eastern Orthodoxy, Roman Catholicism and the Protestant Evangelical and Ecumenical traditions. Thus, they bring a fresh approach to mission, and their sheer numbers and vitality play a role in the changing face of mission today.

Changing Global Realities

The factors leading to a new paradigm of mission are not only those associated with the global transformation of the church. There are also significant global realities and megatrends that set the context for the church's mission. The first is the *collapse of colonialism* in the twentieth century. During the twenty-five year period from 1878 to 1914 European countries seized more than ten million square miles of land and subjugated a half billion people—half of the non-European people in the world—in Asia and Africa. This Western global dominance shaped the missionary enterprise of the late nineteenth and early twentieth centuries. Missionaries flowed along the paths of colonial rule. Beginning in 1947 on the Indian subcontinent and continuing through the next two decades virtually every nation under European colonial rule gained its independence. To the degree that the mindset, strategies, structures and practices of cross-cultural missions had been formed in this Western colonial milieu, its collapse brought the challenge to rethink the entire approach to mission.

> To the degree that the mindset, strategies, structures and practices of cross-cultural missions had been formed in this Western colonial milieu, its collapse brought the challenge to rethink the entire approach to mission.

A second factor is *globalization*.[6] The global dominance of Western civi-

---

[5]Ibid., p. 1.
[6]The theme of globalization and its implications is central in the proposal for a new World Council of Churches Affirmation on Mission and Evangelism submitted by the Commission on World

lization has been a feature of the world for many centuries. However, toward the end of the twentieth century the term "globalization" became quite popular to define a new global reality. Globalization is the spread of the modern Western story of economic progress around the world, especially with the use of new information technology. Globalization is the "single most adequate way of describing the context in which we work today."[7] It has beneficial potential but also has been the source of a consumer society in the West, a growing gap between rich and poor, ecological destruction, a massive displacement of peoples, and a homogenizing force imposing the spirit of Western culture on the cultures of the world. René Padilla believes it to be "the greatest challenge that the Christian mission faces,"[8] and Richard Bauckham agrees, devoting the last chapter of his book *Bible and Mission* to the church's mission in a globalized world.[9]

A third factor, a result of a globalized world, is *urbanization*. In 1800 only 5% of the world's population lived in cities. One hundred years later the number had risen modestly to about 14%. But by the year 2000 over half of the world's population could be counted as urban, and by the middle of the twenty-first century this will rise to 80%. Cities represent powerful centers of cultural, economic and political dominance in the world. The urban setting is also the scene of the enormous social and economic problems facing the world. The 2010 World Disasters Report focused on violence, health problems and other issues facing the urban population.[10] The cities are also the place where people live! We face an urban future, and the city represents mission's "new frontier."[11]

A fourth factor is the *staggering social and economic problems* that afflict

---

Mission and Evangelism (CWME), "Together Towards Life: Mission and Evangelism in Changing Landscapes," dated September 5, 2012 (www.oikoumene.org/en/resources/documents/wcc-commissions/mission-and-evangelism/together-towards-life-mission-and-evangelism-in-changing-landscapes.html).

[7]Robert Schreiter, "Major Currents of Our Time: What They Mean for Preaching the Gospel," *Catholic News Service* 31, no. 11 (August 16, 2001). See www.dominicains.ca/providence/english/documents/schreiter.htm for a shorter version of the larger article.

[8]C. René Padilla, "Mission at the Turn of the Century/Millennium," *Evangel* 19, no. 1 (2001): 6.

[9]Richard Bauckham, *Bible and Mission: Christian Witness in a Postmodern World* (Grand Rapids: Baker Academic, 2003), pp. 83-112.

[10]"World Disasters Report 2010: Focus on Urban Risk" (www.ifrc.org/Global/Publications/disasters/WDR/WDR2010-full.pdf).

[11]Roger S. Greenway and Timothy M. Monsma, *Cities: Mission's New Frontier* (Grand Rapids: Baker Books, 1989).

our world. The level of poverty and hunger in our world is alarming. Three billion people, almost half of the world's population, live on less than $2.50 per day, and 80% of the world's population on less than $10 per day. Thirty thousand children die each day due to poverty, and 1.5 billion people live below the international poverty line. Although enough food is produced in the world to feed everyone, 854 million people do not have enough to eat, and the number is growing each year. Tragically, most of those who are hungry are women and children. And things are not improving; in fact, the gap between the rich and poor is growing. In 1960 the richest billion were thirty times richer than poorest billion, while in 1990 that number had doubled to sixty times, and today it is almost ninety times. The income ratio between the richest to the poorest was 44 to 1 in 1973 but had risen to 74 to 1 by the end of the century. The wealthiest 20% of the world's population accounted for 76.6% of consumption of the world's resources, while the poorest fifth consumed 1.5%. Americans spend $8 billion on cosmetics and $17 billion on pet food, while $6 billion is needed for education for all, $9 billion for water and sanitation for all, and $13 billion for health and nutrition for all. The primary problem driving poverty, hunger and the growing gap between rich and poor are unjust structures—corrupt governments, inequitable global markets, worldwide arms race, structural consumerism, massive third-world debt, and more.

One can add to this a long list of other social and economic problems that boggle the mind: the HIV-AIDS epidemic, which has been called "the greatest human emergency in history";[12] organized crime, heavily involved in human trafficking, the prostitution and the sex "industry," drug trafficking and more, ruining lives and raking in over $1 trillion a year; escalating numbers of wars fueled by racial, ethnic, religious and ideological animosities in which over 75 percent of the victims are civilians; a crisis of uprooted peoples and mass migration caused by conflict, persecution, natural disasters and poverty; gender inequality that leaves women much more vulnerable to violence, illiteracy and poverty; growing violence, terrorism and crises in the areas of food, education and healthcare, along with other areas, could be added.

---

[12]Bryant L. Myers, *Exploring World Mission: Context and Challenges* (Monrovia, CA: World Vision International, 2003), p. 68.

Two crises threaten the very existence of the planet: nuclear and environmental. There are between forty thousand and fifty thousand nuclear warheads in the world, capable of destroying the world sixty times over. Nine countries are armed with nuclear weapons, with the potential of up to twenty more in the next decade. Over $1 trillion is spent annually on arms, an expenditure that could feed the world's hungry for years. A UN environmental study said about a decade ago that "the planet is poised on a precipice, and time is running out for making tough, economic and political choices that can pull it back from disaster."[13] We face global warming, protective ozone layer depletion, acid rain, loss of biodiversity, toxic chemical waste, deforestation, air and water pollution, a depleting energy supply, looming water shortage, unbridled harvesting of resources of ocean floor, and more. Much of the problem is driven by a faith commitment to economic growth and an accompanying runaway consumer culture that lives off designed waste. If the whole world used resources at the rate that North Americans do, the world's resources would last about ten years. If Jesus in his mission "launches an all-out attack on evil in all its manifestations," the church is called to do likewise.[14]

Fifth, the *soaring population* of the last century, which shows no signs of abating, brings new challenges to mission. Although there is decline in parts of the West and in Japan, the overall global picture is one of escalating growth. When William Carey set sail for India in the late eighteenth century, there were not yet 1 billion people in the world. That number would not be reached until 1830. It took another century until in 1930 there were 2 billion people. The third billion came thirty years later (1960), and the fourth fourteen years after that (1974). By 2000 world population passed the 6 billion mark, and we passed 7 billion in 2011. While the global population explosion increases pressure on the limited resources of the earth and contributes to growing poverty, it also heightens the evangelistic challenge of reaching this burgeoning number of people with the good news.

---

[13]Klaus Toephler, director of the UN Environment Programme, Nairobi, Kenya, in "United Nations Environmental Study 2002 Report," quoted in "Transition to a Sustainable Civilisation," *New Paradigm* 1, no. 1 (2006) (www.newparadigmjournal.com/March2006/transition .htm).

[14]David Bosch, *Transforming Mission: Paradigm Shifts in Theology of Mission* (Maryknoll, NY: Orbis Books, 1991), p. 32.

Sixth, we are witnessing a *resurgence in religions* around the world. At the beginning of the twentieth century it was predicted that the "acids of modernity"[15]—science, technology, the new consumer culture—would corrode religious belief, and that all religions would wither away and die. And it seemed in the "secular sixties" that this prediction would be fulfilled. Instead, today we see a renaissance of all religions. Christianity has grown from 558 million people in 1900 to 2.3 billion today, a 1.3% growth rate. At the beginning of the twentieth century both Muslims and Hindus numbered about 200 million.

> WHILE THE GLOBAL POPULATION EXPLOSION INCREASES PRESSURE ON THE LIMITED RESOURCES OF THE EARTH AND CONTRIBUTES TO GROWING POVERTY, IT ALSO HEIGHTENS THE EVANGELISTIC CHALLENGE OF REACHING THIS BURGEONING NUMBER OF PEOPLE WITH THE GOOD NEWS.

At the beginning of the twenty-first century Muslims number 1.6 billion, a growth of about 1.8%, and Hindus number just under 1 billion, a growth rate of 1.4%. There is, moreover, a rebirth of spirituality in the West among those who have abandoned traditional religion. We observe not only the growth of religious commitment but also the increasing tension among religions groups and the advance of fundamentalism in all religious traditions. Not only is religious plurality a fact in many countries of the world, but also the growth of ideological pluralism that has given up on a search for truth is a global phenomenon. All of this leaves the Christian church with a difficult path to navigate in its mission to adherents of other faiths.

Finally, *tectonic cultural shifts in Western culture* establish a new context for mission today. These shifts affect not only the church and its mission in the West but also the global church because the globalization of Western culture especially in urban centers impacts the church in every part of the world. The economic dimension of Western culture that began to emerge as an ascendant power in the eighteenth century has become the dominant spirit overriding all others as it shapes our culture today. The profit motive and market are driving all areas of Western culture. A consumer society that dominates every aspect of life has emerged. Technological changes have

---

[15]Walter Lippmann, "The Acids of Modernity," in *A Preface to Morals* (New York: Macmillan, 1929), pp. 51-67.

been nothing short of dizzying. The digital revolution, information and media technology, medical technology and nanotechnology are raising enormous issues and changing the face of Western culture in many ways. Much technology has been pulled into the wake of economic currents; for example, computers enable global finance, and advertising in media stimulates consumerism. Yet it has done much more. Information overload leads to disorientation, apathy, chronic boredom and decreasing wisdom. We also see a new, postmodern spirit that is suspicious of truth claims and authority, that longs for relationship, that values subjective experience, that is rooted in local context, and that is skeptical of certainty. These and other changes in Western culture demand a fresh look at our context and how it influences mission in the West and also beyond.

A New Understanding of Mission

This book will explore mission today, but by way of preliminary anticipation I can indicate a new understanding that is emerging by way of four definitions. The first definition derives from the World Council of Churches ecumenical missionary conference in Mexico City in 1963, which enunciated its theme as "witness in six continents." If one considers mission from the standpoint of geography, then mission is not to three continents (Asia, Africa, Latin America) from two continents (Europe, North America). Rather, it is *from* all six continents, including Africa and Asia; it is *to* all six continents, including Europe and North America; and it is *in* all six continents. The whole of God's world is a mission field, and the "base" for mission is in every congregation in every part of the world. The definition does not yet tell us what mission is; it simply challenges old geographical notions and opens broader horizons. We can move further along the path of probing the meaning of mission by considering the following definitions.

Christopher Wright offers as a definition "our committed participation as God's people, at God's invitation and command, in God's own mission within the history of the world for the redemption of God's creation."[16] This definition moves us away from misunderstanding mission as first of all what the church does. Rather, the church must understand its mission as partici-

---

[16]Christopher J. H. Wright, *The Mission of God: Unlocking the Bible's Grand Narrative* (Downers Grove, IL: InterVarsity Press, 2006), pp. 22-23 (italics removed).

pation in the mission of the triune God. And this mission has a communal nature: it is a mission of God's people. Often evangelism and cross-cultural missions are understood in individualistic ways. However, mission is the calling of a people. Finally, the scope of mission is as broad as creation because God's mission is the redemption of his whole world.

> THE CHURCH MUST UNDERSTAND ITS MISSION AS PARTICIPATION IN THE MISSION OF THE TRIUNE GOD. AND THIS MISSION HAS A COMMUNAL NATURE: IT IS A MISSION OF GOD'S PEOPLE.

A third definition follows the lead of four Dutch missiologists who want to replace the "the paradigm of 'expansion' with one of 'communication.'"[17] Mission is the communication of the gospel. Mission is no longer primarily understood as the geographical expansion of Christianity, but rather as the task given to God's people everywhere to communicate the good news not only with their words but also with their lives and deeds. Mission is witness in life, word and deed. Putting "life" before "word" and "deed" is intentional: the gospel is first of all communicated in the lives of believers, both in their communal life together and as they are scattered in the world. Flowing from the new power at work transforming their lives will be words and deeds that further communicate the gospel.

A final definition follows a similar path. Mission is the whole church taking the whole gospel to the whole person in the whole world. This definition is a slight variation on the wording found in official documents from the Ecumenical and Evangelical traditions. In 1963 the statement from the ecumenical missionary conference in Mexico City spoke of mission as "the common witness of the whole Church, bringing the whole Gospel to the whole world."[18] In 1974 the evangelical Lausanne Covenant followed suit when it said, "World evangelization requires the whole church to take the whole gospel to the whole world" (paragraph 6). This was affirmed again in 2010 by the Third Lausanne Congress, meeting in Cape Town, in the preamble of the "Cape Town Commitment": "*The Lausanne Covenant* defined

[17]F. J. Verstraelen, A. Camps, L. A. Hoedemaker and M. R. Spindler, *Missiology: An Ecumenical Introduction; Texts and Contexts of Global Christianity* (Grand Rapids: Eerdmans, 1995), p. 1.
[18]Ronald K. Orchard, ed., *Witness in Six Continents: Records of the Meeting of the Commission on World Mission and Evangelism of the World Council of Churches Held in Mexico City, December 8th to 19th, 1963* (London: Edinburgh House Press, 1964), p. 175.

evangelization as 'the *whole Church taking the whole gospel to the whole world.*' That is still our passion."[19]

It is the whole church, not just missionaries or evangelists. It is the whole gospel for the whole person, not a "spiritual" gospel for the soul or a "social" gospel for the body. It is in the whole world, not just in certain parts of the world labeled "mission field."

THE LANDSCAPE OF MISSION STUDIES TODAY

The church's mission is always contextual. The church must always ascertain what the issues of the day are and address those. Missiology must remain rooted in the gospel and the Word of God. But it also must address the times and places in which it lives. Thus missiology will vary from place to place and time to time. If we take seriously the context sketched out in this introductory chapter, we must ask, what kinds of subjects arise that are important to study in missiology today? If we want a relevant and contextual missiology, what are the burning issues that must be part of mission studies today?

First, there must be a *fresh reflection on Scripture and mission.* The opportunity that presents itself to the church today is to return to the Bible and judge our understanding of mission by the scriptural text. When the church is confident of its mission, it is more likely to find texts to support its activity. Uncertainty can drive us back to the text. It is essential at this time that what drives mission not be the global context, as important as that is, but rather the light of Scripture. Whereas in the past a few texts such as the Great Commission (Mt 28:19-20) undergird the church's mission, we now need to see the centrality of God's mission in the biblical story and the missional role that the church plays. Happily, a missional hermeneutic is developing today that attends to the central importance of mission in interpreting Scripture. Moreover, in the past the universalization of an Enlightenment methodology has masked

> MISSIOLOGY MUST REMAIN ROOTED IN THE GOSPEL AND THE WORD OF GOD. BUT IT ALSO MUST ADDRESS THE TIMES AND PLACES IN WHICH IT LIVES.

---

[19]The Lausanne Movement, "The Cape Town Commitment" (www.lausanne.org/ctcommit ment).

the local character of a Western hermeneutical approach to Scripture sup-
pressing other contextual approaches and marginalizing mission. Today the
growing reflection of third-world theology is enabling us to profit from contextual theologies that see mission as central to the biblical story.

And so a return to the biblical story will demand deepened theological
reflection to empower the mission of the church. For too long abstract theological reflection has parted ways with the mission of the church.[20] We certainly will need renewed theological work on the mission of God and of the
church, but it will also be essential to recover the "missional nature of all
theology"[21] and so to address other theological themes that shape the
church's mission at a deep level—biblical themes such as the nature of the
gospel, Christology, kingdom of God and eschatology, pneumatology (doctrine of the Spirit), ecclesiology (doctrine of the church), anthropology
(doctrine of humanity), soteriology (doctrine of salvation) and culture.

A second task for missiology today is to *reassess the way we understand
the history of mission*. An African proverb says that until lions have their
historians, the hunter will always be the hero of the story. History is always
told from some standpoint, and its result is to invite us to participate in a
story. The history of mission in the past most often has been told from a
Western perspective. Moreover, it has been told from the standpoint of the
geographical spread of the gospel, and so this view governed the selection,
organization and interpretation of the narrative. The question that confronts
missiology today is this: how do you write mission history if all of the global
church's life is mission?

A third task that missiology must engage is fresh reflection on the *nature
of mission*. What is mission anyway? Twentieth-century studies have returned to the mission of the triune God as the starting point for mission. As
the people of God participate in God's mission, the church understands
itself to be "missionary by its very nature." Thus, all of life is to make known

---

[20]"Laypersons in the church would perhaps have been within their rights to bring a class-action
suit against systematic theologians for criminal pastoral and missiological negligence" (Kevin
Vanhoozer, "'One Rule to Rule Them All?' Theological Method in an Era of World Christianity,"
in *Globalizing Theology: Belief and Practice in an Era of World Christianity*, ed. Craig Ott and
Harold A. Netland [Grand Rapids: Baker Academic, 2006], p. 93).

[21]Timothy C. Tennent, *Invitation to World Missions: A Trinitarian Missiology for the Twenty-first
Century* (Grand Rapids: Kregel, 2010), pp. 60-61.

the good news in life, word and deed. How do we relate this broader understanding of mission to some of the more narrow tasks that have been studied in mission in the past, such as evangelism, deeds of mercy and justice, and cross-cultural missions? Have we overcome the dualistic heritage bequeathed to us that splits word from deed? When we view the staggering social and economic problems of our world, surely the people of God living in God's new world of justice and shalom cannot be oblivious to these problems but rather will seek ways of embodying and seeking justice and compassion in keeping with the gospel. In a world longing for good news of justice God's people can offer the good news of God's kingdom. How do evangelism, mercy and justice relate to the life of the church and the callings of believers in culture? Is there still a place for cross-cultural mission, and what does that look like in a world where there is a church in every corner of it? In fact, this will be an important issue: with the broadening of mission, it is essential to see the place for taking the gospel to those who have never heard in other parts of the world. These are some of the questions and issues that need continued reflection as missiology struggles toward a biblical vision of mission.

Fourth, the growth of the church in every culture of the world makes the issue of *contextualization*—the relation of the gospel and church to its cul-

---

"The church only becomes the church as it responds to God's call to mission, and to be in mission means to change continually as the gospel encounters new and diverse contexts. Such change, however, is not arbitrary; rather, there have always existed certain *constants* that, while they might differ in content, are always present as a kind of framework by which the church identifies itself and around which the gospel message takes shape."

Stephen Bevans and Roger Schroeder, *Constants in Context*, p. 72

---

tural context—an important one. Today, with a global church, we see many different expressions and theologies as the gospel incarnates itself in various cultures. This creates difficult issues that surround two major sets of questions. The first is the relation of the gospel to cultures (plural). There is one gospel and yet many embodiments in the various cultures of the world. How can we be faithful to one gospel without privileging one cultural expression? How can we honor diverse expressions without falling into relativism? The second is the relation of the gospel to culture (singular). How do we relate the gospel to a particular culture? How can it be both at home and at odds in each context? How can the gospel both affirm the creational good and confront the idolatries of each culture? Contextualization studies that struggle with these questions will be an essential item on the agenda of missiology today.

Fifth, as a particular subset of contextualization studies, the issue of *the gospel and Western culture* must be prominent. The long history of the gospel in the West makes it difficult for us to gain a critical distance on our culture. Much of the church's life, including its missionary enterprise, has been shaped by Western cultural assumptions that are not in line with the gospel. Moreover, how can we recover a missionary consciousness that has been stunted by the false assumption that we live in a Christian or a neutral culture? Where can Western Christians receive the gift of new eyes to see the idolatry that shapes its culture? Further, we are more aware today that we live in a "mission field," if by that term we mean a culture and people who need the gospel. How can the church embody the good news in Western culture? What makes this even more urgent is that Western culture, with all its benefits and distortions, is being transported around the world in the process of globalization. Understanding the spiritual roots of Western culture is essential for the church today.

A sixth item on the agenda of mission studies is to understand what a *missionary encounter with other world religions* looks like. In the past the church was isolated from the various religions of the world, but today the fact of pluralism faces every church. Amidst constant interaction with adherents from other faiths, caricatures are increasingly difficult to maintain. Moreover, with the West losing prestige and power in the global community, a condescending attitude based on cultural superiority is something of the past. Further, our notion of religion as a private department of life is challenged by the comprehensive worldviews of major world religions. All of this opens up complex issues. How are Christ and the gospel unique amidst other religious commitments? How are we to understand religions from the standpoint of the gospel? What is our mission to the members of these faith communities?

Seventh, the explosive growth of cities, their cultural power, and the growing socioeconomic problems that beset them makes *urban mission* a critical issue to be studied by mission studies today. Mission is no longer a rural phenomenon. What does a missional church look like in the increasingly sophisticated Western and Westernized cities of our world? How does the church follow Jesus in the slums, favelas and shantytowns of the cities of our world?

Finally, in a world with a global church it will be important to deepen our understanding of the *world church*. A number of schools today label their mission department with some variation of "mission and world Christianity." Should the subject of world Christianity be part of a mission course? On the one hand, we might say no. After all, this continues to spread the false assumption that anything associated with "overseas" and "Christian" is mission. On the other hand, other areas of theological study have been slow to address this topic. Sadly, issues surrounding the third-world church often are considered to be exotic and something to be taught only in mission classes, which, after all, are in the business of talking about Christianity overseas. Arguably, the whole theological curriculum needs to engage third-world Christianity. What then is an authentic way of addressing world Christianity within the context of mission? It is to examine churches in various cultural contexts in light of the kinds of issues they face in mission today.

> WHAT THEN IS AN AUTHENTIC WAY OF ADDRESSING WORLD CHRISTIANITY WITHIN THE CONTEXT OF MISSION? IT IS TO EXAMINE CHURCHES IN VARIOUS CULTURAL CONTEXTS IN LIGHT OF THE KINDS OF ISSUES THEY FACE IN MISSION TODAY.

In this book I introduce these various areas of mission studies. In the first section I ground the mission of the church in God's mission as narrated in the biblical story and reflect theologically on the church's mission. In the second section I look at the way the church has carried out its comprehensive mission at various times in history. Moreover, I consider the church today in terms of an emerging ecumenical paradigm, current theological traditions and a survey of the global church. Finally, in the last and longest section I address a number of important current issues facing the church today: holistic mission, contextualization, mission in Western culture, world religions, urban mission and cross-cultural missions.

Further Reading

Escobar, Samuel. *The New Global Mission: The Gospel from Everywhere to Everyone.* Downers Grove, IL: InterVarsity Press, 2003.

Myers, Bryant L. *Exploring World Mission: Context and Challenges.* Monrovia, CA: World Vision, 2003.

Pocock, Michael, Gailyn Van Rheenen and Douglas McConnell. *The Changing Face of World Missions: Engaging Contemporary Issues and Trends.* Grand Rapids: Baker, 2005.

Tennent, Timothy C. *Invitation to World Missions: A Trinitarian Missiology for the Twenty-first Century.* Grand Rapids: Kregel, 2010, pp. 18-50.

Discussion Questions

1. Do you think a more traditional view of mission remains prevalent in your church circles? How *is* the word *mission* understood in your church?

2. What seems right about a traditional view of mission? In what ways might it be inadequate for today?

3. What factors do you think are most significant for rendering a traditional view of mission obsolete?

Essay Topics

1. Characterize the traditional view of mission. Why was this understanding and practice of mission important for its time?

2. Discuss the factors that render a traditional approach to mission inadequate. Which are most important? Are there others?

3. Do you find the four preliminary definitions of mission helpful? Why or why not? What characteristics of the shift in mission do they capture?

PART ONE

CƷ

Biblical and Theological
Reflection on Mission

1

Scripture as a Narrative
Record of God's Mission

C03

I REMEMBER WELL MY FIRST COURSE on biblical foundations for mission over thirty-five years ago. We moved rather quickly through the Old Testament because there was little missionary gold to be mined there[1]—or so we believed. Somehow the extermination of the Canaanites just did not fit our view of mission. We dealt more extensively with Jonah, Ruth and Isaiah 40–66 because they more readily lined up with our vision of cross-cultural witness. The New Testament more promptly yielded its missionary gold, but there were still favorite texts: "go and make disciples," "you will be my witnesses to the ends of the earth," and so forth. The problem was that sitting there in that Bible college, situated as it was in the Evangelical tradition, we knew what mission was, and we could not imagine anything but being committed to it. All we needed was a biblical foundation to justify it.

Our point of departure was an already existing missionary enterprise, to which we all joyfully offered our wholehearted support. Through this lens we looked for missionary texts and found those that fit our preexisting paradigm: a geographical expansionist understanding of mission that highlights sending from one place (Christian West) to another place (pagan non-West). We were unaware that on closer scrutiny Jonah did not really fit in any other way beyond crossing the water to a foreign place, or that the "go"

---

[1]I borrow this image of mining missionary gold from David J. Bosch, "Reflections on Biblical Models of Mission," in *Toward the Twenty-First Century in Christian Mission: Essays in Honor of Gerald H. Anderson*, ed. James M. Phillips and Robert T. Coote (Grand Rapids: Eerdmans, 1993), p. 176.

of the Great Commission was not the primary command at all.[2]

These comments are not meant to be disparaging. Indeed, I remain thankful for my early years in that tradition and the fervent commitment to taking the gospel to those who have never heard. My point is simply that when we examined the Bible's teaching on mission, our preexisting understanding of mission dictated what we saw. Thus, we did not bring our missionary practice to the Bible to be scrutinized; rather, familiar endeavors were legitimized by divine authority. I have no interest in hopping on the bandwagon that maligns the modern missionary movement. I am grateful for what was accomplished, and I believe there was much in the way of biblical faithfulness. My purpose at the beginning of this chapter is to raise the question of how to proceed in dealing with mission in the Bible.

THE BIBLE AND MISSION IN A NEW ERA

With the changes in mission today, it is essential to return to the Bible to get our bearings. David Bosch says that in this new era "if we want the missionary enterprise to be authentic and our reflections on mission to be relevant, we will have to pay even more serious attention to this branch of missiology than we used to do."[3] He further observes that in the past a biblical foundation for mission was laid by gleaning certain "missionary texts" from the Old and New Testaments to undergird the contemporary missionary enterprise. Mission was understood primarily as a geographical movement from the West to the non-West. Thus, it was more difficult to find Old Testament passages to fit this understanding, but the New Testament offered more. And yet here also the practice was to isolate missionary texts that fit a geographical-expansion understanding.

Mission should be based not on isolated passages of Scripture but rather on "the thrust of the central message of Scripture. In other words, either mission—properly understood—lies at the heart of the biblical message or it is so peripheral to that message that we need not be overly concerned with it."[4] Bosch advocates a missional reading of Scripture that recognizes the

---

[2]In Greek the "go" in Matthew 28:19 is not an imperative but rather a participle. While this may have the force of an imperative in this text, the main command is "make disciples."
[3]Bosch, "Biblical Models of Mission," p. 175.
[4]Ibid., p. 177.

centrality of mission to the biblical story. So instead of grasping isolated missionary texts, we need to read Scripture as a whole.[5]

In regard to reading Scripture "as a whole," there are two important senses in which this is true. First, there is a *redemptive-historical whole*. Mission must be understood as central to the whole plot of the biblical story.

"What sort of hermeneutic will enable us to enter into the Bible's own missionary direction? . . . It must be, in the first place, a canonical hermeneutic, that is, a way of reading the Bible as a whole. Secondly, it will be a narrative hermeneutic, one which recognizes how the Bible as a whole tells a story, in some sense a single story . . . constituting in its overall direction a metanarrative, a narrative about the whole of reality that elucidates the meaning of the whole of reality."

Richard J. Bauckham, *The Bible and Mission*, pp. 11-12

Second, there is a *literary whole*. Various texts must be read in terms of the whole literary structure of the book. For example, the so-called Great Commission must be set within the whole literary structure of the book of Matthew. It is the first of these "wholes" that will concern us in this chapter.

The Bible is a narrative record of God's mission in and through his people for the sake of the world. It tells a story in which mission is a central thread—God's mission, Israel's mission, Christ's mission, the Spirit's mission, the church's mission. Indeed, "*the whole Bible is itself a 'missional' phenomenon*. The writings that now comprise our Bible are themselves the product of and witness to the ultimate mission of God. . . . Mission is not just one of a list of things the Bible happens to talk about, only a bit more urgently than some. Mission is, in the much abused phrase, 'what it is all about.'"[6] Thus, a faithful reading of Scripture is one that takes seriously a missional hermeneutic. A missional hermeneutic might be defined as "a way of reading the Bible for which mission is the hermeneutical key. . . . A

---

[5]Ibid., pp. 175-78.
[6]Christopher J. H. Wright, *The Mission of God: Unlocking the Bible's Grand Narrative* (Downers Grove, IL: InterVarsity Press, 2006), p. 22.

missionary hermeneutic of this kind would not be simply a study of the theme of mission in the biblical writings, but a way of reading the whole of Scripture with mission as its central interest and goal."[7] In this chapter I will briefly trace the biblical story with mission as a central theme.

> A FAITHFUL READING OF SCRIPTURE IS ONE THAT TAKES SERIOUSLY A MISSIONAL HERMENEUTIC.

GOD'S MISSION TO RESTORE THE WHOLE WORLD

It is not controversial to claim that the Bible tells one story.[8] It is more disputable to say that this is a story with universal validity—the true story of the whole world in which all people in all places at all times must find their place. But that is the claim being made here. To use current terminology, it is a "metanarrative"[9] about the meaning and destiny of universal history. Scripture, as N. T. Wright puts it, "offers a story which is the story of the whole world. It is public truth."[10]

God's mission to restore the world and its peoples is a central theme in the biblical narrative. Christopher Wright offers an approach that "sees the mission of God (and the participation in it of God's people) as a framework in which we can read the whole Bible. Mission is a major key that unlocks the whole grand narrative of the canon of Scripture."[11] Whereas a traditional interpretation of the *missio Dei* revolves around "sending"—the Father sends the Son, and together they send both the Spirit and the church—Wright speaks of God's mission in terms of God's long-term purpose to restore people from all nations and the whole creation. Thus, the Bible tells us

---

[7]Richard Bauckham, "Mission as Hermeneutic for Scriptural Interpretation" (richardbauckham .co.uk/uploads/Accessible/Mission%20as%20Hermeneutic.pdf).

[8]For further elaboration of the Bible as one story, see Michael W. Goheen, "The Urgency of Reading the Bible as One Story," *Theology Today* 64, no. 4 (2008): 469-83; Richard Bauckham, "Reading Scripture as a Coherent Story," in *The Art of Reading Scripture*, ed. Ellen F. Davis and Richard B. Hays (Grand Rapids: Eerdmans, 2003), pp. 40-47.

[9]The term "metanarrative" is coined by postmodern philosopher Jean-François Lyotard. It refers to a "story about the meaning of reality as a whole. . . . A metanarrative is an attempt to grasp the meaning and destiny of human history as a whole by telling a single story about it; to encompass, as it were, all the immense diversity of human stories in a single, overall story which integrates them into a single meaning" (Richard Bauckham, *Bible and Mission: Christian Witness in a Postmodern World* [Grand Rapids: Baker Academic, 2003], p. 4).

[10]N. T. Wright, *The New Testament and the People of God* (London: SPCK, 1992), pp. 41-42.

[11]Wright, *Mission of God*, p. 17.

the story of God's long historical journey to liberate his world from the destructive power of sin.

"The Old Testament tells its story as the story or, rather, as part of that ultimate and universal story that will ultimately embrace the whole of creation, time, and humanity within its scope. In other words, in reading these texts we are invited to embrace a metanarrative, a grand narrative."

Christopher J. H. Wright, *The Mission of God*, pp. 54-55

God announces his intention to restore the creation right after Adam and Eve's treasonous act of rebellion (Gen 3:15). God, as the first to announce good news, proclaims, "Through one of Eve's children I will crush the evil forces you have unleashed by your foolish defection." The story of God's mission is the path he follows to make this good news known to the ends of the earth. The mission of God's people is to take their role in this drama.

The horizon of God's mission is the ends of the earth. God's intention is to restore all nations, all cultures, indeed all of the creation from the sinful rebellion of humankind and its effects. So God's purpose is restorative and comprehensive, and it involves a battle against the corruption and idolatry that befouls his creation.

GOD CHOOSES ISRAEL TO BRING SALVATION TO THE WHOLE WORLD

The election of one people for the sake of all nations. In the Old Testament God chooses and forms Israel as a people with a view to bringing salvation to the ends of the earth. God's way of carrying out his mission is to choose a particular people and then gather all humankind into that community. One way of speaking of God's mission is in terms of a movement from the particular to the universal, or from the one to the many. We must learn to "read the Bible in a way that takes seriously its missionary direction." The story of the Bible "embodies a kind of movement from the particular to the universal, which we as readers need to find ourselves inside. The Bible is a kind of project aimed at the kingdom of God, that is, towards the achievement of God's purposes for good in the whole of God's creation."[12] God travels a particular road—Israel, Jesus, church—to arrive at his universal destination.

> **GOD TRAVELS A PARTICULAR ROAD—ISRAEL, JESUS, CHURCH—TO ARRIVE AT HIS UNIVERSAL DESTINATION.**

Here we are faced with the biblical doctrine of election. Why does God choose one people? First, election must always be understood in terms of God's universalistic intention. Election has to do with God's means of extending his blessing to the many. Second, election must be understood in the context of the covenant as both privilege and obligation, gift and task, grace and responsibility. Election often has been formulated in terms of privilege only. In reaction, some have emphasized only task. Yet in Scripture it is a matter of privilege and responsibility. When God's people forget the purpose of their election, they stand under divine judgment: "You only have I chosen of all the families of the earth; therefore I will punish you for all your sins" (Amos 3:2).

The particular community chosen by God is first the place of God's mission and then the channel. God works out his redemptive purposes first in the community and then through that community for the sake of the whole world. When God graciously saves his people, it is not only for their sake; it is also for the sake of others.

Genesis 12:1-3: Blessed to be a blessing. This story of a chosen people begins with the election of Abraham and the promise that God gives to him (Gen 12:1-3). However, the biblical story does not begin with Abraham. Genesis 1–11 provides the universal backdrop against which Abraham is chosen. To set the story of Abraham in this context is to emphasize "the universal dimensions of a divine plan that embraces all humanity and all creation."[13] A number of important themes that will continue throughout the biblical story are introduced: the God of Abraham and Israel is the creator of heaven and earth; there is only one true God, and there is none other; he is the God not only of Israel, but of all nations; he is the sovereign ruler over the whole earth and all of history; all nations have descended

---

[12]Bauckham, *Bible and Mission*, p. 11.

[13]Lucien Legrand, *Unity and Plurality: Mission in the Bible*, trans. Robert R. Barr (Maryknoll, NY: Orbis Books, 1990), p. 4.

from one man created in God's image to love, worship, and serve him; all peoples are living in revolt against him, shape their cultures and society in rebellion, are accountable to him, and are under his judgment; the scope of God's redemptive intention is creation-wide, with his promise being to undo the deleterious effects of human sin in all creation, for all nations, and all of human life.

Against this universal backdrop God chooses Abraham to be a channel of redemptive blessing to all the families of the earth. God does not reject the nations but rather chooses Abraham precisely for their sake (Gen 12:1-3). The promise of Genesis 12:2-3, referred to as "the gospel in advance" by Paul (Gal 3:8), is summarized later in terms of a twofold promise: "Abraham will surely become a great and powerful nation, and all nations on earth will be blessed through him" (Gen 18:18). God has chosen Abraham; God will form Israel into a nation and bless them. Yet the ultimate purpose is "so that all nations on earth may be blessed" through him.[14] God's people from their inception are a "so-that people"—chosen and graciously blessed so that all people might know God's merciful blessing. It is essential to understand the pivotal significance of these verses. "What is being offered in these few verses is a theological blueprint for the redemptive history of the world."[15] Genesis 12:2-3 offers the two-stage plan by which God will carry out his redemptive purpose.

Although this promise remains central to the following patriarchal narratives, we are not told exactly how God will bring that redemptive blessing. We are given something of a hint in Genesis 18:19. God says, "I have chosen him, so that he will direct his children and his household after him to keep the way of the LORD by doing what is right and just, so that the LORD will bring about for Abraham what he has promised him" (Gen 18:19). The fulfillment of the promise to bless

> GOD'S PEOPLE FROM THEIR INCEPTION ARE A "SO-THAT PEOPLE"— CHOSEN AND GRACIOUSLY BLESSED SO THAT ALL PEOPLE MIGHT KNOW GOD'S MERCIFUL BLESSING.

---

[14]I have followed Walter C. Kaiser's translation of Genesis 12:3 (*Mission in the Old Testament: Israel as a Light to the Nations* [Grand Rapids: Baker Books, 2000], p. 18).

[15]William Dumbrell, *Creation and Covenant: An Old Testament Covenantal Theology* (Nashville: Nelson, 1984), p. 66.

the nations is tied somehow to the way in which Abraham and his household will live. They must keep the way of the Lord and do what is right and just.

Exodus 19:3-6: A display people to the nations. The way God will bless the nations is revealed more clearly in Exodus 19:3-6. The whole of the book of Exodus leads up to these words, which define Israel's role and identity in redemptive history. The imagery that the author of Exodus uses to describe what God does for Israel is that of redemption (Ex 6:6; 15:13). Redemption refers to the recovery of a son who once was part of a family but has been alienated. Redemption is the return of this son to his proper relationship. Israel as God's son (Ex 4:22) is enslaved, but God intervenes to restore Israel to their proper place in God's family. Israel is liberated from slavery to the gods and idols of Egypt and from the tyranny of Pharaoh to serve the living God. He leads them out of Egypt, cares for them in the wilderness, and now brings them to himself at Sinai. Why has God done this for Israel? What role does he have for them to play? This is answered in the critical verses of Exodus 19:4-6.

God chooses Israel as his special possession. Israel will be bound to God in covenant and will hold a special place in God's redemptive purpose. But again, the universal horizon of God's redemptive intention is evident: "for the whole earth is mine" (Ex 19:5).[16] Israel is God's treasured possession for the sake of the whole earth. More specifically, Israel is called to be a priestly kingdom and a holy nation. Holiness refers to being set aside wholly for God's use. Thus, Israel is a nation set apart for God's use in his redemptive work. They are to live holy lives in the midst of the nations. The role that Israel will play is a priestly one. In the same way a priest plays a special role in the midst of a nation, Israel will play a priestly role among the nations. A priest is separated from the rest of the nation to be a model of devotion consecrated to God's service and to be a mediator of God's blessing to the rest of the nation (Num 6:22-26).

In this call Israel is summoned to be a model of what God intends for human life. They are to be an illustration of God's creational purposes for all peoples. In the words of John Durham, God charges Israel to be "a display-people, a showcase to the world of how being in covenant with

---

[16]See ibid., p. 89.

Yahweh changes a people."[17] Israel is to incarnate in the midst of history what God intended in creation at the beginning of history and what he will accomplish in his redemptive work at the end of history. If Israel is faithful, their life will be attractive and draw the nations into the covenant with the Lord. In the later language of Isaiah, Israel is called to be "a light to the nations" (Is 49:6; cf. Mt 5:14).

On the heels of this momentous call God gives Israel the Torah (Ex 20–23). The Torah directs Israel's life and provides the pattern by which they

"It is not the case that *Israel* alone belongs to God and other nations do *not*, or that Israel is more "possessed" by God than they were. For the text expresses God's possession of the world (and by implication the nations) in exactly the same terms as God's anticipated possession of Israel. All nations belong to God, but Israel will belong to God in a unique way that will, on the one hand, demand covenantal obedience, and, on the other hand, be exercised through a priestly and holy identity and role in the world. . . . Or in other words, *the particularity of Israel here is intended to serve the universality of God's interest in the world. Israel's election serves God's mission.*"

Christopher J. H. Wright, *The Mission of God*, pp. 256-57

should live as a holy nation in the midst of the nations. Mosaic law is a divinely authorized way of life, which manifests both the "universal and enduring principles of creation and the historical situation of a particular people (Israel) in a particular place (Palestine) at a particular time (the centuries between Moses and Christ)."[18] The law calls for a communal life of love and justice with a special concern for the poor and weak. "Israel's distinctive practice of justice was meant to shine as a beacon in the ancient Near East, attracting other nations to the distinctive God who wills such

---

[17]John I. Durham, *Exodus* (Word Biblical Commentary 3; Waco, TX: Word Books, 1987), p. 263.
[18]Albert M. Wolters, *Creation Regained: Biblical Basics for a Reformational Worldview; with a Postscript coauthored by Michael W. Goheen* (Grand Rapids: Eerdmans, 2005), p. 40.

justice."[19] Israel was to "function as a people who would show the rest of humanity what being human was all about,"[20] a people called to "model genuinely human existence."[21]

The instruction that Israel received in the law indicates a threefold orientation for their lives visible to the nations. They were oriented *backward* to creation: they were to be a picture of what God originally intended for human life in the creation. All of their social and cultural lives were to conform to God's original creational design. They were oriented *forward*: they were to be a sign or preview of God's goal for humanity and all creation at the end of history. They were oriented *outward*: they were to confront and engage the other pagan cultures of the day, embracing what was good but rejecting the idolatry. So they were to live as a contrast society to the nations that did not know God.

It is hard to overestimate the importance of Israel's call in Exodus 19 for the rest of the Old Testament story. "The history of Israel from this point on is in reality merely a commentary upon the degree of fidelity with which Israel adhered to this Sinai-given vocation."[22] The remainder of the Old Testament history narrates how faithful Israel is to this call.

The book of Exodus ends with God coming to dwell among his people (Ex 25–40). Robert Martin-Achard reminds us that mission "is a matter of presence— *the presence of the People of God in the midst of mankind and the presence of God in the midst of His People.*"[23] A little while later Moses will remind Israel of their missional calling as they are about to enter the promised land. Their distinctive lives are to lead the nations to say, "Surely this great nation is a wise and understanding people" (Deut 4:6). This will lead to questions about the God who dwells in their midst and the righteousness of His laws that direct their lives (Deut 4:5-8). Thus, God will reveal himself to the nations as he dwells in the midst of Israel and transforms their lives with the law.

[19]J. Richard Middleton and Brian J. Walsh, *Truth Is Stranger Than It Used to Be: Biblical Faith in a Postmodern Age* (Downers Grove, IL: InterVarsity Press, 1995), p. 98.
[20]Tom Wright, *Bringing the Church to the World: Renewing the Church to Confront the Paganism Entrenched in Western Culture* (Minneapolis: Bethany House, 1992), p. 59.
[21]N. T. Wright, *Scripture and the Authority of God: How to Read the Bible Today* (New York: HarperCollins, 2011), p. 51.
[22]Dumbrell, *Creation and Covenant*, p. 80.
[23]Robert Martin-Achard, *A Light to the Nations: A Study of the Old Testament Conception of Israel's Mission to the World*, trans. John Penney Smith (London: Oliver & Boyd, 1962), p. 79.

It was difficult for Israel to keep the universal horizon of their mission clear. An exclusivistic nationalism constantly corrupted their understanding of election and covenant, as the book of Jonah shows. And so God gives psalms to Israel to constantly nourish their mission.[24] Their songs in worship reminded them that they were a "so-that people," a people blessed *so that* they might be a channel of blessing to the nations.

> May God be gracious to us and bless us
>   and make his face shine on us—
> *so that* your ways may be known on earth,
>   your salvation among all nations.
> May the peoples praise you, God;
>   may all the peoples praise you. . . .
> May God bless us still,
>   *so that* all the ends of the earth will fear him. (Ps 67:1-3, 7, italics added)

On the land in the sight of the nations. It is important to hold in view the narrative trajectory that Genesis 12:2-3 and Exodus 19:3-6 set as we read the rest of the Old Testament story. In the book of Joshua Israel is given the gift of the land. They are placed at the crossroads of the nations and the navel of the universe[25] as a display people visible to the nations.[26] From this point on, "Israel knew that it lived under constant surveillance of the then contemporary world."[27] This is the way of God's mission: "God's mission involves God's people living in God's way in the sight of the nations."[28]

> ROBERT MARTIN-ACHARD REMINDS US THAT MISSION "IS A MATTER OF PRESENCE—THE PRESENCE OF THE PEOPLE OF GOD IN THE MIDST OF MANKIND AND THE PRESENCE OF GOD IN THE MIDST OF HIS PEOPLE."

---

[24]See Theodore Mascarenhas, *The Missionary Function of Israel in Psalms 67, 96, and 117* (Lanham, MD: University Press of America, 2005).

[25]A number of Jewish and rabbinic texts situate Israel at the center of the world, as the navel of the universe.

[26]Wright, *Mission of God*, p. 467; Richard R. De Ridder, *Discipling the Nations* (Grand Rapids: Baker Books, 1971), pp. 43-44.

[27]J. H. Bavinck, *An Introduction to the Science of Missions*, trans. David Hugh Freeman (Philadelphia: Presbyterian & Reformed, 1960), p. 14.

[28]Wright, *Mission of God*, p. 470.

"Israel did not live in vacuum-sealed isolation from the rest of the world. On the contrary, they could not have lived on a more crowded international stage. The land of Canaan, as the land bridge between three continents, was a veritable public concourse of the nations. Israel's presence there was internationally visible."

Christopher J. H. Wright, *The Mission of God*, p. 467

Thus, the nations appear as witnesses throughout the historical narratives of Israel's history.[29] When God threatens to destroy Israel in the wilderness after redeeming them from Egypt, Moses intercedes: "Why should the Egyptians say, 'It was with evil intent that he brought them out, to kill them in the mountains and to wipe them off the face of the earth'?" (Ex 32:12). When again God threatens Israel with a plague after

> THE NATIONS APPEAR AS WITNESSES THROUGHOUT THE HISTORICAL NARRATIVES OF ISRAEL'S HISTORY. . . . ISRAEL'S HISTORY IS UNDER THE SCRUTINY OF THE NATIONS.

their complaining, Moses intercedes. He fears that the Egyptians and Canaanites will hear about it and conclude that the Lord was unable to bring these people into the land that he promised to give them (Num 14:13-16; cf. Deut 9:28). And so the story continues: Israel's history is under the scrutiny of the nations.

In the book of Judges the people Israel, as so often in their history, are swallowed up by the darkness of the idolatry of the very pagan nations to which they are to bring light. Israel's repeated covenant breaking is a threat to God's mission, and so the situation cries out for a king who will enable Israel to live as a faithful people (Judg 21:25). In the books of Samuel God gives them a king to mediate God's rule to Israel. Israel's request for a king is an act of apostasy; it stands in stark contradiction to God's missional purposes for Israel to be different from the other nations for the sake of the

---

[29]They are witnesses of Israel's covenant obligations, witnesses of God's judgment on Israel, witnesses of God's restoration of Israel (ibid., pp. 467-74).

other nations. But Israel wants a king so that they can "be like the other nations" (1 Sam 8:20; cf. 1 Sam 8:6). God grants them the king, but he incorporates the kingship into his covenantal and missional purposes. God promises David that he will grant an everlasting kingdom to David's descendant (2 Sam 7:11b-16). It is this kingdom that now becomes the universal horizon of God's redemptive purpose—an everlasting kingdom into which all nations will be brought.

The psalms and prophets pick up this theme. The psalms nourish the universal end of Israel's election, but now with the image of a king and a kingdom. Especially significant is the phrase "to the ends of the earth," found in various psalms and prophets to describe the universal reign of Israel's coming king (e.g., Ps 2:8; Mic 5:4; Zech 9:10). One day the reign of God's faithful king will be acknowledged to the ends of the earth (Ps 72:8-11).

The books of Kings narrate the failure of those kings and the consequent failure of Israel to fulfill their mission. The narrative tells of Israel's slide into rebellion as they follow their faithless kings, and it finally culminates in God's judgment—first as the northern kingdom is scattered by Assyria, and then as the southern kingdom is exiled to Babylon. It seems that God's redemptive mission has ground to a halt.

The prophets' message: The future fulfillment of God's mission. It is at this moment in the story that the prophets emerge and point to a time when Israel's mission will be fulfilled for the whole creation and all nations. They speak of an end-time event when God will rule the whole earth and bring salvation to the nations (Is 2:2-5; 52:10). For this to happen, Israel themselves must first be converted. It is only when Israel is gathered, purified, and given a new heart to fulfill their calling that they can be a light to the world (Ezek 36:22-32). This climactic moment will be ushered in by a Messiah, a faithful anointed king, who will come in power and glory as a world ruler (Zech 9:9-13), but who is also, paradoxically, a suffering and lowly servant (Is 53; cf. Lk 24:25-26). God will make his servant "a light for the Gentiles that my salvation may reach to the ends of the earth" (Is 49:6). The kingdom would come in the power of the Spirit as the Spirit is poured out on the Messiah (Is 61:1), on Israel (Ezek 36:26), and on all people (Joel 2:28-32). The Messiah would bring judgment and destruction on the earth (Is 63:1-6; Joel 1:15; Mal

3:2). But it would also be a day of salvation, not only for Israel but for all the nations as well. Isaiah declares, "In the last days the mountain of the LORD's temple will be established as the highest of the mountains; it will be exalted above the hills, and all the nations will stream to it. Many peoples will come and say, 'Come, let us go up to the mountain of the LORD, to the house of the God of Jacob'" (Is 2:2-3).

And what stands out in Old Testament prophecy is that this salvation of the nations is viewed as a spontaneous coming. "This is what the LORD Almighty says: 'In those days ten people from all languages and nations will take firm hold of one Jew by the hem of his robe and say, "Let us go with you, because we have heard that God is with you"'" (Zech 8:23).[30] So "Israel must itself become a living power by means of which the nations would be drawn into the light of the salvation of Israel's God. . . . Israel . . . shall now emit its magnetic light and draw the peoples of the world to itself."[31] Israel will finally fulfill the calling that they were given in Abraham to be a blessing to the nations: "Just as you, Judah and Israel, have been a curse among the nations, so I will save you, and you will be a blessing" (Zech 8:13).

The mission of God through Israel can be described in three terms: universal, centripetal and eschatological. It is *universal:* even though Israel is chosen to be God's covenant people, the whole earth and all nations are clearly in view. It is *centripetal:* Israel's role is to be a light to the nations, to live their lives in such a way that the nations see the true and living God and are attracted to their lives and to their God. It is *eschatological:* although the recognition of Yahweh by the nations in the life of Israel "is the meaning of Israel's history and the contents of her liturgy," it is also true that "during the whole history of Israel this comes to realization little if at all"; thus, the achievement of this goal looks

> THE MISSION OF GOD THROUGH ISRAEL CAN BE DESCRIBED IN THREE TERMS: UNIVERSAL, CENTRIPETAL AND ESCHATOLOGICAL.

[30]Albert M. Wolters, "Mission and the Interpretation of Zechariah 8:20-23," in *That the World May Believe: Essays on Mission and Unity in Honour of George Vandervelde,* ed. Michael W. Goheen and Margaret O'Gara (Lanham, MD: University Press of America, 2006), pp. 1-13.
[31]Bavinck, *Science of Missions,* pp. 21, 23.

to the future: "Israel's history, is eschatologically defined."[32] The final gathering of the nations awaits a future time when God will break into history in an unusually powerful way through the Messiah and by the Spirit to gather and purify Israel as an eschatological people and to bring about a comprehensive salvation for all the peoples of the earth.

GOD SENDS JESUS TO GATHER AND RESTORE ISRAEL TO ITS MISSION

The "already but not yet" era of the kingdom as a time of gathering. The eschatological era of the ingathering of Israel and the nations begins with the kingdom mission of Jesus. The prophets promised that comprehensive salvation and final judgment would come through the Messiah in that great eschatological future when God ushered in his kingdom. As one empire after another oppressed Israel, the flame of hope ignited by the prophets was fanned into a raging inferno of eschatological expectation. In this context of intense expectation Jesus announces the good news: "The kingdom of God has arrived!" (cf. Mk 1:14-15).

All Jews nurtured on the Old Testament prophets expected the kingdom to come immediately in fullness; the old age would draw to a close, and the age to come would dawn (see fig. 1). John the Baptist believed that the ax and the winnowing fork were already in the hands of the Messiah to bring salvation and judgment (Lk 3:9, 17). Yet John, like others, finds himself confused when God's judgment does not fall, and he sends his disciples to enquire whether or not Jesus is in fact the Messiah promised in the Old Testament (Lk 7:18-23). Jesus assures him that he is, and that the works that he is doing are signs that the power of God to renew the creation has indeed broken into history. Jesus' own disciples also struggle to understand, and so he tells them parables so that they might understand that although the kingdom has already dawned, it has not yet arrived in its fullness. The forces of the age to come are flowing into history, but the counterforces of the old age remain a powerful reality. There is an overlapping of the old age and age to come (see fig. 2).

The reason for this overlapping of the ages is mission.

---

[32]Johannes Blauw, *The Missionary Nature of the Church: A Survey of the Biblical Theology of Mission* (New York: McGraw-Hill, 1962), p. 27.

The meaning of this "overlap of the ages" in which we live, the time between the coming of Christ and His coming again, is that it is the time given for the witness of the apostolic Church to the ends of the earth. The end of all things, which has been revealed in Christ, is—so to say—held back until witness has been borne to the whole world concerning the judgment and salvation revealed in Christ. The implication of a true eschatological perspective will be missionary obedience, and the eschatology which does not issue in such obedience is a false eschatology.[33]

Prophetic Expectation

Spirit | Messiah

Sin
Death
Evil
Satan

Knowledge
of God
Love
Joy
Justice

OLD AGE   AGE TO COME

Figure 1. Prophetic expectation

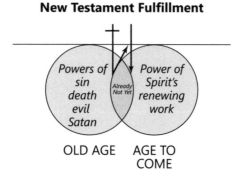

New Testament Fulfillment

Powers of
sin
death
evil
Satan

Already
Not Yet

Power of
Spirit's
renewing
work

OLD AGE   AGE TO
COME

Figure 2. New Testament fulfillment

[33]Lesslie Newbigin, *Household of God: Lectures on the Nature of the Church* (New York: Friendship Press, 1954), p. 153.

Strong words: eschatology apart from missionary obedience is false! The biblical testimony bears this out: this "already but not yet" time period is taken up with the end-time ingathering of the nations. It begins with Jesus' mission to Israel and then continues as a renewed Israel is invited to participate in his mission to the remaining sheep of Israel and then to the nations.

> STRONG WORDS: ESCHATOLOGY APART FROM MISSIONARY OBEDIENCE IS FALSE! THE BIBLICAL TESTIMONY BEARS THIS OUT.

"Contemporary New Testament scholars are thus affirming what the systematic theologian Martin Kähler said eight decades ago: Mission is the 'mother of theology.' Theology, says Kähler, began as 'an accompanying manifestation of the Christian mission' and not as 'a luxury of the world-dominating church.' The New Testament writers were not scholars who had the leisure to research the evidence before they put pen to paper. Rather, they wrote in the context of an 'emergency situation', of a church which, because of its missionary encounter with the world, was *forced* to theologize."

David J. Bosch, *Transforming Mission*, p. 16

Gathering is what gives this interim era meaning. Gerhard Lohfink laments that whereas "the 'gathering of the scattered people of God' has been . . . one of the fundamental statements of Israel's theology," Old Testament theology has paid scant attention to it.[34] This eschatological gathering motif is important for mission. "*The gathering of all peoples into one is the eschatological deed of God. The Old Testament says so, and Jesus remains loyal to this viewpoint. . . . The divine action . . . is now found to be entrusted to human beings—first of all to the human being Jesus, and then to those who, in his footsteps, will be sent forth to the harvest.*"[35]

---

[34]Gerhard Lohfink, *Does God Need the Church? Toward a Theology of the People of God,* trans. Linda M. Maloney (Collegeville, MN: Liturgical Press, 1999), pp. 51-52.
[35]Legrand, *Unity and Plurality*, p. 153.

The Gospels employ three images of gathering from the prophets and intertestamental literature: the gathering of the harvest into the barn, of sheep into the fold, and of guests to the banquet. Isaiah foresaw a time when all peoples would gather on Mount Zion for an end-time banquet of salvation (Is 25:6-9), which is now fulfilled in Jesus (e.g., Mt 8:11). In the parable of the great banquet Jesus describes a delay after the banquet is ready (Lk 14:15-24). J. H. Bavinck comments on this parable,

> The kingdom lay ready . . . in a certain sense all was ripe for the consummation, but there must first come a period in which the servants of the Lord must work. . . . The intervening time is marked by the activity of the servants. According to the above parables such work consists particularly in going out into the highways and byways to invite all to the marriage feast of the king. One may say thus that the interim is preoccupied with the command of missions, and it is the command of missions that gives the interim meaning.[36]

The second image is agricultural: the gathering of the harvest. Jesus invites his disciples to open their eyes to see the fields that are ripe with harvest (Jn 4:35; cf. Mk 4:3-8, 26-29). Jesus says, "The harvest is plentiful but the workers are few. Ask the Lord of the harvest, therefore, to send out workers into his harvest field" (Mt 9:37-38). This is a "missionary prayer" driven by the conviction that "the harvest of the end time is ripe and is entering human history; human harvesters, especially Jesus and his disciples with him, are called to associate themselves with it."[37]

The third image is of a shepherd gathering in lost sheep. Ezekiel and Jeremiah employ the imagery of an eschatological shepherd who will gather his scattered sheep back into the fold on the last day (Jer 23:2-3; 31:10; Ezek 34:12, 23-31). Jesus announces that he was sent only to the lost sheep of Israel (Mt 15:24) and begins to gather them into a little flock (Lk 12:32). But as the good shepherd, he foresees the day when the nations will also be gathered into his flock: "I have other sheep that are not of this sheep pen. I must bring them also. They too will listen to my voice, and there shall be one flock and one shepherd" (Jn 10:16).

Jesus is sent first to gather Israel for their mission. Mission has been

---

[36]Bavinck, *Science of Missions*, p. 32.
[37]Legrand, *Unity and Plurality*, p. 61.

explicated in terms of "the God who sends." The gospel of John portrays God as sending Jesus, and Jesus as the sent one. "It cannot be overemphasized how deeply the sending concept relates to Jesus' identity. Almost every page of the Fourth Gospel breathes with a passage in which Jesus expressed who he is in terms of his sense of being sent, his sense of mission."[38]

Jesus is sent on his mission in the power of the Spirit (Lk 4:18). This period between the first and the second coming of Jesus is the time of the Spirit. Indeed, the prophets envisioned a time when God's Spirit would be poured out on the Messiah to renew Israel and gather the nations. Thus, the Gospels begin with the outpouring of the Spirit on Jesus to carry out his mission (Mk 1:10; Lk 3:21-22; Acts 10:38).

What was the mission that the Father sent him to accomplish? In the first place, it was to gather Israel into an end-time community according to the prophetic promise. Joachim Jeremias makes the astonishing comment that "the *only* significance of the whole of Jesus' activity is to gather the eschatological people of God."[39] The gathering of the end-time people of God begins with Israel. Matthew makes it clear that Jesus' mission is limited to Israel. Jesus says to the Canaanite woman, "I was sent only to the lost sheep of Israel" (Mt 15:24). He sends his disciples only to the lost sheep of Israel (Mt 10:6). The apparent narrowing of Jesus' mission to Jews only has puzzled interpreters. How does this fit in with the clear universalistic horizon of the Old Testament, a horizon that Jesus clearly shares (Mt 8:11; 24:14)?

This anomaly must be read in terms of Old Testament prophecy. "Jesus read in his Bible" that there would be an "eschatological pilgrimage of the Gentiles to the Mountain of God"[40] (e.g., Is 2:2-4). God would reveal his glory to the Gentiles in and through Israel. First, Israel would be gathered to the messianic banquet on this mountain. Only after that would the nations come. When Jesus speaks of the many Gentiles gathering at the banquet table with Abraham, Isaac and Jacob, it is clear that he has this prophetic promise in mind (Mt 8:11). So the prophets looked forward to

---

[38]Francis M. DuBose, *God Who Sends: A Fresh Quest for Biblical Mission* (Nashville: Broadman, 1983), pp. 49-50.

[39]Joachim Jeremias, *New Testament Theology*, trans. John Bowden (New York: Scribner, 1971), p. 170.

[40]Joachim Jeremias, *Jesus' Promise to the Nations*, trans. S. H. Hooke (Studies in Biblical Theology 24; London: SCM Press, 1958), pp. 56-57.

"two successive events, first the call to Israel, and subsequently the redemptive incorporation of the Gentiles in the kingdom of God."[41]

The ministry of Jesus is directed to the first event. For Israel to carry out their role to draw the nations, two things must take place: Israel must be gathered; then Israel must be renewed so that they might live in obedience to God's Torah and shine as a light to the nations. Ezekiel offers a glimpse of both of these features—gathering and purifying—in God's eschatological future. Israel has failed in their mission and profaned the Lord's name among the nations (Ezek 36:16-21). However, God tells Israel that he will act so that the nations would know that he is the Lord when he is "proved holy *through you* before their eyes" (Ezek 36:23, italics added). Thus, God will act to complete his mission through Israel:

> For I will take you out of the nations; I will gather you from all the countries and bring you back into your own land. I will sprinkle clean water on you, and you will be clean; I will cleanse you from all your impurities and from all your idols. I will give you a new heart and put a new spirit in you; I will remove from you your heart of stone and give you a heart of flesh. And I will put my Spirit in you and move you to follow my decrees and be careful to keep my laws. (Ezek 36:24-27)

ACCORDING TO THE OLD TESTAMENT PROPHETS, THE MINISTRY OF THE MESSIAH IS FIRST TO GATHER ISRAEL AND THEN TO PURIFY AND EMPOWER ISRAEL FOR ITS MISSIONAL CALLING.

Thus, according to the Old Testament prophets, the ministry of the Messiah is first to gather Israel and then to purify and empower Israel for its missional calling. The Gospels show the way in which this was fulfilled: salvation is offered first to Israel, and a community is gathered; then the central events of the cross, resurrection and Pentecost accomplish salvation so that gathered Israel is renewed and empowered, ready for their mission to the nations.

Israel gathered and formed to take up their missional calling. Jesus calls this gathered community to take up their missional identity. In the Sermon on the Mount he applies to them the Old Testament images that portray

---

[41]Jeremias, *Jesus' Promise to the Nations*, p. 71.

Israel's mission: "You are the light of the world. A town built on a hill cannot be hidden. Neither do people light a lamp and put it under a bowl. Instead they put it on its stand, and it gives light to everyone in the house. In the same way, let your light shine before others, that they may see your good deeds and glorify your Father in heaven" (Mt 5:14-16). Together, the images of light and city refer to "the eschatological Jerusalem, which the prophets foretell will one day be raised above all mountains and illumine the nations with its light (cf. Is 2:2-5)."[42] In the mission of Jesus Israel is being restored to be a light to the nations.

There are two elements of the missional vocation to which Jesus calls his people. The first is *to embody a distinctive and attractive life.* Jesus announces

---

"We stand in need of an interpretation of salvation which operates within a *comprehensive* christological framework, which makes the *totus Christus*—his incarnation, earthly life, death, resurrection and parousia—indispensable for church and theology. All these christological elements taken together constitute the praxis of Jesus, the One who both inaugurated salvation and provided us with a model to emulate."

David J. Bosch, *Transforming Mission*, p. 309

---

the coming of the kingdom of God. The kingdom can be characterized as the inbreaking of God's dynamic power to defeat all that stands against his rule, and as the arrival of the comprehensive salvation of the world. The announcement calls for a response of radical allegiance. To those who respond in faith and repentance the good news promises the gift of renewal: a restored relationship with the Father, forgiveness, the Spirit, a new heart that will renew their whole lives. As they believe and follow Jesus, the promise is that they will participate in the renewal of the whole creation.

Those who have received the gift of the kingdom are to embody the life of the new creation given by the Spirit. They are to live a distinctive life that embodies God's creational intention for human life in creation, that is a sign

---

[42]Gerhard Lohfink, *Jesus and Community: The Social Dimension of the Christian Faith*, trans. John P. Galvin (Philadelphia: Fortress, 1982), p. 65.

of the coming new creation, and that challenges the idols of culture that stand against that life. And so Jesus spends much of his mission instructing this community in a distinctive way of life as an alternative community (e.g., Mt 5–7; Jn 13). Theirs is to be a life of love, reconciliation, peace, joy, justice, compassion and solidarity with the poor and marginalized. To live in this way will challenge the societal structures of injustice among the Jews and Romans. And so, this disciple community can expect to suffer as the price to be paid for living distinctively (Jn 15:18-21). Such a life can be lived only in communion with the Father and Son, and as a gift of the Spirit. And so, the distinctive lives of God's people can be known only by prayer. The kingdom comes as the Spirit works in response to prayer.[43]

◇◇

"A recognition of this missionary character of the documents will help us to see them in true perspective and to interpret them in the light of their intention. They are at one and the same time the product of a dynamic process of evangelism and nurture and the tools for accomplishing that process. It is the recognition of this organizing principle that enables us to have a coherent understanding of them. Essentially the New Testament is a collection of books that express the gospel or good news that was proclaimed in the Christian mission. . . . Recognition of the missionary orientation of the New Testament will alert us to a more dynamic view of the church as the agent of mission instead of the static view that we sometimes have."

I. Howard Marshall, *New Testament Theology*, pp. 35-36

◇◇

The second element of renewed Israel's missional vocation is *to participate, by word and deed, in Jesus' gathering mission.* Not only is this community gathered and formed to live as an alternative community, but also it is invited to participate in the more intentional task of gathering that Jesus has begun. Jesus says to Simon and Andrew, "Come, follow me, and I will send you out to fish for people" (Mk 1:17). The "calling of the disciples is a

---

[43]Stephen S. Smalley, "Spirit, Kingdom, and Prayer in Luke-Acts," *Novum Testamentum* 15, no. 1 (1973): 59-71.

call to follow Jesus and a being set aside for missionary activities. Calling, discipleship, and mission belong together."[44] Jesus sends out his twelve disciples to proclaim the arrival of the kingdom and to demonstrate its arrival with deeds (Mt 10; Lk 9:1-6; 10:1-16). It is through the words and deeds of the disciples that others would be invited to participate in the salvation of God's kingdom. If such words and deeds are to be the power of God unto salvation, then they too must be accompanied by prayer (Mk 9:29).

The elements of Jesus' kingdom mission. Thus, the kingdom mission of Jesus is to gather and restore Israel to its missional vocation. But it is not only important to see those to whom Jesus directed his mission. It is equally important to understand the way he carried it out—the elements that comprised his kingdom mission. We must look carefully at "the earthly Jesus if we want to elucidate 'the beginnings of the earliest Christian mission.' . . . Here we are confronted with the real starting point of the primitive Christian mission: it lies in the conduct of Jesus himself. If anyone is to be called 'the primal missionary,' he must be."[45] This is significant because Jesus incorporates his disciples into his mission to Israel, and after the major redemptive events of the cross, resurrection, exaltation and Pentecost Jesus sends that little community to continue his mission in the world. "As the Father has sent me, I am sending you" (Jn 20:21). Jesus' mission is a pattern and model for our own.

> "AS THE FATHER HAS SENT ME, I AM SENDING YOU" (JN 20:21). JESUS' MISSION IS A PATTERN AND MODEL FOR OUR OWN.

Jesus' mission is centered in the kingdom of God. He announces the arrival of the kingdom: "Good news! God is breaking into history in power and love in me, the Messiah, by the power of the Spirit to restore the whole creation and all of human life to again live under the gracious rule of God." To this message he invites and commands a response of total commitment: repent, believe, and follow him. When asked by John's disciples if he is the

---

[44]Rudolf Pesch, "Berufung und Sendung, Nachfolge und Mission: Eine Studie zu Mk 1, 16-20," *Zeitschrift für katholische Theologie* 91 (1969): 15, quoted in David Bosch, *Transforming Mission: Paradigm Shifts in Theology of Mission* (Maryknoll, NY: Orbis Books, 1991), p. 36.

[45]Martin Hengel, "The Origins of the Christian Mission," in *Between Jesus and Paul: Studies in the Earliest History of Christianity*, trans. John Bowden (London: SCM Press, 1983), pp. 62-63, quoted in Bosch, *Transforming Mission*, p. 31.

Messiah, Jesus tells them to tell John that his deeds demonstrated that the power of God to heal and liberate was present in him (Lk 7:22-23). Indeed, in his deeds Jesus "launches an all-out attack on evil in all its manifestations."

> God's reign arrives wherever Jesus overcomes the power of evil. Then, as it does now, evil took many forms: pain, sickness, death, demon-possession, personal sin and immorality, the loveless self-righteousness of those who claim to know God, the maintaining of special class privileges, the brokenness of human relationships. Jesus is, however, saying: If human distress takes many forms, the power of God does likewise.[46]

Thus, words of Jesus that announced the salvation of the kingdom were authenticated by deeds. But his life also witnessed to the kingdom: his dependence upon the Spirit (Lk 3:22; Acts 10:38); his loving communion with the Father (Jn 14–17); his glorifying of the Father (Jn 14:13); his life of devoted prayer (Lk 5:16); his compassion, mercy and justice for the poor, sick and marginalized (Lk 4:18-19); his self-giving life of sacrificial service (Jn 13:1-17); his submission and obedience to the Father (Heb 5:8); his love, gentleness and joy (Mt 11:29; Jn 15:11); his suffering for the kingdom's sake as he opposed hostile powers that stood against it (Jn 15:18). All of this, and more, witnessed to a life empowered and controlled by the Spirit.

We might list the components of Jesus' mission thus:

- Jesus announced the kingdom with his words.
- Jesus demonstrated the kingdom with his deeds.
- Jesus "lovingly attacks" every form of evil that he sees in the individual and social lives of people.
- Jesus embodied the kingdom with his life.
- Jesus formed a kingdom community.
- Jesus taught his disciple community about the kingdom and life in it.
- Jesus stands with sinners and outcasts, the poor and marginalized, and welcomes them into the kingdom.
- Jesus prayed for the coming kingdom.
- Jesus suffered as he withstood the powers that opposed the kingdom.

[46]Bosch, *Transforming Mission*, p. 33.

The mission of Jesus provides a model: mission must be in Christ's way. "Mission flows from a desire to follow in the way of Jesus, who healed the sick, associated with outsiders, rebuked the self-righteous, challenged the absolute power of the state, restored people's dignity, opposed legalistic and corrupt religious practices, and ultimately gave his life to demonstrate that even enemies were encompassed in his love. Jesus tells his disciples to 'go and do likewise.'"[47]

"The integral character of salvation demands that the scope of the church's mission be more comprehensive than has traditionally been the case. Salvation is coherent, broad, and deep as the needs and exigencies of human existence. . . . From the tension between the 'already' and the 'not yet' of the reign of God, from the tension between the salvation *indicative* (salvation is already a reality!) and the salvation *subjunctive* (comprehensive salvation is yet to come!) there emerges the salvation *imperative*—Get involved in the ministry of salvation! Those who know that God will one day wipe away all tears will not accept with resignation the tears of those who suffer and are oppressed *now*. Anyone who knows that one day there will be no more disease can and must actively anticipate the conquest of disease in individuals and society *now*. And anyone who believes that the enemy of God and humans will be vanquished will already oppose him *now* in his machinations in family and society. For all of this has to do with *salvation*."

David J. Bosch, *Transforming Mission*, p. 400

Yet, as the church goes to the nations and finds itself in new situations, it must follow the pattern of Jesus with imagination and creativity. "Jesus did not set up a rigid model for action but, rather, inspired his disciples to prolong the logic of his own action in a creative way amid the new and different historical circumstances in which the community would have to proclaim the gospel of the kingdom in word and deed."[48]

---

[47]J. Andrew Kirk, *The Mission of Theology and Theology as Mission* (Valley Forge, PA: Trinity Press International, 1997), p. 52.

[48]Hugo Echegaray, *The Practice of Jesus*, trans. Matthew J. O'Connell (Maryknoll, NY: Orbis Books, 1984), p. 94.

Crucifixion, resurrection and commissioning. The kingdom mission of Jesus climaxes in his death on the cross and his bodily resurrection from the dead. The Torah had been given to Israel to shape them into a faithful people who would be a light to the nations. However, the law could not form that people into a contrast community because of the power of sin. And so, if there was to be a faithful people, sin must be defeated at the cross. "For what the law was powerless to do because it was weakened by the flesh, God did by sending his own Son in the likeness of sinful flesh to be a sin offering. And so he condemned sin in the flesh, in order that the righteous requirements of the law might be fully met in us, who do not live according to the flesh but according to the Spirit" (Rom 8:3-4). It is only after the death of Jesus, who takes upon himself the guilt and power of sin, liberating his people to walk in obedience, that "the law will go out of Zion, the word of the LORD from Jerusalem" (Is 2:3).

> AS THE CHURCH GOES TO THE NATIONS AND FINDS ITSELF IN NEW SITUATIONS, IT MUST FOLLOW THE PATTERN OF JESUS WITH IMAGINATION AND CREATIVITY.

The bodily resurrection is the dawning of the age to come. Jesus is the firstborn from the dead (Col 1:18; Rev 1:5), the firstfruits of the resurrection life (1 Cor 15:20). As God's people are united to Christ by faith, they already begin to share the life of the resurrection (Rom 6:1-14), a life that they will enjoy fully at their bodily resurrection when Christ returns (1 Cor 15:23).

These two events constitute the turning point in universal history: the old age is passing away as the enemies that dominate it—sin, death, Satan—have been defeated, and the life of the age to come has arrived. The forces of the future world of the kingdom are streaming into the present. Now, newly gathered Israel can begin to participate in the life of the age to come. But the import of these events moves beyond Israel. The death and resurrection of Jesus have cosmic scope and universal significance. The cross accomplishes the salvation of the entire creation and all nations; the resurrection is the dawning of the renewed creation. On the basis of these events Jesus draws his disciples together and commissions them to take the good news to all nations, even to the ends of the earth. The eschatological gathering of the nations can now proceed.

The Gospels offer various versions of the commissioning to worldwide mission.[49] In Matthew, Jesus commissions freshly gathered Israel to make disciples who are to be baptized into this newly founded community and to be taught to acknowledge the absolute and comprehensive authority of Jesus, to whom all authority is given, by obeying all that he has commanded (Mt 28:18-20). In Luke, Jesus charges his followers to proclaim repentance and forgiveness in response to the central events of world history—the cross and the resurrection—to all nations in the power of the Spirit (Lk 24:45-49). In John, Jesus sends his people into the world to continue what he has been doing (Jn 20:21). Here the biblical story stands at the threshold of the goal toward which it has been moving: the gathering of all people to a kingdom in which God restores everything.

THE CHURCH'S MISSION TO THE ENDS OF THE EARTH

The church is taken up into God's mission to continue the mission of Israel and of Jesus to the ends of the earth. It is the book of Acts that records the earliest mission of the church as it moves from Jerusalem, to Judea, to Samaria, and through the Roman Empire finally to Rome. Referring to the book of Luke, the writer of Acts opens the narrative with these words: "In my former book, Theophilus, I wrote about all that Jesus began to do and to teach" (Acts 1:1). The implication is that the ensuing narrative is what the exalted Christ will continue to do and teach, now by the Spirit in and through the church.

Jesus, alive from the dead, appears to the disciples, and over forty days speaks to them about the kingdom of God and the coming of the Spirit. For the disciples, like for all Jews of that time, these three things—resurrection, kingdom, Spirit—mean one thing: the end-time kingdom is about to dawn. And so they ask the obvious question: "Lord, are you at this time going to restore the kingdom to Israel?" (Acts 1:6) Jesus' fourfold answer (Acts 1:7-8) is significant for mission. First, the culmination of the kingdom is not yet

---

[49]For a brief elaboration of the various "great commissions" in the four Gospels, see Mortimer Arias and Alan Johnson, *The Great Commission: Biblical Models for Evangelism* (Nashville: Abingdon, 1992).

here. The interim period as a time for gathering will continue for a while yet ("It is not for you to know the times"). Second, until the end does come, your task is to be a witnessing community. "When the Spirit of God comes to them and gives them the gift of power, their very identity will be transformed into that of witnesses"[50] ("you will be my witnesses"). Third, you can carry out this role only if the Spirit comes to equip you, and more importantly as he gives you the life of the kingdom of God ("you will receive power when the Holy Spirit comes upon you"). Finally, the witness will go to "the ends of the earth." It will begin in Jerusalem, then move to Judea, and then to Samaria, but the ultimate horizon for your mission is the ends of the earth.

"The ends of the earth" is a phrase used frequently in the Old Testament, especially in Psalms and Isaiah, to designate the ultimate horizon of God's redemptive purpose (e.g., Ps 72:8; Is 49:6; Zech 9:10). The universal horizon envisioned by the Old Testament in God's great eschatological future is about to be narrated in the book of Acts. The end has come! Beginning at the center of the world (cf. Ezek 5:5), God's word will move from Jerusalem through Judea and Samaria to the ends of the earth. It is this geographical structure that forms the literary structure of the book of Acts—a structure that gives expression to the theological truth that the eschatological promise is being fulfilled.

But before the worldwide mission can surge forth to the ends of the earth, two significant events must take place: the ascension of Christ (Acts 1:9-11) and the outpouring of the Spirit (Acts 2:1-13). Jesus is exalted to the right hand of God. He is given a place of cosmic authority at the right hand of God (Mt 28:18-20; cf. Dan 7:13-14). The church's mission is to proclaim and embody Jesus' reign over all things and to summon others also to submit to his rule. "It is Jesus' Ascension, in particular, that launches the church on its mission. . . . The Ascension launches the church . . . on the task of announcing and inaugurating the sovereign rule of *Jesus* in the whole world."[51] And he will be present with his people in power through the Spirit to carry on his own mission. The Spirit is "the divine power by which the exalted

---

[50]Darrell L. Guder, *Be My Witnesses: The Church's Mission, Message, and Messengers* (Grand Rapids: Eerdmans, 1985), p. 40.
[51]Wright, *Bringing the Church to the World*, p. 195.

Lord . . . is present and active in [and through] his Church."[52] As he sends
his newly gathered people, the exalted Christ pours out on them the same
Spirit who empowered him to carry out his mission. Acts records their
Spirit-driven mission.

Brian Rosner observes, "Acts narrates the progress of the gospel from a
small gathering of Jewish disciples of the earthly Jesus in Jerusalem, across
formidable cultic, ethnic, relational and geographical boundaries, to Paul's
bold and unhindered preaching of the risen and ascended Jesus to Gentiles
in Rome. Acts is unmistakably a story of missionary expansion."[53] Similarly,
Howard Marshall says, "Acts is the story of mission, in the course of which
we learn the theological content of the gospel and the theology on which the
mission to Jews and Gentiles rested."[54] This is indeed true, but we must be
careful not to impose a nineteenth-century view of mission on this book. A
central theme in Acts is the way the Old Testament vision of God's eschatological program will come to fulfillment. The Jews must first be gathered and
established as a faithful covenant community. Then the word of God will go
forth from a renewed community in Jerusalem. The Acts story lingers long
in Jerusalem as scattered Israel is called to join the eschatological people of
God and take up their missionary vocation of being a light to the nations. It
is only "as soon as Israel appears among all the other societies of the world
as the properly constructed . . . society, pagan society will be able to seek and
find God—in Israel, the divine model society."[55]

Only with the coming of the Spirit can this kind of community be formed
and the mission to which God called his people from the beginning take
place (Ezek 36:24-27). When the Spirit is poured out at Pentecost, the people
of God in Jerusalem are given a foretaste of the salvation of the kingdom.
The kingdom banquet has been prepared by the work of Christ, but it waits
for a future time, when all the guests have been assembled. Yet those who
have been gathered by Christ have already begun to taste the powers of the
coming age (Heb 6:5). The eschatological community in Jerusalem receives

---

[52]Hendrikus Berkhof, *The Doctrine of the Holy Spirit* (Atlanta: John Knox, 1964), p. 25.
[53]Brian Rosner, "The Progress of the Word," in *Witness to the Gospel: The Theology of Acts*, ed. I.
   Howard Marshall and David Peterson (Grand Rapids: Eerdmans, 1998), p. 216.
[54]I. Howard Marshall, *New Testament Theology: Many Witnesses, One Gospel* (Downers Grove, IL:
   InterVarsity Press, 2004), p. 157.
[55]Lohfink, *Jesus and Community*, p. 140.

the Spirit as a down payment on the future salvation (2 Cor 1:22; 5:5; Eph 1:14) and thereby becomes the firstfruits of the eschatological harvest (Rom 8:23; Jas 1:18). Thus, the community of Pentecost is the prime exhibit of what the future kingdom will look like. It is like a movie trailer, a few minutes of actual footage from a film not yet released. This preview is shown so that the potential audience can catch a glimpse of a coming future attraction. It will be as their lives emit the radiance of God's intention for human life that first Israel can be gathered and then the nations. With the coming of the Spirit, God's people in Jerusalem are empowered to be a preview of what the future in God's kingdom will be.

> THE COMMUNITY OF PENTECOST IS THE PRIME EXHIBIT OF WHAT THE FUTURE KINGDOM WILL LOOK LIKE. IT IS LIKE A MOVIE TRAILER, A FEW MINUTES OF ACTUAL FOOTAGE FROM A FILM NOT YET RELEASED.

After the Spirit is poured out (Acts 2:1-13) and Peter explains this mighty act of God (Acts 2:14-39), we are given a glimpse of the newly formed and Spirit-filled community in Jerusalem charged with the vocation of gathering Israel. They are what God meant his people to be from the beginning: an attractive community that draws people in. As they commit themselves to the apostles' teaching, fellowship, the breaking of bread, and prayer, they receive the life of the kingdom (Acts 2:42), the Spirit makes their life attractive (Acts 2:43-47), and the Lord adds to their number daily those who are being saved (Acts 2:47). Here in the community of Jerusalem the Old Testament prophets' words are starting to be realized.

The mission of the church in Jerusalem is marvelously successful. But although rapid growth occurs, many within Israel refuse to be gathered and so are cut off from the people of God. Acts tells the story of many in Israel who reject the gospel and are severed from the covenant. Yet the time has also come for Gentiles who believe the gospel to be grafted on like wild shoots (Rom 11:17-21).[56] In Acts Peter lays down the foundations for this universal mission through his affirmation of the extension of the word to

---

[56]"Reading Acts and Romans 11 side by side, one is struck by many suggestive similarities. The interesting thing is that Acts appears the more primitive, setting out the grist from which Paul has milled his extraordinary theology of the destiny of Jew and Gentile" (David Seccombe, "The New People of God," in Marshall and Peterson, *Witness to the Gospel*, p. 371).

Samaria (Acts 8:14-17) and his encounter with the Gentile Cornelius (Acts 10–11:18, esp. 10:34-35; 11:18). Yet the first major move outward from Jerusalem is an unplanned expansion of the gospel into Judea, Samaria and certain Gentile areas (Acts 6:8–12:25). It is especially under persecution of the church in Jerusalem that the gospel spread throughout these areas by the evangelistic endeavors of unknown witnesses (Acts 8:1, 4) until it finally reaches Antioch (Acts 11:19-20). It is only here that for the first time we see a planned effort to take the gospel to places where it has not been heard.

<><><><><><><><><><><><><><><><><><><><><><><><><><><><><><><><><><><><><><><><><><><><>

"The founding of the Church and the beginning of mission coincided (Acts 2). Mission was mission-of-the-Church and Church was missionary Church. In the course of time, however, . . . there developed a tendency to concentrate on parochial problems and neglect the relationship of the Church to the world."

David J. Bosch, *Witness to the World*, p. 95

<><><><><><><><><><><><><><><><><><><><><><><><><><><><><><><><><><><><><><><><><><><><>

The church in Antioch carries on its own mission in the place where it has been set. In words that recall the church in Jerusalem there is evidence of God's work in the community at Antioch, and a great number of people turn to the Lord (Acts 11:21-24). But something different takes place here: they lift their gaze to the ends of the earth. Under the Spirit's direction, they commission Paul and Barnabas to take the gospel throughout Asia Minor (Acts 13:1-3). The remainder of Acts tells the story of an organized expansion from Antioch into Asia Minor.

Paul's missionary pattern is important.[57] He moves throughout Asia Minor as a pioneer church planter preaching the gospel where it has never been heard and establishing witnessing communities in places where there are none (Rom 15:20). He stays no longer than two years in one place. As he plants churches, he says when he leaves, as it were, "Now you are the mission in this place." Here is something new in the story of God's mission: intentional efforts to establish a witnessing community in places where there are

---

[57]On Paul's mission, see the important study by Eckhard Schnabel, *Early Christian Mission*, vol. 2, *Paul and the Early Church* (Downers Grove, IL: InterVarsity Press, 2004), pp. 923-1485.

66

INTRODUCING CHRISTIAN MISSION TODAY

none. Paul does not then abandon them, but rather revisits them and sends letters to encourage them to be faithful to their mission in the place where they have been set.

Throughout the biblical story to this point the mission of God through his people has been centripetal: the people of God are to be attractive so those outside will come, drawn by the salvation visible in Israel.[58] Luke tells his story showing that this is fulfilled in the community at Jerusalem (Acts 2:42-47; 4:32-35) and now in Antioch (Acts 11:21-23). However, with Antioch the mission of God through his people takes a centrifugal direction: the people of God go out to the nations. It is in this going that there lies "the distinctive turning-point, the great change of direction of the gospel."[59] Yet both dimensions of mission remain important: the centrifugal serves the centripetal. Some, like Paul and Barnabas, are sent out to establish witnessing communities. These communities in turn witness in their lives, words and deeds in their local setting to the transforming power of God. Richard Bauckham speaks of the "permanent value of the image of the two directions of movement—centrifugal and centripetal." He continues, "The church's mission requires both the individuals and groups who, authorized by God to communicate his message, go out from the community to others, near or far, *and also* the community that manifests God's presence in its midst by its life together and its relationships to others."[60]

> BOTH DIMENSIONS OF
> MISSION REMAIN IMPORTANT:
> THE CENTRIFUGAL SERVES
> THE CENTRIPETAL.

Another dimension of Paul's ministry is one that is easily overlooked: his deep concern for the poor. When the apostles agree that Paul and Barnabas go to the Gentiles, they ask them to remember the poor, something that Paul says he was eager to do all along (Gal 2:9-10). Central to Paul's "missionary journeys" was the collection of money for the poor believers in Jerusalem and Judea. It is Paul's "*obsession* for nearly two decades," and it is "hard to imagine . . . any project that occupied Paul's attention more

---

[58]"These prophetic passages all envisage *the nations coming to Israel, not Israel going to the nations.* The recurring verb is 'come'" (Charles Scobie, "Israel and the Nations: An Essay in Biblical Theology," *Tyndale Bulletin* 43, no. 2 [1992]: 292).

[59]Blauw, *Missionary Nature of the Church*, p. 85.

[60]Bauckham, *Bible and Mission*, p. 77 (italics added).

than this collection to the saints."[61] Indeed, Paul speaks about this concern more often than about justification by faith (Rom 15:25-31; 1 Cor 16:1-4; 2 Cor 8-9)![62] He uses this collection as a springboard to speak to the churches that he plants about the centrality of generosity (2 Cor 9:6-15). Paul's activity shows his commitment to a ministry of mercy and justice that accompanies his evangelistic efforts, which was also an example to be emulated in the churches that he planted.

Paul's mission establishes many Gentile churches in various cities throughout Asia Minor, but it sets off a firestorm of controversy among the Jews. For two thousand years the divinely established pattern for God's people has been the Jewish law. The church in Antioch was unique in that a majority of believers were Gentiles, not Jews. Barnabas initially quelled fears coming from Jerusalem. Now, in Paul's mission the pattern is being replicated, and the people of God are taking on new cultural forms in the places where they are established. Many Jews oppose this new, Gentile form of the gospel as inconsistent with many centuries of tradition. A council is called to stem the tide of a growing controversy (Acts 15). The conclusion of this council is of tremendous significance for the ongoing mission of the church: it allows for contextual diversity, and "not even the original, divinely sanctioned culture of God's elect nation has the right to universalize its particular expression of Christianity."[63]

Here is a new situation in the mission of God's people: learning to live amidst the cultures of the world. From now on the mission of God's people will involve a missionary encounter with all cultures, embracing the priceless treasures and opposing the destructive idolatries of all cultures. This missionary encounter takes place already in the Old Testament between Israel and the surrounding nations. An encounter with idolatry is evident in the encounter with the divine claims of Pharaoh, with the idolatrous myths that shape ancient

---

[61]Scot McKnight, "Collection for the Saints," in *Dictionary of Paul and His Letters*, ed. Gerald F. Hawthorne and Ralph P. Martin (Downers Grove, IL: InterVarsity Press, 1993), pp. 143-44.

[62]Jason Hood, "Theology in Action: Paul, the Poor, and Christian Mission," *Southeastern Theological Review* 2, no. 2 (2011): 127-42. See also Jason Hood, "Theology in Action: Paul and Christian Social Care," in *Transforming the World? The Gospel and Social Responsibility*, ed. Jamie A. Grant and Dewi A. Hughes (Nottingham: Apollos, 2009), pp. 129-45. This latter book is a collection of essays issuing a biblical call for social responsibility.

[63]Dean Flemming, *Contextualization in the New Testament: Patterns for Theology and Mission* (Downers Grove, IL: InterVarsity Press, 2005), p. 52.

Near Eastern cultures, with the idolatry of Canaan, and with Israel's encounter with world empires in the postexilic period. But there is also already an embrace of the cultural insights of the nations, as is seen in the law and the wisdom literature. Dan Beeby speaks of "transformed borrowing."[64] Christopher Wright speaks of wisdom from the surrounding nations that employs a "staunch monotheistic disinfectant."[65] That is, there is insight in pagan cultures that must be extracted from their idolatrous setting.

> SINCE THE GOSPEL IS TRANSLATABLE BY ITS VERY NATURE, IT CAN TAKE ON MANY CULTURAL FORMS. IN THAT TRANSLATION THE GOSPEL BOTH AFFIRMS THE CREATIONAL GOOD AND JUDGES THE IDOLATROUS TWISTING OF ALL CULTURAL FORMS.

Israel existed as a unified political community under God's law, and the pagan nations were outsiders. But in the New Testament a missionary encounter becomes more problematic. God's people are now nongeographically based and multiethnic; they are sent to and live in the midst of all the cultures of the world. Since the gospel is translatable by its very nature, it can take on many cultural forms. In that translation the gospel both affirms the creational good and judges the idolatrous twisting of all cultural forms.

"Being the original Scripture of the Christian movement, the New Testament Gospels are a translated version of the message of Jesus, and that means Christianity is a translated religion without a revealed language. . . . Without translation there would be no Christianity or Christians. Translation is the church's birthmark as well as its missionary benchmark: the church would be unrecognizable or unsustainable without it. . . . Christianity seems unique in being the only world religion that is transmitted without the language or originating culture of its founder."

Lamin Sanneh, *Whose Religion Is Christianity?* pp. 97-98

---

[64]Harry Daniel Beeby, "A Missional Approach to Renewed Interpretation," in *Renewing Biblical Interpretation*, ed. Craig Bartholomew, Colin Greene and Karl Möller (Grand Rapids: Zondervan, 2000), p. 280.
[65]Wright, *Mission of God,* p. 50.

A missionary encounter also brings suffering. When the church is faithful to the gospel, its life and witness "will overturn the world's most fundamental beliefs." There will thereby "be a challenge by word and behavior to the ruling powers. As a result there will be conflict and suffering for the Church."[66] This dynamic is evident through the story of Acts. Persecution breaks out against God's people in Jerusalem early (Acts 3–4; 8:1). Jesus says that Paul will learn how much he must suffer for Christ's name (Acts 9:16), and indeed, after suffering for the gospel, Paul and Barnabas say to the church at Antioch, "We must go through many hardships to enter the kingdom of God" (Acts 14:22).

GOD'S MISSION CONTINUES BEYOND ACTS

The story of God's mission through his people is an unfinished story in which we are invited to take our place. The book of Acts draws to a close with Paul in Rome, yet it is a puzzling conclusion. Why does it end so abruptly? It is because Luke invites us into the mission to the ends of the earth. Jesus indicates that the spread of the gospel will be from Jerusalem to the ends of the earth (Acts 1:8). But "'the ends of the earth' is not, in fact, a reference to Rome. . . . Acts 1:8 anticipates the vast expansion of the mission throughout Acts and beyond. . . . The gospel is to spread throughout the entire world."[67] Acts portrays the ongoing progress of the gospel, and the sudden ending in Rome invites us into this story to complete the task that is not yet finished. "In effect," Rosner says, Luke "finishes with the subliminal message, 'to be continued,'"[68] and we might add "with you, the reader, as a participant." We are invited to take our part in that mission. "The book of Acts, as a history of the mission of the church, has no ending as long as Jesus' promise to return remains unfulfilled."[69]

N. T. Wright provides a helpful illustration of how the Bible invites us into its narrative.[70] He imagines that the script of a "lost" Shakespeare play is somehow discovered. Although the play originally had six acts, only a

---

[66]Lesslie Newbigin, *The Gospel in a Pluralist Society* (Grand Rapids: Eerdmans, 1989), pp. 107, 136.

[67]Rosner, "Progress of the Word," pp. 218-19.

[68]Ibid., p. 231.

[69]Schnabel, *Paul and the Early Church*, p. 1588.

[70]N. T. Wright, "Can the Bible Be Authoritative?" *Vox evangelica* 21 (1991): 7-32; idem, *New Testament and the People of God* (London: SPCK, 1992), pp. 139-43.

little more than five have been found: the first four acts, the first scene of act five, and the final act of the play. The rest is missing. The play is given to Shakespearian actors who are asked to work out the rest of act five for them-

---

"What a difference it would make to biblical studies if full justice were done to the Bible as a book about mission from beginning to end, written by missionaries for missionaries! Given its content and intent, how could one study it in any other way?"

Andrew Kirk, *What Is Mission?* p. 20

---

selves. They immerse themselves in the culture and language of Shakespeare and in the partial script that has been recovered. They then improvise the unscripted parts of the fifth act, allowing their performance to be shaped by the trajectory, the thrust, of Shakespeare's story as they have come to understand it. In this way they bring the play toward the conclusion that its author has provided in the script's final act.

Here Wright provides a specific analogy for how the biblical story, and Acts in particular, might function authoritatively to shape the life of the believing community. The biblical story consists of four acts—creation, fall, Israel's mission, Jesus' mission—plus the first scene of the fifth act, which narrates the beginning of the church's mission in Acts. Moreover, we are told how the play is to end—the sixth act. The church today is to carry out its mission in a manner

> WE TAKE UP ISRAEL'S MISSION TO BE A LIGHT TO THE WORLD, JESUS' MISSION TO MAKE KNOWN THE KINGDOM OF GOD, AND THE EARLY CHURCH'S MISSION TO BEAR FAITHFUL WITNESS TO JESUS.

that is consistent with the forward impetus of the first acts while at the same time moving toward and anticipating the intended conclusion.

The overarching plot of the biblical story is God's mission in and through Israel, Jesus and the early church. All three parts of this story are significant for us, for it is we who are now called to continue on the mission of Israel, the mission of Jesus, and the mission of the early church. We take up Israel's mission to be a light to the world, Jesus' mission to make known the kingdom of God, and the early church's mission to bear faithful witness to Jesus. We do so first of all immersed in this story so that our witness may be consistent with and faithful to it. We do so also creatively and imaginatively, improvising in our new cultural settings.

FURTHER READING

Bauckham, Richard. *The Bible and Mission: Christian Witness in a Postmodern World*. Grand Rapids: Baker Academic, 2003.

Bosch, David J. *Transforming Mission: Paradigm Shifts in Theology of Mission*. Maryknoll, NY: Orbis, 1991, pp. 15-178.

Flemming, Dean. *Recovering the Full Mission of God: A Biblical Perspective on Being, Doing and Telling*. Downers Grove, IL: IVP Academic, 2013.

Goheen, Michael. *A Light to the Nations: The Missional Church and the Biblical Story*. Grand Rapids: Baker, 2011.

Wright, Christopher J. H. *The Mission of God: Unlocking the Bible's Grand Narrative*. Downers Grove, IL: IVP Academic, 2006.

DISCUSSION QUESTIONS

1. Hans Frei speaks of "The Eclipse of Biblical Narrative" in reading Scripture since the eighteenth century. What do you think are the primary factors that have hindered the church from reading the Bible as one unfolding story?

2. This chapter explores a missional hermeneutic that sees participation in God's mission as a key to unlocking the biblical story. Do you find this a helpful way to read the biblical story? Why or why not?

3. How does a missional reading of Scripture bring fresh insight to the story of Israel? To the ministry of Jesus? To the history of the early church?

ESSAY TOPICS

1. This chapter employs Genesis 12:1-3 and Exodus 19:3-6 as lenses through which to view the whole story of the Old Testament. What are the strengths and weaknesses of this approach?

2. Discuss the mission of Jesus from the standpoint of John 20:21: "As the Father has sent me, I am sending you."

3. How can we read Acts missionally so as to continue the mission of the early church and yet avoid imposing our understanding of mission on the text?

2

Theology of Mission and
Missional Theology

ભ

In this chapter we move from the biblical story to theological reflection to deepen our understanding of mission. The first part of the
chapter is theological reflection on mission. What is mission? I investigate
this question by examining three important distinctions: the mission of
God and the missional nature of the church, missional dimension and intention, and mission and missions. However, it is important to reflect not
only theologically on mission itself but also on other themes in theology
that shape our understanding of mission. And so the second part is missional reflection on theology.

THEOLOGICAL REFLECTION ON MISSION

Just over a half century ago, when it was clear that a geographical understanding of mission was breaking down, mission statesman John Mackay
asked, "What is the Christian mission at this hour? . . . The time is clearly
ripe to probe deeply into the theology of *mission*. . . . The basic question
confronts us: What does *mission—mission of any kind*—mean? What does
it signify to have a sense of mission?"[1]

The question of the nature of mission will occupy our attention in one
way or another throughout the entire book. But in the first part of this
chapter I explicitly tackle the question by reflecting on three major distinc-

---

[1]John Mackay, "The Christian Mission at This Hour," in *The Ghana Assembly of the International
Council: 28th December, 1957 to 8th January, 1958*, ed. Ronald K. Orchard (London: Edinburgh
House Press, 1958), p. 104.

tions that emerge in mission theology during the twentieth century. They
are the distinctions between (1) the mission of God and the missional nature
of the church; (2) missional dimension and missional intention; (3) mission
and missions. These theological distinctions are important because they
provide an ongoing framework that will properly orient us for the remainder
of the book.

The mission of God and the missional nature of the church. To understand mission, we start with two essential theological perspectives: the
mission of God and the missional nature of the church. Both of these theological themes emerged in close association with one another throughout
the twentieth century.

> TO UNDERSTAND MISSION,
> WE START WITH TWO
> ESSENTIAL THEOLOGICAL
> PERSPECTIVES: THE MISSION
> OF GOD AND THE MISSIONAL
> NATURE OF THE CHURCH.

During the nineteenth century
mission was understood to be one
(usually very important) task of the
church. In the twentieth century a
new understanding gradually emerged:
mission is not simply a task of the
church, but rather is something central
to its very nature and being. Mission is not just something that the church
does, but rather is something that it is. Mission is not merely about certain
activities, but rather defines the very identity of the church.

At the dawn of the twentieth century some foundational assumptions
about mission might be characterized as follows. Mission was primarily
about the geographical expansion of the Christian faith from the Christian
West to the non-Christian non-West. With this understanding, mission is
what takes place overseas, and the church is called to play its role in this
enterprise. For the church in the West this means institutional and financial
support for cross-cultural missionary projects. For the church in the non-
West it means functioning as an institution parallel to mission societies that
provides a container into which missions might place their converts.

This view of mission led to a number of problems. Mission is reduced to
the task of taking the gospel to places where it is not known. Moreover,
mission and church are separated. There are two parallel institutional bodies:
mission organizations are committed to the missionary enterprise, and local
congregations are communities that support it. Further, this leads to

churches without mission and to missionary organizations that are not churches. Churches are reduced to their pastoral role and become introverted. Mission organizations carry on their work outside of ecclesial structures. Finally, mission is an activity carried out in non-Western cultures. If the church was to recover its intrinsic missional character, these undergirding assumptions had to break down. This began to happen early in the twentieth century.

In the 1930s Hendrik Kraemer posed the question that would set the tone: "The church and all Christians . . . are confronted with the question, what is the essential nature of the church, and what is its obligation to the world?"[2] William Richey Hogg observes that mission theology answered this question by stressing that "mission is not a segment of the church's life. On the contrary, the church exists to fulfill a divinely ordained mission."[3] Mission could not be separated from the church: the church must be missionary, and mission must be ecclesial.

A consistent missionary ecclesiology did not immediately emerge, however, because there was no theological framework in which to incorporate the growing theological insights about church and mission. This would be resolved with the notion of the *missio Dei*, the "mission of God." Mission was first and foremost the mission of the triune God, and the mission of the church must be understood as participating in his mission. The concept of the mission of God emerged gradually in the middle part of the twentieth century. Since that time "the understanding of mission as *missio Dei* has been embraced by virtually all Christian persuasions"— mainline Protestantism, Eastern Orthodoxy, Roman Catholicism, and evangelical Protestantism.[4]

The concept of God's mission was injected into the bloodstream of mission thinking by the global conference of the International Missionary Council at Willingen, Germany, in 1952. The task at Willingen was to draft a new theological framework for the mission of the church. The final

---

[2]Quoted in Tom Stransky, "*Missio Dei*," in *Dictionary of the Ecumenical Movement*, ed. Nicholas Lossky et al. (Grand Rapids: Eerdmans, 1991), p. 688.

[3]Alfred Richey Hogg, *Ecumenical Foundations: A History of the International Missionary Council and Its Nineteenth-Century Background* (New York: Harper, 1952), pp. 297-98.

[4]David Bosch, *Transforming Mission: Paradigm Shifts in Theology of Mission* (Maryknoll, NY: Orbis Books, 1991), p. 390.

statement, entitled "The Missionary Calling of the Church," opens, "The missionary movement of which we are a part has its source in the Triune God Himself."[5] The concept of God's mission provided a framework for gathering and relating many theological and missiological insights that had developed over the first half of the twentieth century into a unified theological framework for mission.

◇◇◇

"The missionary movement of which we are a part has its source in the Triune God Himself. Out of the depths of His love for us, the Father has sent forth His own beloved Son to reconcile all things to Himself, that we and all men might, through the Spirit be made one in Him with the Father in that perfect love which is the very nature of God."

"A Statement on the Missionary Calling of the Church," p. 189

◇◇◇

A number of new theological developments in biblical studies and systematic theology were employed to construct the notion of God's mission:

• Scripture: A biblical theological approach, which understands the Bible to be a unified narrative of God's saving acts in history, dominated the ecumenical movement at this time.[6] God's triune mission is understood narratively. It manifests itself in the unfolding history of mighty redemptive acts that culminate in Jesus Christ and the sending of the Spirit and church. The church's mission is a part of this story.

• Eschatology: Jesus announced the gospel of the kingdom. The kingdom as the end goal of universal history had entered history in him; it is already here but has not yet arrived in fullness. This meant that the church must understand its participation in Christ's mission in terms of the creation-wide scope of the kingdom. Moreover, mission is the meaning of the "already but not yet" time period of the kingdom.

---

[5]Norman Goodall, ed., *Missions under the Cross: Addresses Delivered at the Enlarged Meeting of the Committee of the International Missionary Council at Willingen, in Germany, 1952; with Statements Issued by the Meeting* (London: Edinburgh, 1953), p. 190.
[6]Ellen Flessemen-van Leer, *The Bible: Its Authority and Interpretation in the Ecumenical Movement* (Faith and Order Paper 99; Geneva: World Council of Churches, 1980), p. 1.

- Christology: Since the mission of the church is to continue the mission of Jesus, it is his forgotten earthly ministry in its many dimensions that receives new emphasis. But this emphasis does not take away from the universal significance of his death and resurrection, wherein he accomplishes and inaugurates the kingdom, nor does it diminish his cosmic authority in his ascension or his divine nature.

- Soteriology: Salvation accomplished by Christ is restorative of and as wide as creation, and thus the church is sent to embody and announce a salvation that is equally comprehensive.

- Pneumatology: The Spirit must be understood in terms of eschatology and mission. The Spirit is a gift of the end time that brings the powers of the age to come into history. The Spirit gives this life of the new creation to the church and empowers it for witness in life, word and deed.

The mission of the church is rooted in the mission of the triune God. There are two sides to this new emphasis. First, mission is first and foremost *God's* mission. The primary emphasis is on what God is doing for the restoration of the world. Only then do we consider the mission of the church as it participates in God's redemptive work. Second, mission is defined in terms of the *triune* work of God. It is this participation in the mission of the triune God that gives the church its role in God's story and thus its missionary identity. The church takes its role in the loving mission of the Father to restore the creation as it is accomplished in the kingdom mission of the Son and realized to the ends of earth in the power of the Spirit.

"If the contemporary church truly grasped and lived by the truth that mission is the mother of theology and theology is the mother of mission, that is, if the church were intoxicated with the triune God, it would be transformed and a powerful transformer of culture."

Ross Hastings, *Missional God, Missional Church*, p. 250

Mission is first of all the activity of God. The missionary impulse flows from the love of God to reconcile his alienated world. The Father sends the Son to reconcile all things to himself. Jesus accomplishes the mission for which he was sent in his life, death and resurrection. On the basis of Christ's finished work, the Father and Son send the Spirit to continue God's renewing work in the world to the ends of the earth. The Spirit is the missionary Spirit of Jesus who works both in the church as the place or locus of salvation and through the church as a channel and instrument of his salvation to others. By gathering his people into his work of salvation, the Spirit constitutes them as a witnessing community. The Son also sends the church in the power of the Spirit: "As the Father has sent me, I am sending you" (Jn 20:21). Thus, the church is taken up into God's mission, his saving work.

The terminology of "sending" is key. The Father sends the Son to accomplish his redemptive work. The Father and the Son send the Spirit to incorporate his people into that redemption. The Son sends the church in the power of the Spirit to continue his mission. The mission is first of all God's, but he includes the church. The mission of the church is participation in the sending of God. Like Jesus, they are constituted as a sent people.

> MISSION IS FIRST OF ALL THE ACTIVITY OF GOD. THE MISSIONARY IMPULSE FLOWS FROM THE LOVE OF GOD TO RECONCILE HIS ALIENATED WORLD.

It is important to prevent a potential misunderstanding that may be present when the mission of God is reduced exclusively to a sending metaphor: it can easily bypass the Old Testament. If the first movement is the Father sending the Son, we are already into the Gospels! And so God's mission needs to be understood in a narrative way as it unfolds in the story of Scripture. The work of the Father begins in Israel, and this cannot be eclipsed. Sending is an important biblical metaphor, especially in the Gospel of John, but it is only one metaphor. Equally important is the metaphor of participation as God's people in God's mission. Of course, those who originally spoke of God's mission understood this well. However, when the mission of the triune God is reduced to a brief theological formula based on the metaphor of sending, the Old Testament and the narrative quality of the *missio Dei* can easily get downplayed.

With this notion of God's mission the colonialist assumptions that captured mission in the earlier part of the twentieth century are shattered and replaced with a new theological framework. Expressing the nature of the church as participating in God's mission frees it from any nonmissionary misconceptions. It also frees mission from being defined exclusively in geographical terms. The church is sent by God to every inhabited area of the world to embody and make known the good news. Mission defines the very identity and being of the church. The church is missional, and mission is ecclesial.

Hendrikus Berkhof offers insightful theological reflection on missional ecclesiology (although he does not call it that) that pulls together systematically many of these formulations and connects it to theological reflection on the church throughout history.

> MISSION DEFINES THE VERY IDENTITY AND BEING OF THE CHURCH. THE CHURCH IS MISSIONAL, AND MISSION IS ECCLESIAL.

Berkhof analyzes the church in terms of its threefold character.[7] First, the church is understood as an institution. Through a number of activities and ministries the church is organized into a particular societal institution that ministers Christ to people. This ministry has various facets, such as preaching and teaching, sacraments and fellowship, leadership and the diaconate. All of these serve one purpose: to minister the new life of Christ to people. Second, the church can be understood as a community. It is a network of relationships in which we have responsibility for one another. A diversity of gifts is given to serve and build up the body. It is a community bound together in a common fellowship that manifests and nurtures new life in Christ together.

Berkhof says, however, "It is not enough to ascertain this twofold character of the church."[8] We must also understand the church in a third way: in terms of its orientation to the world. The final goal of the church cannot be the upbuilding of the individual believer by the church as institution or even the ecclesial community; rather, it must be the renewal of all humankind, of all of humankind's life, and of all creation. This is the goal of God's redemptive work accomplished in Christ. Thus, the church is positioned be-

---

[7]Hendrikus Berkhof, *Christian Faith: An Introduction to the Study of the Faith*, trans. Sierd Woudstra (Grand Rapids: Eerdmans, 1979), pp. 339-422.
[8]Ibid., p. 344.

tween Christ and the salvation of the whole world with the call to mediate the good news to the world.

This third aspect of the church, its orientation to the world, is not simply an addendum or an important ministry of the church; it is far more important than that. Berkhof speaks of a chain running from Christ to the world: Christ is mediated to the congregation as it gathers; the congregation then mediates Christ to the world. "In this chain the world comes last, yet it is the goal that gives meaning and purpose to the preceding links. Everything that has come before serves this goal, even when it is not deliberately stated."[9] Indeed, the church is misunderstood if this aspect of ecclesiology is neglected. The significance of this insight demands the rethinking of all ecclesiology from the standpoint of the relation of the church to the world.

◇◇◇

"The Church is, by its nature and calling, in the first and last instance an apostolic body. . . . By 'apostolic body' we mean the Church is 'sent' into the world, has a specific 'mission'. It has a message for the whole world that must be heralded. Although it may be considered as an unfounded pretension or felt as an unbearable arrogance, the fact is there, and with genuine understanding of this fact there can be no real understanding of the Christian Church. As an apostolic body the Church is commissioned to proclaim—by its *kerygma* of God's acts of salvation in Christ, by its *koinonia* as a new community, living by the bonds of peace and charity—the message of God's dealings with, and purpose for, the world and mankind. This message has to go out to *all* men, in *all* lands, in *all* situations and civilizations, in *all* conditions and spheres and circumstances of life, so witnessing to God's redemptive order in Jesus, by word and deed."

Hendrik Kraemer, *Religion and the Christian Faith*, pp. 17-18

◇◇◇

So the church must be understood in terms of its threefold character: first, the church is an institution, a totality of structures and activities;

---

[9]Ibid., p. 410.

then, it is a community, a totality of personal relationships sharing salvation together; and finally, it is a totality of influences on the world as salt and leaven.

Berkhof narrates the historical development of ecclesiology. The institutional aspect of the church dominated the history of the Western church, while emphasis on community evolved only since the time of the Reformation. Today the missionary movement and the secularization of the West highlight the importance of recovering the dimension of the church's orientation to the world. Theological reflection on this outward orientation of ecclesiology developed in missionary circles throughout the twentieth century, but it did not penetrate official theology except for Karl Barth. It is perhaps excusable for the Reformers not to recognize this missional dimension, but "anyone who today, either theologically or practically, still ignores it as a central mark is without excuse."[10]

There are two ways—sacralization and secularization—by which the church may refuse to embrace its missionary nature. Either path is disobedience and betrayal.[11] In the first, sacralization (or churchism), the people of God remain within the boundaries of the institutional church. They are focused on their rites, language and institutional forms. They are concerned only for their institutional life. In this path the church has become introverted and self-absorbed. In the second, secularization (or worldliness), the people of God are so immersed in the world that they are assimilated and conformed to the idolatrous currents of the culture. Here solidarity with culture trumps antithesis. In both paths the church avoids the clash, the offense and the suffering of a missionary encounter with the world. The second—worldliness or secularization—is one of open betrayal and will soon draw a reaction. But the first—churchism or sacralization—is much more pious and respectable and therefore is concealed. There will not be the same backlash.

> THERE ARE TWO WAYS—
> SACRALIZATION AND
> SECULARIZATION—BY WHICH
> THE CHURCH MAY REFUSE TO
> EMBRACE ITS MISSIONARY
> NATURE. EITHER PATH IS
> DISOBEDIENCE AND BETRAYAL.

---

[10]Ibid., p. 418.
[11]Ibid., p. 421.

Thus, the temptation of the first is much greater but is no less dangerous and unfaithful than the second.

Understanding mission in terms of God's mission and the missional nature of the church will be foundational for the remainder of this book. Mission is first of all the work of God; it is *God's* mission. The church participates in God's mission and therefore is missional by its very nature. Built upon this theological foundation are many different activities that carry out God's mission in the world. In this book I will discuss many of them: evangelism, action for mercy and justice, the calling of believers in the public square, a missionary encounter with culture and with other religions, urban mission, church planting, and cross-cultural missions that takes the gospel to where it is not known. All are rooted in God's mission to the world. All are rooted in the new being of the people of God that constitute them as a missional people. The rest of the book will always assume and be shaped by these foundational theological convictions about mission.

Missional dimension and missional intention. A second distinction between missionary dimension and missionary intention further helps to characterize mission. During the mid-twentieth century the scope of mission continued to broaden to include everything that the church was doing. Mission advocates were concerned that the more specific evangelistic and missionary tasks of the church might be engulfed in this broadening view of mission. Stephen Neill famously warned that if everything is mission, then nothing is mission. On the one hand, there was an appreciation for the comprehensive scope of mission that was emerging. Indeed, it reflected Scripture's teaching on the cosmic scope of the gospel. On the other hand, the broadening of mission had the potential to leave behind intentional activities that had as their deliberate aim a witness to Christ to those who did not yet know him.

> STEPHEN NEILL FAMOUSLY WARNED THAT IF EVERYTHING IS MISSION, THEN NOTHING IS MISSION.

An important distinction emerged between missional dimension and missional intention. Lesslie Newbigin observes that this distinguishes "between mission as a *dimension* of the Church's whole life, and mission as the primary *intention* of certain activities. Because the Church *is* the mission there is a

missionary dimension of everything that the Church does. But not everything the Church does has a missionary intention"; certain activities can be
considered to have a missional intention when they are "an action of the
Church in going out beyond the frontiers of its own life to bear witness to
Christ as Lord among those who do not know Him, and when the overall
intention of that action is that they should be brought from unbelief to faith."[12]

Since the whole life of the church, both as a gathered community and
when it is scattered throughout the world, is the visible means by which the
Holy Spirit carries on his mission in the world, the whole life of the church
partakes of the character of witness. Every aspect of the believer's and the
believing community's life has a missional dimension. However, not all of
the church's life has a missional intention. Not every activity is deliberately
aimed at inviting people to believe the gospel and submit to the Lordship of
Jesus Christ. Worship does not have a missional intention. It may well
witness to the unbeliever (see 1 Cor 14:23-25) and so possesses a missional
dimension as it makes known God's presence present with his people. But
its intention is to bring praise to God. In our daily lives the focus of marriage,
for example, is not evangelistic; it is a sacrificial, loving union between a man
and woman. Yet it has a missional dimension as it points to renewing work
of Christ when a Christian couple embodies God's creational design. So it
is, for example, with our callings in the public square, with our use of leisure
time, with our lives among our neighbors and friends, with the way we treat
the nonhuman creation, with our handling of technology, and so on. If
Christ is Lord of all of human life, then the whole of our lives will be part of
God's mission as it directs others to his sovereign rule and renewing power.
All of Christian life has a missional dimension.

The structure of the Christian Reformed Church's contemporary testimony *Our World Belongs to God* is helpful to consider. Its basic structure
is narrative as it thematically unfolds the biblical story. The largest section
is the next-to-last section, titled "The Mission of God's People."[13] It begins,
"Joining the mission of God, the church is sent with the gospel of the

---

[12]Lesslie Newbigin, *One Body, One Gospel, One World: The Christian Mission Today* (London:
International Missionary Council, 1958), pp. 43-44.

[13]Christian Reformed Church, *Our World Belongs to God: A Contemporary Testimony* (Grand Rapids: CRC Publications, 2008), paragraphs 41-54 (www.crcna.org/welcome/beliefs/contemporary
-testimony/our-world-belongs-god).

kingdom," and makes explicit that "this mission is central to our being." It affirms the comprehensive scope of the church's mission based on the universal lordship of Jesus: "Jesus Christ rules over all. To follow this Lord is to serve him wherever we are, without fitting in, light in the darkness, salt in a spoiling world." The following paragraphs touch on numerous aspects of human life: the sanctity of life and threats to it in today's society, gender and sexuality, singleness, marriage and family, education, work and leisure, global economics and business, science and technology, environmental stewardship, politics, war and peacemaking. In each area it confesses that the church is called to be involved as a healing presence as a witness to the rule of Jesus Christ. Yet the witness to Jesus to summon others to faith will not be the primary intention; rather, faithfulness to God's creational intention for these various sectors of human life will have a missional dimension as a sign of God's renewing power.

However, the church also undertakes certain activities with the deliberate intent of bearing witness to Jesus Christ. Flowing from a church that is aware of its missionary dimension will be words and deeds whose conscious goal is to point to Jesus Christ and invite others to follow him. For example, evangelism as the verbal proclamation of the gospel is an activity defined by the intent to witness to Jesus Christ and invite the hearer to believe. Moreover, a church whose missionary vision extends to the ends of the earth will take on planned projects of establishing a gospel witness among peoples where

"Mission is more than one *activity* of the church among others. We cannot equate the church's mission with instigating an evangelistic outreach program, supporting overseas missionaries, running an inner city soup kitchen, or combatting human trafficking, as worthy as such activities may be. These are merely concrete expressions of something that runs much deeper. We don't simply *do* mission. 'Mission' is who we *are*. We are a people called by God for the sake of the world. The church's being is inseparable from its mission. This basic missional identity integrates everything we say and do as a church."

Dean Flemming, *Recovering the Full Mission of God*, p. 258

there is no witness. These activities will be deliberate and intentional, aimed to witness to the gospel and invite the response of faith. Certain activities, then, have a missional intention.

Both of these aspects of mission are essential. In fact, one without the other will cripple the mission of the church. A church that is not evangelizing and is unconcerned about missions to peoples who have never heard betrays the gospel. A church that reduces mission to evangelistic activities narrows the scope of the gospel. And at the same time it removes the full context in which witnessing words should find their place. Each aspect needs the other.

Mission and missions. Another related crucial distinction is extremely helpful in properly speaking of mission. Throughout the nineteenth and early twentieth centuries mission was reduced to cross-cultural missions, but things changed: the church in the non-Western part of the world grew, and the church in the West receded. A broader vision of mission threatened the cross-cultural missionary task of the church. It was indeed important to broaden mission in light of the church's role in the biblical story. But at the same time it was also essential "to identify and distinguish the specific foreign missionary task within the total Mission of the Church."[14]

Newbigin distinguishes between mission and missions (with an "s").[15] Whereas mission is the total calling of the church to make known the gospel as it participates in God's mission, missions are particular enterprises within that total mission of the church "which have the primary intention of bringing into existence a Christian presence in a milieu where previously there was no such presence or where such presence was ineffective."[16] Thus, missions remain an essential part of the ongoing mission of the church. Since the mission of the church is to the ends of the earth, it will continue to be important to

> NEWBIGIN DISTINGUISHES BETWEEN MISSION AND MISSIONS (WITH AN "S").

[14]Lesslie Newbigin, "Mission and Missions," *Christianity Today* 4, no. 2 (August 1, 1960): 911.
[15]David Bosch also makes a distinction between mission and missions but in a different way. Mission is the mission of God, whereas missions are human activities of the church that participate in God's mission. See Bosch, *Transforming Mission*, p. 391.
[16]Lesslie Newbigin, "Crosscurrents in Ecumenical and Evangelical Understandings of Mission," *International Bulletin of Missionary Research* 6, no. 4 (1982): 149.

identify where there are peoples who have not heard the good news and to establish a witness to the gospel in those places.

A broadening of mission should not eclipse missions. In fact, missions are important for maintaining the missional dimension in all of life. While "the church is mission, we still need 'missions' in order that it may be truly so. . . . This is not in order to relieve the rest of the church of missionary responsibility but to ensure that its whole life is missionary."[17] It is still important to identify need throughout the world and to commission gifted and called individuals to take the gospel to those places. If our response to the modern missionary movement's reducing mission to "missions" ends up eclipsing missions, we have lost sight of the scriptural horizon of the "ends of the earth." There is much more to say about missions, and we will return to this aspect of the missional calling of the church in the final chapter of this book.

MISSIONAL REFLECTION ON THEOLOGY

It is important not only to reflect on mission itself but also to look at other themes in theology that shape our understanding of mission. Our understanding and practice of mission will be fundamentally shaped by foundational theological commitments. For example, our understanding of the gospel, of Christ, of salvation, of the Holy Spirit, of the church, of sin, of humanity, of the nature and interpretation of Scripture, and more will form our views of mission at a deep level, usually unconsciously.

"We are in need of a missiological agenda for theology rather than just a theological agenda for mission; for theology rightly understood, has no reason to exist other than critically to accompany the *missio Dei*. So mission should be the theme of all theology."

David J. Bosch, *Transforming Mission*, p. 494

Earlier in this chapter we noted a fundamental shift in the theology of mission in the middle part of the twentieth century. This new view of

---

[17]Ibid., p. 179.

mission was rooted in God's mission and its necessary correlative, the missional nature of the church. That shift, we observed, took place only because of new insights in other areas of theology: Scripture, eschatology, Christology, salvation and the Spirit. This historical example shows that it is necessary not only to reflect theologically on mission but also to reflect missionally on theology. As Harvie Conn puts it, the "question is not simply, or only, or largely, missions and what it is. The question is also theology and what it does."[18] In this chapter I will take some beginning steps toward a missional theology by briefly addressing a number of theological topics from Scripture that undergird authentic mission today.

"From a theology of mission to a missional theology." David Bosch expresses this in terms of moving from a theology of mission to a missional theology. It is theological reflection not only on mission itself in Scripture but also on the whole range of theological loci that will influence our vision of the missional calling of the church. When one probes reductionist understandings of mission more deeply, one almost always finds at the foundation a deficient Christology, or a misunderstanding of the gospel, or an individualistic understanding of humanity, sin and salvation, or a variety of other theological beliefs that inform our view of mission, even though they usually are held at a subconscious level.

This should not surprise us if we properly understand the missional nature of theology. "The formation of the church for mission should be the motivating force that shapes and energizes our theological labors in all their diversity and distinctiveness."[19] To detach theology from the church's mission distorts the very nature of theology. And so J. Andrew Kirk rightly comments that "theology by its nature is missionary."[20] And likewise Bosch says, "Just as the

> TO DETACH THEOLOGY FROM THE CHURCH'S MISSION DISTORTS THE VERY NATURE OF THEOLOGY.

---

[18]Harvie Conn, "The Missionary Task of Theology: A Love/Hate Relationship?" *Westminster Theological Journal* 45 (1983): 7.

[19]Darrell Guder, "From Mission and Theology to Missional Theology," *Princeton Seminary Bulletin* 24, no. 1 (2003): 48.

[20]J. Andrew Kirk, *The Mission of Theology and Theology as Mission* (Valley Forge, PA: Trinity Press International, 1997), p. 49.

church ceases to be church if it is not missionary, theology ceases to be theology if it loses its missionary character."[21]

<hr>

"Intuitively the Third World church is making a discovery. Systematic theology is not simply a coherent arrangement of supra-cultural universals. It is a compilation from the Western history of dogma. And that history, in the process of compilation, has lost its missiological thrust. The effect of this process on the Western churches is similarly destructive of mission."

Harvie Conn, "The Missionary Task of Theology," p. 19

<hr>

The missional theologies of the third-world church present a challenge to the nonmissional theologies of the West. Following the systematic theologian Martin Kahler, who argued in 1908 that in the early church mission was the mother of theology, Bosch believes that the early church theologians "wrote theology for the sake of mission," and that this "is what is taking place in Africa today."[22] Likewise, Johannes Aagaard says that in Asia "theology has to some extent become missiology, while at the same time missiology has become theology. It is probably the most important thing which has happened in the Asian churches."[23] Latin American theologies—Catholic, evangelical, liberationist—are also products of mission as the church has sought to address its context of injustice and oppression with the gospel. Bosch rightly concludes, "Third World theologies are *missionary* theologies, whereas First World theologies are not," and so, he hopes, "Third World theologies may become a force of renewal in the West."[24]

The importance of a renewed missional reflection on theology is evident when Bosch says that "unless we develop a missionary theology, not just a theology of mission, we will not achieve more than merely patch up the

---

[21]Bosch, *Transforming Mission*, p. 494.
[22]David Bosch, "Missionary Theology in Africa," *Journal of Theology for South Africa* 49 (December 1984): 16
[23]Johannes Aagaard, "The Soft Age Has Gone," *Missiology* 10, no. 3 (1982): 266.
[24]David Bosch, *Believing in the Future: Toward a Missiology of Western Culture* (Valley Forge, PA: Trinity Press International, 1995), p. 36.

church."[25] In the last part of this chapter I briefly consider a number of theological motifs. Guiding my rather selective and brief treatment are questions such as these: What theological issues are important for the mission of the church today especially in the West? How have these significant issues been deformed or neglected because of the Western cultural story? I begin with theological reflection on salvation because of its obvious importance for mission. But it becomes clear that as I discuss the doctrine of salvation (soteriology), a number of other theological themes closely bound up with it necessarily come into view—eschatology, Christology, the Spirit, church, humankind, sin, Scripture—and demand a brief treatment.

Salvation. There is a universal religious craving among human beings for salvation. At the heart of the Christian faith is a story of cosmic salvation: against the backdrop of creation and human rebellion the Bible narrates a story of God's mighty acts finding their center in Jesus Christ that are aimed at the salvation of his creation. It is in this story of salvation climaxing in Jesus as the Savior that the people of God find their identity and role. As a people they are taken up into God's work so that they might experience and mediate his salvation to others. It therefore is no wonder that since salvation is "the deepest and most fundamental question of humanity," the "soteriological motif" has always been "the throbbing heart of missiology."[26]

But what is salvation? And what is its scope? "Christians differ in the way they conceptualize salvation, which in turn determines their approach to mission."[27] Certainly our understanding of salvation greatly influences the way we think about and practice mission. "In fact," writes P. R. Parushev, "our view of salvation is probably the most critical determinant in deciding on our approach to missions."[28] It is both the scope and the nature of salvation that will impact the mission of the church.

Four interconnected misunderstandings of the nature and scope of salvation have often had a detrimental effect on the mission of the church. First,

---

[25]Bosch, *Believing in the Future*, p. 32.
[26]Jerald Gort, "Heil, onheil en bemiddeling," in *Oecumenische inleiding in de missiologie: Teksten en kontektsten van het wereldchristendom*, ed. F. J. Verstraelen et al. (Kampen: Kok, 1988), p. 203, quoted in David Bosch, *Transforming Mission*, p. 393.
[27]P. R. Parushev, "Salvation," in *Dictionary of Mission Theology: Evangelical Foundations*, ed. John Corrie (Downers Grove, IL: InterVarsity Press, 2007), p. 353.
[28]Ibid.

salvation has been reduced to the individual person. Sometimes it is reduced even further to individual souls, conceived as the spiritual part of the
human person.[29] Second, salvation has been understood in otherworldly
terms; it is about escaping this world when you die and going to heaven.
Third, salvation has been cast primarily in future terms; salvation is something that happens at the end of our life when we die. Finally, salvation is
conceived as something that God does in and for us but not through us for
the sake of the whole world. In other words, God's people are recipients, but
not channels, of God's salvation. It is only when we correct these mistaken
notions of salvation that, as N. T. Wright says, "we will discover the historic
basis for the full-orbed mission of the church."[30]

In the New Testament salvation was understood within an eschatological
framework. Salvation was bound up with the coming of the kingdom of God,
the restoration of God's rule over all of human life and all of creation. In
Luke, for example, salvation comes with the arrival of the kingdom of God
in Jesus. Luke uses the word "salvation" in a holistic way to describe the
renewal of the whole of human life—economic, social, political, physical,
religious. For Paul, the new creation has broken into the present, and thus
salvation extends even to the nonhuman creation as well as all of human life.
It is in the early centuries of the church as the gospel encountered Greek
philosophy that this "eschatological expectation waned"; increasingly, "salvation was the redemption of indi-
vidual souls in the hereafter, which
would take effect at the occasion of
the miniature apocalypse of the
death of the individual believer."[31]

> LUKE USES THE WORD
> "SALVATION" IN A HOLISTIC WAY
> TO DESCRIBE THE RENEWAL OF
> THE WHOLE OF HUMAN LIFE—
> ECONOMIC, SOCIAL, POLITICAL,
> PHYSICAL, RELIGIOUS.

This individualistic and otherworldly view of salvation was embraced to some extent by the Pietist
movement of the seventeenth century and is still present in popular evangelicalism today. And so it has had a defining and shaping impact on the

---

[29]Soong-Chan Rah, *The Next Evangelicalism: Freeing the Church from Western Cultural Captivity*
(Downers Grove, IL: InterVarsity Press, 2009), pp. 27-45.
[30]N. T. Wright, *Surprised by Hope: Rethinking Heaven, the Resurrection, and the Mission of the
Church* (New York: HarperCollins, 2008), pp. 200-201.
[31]Bosch, *Transforming Mission*, p. 394.

understanding and practice of mission. But it is clear, even in this brief sketch, that a doctrine of salvation does not stand alone; a number of doctrinal corollaries are woven together with this view of salvation. We have noted that the eschatological setting of salvation—the kingdom of the Gospels—is a casualty. The kingdom is relocated to a future heaven or is confined to the inner person. It is also true that Christology may be made subservient to this individualistic and otherworldly soteriology. Discussions about Christ may center on defining the divinity and humanity of Christ, separating his person from his work. The cross may be interpreted primarily, if not exclusively, in terms of the substitutionary atonement, which provides salvation for the individual person as Christ takes their guilt. Moreover, the Spirit's role in this context is to apply Christ's work to the individual. The church is reduced to a mediator of salvation to the faithful, channeling salvation to individual members through word and sacrament. Humankind is understood primarily as discrete individuals, sin as the disobedience and guilt of individual people, and ethics as personal moral choices and conduct. Such a view eclipses a true understanding of humankind, which is a cultural and communal solidarity around a common worldview and religious faith. It also ignores the way that sinful structures and powers at work in culture subvert communal life.

Although the foregoing portrait is painted with a broad brush, it is helpful in seeing how this type of theology has had a shaping effect on our understanding of mission in popular evangelicalism. The problem is not so much that these emphases are unbiblical. In fact, defending the divinity and humanity of Jesus in our day remains critically important; the substitutionary atonement is central to biblical faith; the Spirit does bring salvation to individual people; human beings are moral agents of responsibility, and sin is individual disobedience. All of these doctrinal affirmations certainly express biblical themes. The problem is that wide swaths of scriptural teaching are neglected and even twisted when salvation is mistakenly reduced to the individual and understood in terms of going to heaven when you die. Or, to put it another way, these truths find their place in the wrong story: the story of how Jesus saves individuals to live in heaven.

G. C. Berkouwer speaks of a "soteriological self-centeredness" that has marginalized the cosmic scope of the biblical story. He continues, "Such an approach does not repudiate what the Bible says about the new earth, it simply pays it no mind. The cosmic perspective is just not assimilated into the larger expectation. . . . It is as if the creation-perspective is obliterated in eschatology and becomes superfluous on account of [individual] salvation."[32] Similarly, N. T. Wright says that in the last two hundred years we have "over-emphasized the individual at the expense of the larger picture of God's creation." The problem is that when "we start with the future hope of the individual, there is always the risk that we will at least by implication, understand that as the real center of everything and treat the hope of creation as mere embroidery around the edges."[33] He thus structures his following argument along biblical lines in terms of the "large-scale hope of the whole cosmos, the great drama within which our little dramas are, as it were, the play within the play. What is God's purpose for the world as a whole?"[34] Likewise, Bosch states that when salvation "refers solely to something which happens to an individual after death," such an "ahistorical and otherworldly perception of salvation is spurious."[35]

A more faithful approach to the theological logic of the biblical story, one that will nourish a robust mission, is cosmic, communal and individual. God's goal is a cosmic, creation-wide, culture-wide renewal; he chooses a community to embody and make known that future; and individuals are called to join this community, take responsibility, and play their role in the bigger story. The individualism of our Protestant theology is the result of "deep personalization of the Christian faith" that took place at the Reformation. This "bringing together of the Word

> GOD'S GOAL IS A COSMIC, CREATION-WIDE, CULTURE-WIDE RENEWAL; HE CHOOSES A COMMUNITY TO EMBODY AND MAKE KNOWN THAT FUTURE; AND INDIVIDUALS ARE CALLED TO JOIN THIS COMMUNITY, TAKE RESPONSIBILITY, AND PLAY THEIR ROLE IN THE BIGGER STORY.

---

[32]G. C. Berkouwer, The Return of Christ, Studies in Dogmatics (Grand Rapids: Eerdmans, 1972), pp. 211-12. "This cosmic aspect of redemption was increasingly lost to Western Christendom since the Age of Enlightenment, and to this day we have been unable to restore it to its strength and clarity" (Adolf Köberle, Der Herr über alles: Beiträge zum Universalismus der christlichen Botschaft [Hamburg: Furche-Verlag, 1957], p. 103).

[33]Wright, Surprised by Hope, p. 80.

[34]Ibid.

[35]Bosch, Transforming Mission, p. 488.

of God and the individual" was unique in Christian history "and can never be undone."[36] However, to prevent this personalization of the gospel from distorting the biblical testimony, it must be properly set in the cosmic and communal context of the narrative of Scripture. It is there that it finds its rightful place and, in fact, comes into its own.

It is important to recognize that these individualistic and otherworldly confessional commitments greatly impact the mission of the church. Under these misguided views, the comprehensive scope of mission across the full range of human life—witness in the whole of our lives, in deeds of justice and mercy, and in word—is limited to evangelism. Further, evangelism is limited to introducing Jesus as Savior to individual people who can find forgiveness because of the substitutionary death of Christ and go to heaven to live with God forever when they die. Again, there remains a necessary and powerful truth in this view. Indeed, evangelism of individual people is essential to the mission of the church; we do find forgiveness from the guilt of sin because Christ has died in our place; we will go to heaven when we die (temporarily as an intermediate state, but one day our bodies will be raised from the dead on the renewed creation, and that is our hope); our relationship with God restored in this life will be realized more fully in the age to come. But again, the problem is not so much what is affirmed as what is left out because of the context or storyline that gives meaning to these truths.

What is needed is a more robust and biblical understanding of salvation. However, this entails an overhaul of more than soteriology. Many theological components are inextricably bound together with this understanding of salvation. Thus, there is a need for a missional renewal of theology that will undergird a more comprehensive and substantial view of mission. Here I can only sketch briefly some of the contours of such an approach.

Gospel. The mission of the church is to embody and announce the gospel. The word "gospel" represents the common Greek word for "good news" (*euangelion*). But what is the good news? It is precisely here that misunderstanding can deform our understanding of mission: in popular evangelicalism there are a number of reductions of the gospel that have had a

---

[36]Hendrikus Berkhof, *The Doctrine of the Holy Spirit* (Atlanta: John Knox, 1964), p. 66.

harmful impact on mission. We have already noted several of them, such as the good news being misrepresented as a message about how an individual can go to heaven. Yet both the otherworldliness and the individualism of this message misrepresent the gospel. The gospel is about the restoration of the whole creation and all of human life in Christ.

There are other ways: the gospel is reduced to the cross and even more narrowly to the substitutionary atonement; the gospel is limited to the benefits of justification by faith and forgiveness. These certainly are true and essential elements of the gospel. Yet the gospel is centered in the whole of Christ's work—his life, death, resurrection, ascension, return—not just his death. Moreover, there are many biblical images that interpret what God has accomplished in the crucifixion of Jesus, not just the substitutionary atonement. And finally, there are many gifts that come to us through the work of Christ, not just justification and forgiveness.

Sometimes this narrowing of the gospel comes because it has been condensed to a formula to be employed in evangelism: "You are a sinner, but there is good news: Christ has died for your sin, and if you believe in him, you will be forgiven and justified." All true! But the gospel is much more than this.

Surely the starting point for understanding the gospel is to recognize that Jesus himself is the first one to proclaim "good news." What did *he* mean by the "gospel"? His was a gospel of the kingdom of God (Mk 1:14-15). Jesus' announcement must be understood as the climactic moment, the fulfillment and center of the whole biblical story. The background of this terminology is found in Isaiah 52:7-10: good news, God reigns! The rule of God over all of creation and all of human life is being restored. This is what the whole story of God's mission has been moving toward from the beginning. It is now here; it is revealed and accomplished in the person and work of Christ.

Thus, the gospel is a message that in the person of Jesus Christ and in the events of his life, death, resurrection and ascension God has revealed and accomplished the goal of redemptive history narrated in the Old Testament: the restoration of the whole creation and the entirety of human life to again live under the rule of God. Note in this description four things: the gospel centers on the person and work of Jesus Christ, especially but not only in his death and resurrection (1 Cor 15:1-8; cf. Rom 1:1-4; 2 Tim 1:10; 2:8);

his work is a fulfillment of the Old Testament story; it is about the restoration of God's rule over his creation, including humanity; it is all-embracing,
thus including the whole creation and the entirety of human life.

Eschatology. Thus, salvation and the gospel must be understood within
their original eschatological context. If we want to follow the logic of the
biblical story that moves from cosmic to communal to individual, the gospel
of the kingdom as the renewal of God's cosmic reign over all things must be
the starting point. Sometimes the word "eschatology" is used to speak only
of the end-time events surrounding the return of Christ; however, in the
announcement of Jesus the kingdom of the end is breaking into history now
in him and by the Spirit.

We must begin with the Jewish world of the time and how its people heard
this announcement. The Jews were ultimately expecting a comprehensive
restoration of God's rule over all creation, over all peoples, over all of human
life that would arrive at the end of history. On the one hand, Jesus says that
his cosmic rule has already arrived. On the other hand, he challenges their
notions of what this looks like and says that God's rule is now present in him.
The kingdom of God now has a human face and a name: Jesus.

"A Kingdom-centered theology worthy of the name is concerned with
every aspect of life and society. Often in the history of the Church and
theology Jesus has been—and in some cases continues to be—proclaimed *without* His Kingdom. In the face of that kind of proclamation,
it should not come as a surprise to discover people attempting to find
the Kingdom and salvation without *Christ.*"

Johannes Verkuyl, "The Biblical Notion of the Kingdom," p. 72

These simple observations begin to correct some distortions that have
taken place in mission history. In the first place, Jesus cannot be separated
from the kingdom. The salvation of the kingdom is restorative in nature and
cosmic in scope. A strong view of creation undergirds the Jewish (and
therefore Jesus') approach to the kingdom. It is the restoration of God's rule
over creation. Separating Jesus from the kingdom and recasting him merely

as a personal Savior can lead to mission understood exclusively as an evangelistic announcement of personal salvation, which loses sight of mission in the public life of culture. It severs salvation from its kingdom context.

> JESUS CANNOT BE SEPARATED FROM THE KINGDOM. THE SALVATION OF THE KINGDOM IS RESTORATIVE IN NATURE AND COSMIC IN SCOPE.

But if some have introduced a Jesus stripped of his kingdom context, others have focused on the kingdom and have allowed the person of Jesus to fade into the background: the kingdom is separated from Jesus. Thus, the kingdom becomes an ideological program or triumphalistic crusade of societal development that is no longer anchored in the person and work of Jesus—his cross, resurrection, exaltation. Sometimes within the mainline churches mission, separated from Jesus, becomes a matter of changing structures and seeking justice as primarily a human task. A relationship to a person recedes into the background.

Herman Ridderbos shows how the message of the Gospels holds together the person of Jesus and the kingdom, the personal and eschatological context of the gospel. In the Synoptic Gospels—Matthew, Mark, Luke—"the coming of God's kingdom constitutes the great ('eschatological') issue at stake and [is] the central content of Jesus' preaching"; however, "that all-controlling 'eschatological' background is missing" in the Gospel of John.[37] It is rather the *person* of Jesus that provides the entire background for John's Gospel—the "personal concept."[38] But this is not to narrow salvation to simply a personal relationship: the Gospel of John deals with the identity of Jesus by "revealing in him God's salvation in its 'eschatological' all-embracing significance."[39] Thus, the person of Jesus and the kingdom of God both define the Gospel accounts. Salvation is a personal encounter yet carries eschatological, creation-wide significance.

And the gospel that is revealed in the person of Jesus the kingdom is already here. God's power to restore the whole of human life and all creation

---

[37]Herman Ridderbos, *The Gospel of John: A Theological Commentary*, trans. John Vriend (Grand Rapids: Eerdmans, 1997), p. 8.
[38]Ibid., p. 125.
[39]Ibid.; see also p. 9.

from the damaging effects of sin is now present in the world; the future eschatological world has flowed into history in the work of Jesus. In the theology of Paul it is in the death and resurrection of Jesus that the powers of the old age are defeated and the new creation begins, and in the Spirit that the salvation of the new creation is made present now. For Paul and the Gospel writers, the final victory and arrival of complete salvation await the return of Christ. So salvation is not simply a future reality, but also present. And the mission of the church is to embody and mediate that present salvation in the world until Jesus returns.

Christology. We have just noted that the kingdom comes into the world in the person and work of Jesus the Christ and is made present by the Spirit. Thus, eschatology shapes Christology and pneumatology. An eschatological context for salvation has a number of implications for our Christology. N. T. Wright comments, "The church has again and again tried to fit its 'Jesus' into a different narrative, the story of how the second person of the Trinity revealed his divinity and saved people from their sins into a disembodied heaven."[40] When the focus of Christology is on the divine and human nature of Christ and on the atonement for individual sinners—both biblical—other dimensions of Christology are crowded out. For example, the importance of Jesus' life is neglected. The Gospels often are viewed as passion stories with an introduction. Sometimes we simply do not know what to do with the life of Jesus. Yet the words of Jesus in John 20:21 offer a clue: "As the Father has sent me, I am sending you." Jesus' kingdom mission becomes a model for our mission, and we must mine the Gospels to understand how Jesus revealed the kingdom in his life, words and deeds.

> "AS THE FATHER HAS SENT ME, I AM SENDING YOU." JESUS' KINGDOM MISSION BECOMES A MODEL FOR OUR MISSION, AND WE MUST MINE THE GOSPELS TO UNDERSTAND HOW JESUS REVEALED THE KINGDOM IN HIS LIFE, WORDS AND DEEDS.

Two important aspects of mission are lost when an emphasis on the life

---

[40]N. T. Wright, "Whence and Whither Historical Jesus Studies in the Life of the Church?" in *Jesus, Paul and the People of God: A Theological Dialogue with N. T. Wright,* ed. Nicholas Perrin and Richard B. Hays (Downers Grove, IL: InterVarsity Press, 2011), p. 132.

of Jesus is reduced. On the one hand, we miss the importance of the gathered community that was central to Jesus' mission. Gerhard Lohfink claims that the restoration of a holy people in the midst of the nations "was for Jesus the self-evident background of all his actions."[41] On the other hand, we may fail to see Jesus' deep concern for the poor and marginalized. Evangelical, Catholic, and liberationist theologies coming out of Latin America have alerted us to the way Jesus demonstrated a special concern for the poor and marginalized.[42] If gathering a people and seeking the justice of the marginalized was central to Jesus' mission, then neglecting these components in Christology may lead us to neglect these very things in our mission as well.

Along with neglecting the life of Jesus there is a second christological issue that may not receive its due emphasis. Often the cross and resurrection are separated from the life and kingdom mission of Jesus. In the Gospels the cross and resurrection narratives are not detached stories to be interpreted in terms of later theological categories or in terms of an evangelistic message. Rather, the cross is the place where the kingdom mission of Jesus narrated in the Gospels is completed and realized. All the powers that oppose the rule of God in the Gospel narratives meet their defeat in the death of Jesus. The resurrection is the inauguration of the end-time kingdom of God in history that Jesus has announced. These events must be part of the ongoing narrative of the coming kingdom of God announced at the beginning of the ministry of Jesus. Thus, the cross and resurrection have the same cosmic and communal dimensions that are evident in the ministry of Jesus.[43]

René Padilla notes that classic theories of the atonement have "concentrated on the salvation of the individual soul but have frequently disregarded God's purpose to create a new humanity marked by sacrificial love and justice for the poor."[44] The cross and resurrection are cosmic events: the old age is decisively defeated, and the kingdom is inaugurated. These are communal events: the community gathered by Jesus shares in the cosmic sal-

---

[41]Gerhard Lohfink, *Jesus and Community: The Social Dimension of the Christian Faith*, trans. John P. Galvin (Philadelphia: Fortress, 1982), p. 123.

[42]See, for example, Hugo Echegaray, *The Practice of Jesus*, trans. Matthew J. O'Connell (Maryknoll, NY: Orbis Books, 1984).

[43]See Michael W. Goheen, *A Light to the Nations: The Missional Church and the Biblical Story* (Grand Rapids: Baker Academic, 2011), pp. 101-14.

[44]C. René Padilla, foreword to *Understanding the Atonement for the Mission of the Church*, by John Driver (Scottdale, PA: Herald Press, 1986), p. 9.

vation of the kingdom. But not only do we need to set these events firmly in the narratives of the Gospels; we also need the numerous New Testament images of the atonement and the resurrection scattered throughout the Epistles to rightly understand these events. Single images, such as the substitutionary atonement, while biblical, when isolated from other images, as well as extracted from their original literary and redemptive-historical context, are easily reread into the narrative of individualized and spiritualized salvation. We need the atonement image of Christ's victory, for example, to help us understand the broad scope of what the cross has accomplished: the defeat of all the powers arrayed against God's kingdom. We need to see the death and resurrection of Jesus as the conclusion of the Gospels, in which the central theme is the coming of the kingdom. We need to see these events as the center of the redemptive history of cosmic renewal, in which sin and the powers are defeated and a new creation is inaugurated.

Two other aspects of Christology, frequently obscured, are also important for the mission of the church. First, the historical and human Jesus of the Gospels is the same person as the exalted Christ of Acts and the Epistles. Sometimes a Christology "from above" that emphasizes the divinity and lordship of Christ is set off against a Christology "from below" that stresses the humanity of Jesus. But this is to distort the scriptural testimony.[45] The mission of the historical Jesus is continued and extended through the work of the exalted Christ by the Spirit in and through the church. Thus, the church is connected with Jesus Christ in two ways: to Jesus historically as the church is called to continue his saving work in the world, and to Christ eschatologically in the present as the church is the place and agent of his saving work through the Spirit. The same Jesus who commissioned his people two millennia ago is still present to work in power and love in and through them now.

A second aspect of Christology is equally important: Jesus is also the Creator. The Jesus of history who is now exalted to the right hand of God and

---

[45]Konrad Raiser believes that a classical Christology "from above" that focuses on the divinity of Christ and his lordship over creation has obscured a Christology "from below" that attends to the earthly ministry of Christ. His solution is to turn the tables. He so stresses the humanity of Jesus that the emphases of a classical Christology disappear. This fits his pluralist vision (*menism in Transition: A Paradigm Shift in the Ecumenical Movement?* [Geneva: WCC tions, 1991], p. 59).

rules all of history is also the Creator of the world. Creation and salvation are equally the work of the same Jesus (Col 1:15-20). Jesus reconciles and restores what he has created. Too often a redemption-centered theology sidelines a vigorous theology of creation, and this has detrimental implications for the church's mission. Yet the biblical testimony witnesses to the restoration of the creation; salvation is its full recovery, not an escape from it.

Pneumatology. A more hearty and scriptural understanding of salvation must attend not only to eschatology and Christology but also pneumatology: the work of the Spirit too often has been limited to the application of Christ's salvation to individuals. Berkhof notes that in Protestant theology the Spirit is limited to the awakener of individual spiritual life in justification and sanctification. For him, this very problem arises because of the "theological neglect of mission."[46]

"Paul relies for the 'success' of his missionary work not on the powers of rhetorical strategies and techniques, and certainly not on social or psychological factors. He relies on the power of God which is present in the preaching of the gospel of the crucified and risen Jesus Christ. The 'proof' for the validity of the gospel of Jesus Christ is not to be found through the application of logical inference or deduction, or in mere rhetorical brilliance. The 'proof' for the truth of the gospel is to be found in the power of the Holy Spirit. When Paul proclaims the gospel, he speaks 'not with plausible words of wisdom' but he relies 'on the demonstration of the Spirit and of power' (1 Cor 2:4). The preaching of the gospel is a demonstration effected by the Spirit and by the power of the presence of God."

Eckhard Schnabel, *Paul the Missionary*, p. 371

---

a sound pneumatology, we must locate the Spirit first in
tology and mission.[47] In his resurrection Christ inau-
gical age of salvation. He pours out the Spirit at Pen-

---

v *Spirit*, p. 32.

tecost, and with that action the last days have dawned. The Spirit belongs properly to the future and thus brings into the present a foretaste of the salvation of the end time.

However, the Spirit is not only es-chatological, but also the missionary. His work moves from the One on the way to the many, from Christ to the whole world. This end-time salvation moves from Christ to the church and on to the world. And so mission is first of all a work of the Spirit that takes up the church into that work as it moves from Christ to the world. The Spirit is like a powerful river of kingdom salvation that flows from the work of Jesus as the source to the ends of the earth, carrying the church along in its eschatological current. Specifically, this means that the church is taken up into the missional work of the Spirit in two ways: as a provisional result to be a preview of the coming age of salvation, and as an instrument of mission of the Spirit in the world.

> IF WE ARE TO HAVE A SOUND PNEUMATOLOGY, WE MUST LOCATE THE SPIRIT FIRST IN THE CONTEXT OF ESCHATOLOGY AND MISSION.

Thus, the mission of the Spirit is one of the mighty acts of God along with the incarnation, atonement and resurrection. It is the mighty deed of God whereby his salvation is passed along to the next generation and to the ends of the earth. "We cannot say that the other mighty acts are God's deeds and that the missionary work is merely the human response to these deeds as an activity of men"; rather, "mission is itself a mighty act as well as atonement and resurrection." In fact, "all these other acts would never be known as mighty acts of God without this last one: the movement of the missionary Spirit."[48]

Ecclesiology. There is a need for the missional renewal of ecclesiology as well. Bosch observes that in the Protestant understanding of the church from the Reformation period on, "The church was defined in terms of what happens inside its four walls, not in terms of its calling in the world. . . . It is a place where something is done, not a living organism doing something."[49] Throughout the history of the church God's work of salvation often was reduced to his work in and for the church, neglecting that it is also through

[48]Ibid., p. 35.
[49]Bosch, *Transforming Mission*, p. 249.

the people of God. God's people thus have been seen as beneficiaries, but not channels, of God's salvation. In consequence, the church is considered exclusively as an institution that dispenses salvation to the people of God.

Thus, the institutional dimensions of the church have been highlighted in ecclesiology. The focus is on a number of activities and ministries of a societal institution that ministers Christ to individual people—things such as preaching, sacraments and prayer. The marks of the true church in the Belgic Confession are the pure preaching of the gospel, the pure administration of the sacraments and the practice of discipline. And so the church is understood in terms of what happens within the four walls of the institutional church and not in terms of its missional calling.

Surely, these institutional dimensions of the church are important. In Acts 2:42 we see that it is the devotion to the practices of teaching, the Lord's Supper, prayer and fellowship that nourished the Jerusalem church to be a vibrant missional community. However, when the nurturing of our new life in Christ is separated from our identity as a people sent to be good news, it is distorted. A theological understanding of the church primarily in terms of its pastoral and institutional role will lead to an introverted church concerned only with the personal salvation of its individual members. However, the need for the eschatological salvation of Christ to be mediated to the members of the congregation through the means of grace—a topic that has dominated historical ecclesiology—finds its rightful place when it is put in this missional context.

"A colony is a beachhead, an outpost, an island of one culture in the middle of another, a place where the values of home are reiterated and passed on to the young, a place where the distinctive language and life-style of the resident aliens are lovingly nurtured and reinforced. We believe that the designations of the church as a colony and Christians as resident aliens are not too strong for the modern American church—indeed, we believe it is the nature of the church, at any time and in any situation, to be a colony."

Stanley Hauerwas and William Willimon, *Resident Aliens*, p. 12

Winston Crum uses a helpful image:

> The Church is rather like an ellipse, having two foci. In and around the first she acknowledges and enjoys the Source of her life and mission. This is an ingathering and recharging focus. Worship and prayer are emphasized here. From and through the other focus she engages and challenges the world. This is a forth-going and self-spending focus. Service and evangelization are stressed. Ideally, Christians learn to function in both ways at once, as it were making the ellipse into a circle with both foci at the center.[50]

Similarly, Karl Barth says that the church's "mission is not additional to its being. It is, as it is sent and active in its mission. It builds up itself for the sake of its mission and in relation to it."[51] Both authors emphasize the missional nature of the church and the importance of its communal life to empower it to be missional. Various aspects and insights of historical ecclesiology that focus on the institutional life of the church find a proper context when the missional identity of the church is firmly in place.

A second aspect of ecclesiology is important. When one says "church," the popular understanding is, again, the institution or the community gathered and organized around certain religious activities. A dualistic assumption resides at the heart of Western culture, separating private religion from public life. And it bears rotten ecclesial fruit: the church belongs to the private realm. It is an institution engaged in private religious activities. But the Bible speaks of church not only in terms of a gathered community committed to certain nurturing activities (that might be termed "religious"); rather, first and foremost the church is the new humankind. They are a people that have begun to experience the eschatological power of the Spirit to renew the whole spectrum of their lives. They are as much the church throughout the week in their various callings as when they are gathered for worship.

> A DUALISTIC ASSUMPTION RESIDES AT THE HEART OF WESTERN CULTURE, SEPARATING PRIVATE RELIGION FROM PUBLIC LIFE.

A biblical understanding of church as a people whose whole lives are

---

[50]Winston F. Crum, "The Missio Dei and the Church: An Anglican Perspective," *St. Vladimir's Theological Quarterly* 17, no. 4 (1973): 288.
[51]Karl Barth, *Church Dogmatics* IV.1.62.2 (Peabody, MA: Hendrickson, 2010), p. 725.

being renewed in Christ is essential for a proper understanding of mission. When one says, for example, that the church should become involved (or, to the contrary, that it should not become involved) in politics or education, it is often assumed that this means the institutional church. It is forgotten that the church is already deeply involved in education and politics—and every other area of culture—through the people of God who work in these sectors of life. A misunderstanding of the church truncates mission.

Humankind. Our doctrines of humankind and sin must be renewed to shape mission more faithfully. A number of areas need to be addressed. Specifically, the religious nature of humanity has been undermined by secularism, and the communal nature of human life has been undermined by individualism. Yet the religious and communal nature of humankind feature prominently in the first chapters of the Bible, which sets the stage for the mission of God's people in Genesis 12.

The first chapter of Genesis (Gen 1:26-28) describes God's original design for human life in the creation. Human beings were to image God as they continued his task of ruling the creation by forming and filling it, by developing culture and society. They were entrusted with God's world as stewards and invited to advance God's purposes in history. Humankind was "blessed" (Gen 1:28), but, as is always the case in God's program, they were blessed in order to be a blessing. In order to image their Creator they were to use their historical power and rule to serve and benefit others. The call of humankind was to form a cultural community or civilization that would image the self-giving love and rule of God.

Two aspects of this original design are important to note. First, human beings are, at the deepest level of their being, religious. That is, they are created to serve God and to image him in the world. This is how human beings are constituted, as religious creatures whose original created purpose is to direct and orient their whole cultural and social task to God for his glory. When human beings stop directing their lives—public and private, social and cultural, individual and communal—to God, they will redirect their efforts toward a God-substitute. Scripture calls this idolatry. It is precisely cross-cultural missionaries who have long drawn our attention to this. Their experience in other cultures that are not secularized has sensitized them to the fact that all social, cultural and public life is shaped by the gods that are served.

The second aspect is that human life is fundamentally communal. Our historical and cultural task is inherently a communal and social phenomenon in which all people contribute to the ongoing task of societal and cultural formation. And the direction of that cultural formation is set by a shared vision of life: "True community is possible only when people are bound together by a common way of life rooted in a shared vision of life."[52] When we connect this communal nature of humankind with the religious, we can see that societies develop historically as a cultural community who together serve some god or gods. In Romans 1:18-32, when Paul offers a cultural critique of the Roman Empire, he points to the centrality of idols (Rom 1:22-23, 25).

A central thread of the story of Genesis 3–11 is how God's historical purposes were misdirected by the rebellion of humankind. Human beings misuse their cultural power for selfish and exploitive purposes. They do not image the self-giving love of God in their rule of the creation and the creation of cultural and social life. The whole sordid tale culminates in the story of Babel, where God thwarts the intention of humankind to build an oppressive, monolithic civilization in which God's original purposes for human life are terribly distorted. Human cultural power in the service of idolatry now oppresses rather than blesses all the human and nonhuman inhabitants of the world.

It is against this backdrop that God chooses and calls Abraham for the larger and universal purpose of again bringing blessing to all the nations of the earth (Gen 12:2-3). Their election is so that God's original design for the creation might be realized: human life together in society is to serve God so that all inhabitants of the world are blessed and God is glorified. The mission of God is to choose and form another community that will manifest in their lives God's original intention for human life. Israel is to be a community in which their cultural and social life is centered in the loving service of God and one another. When the church is gathered and renewed and sent to live in the midst of the nations, its call remains the same but, in a sense, much more complicated. Now the people of the church must carry out this calling and task as members of a community that serves other gods. So at the heart of their mission they are called "not to be conformed to this world" (Rom 12:2).

---

[52]Brian J. Walsh and J. Richard Middleton, *The Transforming Vision: Shaping a Christian Worldview* (Downers Grove, IL: InterVarsity Press, 1984), p. 32.

"In Paul's understanding, the church is 'the world in obedience to God', the 'redeemed . . . creation.' . . . Its primary mission in the world is to *be* this new creation. Its very existence should be for the sake of the glory of God. Yet precisely this has an effect on the 'outsiders.' Through their conduct, believers attract outsiders or put them off. . . . Their conduct is either attractive or offensive. When it is attractive, people are drawn to the church, even if the church does not actively 'go out' to evangelize them."

David J. Bosch, *Transforming Mission*, p. 168

This brief taste of the early chapters of the Bible again reminds us of theological issues that are important for a proper understanding of humankind and sin that will shape the mission of the church: human beings are structurally religious and communal creatures; humankind was created with historical power to shape a culture that imaged God's self-giving rule, and this is constitutive of what it means to be human; human rebellion and sin are not simply a matter of individual ethics but rather involve sinful structures and institutions, communal idolatry, shared practices and customs; the believing community is created to be part of a cultural community and to serve God precisely in contributing toward its healing while participating in its formative development; social ethics will be central to the mission of God's people as they live under Christ's rule; and there will of necessity be an encounter with the dehumanizing gods that rule in the various cultures of the world.

Scripture. "The Bible is the Word of God, the record and tool of God's redeeming work."[53] The words "record" and "tool" are important. As a record, Scripture narrates the story of God's mission to bring salvation to the world through the mission of Israel, Jesus and the church. But the Bible does not only record God's mission; it is also a tool to effectively bring it about. It not only tells us the story of God's mission but also takes an active part in shaping us to play our part. The "apostolic writings . . . were not simply *about* the coming of God's Kingdom into all the world; they were,

---

[53]Christian Reformed Church, *Our World Belongs to God*, paragraph 32.

and were designed to be, part of the *means whereby that happened.*"[54] Scripture as both record and tool is essential to a proper understanding of the nature of biblical authority. N. T. Wright's reflection on biblical authority is a helpful model for the way we can reformulate Scripture in a missional way.[55]

The story of God's purpose to renew all things is told in the Bible. The authority of Scripture must be understood in terms of its role in this story: what part does Scripture play in God's work of renewal? Over against many post-Enlightenment options, God's "self-revelation is always to be understood within the category of God's mission to the world, God's saving sovereignty let loose through Jesus and the Spirit and aimed at the healing and renewal of the creation."[56] So, biblical authority is a "sub-branch . . . of the mission of the church."[57] To understand the authority of Scripture, then, is to understand its formative role, how it powerfully works to shape a missional people for the world. To miss this purpose of Scripture is to misunderstand it.

First, the Old Testament Scriptures were written to "equip" God's people for their missional calling to be a distinctive people. "A full account of the role of scripture within the life of Israel would appear as a function of Israel's election by God for the sake of the world. Through scripture, God was equipping his people to serve his purposes."[58] "Equipping" is shorthand for the many tasks that Scripture accomplished.

> TO UNDERSTAND THE AUTHORITY OF SCRIPTURE, THEN, IS TO UNDERSTAND ITS FORMATIVE ROLE, HOW IT POWERFULLY WORKS TO SHAPE A MISSIONAL PEOPLE FOR THE WORLD.

It is precisely in order that Israel might fulfill its calling to be a light to the nations that the law was given to order its national, liturgical and moral life; that wisdom was given to help shape the daily conduct in conformity to God's creational order; that the prophets threatened and warned the people Israel in their disobedience and promised blessing in obedience; that the

---

[54]N. T. Wright, *Scripture and the Authority of God: How to Read the Bible Today* (New York: HarperCollins, 2011), p. 51.

[55]Ibid., chapters 2-4.

[56]Ibid., p. 29.

[57]Ibid., pp. 27-28.

[58]Ibid., p. 35.

psalms brought all of Israel's life into God's presence and kept the horizon of the nations firmly before them; that the historical books continued to tell the story of Israel at different points, reminding Israel of and calling Israel to its missional place in the story.

Second, the New Testament Scriptures tell the story of God's mission through Israel as it climaxes in Jesus and bring that story to bear in various ways on the early church to form and equip them for their missional calling. We observe three movements. The first movement is that Jesus fulfills the purpose of the Old Testament. Here the word "fulfill" is broader than what we normally think. It is much more than simply the fulfillment of predictive prophecy; rather, he accomplishes what the entire Old Testament Scriptures had been trying to do: bring salvation to God's people and through them to the world.

The Old Testament arose as a tool to shape God's people into a faithful missional people, but Israel failed because of the sin of their hearts. But now Christ accomplishes what the Old Testament could not. Paul puts it this way: "For what the law was powerless to do because it was weakened by the flesh, God did by sending his own Son in the likeness of sinful flesh to be a sin offering" (Rom 8:3). We might substitute "wisdom" or "prophecy" or "history" for "law" in Paul's words. Jesus accomplishes what the Torah, and the rest of the Old Testament, could not. The "work which God had done through scripture in the Old Testament is done by Jesus in his public career, his death and resurrection, and his sending of the Spirit. . . . Jesus thus does, climactically and decisively, what scripture had in a sense been trying to do: bring God's fresh Kingdom order to God's people and thence to the world."[59]

The second movement is that the apostles' teaching and preaching make Christ present in his transforming power. The gospel or the word of God was the proclamation of the fulfillment of Israel's story in Jesus. As such, it makes Jesus present in all his saving power. Initially, Jesus is present in his saving power in person, but now it will be through the preaching of the gospel that will shape God's people for their mission in the world.

Thus, it carried life-changing power as an instrument of the Spirit to make Christ and his saving power present to transform the church into a faithful people for the sake of the world. This is why Paul can refer to the gospel not

---

[59]Ibid., p. 42.

simply as a verbal message but rather as the "power of God unto salvation" (Rom 1:16 KJV; cf. 1 Cor 1:18; 2:4-5; 1 Thess 1:5). The book of Acts shows us that as this word is proclaimed, its power calls into existence a missional community and transforms them into a faithful and attractive people. We can summarize in this way: God's powerful word called into existence a people, shaped that people as a faithful community, and worked through them to draw others to faith. It carried eschatological power as the Spirit employed it as an instrument of salvation.

The New Testament refers to this proclamation as the apostles' teaching and proclamation, as the gospel, and as the word of God. For the apostles, the word of God "was the story of Jesus (particularly his death and resurrection), told as the climax of the story of God and Israel and thus offering itself as both the true story of the world

> GOD'S POWERFUL WORD CALLED INTO EXISTENCE A PEOPLE, SHAPED THAT PEOPLE AS A FAITHFUL COMMUNITY, AND WORKED THROUGH THEM TO DRAW OTHERS TO FAITH. IT CARRIED ESCHATOLOGICAL POWER AS THE SPIRIT EMPLOYED IT AS AN INSTRUMENT OF SALVATION.

and the foundation and energizing force for the church's mission";[60] as such, it "called the church into being and shaped its mission and life."[61]

―――――――――――――――――――――――――――――

"Whatever the language, Christians found themselves propelled toward a popular mode for translation and for communicating the message. The general rule that people had a right to understand what they were being taught was matched by the view that there was nothing God wanted to say that could not be said in simple every-day language. God would not confound people about the truth, and that made the language of religion compatible with ordinary human understanding. The gospel proclamation stripped religious discourse of the hocus-pocus and elevated the voice of the *Volk*."

Lamin Sanneh, *Whose Religion Is Christianity?* p. 98

―――――――――――――――――――――――――――――

[60]Ibid., pp. 48-49.
[61]Ibid., p. 47.

The third movement is that the New Testament authors committed the apostolic preaching and teaching to written form. The New Testament canon is the literary expression of this word of God written to form, equip and renew the church for its mission in the world. The verbal proclamation and teaching of the apostles is now expressed in the written documents of the New Testament. The New Testament authors, conscious of their authority and inspired by the Spirit, wrote books that gave written expression to the apostolic testimony. The purpose of these books, like the apostolic proclamation and teaching, is to shape the church for its mission. Howard Marshall urges us to see the books of the New Testament as "documents of mission." He continues, "New Testament theology is essentially missionary theology. By this I mean that the documents came into being as the result of a two-part mission, first, the mission of Jesus . . . and then the mission of his followers called to continue his work. The theology springs out of this movement and is shaped by it, and in turn the theology shapes the continuing mission of the church."[62]

The message of these books called the church into existence, sustained them as God's faithful people, and equipped them for their missional calling. As Marshall puts it, the New Testament "show how the church should be shaped for its mission, and they deal with those problems that form obstacles to the advancement of the mission. In short, the people who are called by God to be missionaries are carrying out their calling by the writing of Gospels, letters and related material. They are concerned to make converts and then to provide for their nurture, to bring new believers to birth and nourish them to maturity."[63]

The New Testament authors believed themselves to be authorized teachers, who, by the guidance and power of the Spirit, wrote books and letters to sustain, energize, shape, judge and renew the church. As such, these books carried the same power that had characterized the original apostolic preaching of the word as the Spirit makes Christ's saving power present. The two giants of the Reformation articulate their understanding of Scripture in these terms. Martin Luther says, "For Holy Scripture is the garment which

---

[62]I. Howard Marshall, *New Testament Theology: Many Witnesses, One Gospel* (Downers Grove, IL: InterVarsity Press, 2004), pp. 34-35.
[63]Ibid., p. 35.

our Lord Christ has put on and in which He lets Himself be seen and found."[64] Similarly, John Calvin says, "This, then, is the true knowledge of Christ, if we receive him as he is offered by the Father: namely, clothed with his gospel."[65]

The redemptive-historical form of the apostolic testimony finds expression in the literary genres of the New Testament canon. In the Gospels we find the apostolic proclamation and witness, and in the Epistles the teaching of the apostles. Thus, the "writings that became the canonic New Testament all functioned basically as instruments for the continuing formation of these communities for the faithful fulfillment of their missional vocation."[66]

A proper interpretation of the Bible, then, will depend on recognizing how central mission is to its formation and purpose. "A recognition of this missionary character of the documents will help us to see them in true perspective and to interpret them in the light of their intention. They are at one and the same time the *product* of a dynamic process of evangelism and nurture, and the *tools* for accomplishing that process."[67] And so the proper question to ask as we interpret Scripture is this: "How did this written testimony form and equip God's people for their missional vocation then, and how does it do so today?" Darrell Guder continues, "All the resources of historical, critical, and literary research on the biblical testimony can and must contribute to the church's formation by illumining all the dimensions of this fundamental question."[68]

CONCLUSION

If the church's mission is to remain authentic and faithful, each generation must return to the Bible and carry out rigorous and fresh theological reflection on the nature and scope of mission, and on other central theological themes as well. What is needed is a theology of mission and a missional theology that are attentive to the centrality of mission in the biblical story that will nourish and support the calling of the church in the world.

---

[64]Quoted in Karl Barth, *Church Dogmatics* I.2 (Peabody, MA: Hendrickson, 2010), p. 484.
[65]John Calvin, *Institutes of the Christian Religion* 3.2.6, trans. Ford Lewis Battles, ed. John T. McNeill (Philadelphia: Westminster, 1960), p. 548; cf. also 2.9.3, p. 426.
[66]Guder, "From Mission and Theology," p. 48.
[67]Marshall, *New Testament Theology*, pp. 35-36 (italics added).
[68]Guder, "From Mission and Theology," p. 48.

FURTHER READING

Bosch, David J. *Transforming Mission: Paradigm Shifts in Theology of Mission.* Maryknoll, NY: Orbis, 1991, pp. 489-98.

Conn, Harvie M. "The Missionary Task of Theology: A Love/Hate Relationship," *Westminster Theological Journal 45* (1983): 1-21.

Guder, Darrell. *Be My Witnesses: The Church's Mission, Message, and Messengers.* Grand Rapids: Eerdmans, 1985.

Guder, Darrell, "From Mission and Theology to Missional Theology," *The Princeton Seminary Bulletin 24,* no. 1 (2003): 36-54.

Newbigin, Lesslie. *The Open Secret: An Introduction to the Theology of Mission.* Grand Rapids: Eerdmans, 1995.

Ott, Craig, and Stephen J. Strauss, with Timothy Tennent. *Encountering Theology of Mission: Biblical Foundations, Historical Developments, and Contemporary Issues.* Grand Rapids: Baker, 2010.

Tennent, Timothy C. *Invitation to World Missions: A Trinitarian Missiology for the Twenty-first Century.* Grand Rapids: Kregel, 2010.

DISCUSSION QUESTIONS

1. Why are both a theology of mission and a missional theology important for equipping the church for its mission today?

2. In what ways do you find the distinctions between missional intention and dimension, and between mission and missions, helpful for uncovering a biblical view of mission?

3. Consider the differences between the various theological themes noted in this chapter when they are treated missionally and when they are not. How does a missional reflection on theology enrich theology?

ESSAY TOPICS

1. How does the distinction between missional intention and missional dimension clarify a biblical notion of mission?

2. Take one of the theological motifs discussed in this chapter. Compare a more traditional theological treatment with a missional articulation of that same doctrine. Does leaving mission out distort the theological endeavor?

3. Bosch says that "unless we develop a missionary theology, not just a theology of mission, we will not achieve more than merely patch up the church." Discuss and evaluate what he means by this. Does the illustration from the twentieth century help clarify this?

PART TWO

⁊

Historical and Contemporary
Reflection on Mission

3

Historical Paradigms of Mission

෬

Mission is the participation of God's people in God's mission to renew the whole creation and the whole lives of all its peoples and cultures. Yet mission takes different shapes depending on its historical and cultural context. Already in the Bible we see different forms and emphases depending on the situation. For example, the book of Revelation is written to equip a suffering church to remain faithful in their witness to the lordship of Jesus Christ amidst persecution and pressure to compromise or apostatize in a hostile world empire. The book of 1 Corinthians is written to prepare the church to withstand the molding power of the Hellenistic cultural worldview that is ripping apart the congregation in various ways and compromising its witness. The mission of God's people will always be worked out in a particular context at a particular time.

What should mission look like today at the beginning of the twenty-first century? How does our context shape our mission today? It would be tempting to move directly from Scripture to treat our contemporary situation. But such an approach would be ahistorical. We would be prevented from seeing how our view of mission has been shaped by a two-thousand-year history. Moreover, we would miss the opportunity to learn from the failures and foibles, the successes and faithfulness of the church through history. We would lose the possibility of being corrected or enriched by the mission of the church in other historical epochs and cultural contexts that differ from our own. Thus, to be faithful today it is important, indeed essential, to trace how the church has carried out its mission through the last two thousand years in various circumstances and settings.

What Story Do We Want to Tell?

If we want to tell the story of mission, we must first answer "What is mission?" This will, of course, influence the story we are trying to tell, including the events that we emphasize and the way we shape that story. Here I return to the key distinction between mission and missions. Mission is the whole life of the church, witnessing to the whole gospel in the whole world. Missions is one part of mission, establishing a gospel witness where there is none or where it is weak. This normally will be cross-cultural. For the past two hundred years missions have dominated the imagination of the church as cross-cultural expansion. If we begin with a notion of mission exclusively as cross-cultural, geographical expansion will then be the story we tell.

> MISSION IS THE WHOLE LIFE OF THE CHURCH, WITNESSING TO THE WHOLE GOSPEL IN THE WHOLE WORLD.

The history of mission usually has been told from this standpoint. Perhaps the best-known and most nuanced missions histories from this angle are those by Stephen Neill and Kenneth Scott Latourette.[1] From the standpoint of missions or the geographical expansion of Christianity, something like the following story emerges:

- Spread through Roman Empire
    As persecuted religion (100-313)
    As state religion (313-500)

- Christianizing of Europe
    Germanic, Frankish, Anglo-Saxon peoples (500-800)
    Slavonic peoples (800-1000)
    Scandinavian peoples (1000-1200)

- From Europe to the world
    Roman Catholic European missions (1500-1700)
    Pietist European missions (1700-1800)
    European/North American Protestant missions (1800-1950)

- Ecumenical partnership of worldwide church: unreached peoples

[1]Stephen Neill, *A History of Christian Missions* (rev. ed.; New York: Penguin Books, 1986); Kenneth Scott Latourette, *A History of the Expansion of Christianity* (7 vols.; New York: Harper, 1937-1948).

This kind of history is missions history, the story of Christianity's expansion from one culture or location to another. For Latourette and Neill, expansion is more than simply crossing boundaries; they are equally concerned with how the gospel takes root in various cultures. Expansion is not the simple notion of ever-expanding territory, as in the story of Muslim expansion, nor the history of incremental progress from Jerusalem to the ends of the earth, as might be narrated in post-Enlightenment categories. Indeed, for Latourette, it is expansion and recession, and expansion is a rich notion that includes the growth and vitality of the church as well as its influence on society.[2] With this, Latourette has begun to move beyond missions history. Nevertheless, expansion remains the central lens for his historical narrative as that history is structured. Certainly this is a valid and important story to tell: understanding the way the gospel has spread geographically and taken root is an important part of the bigger story of mission. But there is a need for a wider-angle lens.

"In principle, therefore, it appears to me more correct to derive our divisions from an entirely different aspect of the history of missions. The great question of the history of missions is: How did the church view and accomplish its task throughout the course of centuries? In our judgment the criterion of periodization ought not to be the transmission of the gospel from one culture to the other, but rather the principles employed by the church in its conduct of mission work."

J. H. Bavinck, *The Science of Missions*, p. 287

A fuller approach is offered by Andrew Walls (followed by Samuel Escobar), who notes the way the cultural diffusion of the gospel through history and in various cultures both deepens and enriches the Christian faith.[3] The key for these authors is the movement and translation of the

---

[2]Andrew F. Walls, "A History of the Expansion of Christianity Reconsidered: Assessing Christian Progress and Decline," in *The Cross-Cultural Process in Christian History: Studies in the Transmission and Appropriation of Faith* (Maryknoll, NY: Orbis Books, 2002), pp. 3-26.
[3]Andrew F. Walls, "Culture and Coherence in Christian History," in *The Missionary Movement in Christian History: Studies in the Transmission of Faith* (Maryknoll, NY: Orbis Books, 1996), pp.

gospel from one cultural center to another. Christian history may be divided into six phases (five for Escobar), and in each era the Christian faith is shaped by the culture in which it is embodied. The gospel first takes form in the Jewish cultural context. Already in the New Testament and increasingly over the next few centuries the gospel spreads throughout the Roman Empire and takes root in Hellenistic soil. The invasion of the barbarians brings a new tribal culture that gives the gospel yet another cultural form. Various cultural streams flow together to form Western Europe, and here the gospel finds a home for centuries. The next period sees an expansion from Europe in the cross-cultural transplantation of the gospel into other cultures of the world. But at the same time the gospel is taking root in other parts of the world it is under attack in its European homeland. Today the church is in every culture of the world, with expressions of faith from the Southern hemisphere being the dominant forms. Thus, Walls and Escobar tell the story of mission in the following way.

Table 3.1

Andrew Walls	Samuel Escobar
Jewish	A Jewish church in mission
Hellenistic-Roman	Missionary expansion into the Greco-Roman world
Barbarian	The evangelization of barbarians and the making of Europe
Western European	
Expanding Europe and Christian recession	Empire and mission from expanding Europe
Cross-cultural transmission	The shift of Christianity to the South

This too is a valuable way to tell the story of mission. It is a more nuanced story of the geographical expansion of Christianity that attends more sensitively to culture as well as the benefits to the gospel of various cultural contextualizations. But its primary purpose is not to clarify how the church understood and carried out its mission and more particularly its mission in the area in which it is located.

A third and even broader way of telling the history of mission is offered

---

16-25; Samuel Escobar, *The New Global Mission: The Gospel from Everywhere to Everyone* (Downers Grove, IL: InterVarsity Press, 2003), pp. 28-53.

by David Bosch and is followed by Bryant Myers.[4] This approach utilizes the notion of paradigm. Darrell Guder notes that this paradigm approach "in effect transform[s] church history into mission history."[5] Simply put, a paradigm can be described as a way of understanding and practicing mission in a certain historical context. This understanding of mission is shaped not only by the church's place and role in its cultural setting but also by a host of cultural and theological assumptions. This approach traces history in terms of the various ways the church has understood and carried out its missional calling (including missions) in varied cultural settings.

Various important events signal a seismic change and henceforth a new way forward for the church's missional life. The translation of the gospel from a Jewish to a Greek setting, the conversion of Constantine and the church's new place as a powerful and wealthy institution, the Reformation, the momentous conversion of Europe to rationalistic humanism in the eighteenth-century Enlightenment, and the growth of the global church in every part of the world, but especially in the Southern hemisphere—these brought about such significant changes that the church's understanding of itself and its mission was fundamentally altered. Bosch and Myer tell the story as a successive change of (overlapping) missional paradigms.

Table 3.2

David Bosch	Bryant Myers
33-313: Early church paradigm	33-200: Apocalyptic—early church paradigm
150-1453: Eastern church paradigm	200-500: Greek—patristic Orthodox paradigm
313-1800: Roman Catholic/medieval paradigm	600-1400: Christendom—medieval Roman Catholic
1517-1800: Reformation paradigm	1500-1750: Reformation—Protestant
1800-1918: Mission in the wake of the Enlightenment	1750-1950: Modern mission era
1918-today: Ecumenical or postmodern paradigm	1950-today: Emerging mission paradigm of the third millennium

---

[4]David Bosch, *Transforming Mission: Paradigm Shifts in Theology of Mission* (Maryknoll, NY: Orbis Books, 1991), pp. 181-510; Bryant L. Myers, *Exploring World Mission: Context and Challenges* (Monrovia, CA: World Vision International, 2003), pp. 16-17. This chapter makes grateful use at many points of the historical section of Bosch's work above.
[5]Darrell Guder, "Missional Theology for a Missionary Church," *Journal for Preachers* 22, no. 1 (1998): 6.

Alan Kreider accepts Bosch's way of telling mission history in terms of paradigms but offers a correction.[6] He believes that the Eastern, Roman Catholic, Reformation and Enlightenment paradigms are strikingly similar to one another and can be termed Christendom, and so these four represent variations of the same basic paradigm. Thus, he suggests three basic mission paradigms: pre-Christendom, Christendom, post-Christendom. The key for Kreider is his Anabaptist understanding of the church's relationship to its broader political and cultural context and especially the degree of power the church holds in its setting. Lamin Sanneh agrees with Kreider that the Eastern and Roman Catholic are essentially one but sees the Reformation and post-Enlightenment liberalism as offering different approaches. So for Sanneh, there are five: the Judaic phase, the Gentile breakthrough in Hellenistic culture, the Reformation, nineteenth-century laissez-faire liberalism, and a more ecumenical phase in which the gospel has been faithfully translated into African and Asian culture. Sanneh's key is the translation of the gospel into a new setting.[7]

Each of these ways of telling the story (others could be mentioned) offers insights into different aspects of the church's mission. The next two chapters will offer a brief narrative of mission history based on four paradigms: early church, Christendom, Enlightenment, Ecumenical.

EARLY CHURCH PARADIGM

The early church paradigm arose out of the Jewish context into which it was born. While already in the first century the gospel began to translate itself anew within classical culture, the dominant form remained Jewish. The gospel was the good news that in Jesus Christ the end of cosmic history had been revealed and accomplished. The power of that victory was now experienced in foretaste by the church, and its mission was to make known the end of history through its members' lives, deeds and words. Mission was shaped by this eschatological and historical context.

The most characteristic element of mission in the early church of the first

[6]Alan Kreider, "Beyond Bosch: The Early Church and the Christendom Shift," *International Bulletin of Missionary Research* 29, no. 2 (2005): 59-68.
[7]Lamin Sanneh, *Translating the Message: The Missionary Impact on Culture* (Maryknoll, NY: Orbis Books, 1990), p. 6.

three centuries was the attractive power of the local congregation. In this early period "we may take for granted that the mere existence and persistent activity of the individual Christian communities did more than anything else to bring about the extension of the Christian religion. . . . These communities exerted a magnetic force on thousands, and thus proved of extraordinary service to the Christian mission."[8] Living close to the time of Jesus, those in the early church saw themselves as continuing the mission of Jesus and living in the newly inaugurated kingdom. Thus, as citizens of the kingdom, they viewed themselves as resident aliens (*paroikoi*) or a "third race" in the Roman Empire. Although residents of their cultural communities, their primary identity was found as inhabitants of God's kingdom, and thus they found themselves at odds with the way of life of their contemporaries. They recognized that "acceptance of the gospel of Jesus Christ creates a gap between Christians and the values and behaviors of pagans, and it underscores the exhortation not to assimilate to 'this world' (Rom 12:2) is critically important."[9] It is this emphasis on difference, on the prophetic-critical stance within culture, which made them distinctive, that was one of the most salient features of the early church's missional life.

> THE MOST CHARACTERISTIC ELEMENT OF MISSION IN THE EARLY CHURCH OF THE FIRST THREE CENTURIES WAS THE ATTRACTIVE POWER OF THE LOCAL CONGREGATION.

This critical stance of the early church against the idolatry of its cultural context was evident in their battle with pagan religion and philosophy, the imperial cult and cultural practices such as the theater and games. A particularly interesting example can be seen in the struggle in the early second century with how far Christians could take part in various occupations without incurring the stain of idolatry.[10] There were differences, of course, but the struggle itself shows a critical posture toward their pagan environment. The manufacture of idols was forbidden, but more difficult were those trades that indirectly contributed to idol worship—carpentry, painting, engraving,

---

[8] Adolf Harnack, *The Mission and Expansion of Christianity in the First Three Centuries*, trans. and ed. James Moffatt (New York: Harper, 1962), pp. 434, 439.

[9] Eckhard Schnabel, *Early Christian Mission*, vol. 2, *Paul and the Early Church* (Downers Grove, IL: InterVarsity Press, 2004), p. 1537.

[10] Harnack, *Mission and Expansion of Christianity*, pp. 303-11.

stucco work, and so on. Some prohibited these trades, along with being a schoolmaster or professor, because they too would be stained by idolatry. Some also were inclined to prohibit trade because of covetousness and idolatry as well as civil appointments and military service because of the temptation to emperor sacrifice or fulfilling other cultural expectations that stood opposed to the gospel. This anxiety began to relax somewhat as the third century came in, but it is instructive to see how the early church recognized the pervasive influence of pagan idolatry. In his treatise on idolatry Tertullian says, "Idolatry is the chief crime of mankind, the supreme guilt of the world. . . . For even if every sin retains its own identity and even if each is destined for judgement under its own name, each is committed within idolatry."[11]

The "intriguing attraction of early Christianity" was the result of a distinctive people who did not fit into their culture, but this countercultural stance did not come naturally.[12] Rather, it was instilled by way of a painstaking catechetical process that had the purpose of forming a missional identity. This demanding teaching process, which could take as long as three years, was designed to reshape the convert's behavior to conform to the teaching and life of Jesus, to reorient the convert's beliefs with an alternative story to the cultural story, and to deepen the convert's sense of belonging in the church community. Thus, the community was carefully formed into a distinctive people who would manifest the attractive life of Jesus Christ over against the idolatry of the Roman Empire. A second- or third-century Christian responds to a person hostile to the gospel that "beauty of life encourages . . . strangers to join the ranks. . . . We do not preach great things, but we live them."[13] Even the enemies of Christianity conceded that there was an attractive power in the distinctive communal lives of the early church—men such as the emperor Julian (the Apostate), Celsus, Lucian, Pliny and Caecilius.

What was the content of this exemplary life?[14] The early church broke

---

[11]Tertullian, *On Idolatry* 1.1, in J. H. Waszink and J. C. M. Van Winden, *Tertullianus, De Idololatria: Critical Text, Translation and Commentary* (Supplements to Vigiliae Christianae 1; Leiden: Brill, 1987), p. 23.

[12]Alan Kreider, *The Change of Conversion and the Origin of Christendom* (Harrisburg, PA: Trinity Press International, 1999), pp. 10-20. Much of what comes in the following paragraphs is indebted to this book and Kreider's *Worship and Evangelism in Pre-Christendom* (Cambridge: Grove Books, 1995).

[13]Kreider, *Change of Conversion*, p. 18.

[14]See Schnabel, *Paul and the Early Church*, pp. 1555-61; Rodney Stark, *The Rise of Christianity:*

down the barriers that had been erected in the Roman Empire between rich and poor, male and female, slave and free, Greek and Barbarian, creating a confounding "sociological impossibility."[15] A potent "gospel of love and charity" was exercised toward the poor, orphans, widows, sick, miners, prisoners, slaves and travelers.[16] The exemplary moral lives of ordinary Christians stood out against the rampant immorality of Rome. Their hope, joy and confidence shone brightly in the midst of the despair, anxiety and uncertainty that characterized a crumbling empire. Christian unity stood in sharp contrast to the fragmentation and pluralism of Rome. Christians exhibited chastity, marital faithfulness and self-control in the midst of a decadent, sex-saturated empire. Generosity with possessions and resources, along with simple lifestyles, marked their lives in a world dominated by accumulation and consumption. Forgiving love toward each other and toward their enemies witnessed to the power of the gospel. The lives of the believing community, nursed and shaped by the biblical story, enabled them to live as resident aliens, as lights in a dark world. In the cultural context of the Roman Empire their "contrary values" led to a "contrary image of community" that was attractive.[17] The Canons of Hippolytus express the missional goal that the lives of Christians "may shine with virtue, not before each other [only] but also before the Gentiles so they may imitate them and become Christians."[18]

> THE LIVES OF THE BELIEVING COMMUNITY, NURSED AND SHAPED BY THE BIBLICAL STORY, ENABLED THEM TO LIVE AS RESIDENT ALIENS, AS LIGHTS IN A DARK WORLD.

How the Obscure, Marginal Jesus Movement Became the Dominant Religious Force in the Western World in a Few Centuries (San Francisco: HarperSanFrancisco, 1997); See also Harnack, *Mission and Expansion of Christianity*, pp. 147-98; Michael Green, *Evangelism in the Early Church* (Grand Rapids: Eerdmans, 1970), pp. 178-93.

[15]Johannes Hoekendijk, *Kirche und Volk in der deutschen Missionswissenschaft* (Munich: Kaiser, 1967), p. 245, quoted in Bosch, *Transforming Mission*, p. 48; cf. Danny Praet, "Explaining the Christianization of the Roman Empire: Older Theories and Recent Developments," *Sacris Erudiri* 33 (1992-1993): 45-49.

[16]"Pagan and Christian writers are unanimous that not only did Christian scripture stress love and charity as the central duties of faith, but that these were sustained in everyday behavior" (Rodney Stark, "Epidemics, Networks, and the Rise of Christianity," *Semeia* 56 [1991]: 169 [see also pp. 166-70]).

[17]Robin Lane Fox, *Pagans and Christians* (San Francisco: Harper & Row, 1986), p. 323.

[18]Kreider, *Worship and Evangelism*, p. 19.

We must not acquiesce at this point to a common misunderstanding that the early church withdrew from public life. In fact, the early church was for the most part publicly subversive; it did not allow itself to be pushed into a private realm in some obscure religious corner of Roman society. It refused to be conformed to the public doctrine of the Roman Empire. Its confession "Jesus is Lord" stood in stark opposition to the confession "Caesar is Lord," which bound the empire together. Its courageous refusal to be domesticated by the emperor cult of the Roman Empire was a political stance with public consequences. Moreover, it called itself an *ekklēsia*—a public assembly called out by God as the vanguard of the new humanity—explicitly rejecting the notion of being merely a private religious community (a *thiasos* or *heranos*, as their enemies referred to them) interested only in future and otherworldly salvation.

The church grew during the first centuries not only by the life and deeds of the church but also by its words. The historian Eusebius (260-340) tells us that at the beginning of the second century many Christians sold their possessions and left their homes to fulfill the work of an evangelist, preaching the word to those who had not yet heard and planting churches before moving on to new areas.[19] Thus, in the way of the apostles the gospel spread into new areas by deliberate missionary activity of itinerant preachers, a role that would soon be taken over by monks. But the most numerous and successful evangelists of the gospel were not these people who devoted their lives to missions far away from home but rather the ordinary Christians themselves who in their own contexts chattered the gospel among the common folk of the empire, a sufficiently widespread activity with enough success to draw the irate scorn of the second-century Greek philosopher Celsus.[20]

Other aspects of the early church's missional life can be mentioned briefly. In the midst of persecution the martyr who was willing to shed his or her own blood drew others to the gospel by this bold and sacrificial testimony.[21] Miracles and exorcisms demonstrated the power and truth of the gospel.[22]

---

[19]Neill, *History of Christian Missions*, p. 35.

[20]Origen, *Against Celsus* 3.49-55.

[21]Danny Praet, "Explaining the Christianization of the Roman Empire: Older Theories and Recent Developments," *Sacris Erudiri* 33 (1992-1993): 29-35.

[22]Ramsey MacMullen, *Paganism in the Roman Empire* (New Haven: Yale University Press, 1981),

The educated apologists and catechetical teachers of the early church engaged the more educated pagans as they elucidated the truth of the gospel in their oral teaching and writings over against the pagan culture in a variety of ways.[23] Their writings illustrate further how the church contextualized the gospel and engaged the Hellenistic culture of their day. The early church was more successful, however, in challenging the pagan religion of Roman culture than Greek philosophy, which began to recast the gospel in a more Platonic form. Nevertheless, these early Christian intellectuals engaged the culture and used its forms and thought patterns to present the gospel in rigorously scholarly ways.

> EARLY CHRISTIAN INTELLECTUALS ENGAGED THE CULTURE AND USED ITS FORMS AND THOUGHT PATTERNS TO PRESENT THE GOSPEL IN RIGOROUSLY SCHOLARLY WAYS.

We should not think that there was only faithfulness, of course. Here I have highlighted what is praiseworthy, but other dimensions of the early church's life are not so attractive. The rebuke of a second-century sermon shows that the church often failed to live up to its own ideals: "When the heathen hear God's oracles on our lips they marvel at their beauty and greatness. But afterwards, when they mark that our deeds are unworthy of the words we utter, they turn from this to scoffing, and say that it is a myth and a delusion."[24]

The early church failed at many points, and I mention only a few. It capitulated increasingly to the Greek worldview, which diminished the significance of history and the material world. Thus, for too many, immortality of the soul in a celestial home, salvation from rather than of the world, replaced the coming of the kingdom into history. This spiritualized eschatology weakened interest in the desire to see the gospel as a transformative power in the world. Ecclesiology became increasingly concerned with its own inner life; order and office, orthodoxy and institution took priority over the call of the community in the world. The dynamic and flexible forms of

pp. 49-112; idem, *Christianizing the Roman Empire (A.D. 100-400)* (New Haven: Yale University Press, 1984), pp. 17-42.
[23]Harnack, *Mission and Expansion of Christianity*, pp. 354-66.
[24]2 *Clement* 13:4, quoted in Kreider, *Change of Conversion*, p. 18.

the early church in mission to the world gave way to an institution that was a custodian of orthodox doctrine against heresy. An understanding of the Spirit lost its connection to mission and instead was linked with individual salvation, with the illumination of Scripture, and with various "supernatural" manifestations. But perhaps the most tragic failure of the early church was its dreadful treatment of the Jews, a regrettable attitude that would sow seeds of a later anti-Semitism throughout Europe for many years to come.

CHRISTENDOM PARADIGM

The shift to a new paradigm of mission came from at least two fundamental factors. First, the Christian faith, which had arisen in a Jewish worldview, was contextualized in the classical culture of the Roman Empire. This transformed the Christian faith, impacting the church's understanding of the gospel and the nature of salvation, its view of the kingdom and history, and even its understanding of Christ. These theological changes could not but alter the church's understanding of mission. Second, the conversion of the Roman emperor Constantine in the fourth century transformed the church's self-understanding and its relation to its political-cultural context. All of these factors merged together in a complex interplay for over a millennium to forge a different understanding and practice of mission. This brief chapter does not allow an exploration of this complicated history, so I will confine the discussion to a few of the main lines of the Christendom paradigm.

In A.D. 312 the Roman emperor Constantine was converted to Christianity, and the following year he legalized the Christian faith. By the end of the fourth century Christianity had become the religion of the empire, and the church grew sixfold throughout this period. This paved the way for the church to find a new place in its cultural context. The changes led to a very different paradigm of mission.

There was a change in the position of the church from the second century to the fourth century.[25] Whereas the church had primarily been a weak and poor community at the margins of the empire, it now became a wealthy and

---

[25]Eckhard Schnabel comments, "Historians of the Roman Empire debate whether the Christian movement needed the conversion of Constantine in A.D. 312 (or slightly earlier) to be transformed from a 'minority religion' to a 'world religion,' or whether the decisive period was the third century, in which the church grew rapidly and was increasingly accepted in the wider population" (*Paul and the Early Church*, pp. 1560-61).

dominant institution at the very center of power. The church moved from being an illegal religion to the established religion of the state. Its members' position moved from being resident aliens to full-fledged citizens of a "Christian" empire. The Constantinian church was now an established church enjoying political and cultural power. A new ecclesial and missional identity was inevitable.

The ambiguity of the Christendom paradigm of mission. This new situation, often referred to as Christendom or Constantianism or *corpus Christianum*, has been vigorously criticized because of the ways the church's mission was compromised by its new position of power.[26] Yet Oliver O'Donovan is correct in locating the emergence of Christendom precisely in mission.[27] The universal rule of Christ is disclosed in the gospel, and the mission of the church is to announce and embody his lordship. In the first few centuries this led to martyrdom as a dissident church challenged the Roman powers. However, when the political and cultural powers finally acknowledged the Lord of the martyrs, the church was prepared to welcome and embrace their homage. They seized the opportunities made available to them to reconstruct cultural practices and institutions under the lordship of Christ. The problem was not with the newly acquired power of the church in the fourth century but rather with the fact that in their established position they lost a missional focus. The contrast between the story of the empire and the

> THE CONSTANTINIAN CHURCH WAS NOW AN ESTABLISHED CHURCH ENJOYING POLITICAL AND CULTURAL POWER. A NEW ECCLESIAL AND MISSIONAL IDENTITY WAS INEVITABLE.

---

[26]There is a stream of literature to counter, correct and bring balance to the overstatement of this position, for example, Peter Leithart, *Defending Constantine: The Twilight of an Empire and the Dawn of Christendom* (Downers Grove, IL: InterVarsity Press, 2010). Yet it remains a debated area, and not all are convinced by Leithart and others. See, for example, Alan Kreider's analysis, "'Converted' But Not Baptized: Leithart's Constantine Project," in *Mennonite Quarterly Review*, 84, no. 4 (October 2011): 575-617, along with Leithart's response that follows. The problem is that Christendom was ambiguous. And so there is a need for a careful nuance that is difficult to reach in this short section. See Dale Irvin and Scott Sunquist, *History of the World Christian Movement Vol. 1* (Maryknoll, NY: Orbis, 2013), Part 4, "The Age of the Imperial Church" for a more nuanced treatment.

[27]Oliver O'Donovan, *The Desire of the Nations: Rediscovering the Roots of Political Theology* (Cambridge: Cambridge University Press, 1996), pp. 212-17. Cf. Lesslie Newbigin, *Foolishness to the Greeks: The Gospel and Western Culture* (Grand Rapids: Eerdmans, 1986), pp. 100-101.

church was toned down. There seemed to be less need to issue a challenge to the political and cultural powers in the name of the Lord Christ. This is what led to the ambiguities of this era when we consider it from the standpoint of the church's mission.

⬦⬦

"Historical evangelicalism is a religion of protest against a Christian society that is not Christian enough. . . .

"Evangelical Christianity . . . assumes Christendom, the territorial conception of the Christian faith that brought about the integration of throne and altar that began with the conversion of the barbarians of the North and West. Perhaps we have not fully faced the extent to which all subsequent Western Christianity was shaped by the circumstances under which the people of northern Europe came into the Christian faith—coming not as individuals, families, or groups but as whole societies complete with their functioning political and social systems integrated around their ruler."

Andrew F. Walls, *The Missionary Movement in Christian History*, p. 81

⬦⬦

The ambiguity of Christendom can be viewed in terms of the way the church is called to engage its cultural context. There is a positive side: the church must assume a posture of solidarity with its culture. The church may not withdraw from participation in cultural development into a ghetto. And so the first words that must be spoken are of *solidarity* and *participation* in the cultural process. The church must be "at home" in its cultural environment. But to speak only these words would be to accommodate to the idolatrous cultural patterns and assume a chameleon existence within its culture. Therefore, there is also a negative side: with equal force one must speak also words of *separation* and *rejection*. Since idolatrous religious beliefs shape every aspect of culture—and this includes the classical and Germanic streams that shaped medieval culture—the church may not simply say yes and immerse itself uncritically in cultural development. Rather, it must also say no and reject the corrupted development that has taken place. The church must also be "at odds" with its cultural milieu because it lives under the authority of a different lord. In Christendom the church attempted to bring levers of cultural power under the lordship of Christ, but too often it sacrificed the critical and antithetical edge of its engagement.

Karl Barth assesses the negative and positive aspects of Christendom's legacy: negatively as accommodation to the world, and positively as an anticipation of a world subject to Christ. The positive element, then, in the Christendom paradigm of mission was the way the gospel came to shape much of culture as the church used its newly found cultural power.[28] Lesslie Newbigin describes the Christendom period as "the first great attempt to translate the universal claim of Christ into political terms."[29] And although harm was done to the gospel and the church's mission by the settlement between the church and cultural power, it is also true that the gospel shaped the cultural life of Europe, and that we are still indebted to that legacy.

> IN CHRISTENDOM THE CHURCH ATTEMPTED TO BRING LEVERS OF CULTURAL POWER UNDER THE LORDSHIP OF CHRIST, BUT TOO OFTEN IT SACRIFICED THE CRITICAL AND ANTITHETICAL EDGE OF ITS ENGAGEMENT.

After his conversion Constantine ended the violent gladiatorial games, punished sexual crimes more harshly, improved the lot of women, protected the weak, bettered the life of slaves and children, outlawed the inhumane treatment of animals, and reformed the justice system.[30] Peter Leithart notes, "The church was able, through example and exhortation, to infuse the evangel into the very structures of civil order, so as to render them more just and compassionate. For planting the seeds of that harvest, we have Constantine to thank."[31] Richard Tarnas, who makes no profession of Christ, notes in later Christendom the "omnipresence of the Church and Christian religiosity in every sphere of human activity" and goes on to say that "all this can hardly fail to elicit a certain admiration for the magnitude of the Church's success in establishing a universal Christian cultural matrix and

---

[28]Karl Barth, "Das Evangelium in der Gegenwart," *Theologicisch Existenz heute* 25 (1935): 30, referenced in Darrell Guder, "From Mission and Theology to Missional Theology," *Princeton Seminary Bulletin* 24, no. 1 (2003): 50.

[29]Lesslie Newbigin, *Sign of the Kingdom* (Grand Rapids: Eerdmans, 1980), p. 47.

[30]Leithart, *Defending Constantine*, pp. 196-232.

[31]Ibid., p. 232.

fulfilling its earthly mission." He says that "whatever Christianity's actual metaphysical validity," the cultural impact of Christianity must be seen in a positive light: "the living continuity of Western civilized culture itself owed its existence to the vitality and pervasiveness of the Christian Church throughout medieval Europe."[32] Later he lists the numerous benefits of the impact of the Christian faith on Western culture as a result of the Christendom era: Christian ethical values, a high estimation of reason, the intelligibility of the world, the human calling to exercise dominion, humanity's intrinsic dignity and inalienable rights, the moral responsibility of the individual, the imperative to care for the helpless and less fortunate, and the orientation toward the future and belief in historical progress.[33]

There is also the negative side of the Christendom paradigm, much publicized today. The prophetic-critical and antithetical side of the church's relation to culture diminished. The church took its place alongside the political, economic, military, social and intellectual powers within the empire. The church's identity was too often shaped by the story of society rather than the *missio Dei*. It became an uncritical arm of state policy rather than an instrument for God's redemptive purposes. Its task was to contribute to the maintenance of the existing political order and uphold the status quo rather than prophetically challenge it. It became a domesticated church wherein critical engagement subsided in what was assumed to be a Christian culture. The unfortunate legacy of Christendom continues to leave its mark on the church even today.

The close alliance with the state affected the church's mission both within the "Christian" empire and outside its boundaries. Within the empire pastoral activity in the church's communal life trumped the outward missional orientation. The healthy church revolves around two mutually dependent focal points: inner pastoral activity and outer missional engagement. In the established church of Christendom the second of these is diminished. This is the result of being at peace with the status quo of a Christian society with no missional task to carry out. It is also the result of a changed view of salvation and the church: the task of the institutional church is to dispense an

---

[32]Richard Tarnas, *The Passion of the Western Mind: Understanding the Ideas That Have Shaped Our World View* (New York: Ballantine Books, 1991), p. 169.
[33]Ibid., p. 321.

otherworldly and future salvation to individuals primarily through the sacraments. Roman Catholic theologian Roger Haight describes the established church of Christendom in these terms:

> The word established indicates a theological category which characterizes a church whose mission has ceased; an established church is at peace with society and content with and in its own forms and inner life. The term is negative for it implies the presumption that the missionary task has been completed so that the church is no longer a mission but simply a community. In terms of missionary and pastoral activity . . . an established church assumes only pastoral responsibilities.[34]

Outside the empire (and sometimes within) the mission of the church was corrupted by a misuse of power. Violence and coercion often were used in the service of the missionary endeavors. The story of "missionary wars" in the Christendom period is a sad one.[35] Coercion and political power were first used in the fifth century within the empire to "persuade" or "compel" (Lk 14:23 was invoked here) heretics and apostates who had been baptized to return to the fold of mother church. In the sixth century Gregory the Great (540-604) authorized the use of coercion for pagans and unbelievers as well. This is the beginning of forced conversions that swept Europe from the fourth to the eleventh centuries. The use of war by a Christian empire is justified by Augustine when it is conducted for self-defense, but he did not yet envision a war to expand the Christian religion. Gregory the Great believed that an "indirect missionary war" was appropriate for a Christian empire: pagans subjugated politically could be noncoercively evangelized under the protection of the state. Indirect wars gave way to "direct missionary wars" in which the Christian power subjugated people and compelled them to be baptized under violence.

> THE HEALTHY CHURCH REVOLVES AROUND TWO MUTUALLY DEPENDENT FOCAL POINTS: INNER PASTORAL ACTIVITY AND OUTER MISSIONAL ENGAGEMENT. IN THE ESTABLISHED CHURCH OF CHRISTENDOM THE SECOND OF THESE IS DIMINISHED.

---

[34]Roger Haight, "The Established Church as Mission: The Relation of the Church to the Modern World," *The Jurist* (1980): 10.

[35]Bosch, *Transforming Mission*, pp. 222-26.

Charlemagne is an example of this; he could not conceive of a Christian ruler ruling over pagan people, and so when he defeated the Saxons, he forced them at the point of a sword to be baptized. Sadly, this pattern was too often repeated in the "Christianization" of Europe.

Monastic mission. A more edifying side of the story of mission in the Christendom period is found in the story of monasticism. Monastic orders began to develop in the fifth and sixth centuries with the Celtic or Irish monks in Iona and the founding of the Benedictines by Benedict (480-543). The fusion of these two groups created another group: the Anglo-Saxon monks. These monastic groups dominated the mission work of the church from the fifth to the twelfth centuries. From the thirteenth century onward that work would be carried on by three more great orders: the Franciscans and Dominicans, founded in the thirteenth century, and the Jesuits, founded in the sixteenth century.

The mission of the monks was both domestic and foreign, a comprehensive witness to Christ in Christian realms as well as missionary and evangelistic work beyond the borders of Christian rule, among pagan tribes. The gospel spread throughout the various barbarian groups in Europe: to Germanic, Frankish and Anglo-Saxon people (500-800), to the Slavonic peoples in Eastern Europe (800-1000), and to the Scandinavian people in Northern Europe (1000-1200). The monks were the primary agents in spreading the gospel and the conversion of the barbarian peoples. Here, for example, we think of Ulfilas (311-388) to Goths, Martin of Tours (316-396) to Gauls, Patrick (396-493) to Ireland, Columba (521-596) to Scotland, Augustine (505-605) to England, Willibrord (657-739) to Holland, Boniface (680-755) to Germany, and Cyril and Methodius (815-885) to Slavs.

According to Stephen Neill, the pattern of conversion was often quite similar.[36] The first monk to bring the gospel to the savage tribes would face hostility and be martyred. This martyrdom would bring some small successes that in turn led to a violent pagan reaction to these initial conversions. Then the gospel would gain a foothold when a ruler was converted to the faith. As a result, sometimes the whole tribe was converted, but at least there would be the opportunity to send bishops to build churches. Although the

---

[36]Neill, *History of Christian Missions*, pp. 77-78.

initial Christianization was superficial, through the patient work of monks and bishops the peoples were discipled, and the Christian faith became part of the fabric of tribal life.

Thus, the mission work of the monks continued beyond the initial evangelization. Within the realm the monks played a significant role in reshaping

---

"The significance of the monastic movement can, nevertheless, hardly be over-emphasized. Europe sank into chaos in about A.D. 450 and remained in turmoils for many years. Tribal incursions and migrations virtually destroyed the fabric of society. The most creative response of the Church to the challenge of the times took the form of monasticism. The disciplined and tireless life of the monks turned the tide of barbarism in Western Europe. Of these, perhaps the most famous was Winfrith, better known as Boniface, a man who, to quote Christopher Dawson, 'had a deeper influence on the history of Europe than any Englishman who has ever lived.'"

David J. Bosch, *Witness to the World*, p. 112

European culture with the gospel. This might seem initially implausible when we consider the stereotype of the monk—one withdrawn from society into a cloistered existence. But that is not the whole story. Bosch offers four reasons why monks were able to play a crucial role in shaping culture with the gospel.[37] First, the general populace held the monks in high esteem. In the peasant's mind the monks replaced the martyrs as committed and uncompromising Christians in a world where the church seemed so compromised by power and wealth. Second, their exemplary lives made a profound impact on people, especially peasants. The monks were poor by choice and worked very hard, and their work was of great public benefit. They plowed and hedged fields, drained swamps, cleared away forests, built and thatched buildings, and built roads and bridges. They did the lion's share of agricultural restoration in Europe. Third, monasteries were centers for culture and

---

[37]Bosch, *Transforming Mission*, pp. 231-33.

education. When the educational institutions were swept away by the barbarian invasions, the monastery became the center of learning. Moreover, each "monastery was a vast complex of buildings, churches, workshops, stores and almshouses—a hive of activity for the benefit of the entire surrounding community."[38] Finally, the monks exhibited tenacity, patience and perseverance amidst waves of violence and destruction. Whenever their work was destroyed, they would begin again. "The monks knew that things took time, that instant gratification and a quick fix mentality were an illusion, and that an effort begun in one generation had to be carried on by generations yet to come, for theirs was a 'spirituality of the long haul' and not of instant success."[39]

The thirteenth century saw a fresh renewal of missions in the formation of two famous monastic orders, the Franciscans and the Dominicans. Both were infused with a missionary spirit from the beginning, communities formed for the conversion of unbelievers. Francis of Assisi, without knowledge of the language, went to a sultan in Egypt and attempted to persuade him to become a Christian. The most famous personality of this time was Raymond Lull (1235-1315), a so-called secular or tertiary Franciscan. He articulated by far the most advanced understanding of foreign missions to date, arguing for a thorough knowledge of the Muslim culture and language as well as the need for preaching and martyrdom as the most effective means for making known the gospel. He himself was martyred on his fourth missionary journey to Northern Africa.

> THE THIRTEENTH CENTURY SAW A FRESH RENEWAL OF MISSIONS IN THE FORMATION OF TWO FAMOUS MONASTIC ORDERS, THE FRANCISCANS AND THE DOMINICANS. BOTH WERE INFUSED WITH A MISSIONARY SPIRIT.

Colonialism and missions. The "age of discovery" brought a new period in the Christendom era. Europe had been isolated from the rest of the world since the seventh century, hemmed in by Islam to the south and east. In the fifteenth century developments in sailing technology allowed Portugal and Spain to sail around Africa to Asia and across the Atlantic Ocean to the

---

[38]Ibid., p. 232.
[39]Ibid., pp. 232-33.

Americas. Europe entered a new stage of expansion. The development of gunpowder gave Europe a superior military power, and so this expansion developed in the way of conquest, subjugation and colonialism. This had significant implications for the mission of the church.

〰〰

"It is difficult to make any generalizations. The slapdash assertion that the penetration of the world by the political power and the culture of the West has nowhere produced anything but destruction, and that Christian missions without distinction have been involved in the guilt of that destruction, will not stand up to the light of sober historical investigation. On the other hand, idealizing representations, whether of colonial expansion as the bearing of the white man's burden, or of missionary progress in which the good missionary always appears as the friend of the simple Asian or African, are gravely distorted by mythological importations."

Stephen Neill, *Colonialism and Christian Missions*, p. 412

〰〰

Since the alliance of church and state remained intact, mission often became the religious side of colonial expansion. Expansion meant that mission was now redefined. To this point mission had been confined to Europe, but by the fifteenth century all tribes had been baptized. Now mission became a matter of Christianizing the peoples being subjugated by European expansion and colonialism. Missions flowed along colonial lines.

The most powerful countries of this era were the maritime and Roman Catholic countries of Portugal and Spain. In 1493 Pope Alexander VI divided the world, allocating to Spain and Portugal their own territories, requiring the monarchs of each country to evangelize their newly acquired areas. This is called the "right of patronage." Religion and politics remained closely fused, and so in the early period of expansion the missionaries remained responsible to the king for their activity. Sadly, the subjugated people often viewed political authority and missionary activity as two sides of the same imperialist coin. The brutal conquest of Central and South America, for example, saw missionary work and political subjugation go hand in hand. It is important, though, to recognize that there were a number of committed and brave missionaries who challenged colonial authorities, men such as Antonio de Montesinos and Bartholomew de las Casas.

In the sixteenth century the Portuguese and Spanish kings governed mission. In the seventeenth century Pope Gregory established the *Sacra Congregatio de Propagande Fide* as the authoritative missionary body of the Catholic Church, and control of the missionary enterprise shifted to the pope. The Jesuits became the primary instrument for mission during this time. Ignatius Loyola founded the Jesuits in 1534 to regain Protestant areas and to take new territory for the Roman Catholic Church. The famous missionaries of this order at this time were Francis Xavier (1506-1552) to India, Matteo Ricci (1583-1610) to China, and Roberto de Nobili (1577-1656) to India. One of the new strategies of these Jesuit missionaries was to adapt the faith to these new cultures. They argued, for example, that the Chinese rite of ancestor worship and offerings to the emperor were social and not religious ceremonies, and so a Christian could participate. They employed the Confucian term for "High God" (*Shangti*) for God and believed that worship of God in Confucian temples was permissible. This way of cultural adaptation brought vigorous criticism especially from the Dominicans, who saw it as syncretistic compromise with Confucianism. This ignited the so-called Chinese Rites controversy, which raged on for over a hundred years until several popes condemned the experiment in 1715 and 1742. Finally, in 1773 Pope Clement XIV dissolved the Society of Jesus and recalled 3,500 Jesuit missionaries. This effectively ended this period of missions.

The Protestant Reformation and its aftermath. Meanwhile, new winds were also blowing in the Protestant Reformation, but it too belongs to the Christendom era of mission. The close relationship of church and state remained, but now Europe was fragmented into Roman Catholic, Lutheran and Calvinist states. The terrible religious wars between these confessional states finally ended in the Peace of Augsburg (1555) and in the Peace of Westphalia (1684), treaties that mandated that each region follow the confessional tradition of its ruler. And so the main features of the Christendom paradigm carried on.

Nevertheless, there were at least two developments that began to break with Christendom assumptions and would gradually transition the church into a new paradigm of mission. First, the rediscovery of some biblical themes by the mainline Reformers would lay the theological groundwork for a new view of mission: salvation by grace through faith, *sola Scriptura* ("by Scripture alone"), the priesthood of all believers, the calling of believers in the world, the kingship of Christ, and a more historical creation-fall-redemption framework. But it was especially a second development that proved significant: the new Reformational consciousness of the individual's relationship to God would challenge the tribal identity of medieval communities and open up into a new view of mission.

> THE NEW REFORMATIONAL CONSCIOUSNESS OF THE INDIVIDUAL'S RELATIONSHIP TO GOD WOULD CHALLENGE THE TRIBAL IDENTITY OF MEDIEVAL COMMUNITIES AND OPEN UP INTO A NEW VIEW OF MISSION.

Although these recovered biblical themes would influence future mission, the practice of the Reformers is more debated. Of course, it depends on how one defines mission. If it is seen entirely from the standpoint of intentional cross-cultural missions, then they seem to have failed. Cardinal Bellarmine of the Counter-Reformation said of the Protestants, "Heretics are never said to have converted either pagans or Jews to the faith, but only to have perverted Christians."[40] There are a variety of reasons the Reformers were not involved in cross-cultural missions: a theology that concluded that the apostles had already taken the gospel to the ends of the earth, the continuing strife with Roman Catholics and with other Protestants that occupied their energy, the rejection of monasticism, which was the primary organ of crosscultural mission, the lack of government backing, and the inability to cross the seas as a maritime and colonial power.[41] However, this is to summon the Reformers before the court of Roman Catholic colonial mission as well as the modern missionary movement and find them guilty of not fitting that single pattern of mission.[42]

---

[40]Robertus Bellarminus, *Controversiae* book 4, quoted in Neill, *History of Christian Missions*, p. 188.

[41]Cf. Justice Anderson, "Medieval and Renaissance Missions (500-1792)," in *Missiology: An Introduction to the Foundations, History, and Strategies of World Missions*, ed. John Mark Terry, Ebbie Smith and Justice Anderson (Nashville: Broadman & Holman), pp. 194-95; Bosch, *Transforming Mission*, pp. 243-48.

[42]See Bosch, *Transforming Mission*, p. 244.

If we consider other dimensions of the church's mission under the Reformers, we can see that they defined their task within Europe: efforts at renewing the church and at shaping the public life of culture with the gospel (especially John Calvin) commanded their attention.[43]

The second development was the challenge to Christendom by the Anabaptists. They rejected the symbiotic relationship between church and state and defined the church as a pilgrim, missionary and martyr church. Consequently, other assumptions of the Christendom view of mission also were brought into question: Europe was not Christian but rather a mission field; neither the ruler nor the pope was responsible for initiating mission, as this was the obligation of each believer; the Great Commission was not fulfilled by the apostles and thus was still in effect. All of these things would appear again in Pietism and later significantly shape evangelical missions in the post-Enlightenment era.

"The various *constants* of the church's one mission throughout its history have both shaped and been shaped by the historical-cultural *context* and the corresponding theological thought of particular times and places. The history of mission, the movements of culture and the history of theology intersect, and, depending on the *way* they intersect, various 'models' of mission can be discerned."

Bevans and Schroeder, *Constants in Context*, p. 73

Pietism was a reaction to what was perceived to be a cold and cerebral faith of Protestant scholastic orthodoxy that developed in the next century after the Reformation. Lutheran and Calvinist orthodoxy turned inward and lost much of its missionary fire.[44] The Pietist reaction stressed a crisis con-

---

[43]See, for example, James Scherer's treatment of Martin Luther's missionary theology, *Gospel, Church, and Kingdom: Comparative Studies in World Mission Theology* (Minneapolis: Augsburg, 1987), pp. 54-56.

[44]There were exceptions in Dutch and Anglo-Saxon Calvinism. Bosch points to the Second Reformation in Holland, with Gisbert Voetius as the first Protestant to develop a theology of mission, and the Puritan theology of mission and work in the Americas (*Transforming Mission*, pp. 256-60).

version experience for each individual and subsequent personal piety to nourish the new birth and growing sanctification. Out of the warmth of this commitment to Christ would flow evangelistic zeal and a missionary vision.[45] Thus, each individual Christian was responsible for mission, not the state or the church. Mission was carried out by gathering serious individuals together to support one another in this enterprise. Conversion of individual people was the goal of mission, and church planting or transforming society was at best minimally important. The best-known early Pietistic groups were the Methodists, the Danish-Halle mission, and the Moravian movement associated with Nikolaus von Zinzendorf.

The key to understanding a Pietistic approach to mission is its strong individualism. As J. H. Bavinck puts it, "All efforts were concentrated on a very small front. . . . The entire work was dominated by the powerful and gripping idea of saving individual souls."[46] This individualistic turn in Pietism is both its strength and weakness. In terms of its strength, the responsibility of each individual Christian enabled Pietism to break with the idea of missions being the responsibility of the clergy or rulers. "The most striking feature of pietism is that it wrested missions free from the political and cultural alliance in which it had become enmeshed."[47] Pietism motivated individuals to become involved in the missionary enterprise. Indeed, it enabled Germany to become the primary missionary-sending nation in the eighteenth century, with the Moravians alone sending more missionaries in just two decades than did all of Protestantism in the previous two centuries.[48] The stress on individual piety led to evangelistic zeal, love, prayer and the willingness to sacrifice for the sake of Christ.

However, individualism was also its weakness. It narrowed the goal of mission to the initial conversion of individuals; political, cultural and social issues diminished in importance. The creational breadth of salvation was beyond the scope of their theology. Early Pietists were deeply involved in

---

[45]For an excellent expression of this position, see Andrew Murray, *Key to the Missionary Problem*, contemporized by Leona F. Choy (Fort Washington, PA: Christian Literature Crusade, 1979).

[46]J. H. Bavinck, *An Introduction to the Science of Missions*, trans. David Hugh Freeman (Philadelphia: Presbyterian & Reformed, 1960), p. 295.

[47]Ibid., p. 294.

[48]Gustav Warneck, *Abriß einer Geschichte der protestantischen Missionen von der Reformation bis auf die Gegenwart: Ein Beitrag zur neueren Kirchengeschichte* (8th ed.; Berlin: Warneck, 1905), p. 65.

mercy ministries, but this began to change as Pietism narrowed its vision under the powerful reach of the Enlightenment worldview. The importance of the church was also depreciated. Nikolaus von Zinzendorf associated "church" with the lifeless and formal institutions of Lutheran scholasticism and did not want his followers to be a church or plant them in their missionary work. The emphasis on individuals being responsible for mission would further lead to a voluntarism that made mission the job of special-interest groups.

THE ENLIGHTENMENT PARADIGM

The primary factor that led to a new paradigm of mission was the cultural conversion of Europe to the powerful and all-encompassing secular humanist worldview of the eighteenth-century Enlightenment. While humanism, rooted in classical culture, had lived harmoniously in a cohesive synthesis with, but perhaps subordinated to, Christianity during the medieval period, it began to reassert itself during the Renaissance in the fourteenth and fifteenth centuries. In subsequent centuries it gained momentum until it finally triumphed in the eighteenth and nineteenth centuries. By this time secular and rationalist humanism had become a comprehensive vision of the world that stood in opposition to a worldview rooted in the gospel and biblical story. In the eighteenth century Enlightenment European culture converted to this new all-embracing faith, and it would transform every aspect of Western civilization in the nineteenth and twentieth centuries.

The Enlightenment faith was a secular version of the Christian faith. An Augustinian vision of history moving toward the city of God under God's providential rule that had dominated the medieval period was dismantled and rebuilt with a secular understanding of progress toward a paradise constructed by human effort. Salvation could be found in human ability. It was especially science and technology that would give Western people the control and mastery needed to move history toward this utopian goal. This worldview conflicted at numerous points with the Christian faith. It was secular and naturalistic and had no place for a God who is present and acting in history. It was rationalistic and found in human reason and the scientific method the only avenue to truth. Human beings were not dependent creatures subjected to God and his authority, nor were they sinful.

Rather, humanism was built on an understanding of humankind that exalted autonomy and individual freedom and was highly optimistic with a naive confidence in human goodness and ability. This view of the world did not remain simply a dream for a better world. Over the nineteenth and twentieth centuries, in a series of revolutions, this vision for human society was institutionally incarnated in more and more areas of human society.

Mission in Western culture. In time the broadly Christianized vision of the world that had held sway for well over a millennium began to recede, and the church found itself in a new environment. With a dominant cultural worldview that offered a significantly different view of humankind and the world, the Christian community had to redefine its relationship to its religio-cultural environment. Unfortunately, the legacy of Christendom crippled the church's ability to respond in terms of a missionary encounter. The church had lived so long and uncritically in its cultural setting that it was difficult to challenge the beliefs and institutions that now controlled Western culture. The Christian faith was judged by the increasingly dominant secular faith of humanism and was considered by many to be implausible. Growing numbers abandoned the gospel, but the general trend was to compartmentalize the faith into the private, interior, individual and moral life of human beings. This was clearly evident in the more liberal traditions that abandoned theological orthodoxy and the historical facticity of the gospel. Here the Christian faith was confined to ethics and religious feeling. However, it was also evident in early movements such as Pietism in Germany, Methodism in England, and the Great Awakening in the United States, where a more orthodox and vibrant Christian faith continued to live on albeit often narrowed from the cosmic scope of the biblical gospel. Both the liberal and evangelical traditions to some degree reduced the scope of the gospel under the powerful impact of the Enlightenment faith.

This is not to say we must write off the Western church as a wholesale sellout of the gospel. There were, of course, varying levels of faithfulness throughout the last two centuries, as there always has been. There was vibrancy to the Christian faith evident in various religious movements and in many Christian traditions. And although we see in general accommodation to the all-encompassing power and growing ascendance of secular humanism, faithfulness to the gospel spilled over the boundaries that confined the Christian faith to the private realm. Seldom did the church articulate its mission in terms of a clash between incompatible and all-embracing visions of life. In general, the church did not understand mission to its culture beyond evangelism. Nevertheless, the vitality of the Christian faith often produced unintentional yet real formative influence on Western culture. This influence, as well as both vitality and numbers, would dissipate under the encroaching pressure of humanism through the decades of the twentieth century.

Missions outside the West: The modern missionary movement. While the post-Enlightenment church in the West did not sufficiently understand that mission is within and to its own culture, the same cannot be said of cross-cultural and foreign missions. Indeed, the nineteenth and twentieth centuries saw an unprecedented outpouring of financial and human resources toward the cross-cultural missionary enterprise. Like every era before, the modern missionary movement is marked by ambiguity. There is much to be grateful for, and much that makes us uncomfortable. There were both "unspeakable horrors" and "great achievements."[49]

THE NINETEENTH AND TWENTIETH CENTURIES SAW AN UNPRECEDENTED OUTPOURING OF FINANCIAL AND HUMAN RESOURCES TOWARD THE CROSS-CULTURAL MISSIONARY ENTERPRISE.

In spite of overseas efforts by the Roman Catholics in the sixteenth and seventeenth centuries and by the Pietists in the eighteenth century, at the beginning of the nineteenth century Christianity was primarily a "white" religion confined to Europe and its Western colonies. Many in the church rightly understood the horizon of the church's mission to be the ends of the earth and thus acted on the need to take the gospel to places where it was unknown. During the nineteenth and twentieth centuries there was an incredible outpouring of Protestant missionary activity in the third world. The modern missionary movement that developed in the wake of the Enlight-

---

[49]Lesslie Newbgin, "Report of the Division of World Mission and Evangelism to the Central Committee," *Ecumenical Review* 15 (1962): 90; see also idem, "Mission to Six Continents," in *The Ecumenical Advance: A History of the Ecumenical Movement*, vol. 2, *1948-1968*, ed. Harold Fey (London: SPCK, 1970), p. 173; idem, "The Future of Missions and Missionaries," in *Review and Expositor* 74, no. 2 (1977): 210; idem, preface to *Toward the 21st Century in Christian Mission*, ed. James M. Phillips and Robert T. Coote (Grand Rapids: Eerdmans, 1993), pp. 1-6.

enment was primarily about geographical expansion from the "Christian" West to the non-Christian non-West. The mission paradigm that developed, theologically speaking, was primarily about cross-cultural missions. Indeed, in some Christian circles this remains the primary understanding of mission today: anything that takes place overseas—the "salt water myth"—is mission.

Mission was from the West to other parts of the world. Thus, the gospel that was taken to the rest of the world was clothed in Western dress. This should occasion no surprise, as the gospel always is expressed in some cultural form. It is inevitable that when any missionary introduces Christ in other cultures, this will take the cultural form of the missionary. Rather, the problem was twofold. First, scientific and technological progress in the wake of the Enlightenment had made Europe a dominant global civilization. This led to a great confidence in the superiority of Western culture. Second, the gospel had been housed in Western culture for so long that little distinction was made between the gospel and its Western form. "Events so welded Christianity and the West together, and the domestication of Christianity in the West was so complete, the process of acculturation there so successful, that the faith seemed inseparable from the categories of European life and thought."[50] Thus, when missionaries went to other lands, they often were uncritical of the Western form of the gospel that they communicated to others. Moreover, they were not sufficiently aware of the positive aspects of other cultures. Missionary practice imposed a Western form of Christianity on African and Asian peoples. For example, in Africa drums and the *sangoma* (medicine man) were simply associated with pagan religion and summarily condemned.

A more sinister expression of an uncritical acceptance of Western culture emerged at the end of the nineteenth century when missions became intertwined with colonialism and imperialism. During the years 1878-1914 European countries seized more than ten million square miles of land and subjugated half a billion people in Asia and Africa. In the colonialism of the Roman Catholic countries of the fifteenth century the theocratic impulse, created by Christendom's connection between politics and religion, dominated. But in the nineteenth and twentieth centuries it was the commercial

---

[50]Walls, *Cross-Cultural Process*, p. 49.

and economic worldview emerging from the Enlightenment that shaped colonialism. Progress and economic growth reached a high point in Western culture at the end of the nineteenth century. Driven by economic interest, Western Europe and its overseas colonies imposed their political rule, cultural ideals and especially their commercial dominance on the rest of humankind. Sadly, missions usually flowed along the channels dug by colonialism. And so three threads—David Livingstone's "three Cs"—were woven together in colonialism: Christianity, commerce, civilization.

Modern missions comprise an easy target for scathing criticism because of their accommodation to colonialism. Some of that criticism is justified; indeed, missionaries were children of their time, and they accepted the cultural assumptions and social, economic and political practices of their era. But that is not the whole story. Livingstone's concerns to liberate Africans from debilitating cultural practices such as slavery (civilization) and from poverty (commerce) were admirable goals. Much good flowed to non-Western nations through missionary work. Further, many missionaries were critical of colonialism and often championed the peoples they loved. A balanced assessment of this colonial period recognizes ambiguity: as people of their time, missionaries were complicit in colonialism, but for the most part their primary concern was the well-being of the people they served.[51]

> A BALANCED ASSESSMENT OF THIS COLONIAL PERIOD RECOGNIZES AMBIGUITY: AS PEOPLE OF THEIR TIME, MISSIONARIES WERE COMPLICIT IN COLONIALISM, BUT FOR THE MOST PART THEIR PRIMARY CONCERN WAS THE WELL-BEING OF THE PEOPLE THEY SERVED.

Colonial motivations were not the only ones at work; a strong biblical motivation was operative as well. Johannes Verkuyl casts his eye back over the modern missionary movement and observes many of the impure motives mentioned here: the imperialist motive to dominate a people, the cultural motive to transfer one's culture to others, the commercial motive to

---

[51]Such a balanced assessment is available in Stephen Neill's *Colonialism and Christian Missions* (New York: McGraw-Hill, 1966), pp. 412-25. See also Andrew Porter, *Religion versus Empire? British Protestant Missionaries and Overseas Expansion, 1700-1914* (Studies in the History of Christian Missions; Manchester: Manchester University Press, 2004); Andrew Porter, ed., *The Imperial Horizons of British Protestant Missions, 1880-1914* (Grand Rapids: Eerdmans, 2003), especially the chapter by Brian Stanley, "Church, State, and the Hierarchy of 'Civilization.'"

further economic benefit, and the ecclesiastical colonial motive to impose one's own model of Christianity on others. However, he also lists a number of pure or biblical motives at work in this period: obedience, love, doxology, eschatological hope, haste, personal blessing.[52]

Bosch has made a detailed study of the various motives operative in the modern missionary period.[53] I will briefly mention three. First, the motive

~~~~~~

After the American victory over the Spanish in Manila Bay in 1898, President William McKinley considered his options: "I went down on my knees and prayed . . . And it came to me this way . . . (1) . . . we could not give [the Philippine Islands] back to Spain—that would be cowardly and dishonourable; (2) . . . we could not turn them over to France or Germany—our commercial rivals . . . (3) . . . we could not leave them to themselves—they were unfit for self-government—and they would soon have anarchy and misrule worse than Spain's . . . (4) . . . there was nothing left but to take them . . . and civilize and Christianize them . . . as our fellow-men for whom Christ also died. And then I went to bed and went to sleep, and slept soundly."

President William McKinley, 1903

~~~~~~

of obedience to the Great Commission challenged many to take the gospel to the nations. Matthew 28:18-20 was not used throughout church history until the time of the Anabaptists. But it was William Carey's little tract *An Enquiry into the Obligations of Christians to Use Means for the Conversion of the Heathen* (1792) that really put this biblical text front and center. It is unfortunate that this text is removed from its literary context in Matthew, and that, in keeping with the cross-cultural reduction of mission, the emphasis has been put on "go," which is not the primary command in the Greek text. It has also sometimes simply provided a legalistic foundation for mission. Nevertheless, it does issue a missionary command, and the

---

[52]Johannes Verkuyl, *Contemporary Missiology: An Introduction*, trans. Dale Cooper (Grand Rapids: Eerdmans, 1978), pp. 163-75.
[53]Bosch, *Transforming Mission*, pp. 284-345.

churches of this period heard it loud and clear and obeyed.

Second, many were motivated by love for Christ and for people. One author who examines mission in the eighteenth and early nineteenth centuries titled his book *Constrained by Jesus' Love*.[54] Indeed, there is much evidence of a love for Christ and a love for people who were lost souls but also faced great physical need that moved many to great sacrifice and dedication to bring the good news to them in word and deed. It is unfortunate that through the nineteenth century a subtle shift took place that was tied to the growing sense of Western superiority. The motivation of love began as compassion and solidarity with those in need but increasingly was tainted by a condescending and patronizing benevolence for the helpless heathen. The man from Macedonia who pleads, "Come over and help us" (Acts 16:9), became the archetype of non-Christians imploring Christ's messengers to come to their aid. Then mission becomes, as Hendrik Kraemer described it, a matter of "controlling benefactors to irritated recipients of charity."[55] Yet love remained a powerful incentive for missions.

A third motivation was the millennial expectations. John Calvin and the Puritans worked with a threefold epochal scheme: the apostolic era, the era of the antichrist, the era of extending the kingdom to the ends of the earth. The Puritans believed that they were living at the dawn of the third era, and they were on an errand to spread the knowledge of God to the ends of the earth. They were workers bringing in the harvest of this last era. Unfortunately, this progressive understanding of the coming kingdom became infected by an Enlightenment view of progress. The golden age would be ushered in by human effort, and sometimes missions submitted to this view. In the complex history that followed a more evangelical wing challenged this postmillennialism with a more pessimistic premillennialism. This reduced missions to evangelism that was directed toward getting souls off the sinking ship of creation. Thus, the postmillennial optimism of the mainline churches and the premillennial pessimism of the evangelical churches envisioned mission in different ways throughout the twentieth century: the more liberal

---

[54]Johan van den Berg, *Constrained by Jesus' Love: An Inquiry into the Motives of the Missionary Awakening in Great Britain in the Period between 1698 and 1815* (Kampen: Kok, 1956).

[55]Hendrik Kraemer, *The Christian Message in the Non-Christian World* (London: Edinburgh House Press, 1938), p. 426.

church was committed to social and political action, while the more conservative church occupied itself with evangelism. Yet both were driven by an understanding of the kingdom of God—one an exclusive emphasis on the "already," and the other on the "not yet."

During the Christendom era the initiative for mission was taken by the political leader or by the pope. However, with the Reformation the Christian church was fragmented and lost a centralized ecclesial authority to initiate and facilitate mission. Nor was there a political authority to shoulder the task: with the advent of the Enlightenment the church-state alliance was broken, and the fifteen-hundred-year Constantinian settlement was officially shattered. It would be the emergence of missionary societies that would provide the infrastructure for missions.

Bosch refers to these missionary societies as an "astonishing phenomenon,"[56] and yet for many Christians today they are so commonplace and their role in mission so accepted that they are far from astonishing. The first mission society appeared in 1792 (William Carey's Particular Baptist Society for Propagating the Gospel among the Heathen). This new phenomena emerged onto the scene rather apologetically but grew in momentum through the nineteenth century, and their numbers and influence peaked in the first half of the twentieth century.

A number of factors led to the rise of these societies, probably the most important of which was the stubborn refusal of the church to take up its missionary obligation. With much of the church blind and even hostile to its missionary responsibility, those who did believe that mission was obligatory came together to form societies dedicated to taking the good news to places where it had not been heard. There remains an ongoing debate as to the validity of these institutions. Advocates for missionary societies point to the fact that few churches actually undertake missionary work, and when they do, a rigid bureaucracy at home seeks to replicate churches after their own image in other parts of the world. Moreover, mission societies are smaller and can be more imaginative and flexible and also reflect a more ecumenical vision. Opponents point to their absence from Scripture and the way they detract from the missionary nature of the church. There might

---

[56]Bosch, *Transforming Mission*, p. 327.

have been a time when they had a right to exist because of a historical necessity occasioned by the church's failure, but that time is past. Referring to the creation of mission societies that were separate from the church, Newbigin says that this fracture "is one of the great calamities of missionary history, and the healing of this division one of the greatest tasks of our time."[57] J. H. Bavinck believes that "the difficult responsibility of missions must rest upon the church, and whenever a church degenerates to the point that it can no longer serve as an organ of Christ's redeeming love, the task of missions ought not to be assumed by a group of church members, but the church itself ought rather to be reformed, so that it can again become what it ought to be."[58] Whether and how this division will be healed, along with what role these groups will play in the future, remains to be seen. Meanwhile, these bodies remain a central organ of the missionary enterprise today, and the question of how they can function in an authentic way in God's mission continues to be an important discussion.

Today the Enlightenment mission paradigm is no longer adequate. Among other reasons, the growth of the non-Western church, the decline of the Western church, and the collapse of colonialism have placed the church in a new situation. It is essential that the church rethink its missional calling. We turn to this new era in the next chapter.

FURTHER READING

Bevans, Stephen B., and Roger P. Schroeder. *Constants in Context: A Theology of Mission for Today.* Maryknoll, NY: Orbis, 2004, pp. 73-280.

Bosch, David J. *Transforming Mission: Paradigm Shifts in Theology of Mission.* Maryknoll, NY: Orbis, 1991, pp. 181-345.

Neill, Stephen. *A History of Christian Missions.* Revised edition. New York: Penguin, 1986.

Sunquist, Scott W. *Understanding Christian Mission: Participation in Suffering and Glory.* Grand Rapids: Baker, 2013, pp. 23-175.

Walls, Andrew F. *The Missionary Movement in Christian History: Studies in the Transmission of Faith.* Maryknoll, NY: Orbis, 1996.

---

[57]Lesslie Newbigin, *One Body, One Gospel, One World: The Christian Mission Today* (London: International Missionary Council, 1958), p. 26.
[58]Bavinck, *Science of Missions,* p. 61.

Discussion Questions

1. All historical accounts select, interpret and arrange facts from the past to tell a story. What are some of the different story lines that could be told under the general heading "mission history"?

2. Discuss the developments that caused a paradigm shift between the early church and Christendom, between Christendom and the Enlightenment approach to mission, and between the Enlightenment and the ecumenical paradigm.

3. What can we learn from the early church about mission? From the Christendom period? From the Enlightenment?

Essay Topics

1. Explain and illustrate why the distinction between mission and missions is important for telling the story of mission.

2. What was the Christendom church's paradigm mission and what can we learn from it?

3. The modern missionary movement has had its strong critics and ardent defenders. Evaluate the modern missionary movement in terms of its strengths and weaknesses.

4

An Emerging Ecumenical
Paradigm of Mission

ଓଷ

IN THE MOST RECENT *World Christian Encyclopedia* the authors comment, "During the 20th century . . . Christianity has become the most extensive and universal religion in history. There are today Christians and organized Christian churches in every inhabited country on earth. The church is therefore now, for the first time in history, ecumenical in the literal meaning of the word: its boundaries are coextensive with the *oikoumene*, the whole inhabited world."[1] It is this fact—the church now exists as a worldwide body—that is shaping a new paradigm of mission today.

In the introductory chapter we briefly examined a number of issues that have led to the changing paradigm of mission today. The collapse of colonialism eliminated the basic structural framework that provided the channels along which mission flowed for several centuries. Moreover the decline of the church in the West coupled with an increasing awareness of its syncretistic accommodation to the religious public doctrine of humanism made implausible any claim that the Western church was at the center of the global church and its missionary enterprise. Finally, the growth and vitality of the church in Africa, Asia and Latin America meant that the third world could not simply be considered a mission field for the West. These changes rendered the Enlightenment paradigm of mission obsolete. What is required is a rethinking of the theory and practice of mission—a new, ecumenical paradigm.

---

[1]David B. Barrett, George Kurian and Todd M. Johnson, *World Christian Encyclopedia: A Comparative Survey of Churches and Religions in the Modern World* (2nd ed.; New York: Oxford University Press, 2001), p. 3.

This chapter sketches a portrait of this emerging ecumenical paradigm by exploring two things. First, we will note some of the reactions and responses of twentieth-century mission thinking to the Enlightenment era of mission. Second, we will examine five traditions of mission that are contributing to the development of an ecumenical paradigm.

RESPONSES TO THE MODERN MISSIONARY MOVEMENT: TOWARD A NEW PARADIGM

During the twentieth century it became increasingly clear that the paradigm of mission that had molded the church's understanding and practice for over a century was inadequate. There were various theological responses to what was perceived to be flaws in the existing missional thinking and practice of the church. This is not to say that the church today has put all of this into practice—far from it! Rather, the response that we note in this section has been theological or missiological, the response of mission thinkers to the mission practice of the past two centuries.

Mission in, to, and from all six continents in response to mission as unidirectional. At the dawn of the nineteenth century the massive majority of the church lived in Europe and North America. There was the proper missionary impulse to take the gospel to those places that had not heard, the countries of the South and the East. Mission was defined by this unidirectional enterprise that moved from a Western home base to the mission field in the third world. Throughout the twentieth century, however, it became increasingly clear that the West was not as Christian as was supposed, and the church in other parts of the world was growing. Thus, mission was in need of an overhaul. One way this has been expressed is mission in, to, and from all six continents. Or alternatively, as the title of Bishop Michael Nazir-Ali's book puts it, mission is "from everywhere to everywhere."[2]

Missiology of Western culture as a response to exclusively cross-cultural mission. Mission as an exclusively cross-cultural enterprise was legitimate during a time when Christ was unknown throughout much of the globe, and it remains an essential component of mission today. However, reducing mission to cross-cultural work led to the illusion that there was no mission

---

[2]Michael Nazir-Ali, *From Everywhere to Everywhere: A World View of Christian Mission* (London: Collins, 1990).

to be done in the West. There was a loss of a missionary consciousness in the church and an eclipse of a missionary encounter with Western culture.

> REDUCING MISSION TO CROSS-CULTURAL WORK LED TO THE ILLUSION THAT THERE WAS NO MISSION TO BE DONE IN THE WEST.

The assumption that this culture was either Christian or, at worst, secular and neutral led to blindness to the idolatry of the Western worldview. In the latter part of the twentieth century, especially as a result of the pioneering work of people such as Lesslie Newbigin and Wilbert Shenk, a missiology of Western culture has emerged as an important component in mission studies today. But a missiology of Western culture is important not only for the Western church. Because of the ongoing process

David Bosch articulates several elements of an emerging ecumenical paradigm of mission:

- Mission as the church-with-others
- Mission as *missio Dei*
- Mission as mediating salvation
- Mission as the quest for justice
- Mission as evangelism
- Mission as contextualization
- Mission as liberation
- Mission as inculturation
- Mission as common witness
- Mission as ministry by the whole people of God
- Mission as witness to people of other living faiths
- Mission as theology
- Mission as action in hope
- Mission in Western culture

Bosch, *Transforming Mission*, pp. 368-510; *Believing in the Future: Toward a Missiology of Western Culture*

of globalization the churches in other parts of the world, especially those in growing cities, face a "globally dominant Western culture, which has become the shared culture of at least the urbanized part of humankind."[3] In many countries of the world the church must negotiate a faithful embodiment of the gospel in a place where their traditional culture meets a globalizing Western culture.

Missionary ecclesiology as a response to separation of mission and church. The failure of the church to take up its missionary task led to the formation of missionary organizations that carried the task of mission. Thus, mission was separated from the church. The result was that in the West the church was considered to be an institution that nobly supports missionary projects, and in the third world a parallel institution alongside of mission that functions as a container in which to place converts. Moreover, the heritage of Christendom has also led to a church that lacks a sense of its missionary identity. Throughout the twentieth century various developments took place that have fostered a growing sense among mission thinkers that the church is missionary by its very nature. The debate over the continuing role of pervasive mission societies remains an ongoing one.

Contextualization as a response to an exclusively Western gospel. With Western culture as virtually the exclusive host of the majority of the church prior to the twentieth century, it was inevitable that the gospel was embodied in Western form. Without the challenge of alternative cultural embodiments there was little awareness that the gospel in fact was contextualized in a particular culture. When missionaries traveled to other parts of the world, it was unavoidable that the gospel they shared was delivered in Western form. Sometimes missionaries were aware of the issue, but at other times they were blind to their own cultural assumptions. Throughout the twentieth century it became increasingly clear that the church in the West embodied only one form of the gospel. The Western gospel was alien to these other contexts, and the need was for the gospel to be authentically translated into all the other cultures in which the church existed. Thus, there was a growing sensitivity to the problems of the gospel and other cultures.

---

[3]Lesslie Newbigin, "The Christian Message versus 'Modern' Culture," in *Mission in the 1990s*, ed. Gerald H. Anderson, James M. Phillips and Robert T. Coote (Grand Rapids: Eerdmans; New Haven: Overseas Ministries Study Center, 1991), p. 24.

As Lamin Sanneh observes, mission as diffusion increasingly gives way to mission as translation. Diffusion takes place as one cultural expression of the gospel expands and spreads its particular form, incorporating others into it. Translation takes place when the gospel is distinguished from the cultural mold and interacts with the culture producing new forms in a new context.[4] Today a torrent of literature struggles with the problem of contextualization. What does a faithful embodiment of the gospel in each culture look like? How can there be one gospel and yet many faithful cultural expressions?

> As Lamin Sanneh observes, mission as diffusion increasingly gives way to mission as translation.

"Christianity is remarkable for the relative ease with which it encounters living cultures. It renders itself as a translatable religion, compatible with all cultures. It may be imposed or resisted in its Western form, yet it is not uncongenial in any garb. Christianity broke free from its exclusive Judaic frame and, taking a radical turn, it adopted Hellenic culture to the point of complete assimilation. Christian thought was Greek thought. In the expansion of mission beyond Rome and Byzantium, however, we find evidence of how that cultural captivity was challenged."

Lamin Sanneh, *Translating the Message*, p. 56

***Missio Dei* as a response to anthropocentric mission.** Flowing from the eighteenth-century Enlightenment, the story of progress became an article of faith in Western countries. It is not surprising to see the postmillennial eschatology of the nineteenth century that shaped the missionary enterprise corrupted by this faith in progress. Progress ideology is inherently humanistic, with a great deal of confidence in human power and ability to direct history. This meant that planning, strategies, human effort and the benefits

---

[4]Lamin Sanneh, *Translating the Message: The Missionary Impact of Culture* (Maryknoll, NY: Orbis Books, 1999), p. 31.

of Western civilization played a large role in mission in the nineteenth and twentieth centuries. The theological response to such anthropocentrism was a move to understand mission in terms of the *missio Dei*: mission is first of all God's work. The church's mission is more modest: to participate in what God is doing.

Liberation as a response to development. A colonial framework was firmly in place throughout much of the modern missionary movement. As colonial countries gradually gained their political independence from Western countries, it seemed clear to many that a new form of economic colonialism still bound the Southern countries to the West. The continuing Enlightenment story of progress, with its concomitant notion of development, was exposed as imperialistic itself. Much of the church's social engagement overseas was blind to and uncritical of the notion of development and its debt to the humanistic cultural story of progress. The problem was not underdevelopment and the need for development; it was domination and dependence created by unjust global economic structures. The need was for liberation that recognized "dependence and structural injustice as the root problem" that impoverished non-Western nations.[5] This is one of the factors that gave rise to the liberation movements that have developed since the middle part of the century. Liberation has shaped the various contextual theologies in Latin America, Africa and Asia and has called for a new way of doing missional theology and practicing mission. However one evaluates this movement, it has played and continues to play an important role in modern mission.

Mission in weakness and suffering as a response to mission from strength. The economic, technological and military superiority that backed the Western colonial enterprise meant that missions approached other cultures from the standpoint of wealth and strength. Kosuke Koyama believes that the relationship of Western missionaries to the non-Western church has suffered from a "crusading mind" and a "teacher complex."[6] Already early

---

[5]José Míguez Bonino, *Doing Theology in a Revolutionary Situation* (Philadelphia: Fortress, 1975), p. 57.
[6]Kosuke Koyama, "What Makes a Missionary? Toward Crucified Mind, Not Crusading Mind," in *Crucial Issues in Mission Today*, ed. Gerald H. Anderson and Thomas F. Stransky (Mission Trends 1; Grand Rapids: Eerdmans, 1974), pp. 117-32; idem, "Christianity Suffers from 'Teacher Complex,'" in *Evangelization*, ed. Gerald H. Anderson and Thomas F. Stransky (Mission Trends 2; Grand Rapids: Eerdmans, 1975), pp. 70-75.

in the twentieth century Roland Allen compared the practice of modern Western missions to Paul and said, "We have approached them as superior beings, moved by charity to impart our wealth to destitute and perishing souls. . . . We have preached the gospel from the point of view of the wealthy man who casts a mite into the lap of a beggar."[7] David Bosch invites mission advocates to move from being missionary masters to become weak and vulnerable, to take up the cross and embrace suffering.[8]

V. S. Azariah (1874–1945), who would later become the Anglican bishop of Dornakal, India, was among the few non-Westerners invited to speak at the Edinburgh Missionary Conference of 1910: "Azariah pled for a new approach to missions and a new conception of world Christianity: 'The exceeding riches of the glory of Christ can be fully realized not by the Englishman, the American, and the Continental alone, nor by the Japanese, the Chinese, and the Indian by themselves—but by all working together, worshipping together, and learning together the Perfect Image of our Lord and Christ. . . . This will be possible only from spiritual friendships between the two races. We ought to be willing to learn from one another and to help one another.' From addressing the world's largest ever gathering of Protestant missionaries, Azariah returned to his work of evangelization by bullock cart in dirt-poor Dornakal."

Mark A. Noll and Carolyn Nystrom, *Clouds of Witnesses*, p. 149

Missions as partnership in response to missions as the task of the Western church. As the church grew in the non-Western world, it became clear that cross-cultural mission was no longer solely the task of the Western church. The "one-way street mentality" that dominated Western missions had to change.[9] At the International Missionary Council in Whitby (1947) the mem-

---

[7]Roland Allen, *Missionary Methods: St. Paul's or Ours?* (Grand Rapids: Eerdmans, 1962), pp. 142-43.
[8]David J. Bosch, *The Vulnerability of Mission* (Birmingham: Selly Oak Colleges, 1991), pp. 10-11.
[9]Orlando Costas, "Unchartered Waters: The Evolution of Mission," in *The Story of the Community of Latin American Ministries*, ed. Paul E. Pretiz and W. Dayton Roberts (San Jose, Costa Rica: CLAME, 1997), p. 35, quoted in James F. Engel and William A. Dyrness, *Changing the Mind of Missions: Where Have We Gone Wrong?* (Downers Grove, IL: InterVarsity Press, 2000), p. 51.

orable phrase "partnership in obedience" was coined to give expression to the fact that "the tasks which face the churches in all parts of the world are the same"; each church, wherever it was in the world, was "to be a worthy partner in the task of evangelism."[10] The distinctions between younger and older churches, and between the Christian West and non-Christian

> THE "ONE-WAY STREET MENTALITY" THAT DOMINATED WESTERN MISSIONS HAD TO CHANGE.

non-West, had become obsolete. All churches were to be full participants and partners in the cross-cultural missionary calling of the church. Yet the continuing spiritual, financial and administrative dominance of the older churches continue to make it difficult for newer churches to achieve a sense of responsibility for the missionary task in their area or throughout the world. Sri Lankan missiologist Vinoth Ramachandra believes that a "partnership that involves thoughtful, mutual listening among Christians from every tradition and culture within the worldwide Church is indispensable for a faithful united witness to Christ," but he is pessimistic that this will happen any time soon.[11] Nevertheless, the Western church is increasingly aware of the need and is struggling toward a faithful way forward.

Holistic salvation as a response to spiritualized or humanistic salvation. Salvation during the Christendom period was viewed primarily as spiritual and future. The church in its mission has never lacked compassion for the present physical needs of human beings, but this was considered to be something separate from salvation. It was either a byproduct of salvation or a bridge to preaching the good news that leads to salvation. The Enlightenment brought a challenge to the idea of salvation as life in the hereafter with its notion that human betterment could be achieved by human capability. Progress would be generated by science and technology. An uneasy combination of a traditional view of future, spiritual eternal life with material salvation by human ingenuity can be seen in the notion of the "comprehensive approach" introduced at the International Missionary Council

---

[10]Charles W. Ranson, ed., *Renewal and Advance: Christian Witness in a Revolutionary World* (London: Edinburgh House Press, 1948), p. 174.

[11]Vinoth Ramachandra, *Gods That Fail: Modern Idolatry and Christian Mission* (Downers Grove, IL: InterVarsity Press, 1996), p. 219.

in Jerusalem (1928). Here it appeared as if salvation was broadening out to include the physical, mental, social and political life of society. Mission now includes preaching, education, medical care and sociopolitical aid. J. H. Bavinck exposes the dualism at work in this notion. In fact, preaching and spiritual salvation stand alongside of Enlightenment notions of progress and inform approaches to education, medicine and sociopolitical aid.[12] We will observe in a later chapter how this division widened between two traditions that held to one side of the dualism or the other: the Ecumenical tradition championed social, political and economic action with an insufficient critique of modern progress, and the Evangelical tradition held fast to evangelism and a traditional view of salvation but were equally captive to modernity with a spiritualized and privatized gospel.

The move today for many in mission circles is to try to understand how present and future salvation, evangelism and social concern, and political and economic action all flow from the gospel. An ecumenical paradigm struggles toward a comprehensive salvation that is rooted in a comprehensive Christology. The proliferation of words such as "comprehensive," "integral," "holistic" and "total" in missiology are indicative of this desire to overcome the inherent dualisms of the past—individual and society, soul and body, present and future, vertical and horizontal, evangelism and seeking justice, word and deed.[13] This will happen only if the church itself "has conquered the dualism of our culture" in its own life. As Bavinck maintains, it will be "necessary above all else that our entire life be presented as a fundamental unity in which faith in God, love to God, and obedience to God controls our every activity." Only as the church itself "experiences all of life in a fellowship with God in Jesus Christ" instead of standing "with one leg on the gospel and the other on our modern culture" will the dualisms that corrupt our mission be overcome.[14] Surely, at a time when injustice, oppression, social need and suffering are pervasive this is an urgent task for the church today.

Unity as a response to proliferation of denominational traditions. Perhaps it is a bit optimistic to identify a concern for unity as an element

---

[12]J. H. Bavinck, *An Introduction to the Science of Missions*, trans. David Hugh Freeman (Philadelphia: Presbyterian & Reformed, 1960), pp. 107-16.

[13]David Bosch, *Transforming Mission: Paradigm Shifts in Theology of Mission* (Maryknoll, NY: Orbis Books, 1991), p. 399.

[14]Bavinck, *Science of Missions*, pp. 112, 115.

of the ecumenical paradigm. The surge of ecumenical energy from the early twentieth century seems to have dissipated in the last few decades for a variety of reasons. Yet when one looks at the last century, the growing worldwide church along with an acute sense of the scandal of division exposed by mission has led the church to respond to the burgeoning denominationalism of the last two centuries. During the last century it became clear that unity and mission were bound together. Prior to the late nineteenth century any concern for unity was a matter of doctrinal harmony internal to the church. Yet out of late nineteenth-century missions and then from the first global missionary conferences at the beginning of twentieth century arose a concern for unity born of missionary concern. Kenneth Scott Latourette rightly insists, "It cannot be said too often or too emphatically that the ecumenical movement arose from the missionary movement."[15] As clearly expressed in Jesus' prayer in John 17:20-23, unity and mission belong together.

The Ecumenical tradition led the way adopting a strong statement at the New Delhi meeting of the World Council of Churches (1961), which stressed that unity is essential to the church, that unity is for the sake of mission, that unity must have as its goal one visible body, and that unity has local and universal dimensions that must be expressed. Evangelicals, on the other hand, stress spiritual unity and are much more concerned for doctrinal agreement. The Roman Catholic Church has come a long way in acknowledging believers from other traditions since Vatican II (1962-1965), especially evident in its Decree on Ecumenism. The term "common witness," coined by a joint group of Roman Catholic and Ecumenical Protestant Christians, expresses the connection between mission and unity. Mission is an impetus to unity, and unity is part of the church's witness to the coming kingdom, when all things will be

> MISSION IS AN IMPETUS TO UNITY, AND UNITY IS PART OF THE CHURCH'S WITNESS TO THE COMING KINGDOM, WHEN ALL THINGS WILL BE RECONCILED AND UNITED IN CHRIST.

---

[15]Kenneth Scott Latourette, "Ecumenical Bearings of the Missionary Movement and the International Missionary Council," in *A History of the Ecumenical Movement, 1517-1948*, ed. Ruth Rouse and Stephen C. Neill (4th ed.; Geneva: World Council of Churches, 1993), p. 362.

reconciled and united in Christ (Eph 1:10; Col 1:20). Yet questions for our
time are rife: Have justice and peace issues become more urgent than ecclesial unity? Has a broader ecumenism eclipsed the centrality of Christ,
which offers the only possibility for authentic unity? Which model of unity
is truly biblical? Can denominational institutions transcend their self-
preservation? How can the Roman Catholic and Orthodox traditions embrace other confessional groups with their traditional ecclesiologies? Yet
there is no going back; this remains on the agenda for an ecumenical church
in mission in the twenty-first century.

*Theology of religions as a response to superiority of Western Christi-
anity.* For much of church history religions remained confined to their geographical homes, and the church could safely stay on the path of "out of sight,
out of mind." When Western missions came into close contact with adherents of world religions, a colonial mentality often surrounded their
vision. Western religion, Christianity, was superior and would gradually
displace other religions. The issue was not only the truth of the gospel;
Christianity was linked to a superior culture. However, contrary to Walter
Lippmann's prediction, the acids of modernity did not dissolve the world
religions.[16] Instead, there was an explosion of growth in all religions, and
modern technology brought adherents together in close proximity
throughout the world. The church faced a new religious pluralism and the
reality of flourishing religions. These religions were studied with growing
academic sophistication. Various positions arose in response to this phenomenon that range from a relativistic pluralism to an outright rejection of
all non-Christian religious insight. It remains an ongoing conversation: how
does the church in its mission approach the adherents of the world's religions? More importantly: what the does the Bible say about the issue? This
is perhaps one of the thorniest issues facing the church in mission today.

Global urban mission instead of missions in third-world villages.
Massive demographic changes have been taking place throughout the twentieth century that must be accounted for in a new ecumenical paradigm. In
the introductory chapter we noted the remarkable growth of cities
throughout the world in the twentieth century. David Livingstone's picture

---

[16]Walter Lippmann, "The Acids of Modernity," in *A Preface to Morals* (New York: Macmillan,
1929), pp. 51-67.

of "the smoke of a thousand villages which had never heard the gospel" was an appropriate symbol in an age when most of the world's people lived in villages.[17] All that has changed: the people from the villages are all moving to the cities. The sheer size of today's urban populations demands the church's attention. Moreover, the process of globalization is connecting the cities of the world in many ways. This gives urban centers increasing global importance. It is without question that an ecumenical paradigm must address theologically the issue of urban mission.

"The UN now divides the very largest cities into four categories: megacities, supercities, super-giant cities and meta-cities. These last are so large that they function across provincial boundaries and even national borders. There was only one meta-city [Tokyo] in 2000, but they will increasingly dominate the world in the latter part of this century. . . . By 2050 only Tokyo will remain in that list. There will probably be 23 metacities. All of the 10 most populous cities will be in Asia or Africa, and five of them will be in S Asia."

Patrick Johnstone, *The Future of the Global Church*, p. 6

Pentecostal mission as an addition to Roman Catholic and Protestant mission. During the nineteenth and twentieth centuries it has been primarily the work of two traditions—Protestant, in both its ecumenical and evangelical expressions, and Roman Catholic—that has carried the global mission of the church forward. Midway through the twentieth century the term "third force" was coined to account for the phenomenal vitality and growth of the Pentecostal and Charismatic movements and their unique contribution to mission.[18] It is the growth of Pentecostalism not only in the West but also, and perhaps even more importantly, in Africa, Latin America and Asia that has significant implications for mission. The Pentecostal tra-

---

[17]Lesslie Newbigin, *One Body, One Gospel, One World: The Christian Mission Today* (London: International Missionary Council, 1958), p. 12.
[18]Paul A. Pomerville, *The Third Force in Missions: A Pentecostal Contribution to Contemporary Mission Theology* (Peabody, MA: Hendrickson, 1985), p. xi.

dition offers new insight and approaches to mission theology, not least its emphasis on the missional role of the Holy Spirit, which is already having an enriching effect on the emerging ecumenical paradigm of mission.

We will have occasion in later chapters to look at many of these issues more fully. Here I simply highlight elements of an ecumenical paradigm of mission. Every one of these items remains an unfinished agenda today in terms of ongoing discussion and the need to implement and embody these changes.

MISSION TRADITIONS TODAY

Missiological reflection on these emerging issues is taking place in a number of missionary and theological traditions. In this last section I will briefly look at five of them—the Protestant Evangelical and Ecumenical traditions, the Roman Catholic tradition, the Eastern Orthodox tradition, the Pentecostal tradition—attending to the major missional distinctives of each. It should be noted, of course, that there is a wide diversity within these traditions that defies simple description. It is helpful, nevertheless, to draw big-picture generalizations both to offer a taste of the traditions and to get a sense of their contributions and dangers to the developing paradigm of mission. It should also be clear that no one can offer a historical portrait in a neutral way; one's own confessional commitment will shape the selection and interpretive process. I approach this section from within the Evangelical tradition.

Protestant Ecumenical tradition. A major contributor to the rise and development of the ecumenical paradigm is the broader Protestant Ecumenical tradition or, as it is also known, the Conciliar tradition. This tradition is represented institutionally in the World Council of Churches (WCC) and especially its missionary arm, the Commission on World Mission and Evangelism (CWME). The origins of this tradition can be traced back to a remarkable international missionary conference held in Edinburgh in 1910. Out of this conference emerged three streams: one committed to world missions (International Missionary Council [IMC]), one devoted to meeting social needs (Faith and Life), one concerned with solving doctrinal and polity problems to further unity (Faith and Order). The latter two joined to form the World Council of Churches (WCC) in 1948, but the IMC remained as an independent body.

The IMC finally joined the WCC in 1961. The conviction on the part of those who favored this merger was that both mission and unity belonged to the very essence and nature of the church and therefore belonged together. However, there was vigorous opposition from evangelicals within the IMC ranks. There was already a growing polarization between "ecumenicals" and "evangelicals" in the early twentieth century. Evangelicals were concerned especially about the liberal theological direction of the WCC and feared that the missionary calling of the church would be submerged by waves of fruitless efforts for the visible unity of the church. Many mission groups refused to participate in the merger. Nevertheless, the IMC was incorporated into the WCC, and from that point on it became one of the three major arms of the WCC, organized as the Commission on World Mission and Evangelism.

Ecumenical mission theology has developed through the various meetings of the IMC and the continuing meetings of the CWME. Many documents have emerged from these meetings, but one way to understand the missional trends within this tradition today is to look at three significant statements on mission by the CMWE. In 1982 a document entitled "Mission and Evangelism: An Ecumenical Affirmation" was adopted by the WCC. It is, as Jacques Matthey says, "a genuine convergence document" between the ecumenical and evangelical communities because it emphasizes evangelism along with ecumenical concerns for the poor, justice and social concern.[19] Indeed, it has been a high point in the ecumenical mission movement. In 2000 the CMWE adopted another document, "Mission and Evangelism in Unity Today" (MEUT), as an update to the earlier document. Finally, in 2012 the Central Committee adopted another statement, "Together Towards Life: Mission and Evangelism in Changing Landscapes" (TTL). This latter document was presented to the tenth assembly of the WCC in Busan, South Korea, in November 2013. It is meant to update the earlier documents and become a definitive statement on mission and evangelism for the ecumenical movement.[20] These documents are generally more committed to the mis-

---

[19]Jacques Matthey, "Milestones in Ecumenical Missionary Thinking from the 1970s to the 1990s," *International Review of Mission* 88, no. 350 (1999): 296.

[20]World Council of Churches, "Together Towards Life: Mission and Evangelism in Changing Landscapes" (www.oikoumene.org/en/resources/documents/wcc-commissions/mission-and-evangelism/together-towards-life-mission-and-evangelism-in-changing-landscapes.html).

sional and evangelistic task of the church than the broader ecumenical constituency, but a careful reading, especially of the latter document, reveals ongoing questions that exist within the Ecumenical tradition. Nevertheless, these documents are rich with insight on the missional task of the church.

The title "Mission and Evangelism in Unity Today" displays what has been one of the most important commitments of this tradition: the close connection between mission and unity. There remains much disagreement on what such unity looks like and whether or not there is an equal commitment to truth. Nevertheless, the biblical stress on mission and unity remains a foundational commitment and an important challenge to the rest of the church.

The Ecumenical tradition is marked by careful attentiveness to current trends and contemporary issues. If the church is called to be both faithful and relevant, the Ecumenical tradition is especially characterized by relevance. In both MEUT and TTL the missional conversation is set in the context of globalization, postmodernity and pluralism. Indeed, an abiding feature of ecumenical

> CAREFUL ATTENTIVENESS TO CURRENT ISSUES AND TRENDS OFFERS TWO POSSIBILITIES: BEING BLOWN ABOUT AIMLESSLY BY EVERY PREVAILING WIND, OR HARNESSING THE WINDS TO SAIL ON COURSE.

documents is their diligent consideration of the winds blowing at the time. This careful attentiveness to current issues and trends offers two possibilities: being blown about aimlessly by every prevailing wind, or harnessing the winds to sail on course. On the one hand, it keeps missiology on the cutting edge, answering important questions and facing current issues. In fact, many of the current issues that are mainstays in every missiological tradition were first thoroughly discussed in the Ecumenical tradition: missionary ecclesiology, *missio Dei,* contextualization, interreligious dialogue, and so on. On the other hand, it opens this tradition to the danger of syncretism and compromise. The desire to be relevant can lead to ingesting the contemporary idols of the day. There certainly would be more openness and tolerance to a breadth of views on various issues that would cause grave concern within more evangelical circles. We can identify six such areas in regard to mission: evangelism and social concern, *missio Dei* and the *missio ecclesiae* (mission of the church), Christ and the Spirit, Christian approach to other religions, gospel and culture, and worldwide evangelism. In each case there is a breadth of views that evangelicals, for example, could not tolerate. Yet important issues are raised in the discussion, and here we briefly look at the six areas.

First, in the area of evangelism and social concern it is clear that social, economic and political issues have dominated the agenda. Some believe that the concern for social issues has eclipsed a commitment to evangelism. While the documents mentioned above do make clear a commitment to evangelism, it is the social issues of the day that are front and center. Today it is recognized that the threat of the global arms race, war, violence, unjust economic and political structures, poverty, and the threat of environmental and ecological disaster call the church to address these issues as a priority in its mission. Thus, justice, peace and the integrity of creation are central to the church's mission. Salvation is comprehensive, includes structures as well as people, and can be described in terms of shalom and liberation.

Second, from the middle of the century there have been two interpretations of the *missio Dei* and *missio ecclesiae*. The traditional vision makes the church and its mission central to what God is doing in the world. Another view, which arose in the 1960s, believes that the world sets the agenda for the church. It is in various social movements in society and culture where God is most at work, and the church's task is to discern the signs of the times and participate. Such a view marginalizes the church and downplays its distinctiveness. These two visions of the *missio Dei* remain part of the ecumenical movement, and the MEUT and TTL documents try to mediate between them.

Third, closely associated with the differing views of the *missio Dei* are different ways of understanding the work of Christ and the Spirit. Again, a more traditional view sees the work of the Spirit carrying forth the work of Christ in and through the community that Christ founded. Another view stresses the work of the Spirit in the world that appears to be detached from the work of Christ. Thus, mission is working with the Spirit in the world for justice, peace and the protection of the nonhuman creation.

Fourth, in the areas of world religions the Ecumenical tradition is much more comfortable with positively affirming the work of God in other religions and with an agnostic position on the final destiny of its adherents. We boldly witness to the gospel "without setting limits to the grace of God" (LLT, 80). In this tradition there is wide latitude for the inclusivistic and even pluralistic positions. The uniqueness of Christ and his relation to world religions remain a major difference with evangelicals.

Fifth, likewise in its treatment of gospel and culture the rightful celebration of a rich cultural diversity makes the Ecumenical tradition vulnerable to the problem of syncretism. If the two dangers of contextualization are irrelevance and syncretism, it is the latter that would threaten this tradition.

Sixth, concern for worldwide evangelism does not seem to be a pressing issue. It is mentioned and affirmed in the mission documents, but in the broader context a wider ecumenism, tolerance for pluralism, and discomfort with the exclusive claims of the gospel certainly erode a passion for global missions. Within ecumenical mission circles there is more embarrassment with the colonial and aggressive missionary movements of the past.

The future of this tradition may well be determined by the influx of third-world Christians into its ranks. If Philip Jenkins is correct that third-world Christianity is more theologically orthodox, this bodes well for the future. But the question is which Christian communities from the South will become involved in the ecumenical movement.

Protestant Evangelical tradition. Evangelicals were an integral part of the International Missionary Council throughout the first half of the twentieth century. However, out of fear of theological liberalism many evangelicals baled out of the IMC when it joined the WCC in 1961. The evangelical missionary tradition continued in a series of congresses beginning with the Wheaton Congress and then the Berlin Congress, both held in 1966 and both drawing large numbers of missionary advocates. In these early congresses a new Evangelical tradition was being forged over against the growing Ecumenical tradition.

THE INTERNATIONAL CONGRESS ON WORLD EVANGELIZATION, HELD IN 1974 IN LAUSANNE, SWITZERLAND, WOULD PROVE TO BE THE DEFINING EVENT OF THE EVANGELICAL MISSION TRADITION.

Following a series of smaller conferences, the International Congress on World Evangelization, held in 1974 in Lausanne, Switzerland, would prove to be the defining event of the evangelical mission tradition.

Over 2,300 delegates from more than 150 nations attended, and a statement entitled the "Lausanne Covenant" was drafted and signed by the delegates. The Lausanne Covenant has continued to play an authoritative role in defining the Evangelical tradition of mission for almost four decades. The Lausanne congress took place at the height of tension between the Evangelical and the Ecumenical traditions and thus distanced itself from the WCC and concentrated on biblical themes that the participants believed were ignored.

"We, members of the Church of Jesus Christ, from more than 150 nations, participants in the International Congress on World Evangelization at Lausanne, praise God for his great salvation and rejoice in the fellowship he has given us with himself and with each other. We are deeply stirred by what God is doing in our day, moved to penitence by our failures and challenged by the unfinished task of evangelization. We believe the Gospel is God's good news for the whole world, and we are determined by his grace to obey Christ's commission to proclaim it to all mankind and to make disciples of every nation. We desire, therefore, to affirm our faith and our resolve, and to make public our covenant."

Introduction to "The Lausanne Covenant"

The next major meeting (Lausanne II) was held in Manila in 1989, but in between came a series of issue-based gatherings, chief among them consultations on gospel and culture, on unreached peoples, on simple lifestyles, and on holistic mission. Lausanne II in Manila (1989) drew 4,300 attendees from 173 countries. Lausanne III was convened in Cape Town in 2010, with 4,000 leaders from 198 countries. The Lausanne Movement has become the recognized mouthpiece of the Evangelical tradition of mission, and its documents and meetings give us a window into its theology.

The catchphrase that has guided this tradition is "the whole church taking the whole gospel to the whole world," and the Lausanne Movement describes itself as "a worldwide movement that mobilizes evangelical leaders to collaborate for world evangelization."[21] And it is these phrases that define what is most precious to that movement—"world evangelization" understood especially as verbal proclamation of the gospel. This is not to say that the Evangelical tradition is little interested in deeds and lives of justice and mercy. Indeed, its adherents have devoted a number of consultations to deal with holistic mission, simple lifestyle, conversion and transformation. Nevertheless, in response to the perceived abandonment of evangelism in the Ecumenical tradition, Lausanne made it clear that evangelism takes priority over social concern: in the church's mission evangelism is primary.

This commitment to evangelism is nourished by a firm devotion to the uniqueness and universality of Christ along with the importance of explicit faith in Christ for salvation and of individual conversion. They find distressing the presence of pluralism in the WCC, inclusivism in the Roman Catholic communion, and an understanding of dialogue found in both that relativizes the gospel. An exclusivist position on the relationship between the gospel and world religions is the dominant position. This commitment to the finality of Christ and to evangelism has fueled interest in cross-cultural missions. While there is a clear decline in cross-cultural missions in more mainline churches associated with the WCC and in the Roman Catholic communion, there remains in evangelicalism a great outpouring of money, time and personnel to the missions cause. It is within the evangelical tradition that one finds the desire to locate and reach unreached peoples and where church planting and growth continue to play an important role.

Concern for world evangelism is sometimes part of an individualistic and future-oriented and spiritualistic approach to the Christian faith. Many, but not all, see the evangelistic task as getting individuals saved for a future and eternal salvation. The cosmic and corporate dimensions of the gospel can be neglected. This individualism leads to a weaker ecclesiology accompanied by less urgency for unity; indeed, unity is viewed as a spiritual or ethereal reality. Moreover, individualism leads to less interest in sin as it is embodied in oppressive and unjust structures. This is often simply equated with a "social gospel" and dismissed. In this view, sin often is limited to the individual.

---

[21]See the Lausanne Movement website (www.lausanne.org/en/).

Evangelicals' fear of the syncretism they see in the Conciliar tradition has reinforced their stress on older forms of orthodoxy that are faithful to the gospel. This does not mean, of course, that evangelicals have not been deeply shaped by the Enlightenment paradigm. To the contrary: as the powerful humanist story relegates religion to the private realm (privatism), reduces sin and the gospel to the individual person (individualism), and locates renewing power exclusively inside the person (interiorism), the evangelical church has sometimes simply quietly accepted that place assigned to it. And in some cases they see an extension of the gospel beyond this sphere as politicizing the gospel and capitulating to a liberal social gospel. This has begun to change, with evangelicals giving far more attention to social, economic and political issues (we will note this in a later chapter). Nevertheless concern over this emphasis remains part of the evangelical landscape.

> EVANGELICALS' FEAR OF THE SYNCRETISM THEY SEE IN THE CONCILIAR TRADITION HAS REINFORCED THEIR STRESS ON OLDER FORMS OF ORTHODOXY THAT ARE FAITHFUL TO THE GOSPEL.

Roman Catholic tradition. In order to grasp the Roman Catholic understanding of mission today, one must begin with the dramatic changes that took place at Vatican II. During the years 1962-1965 a worldwide council of bishops, usually numbering over two thousand, was held in Rome. The council produced important documents that introduced an entirely different spirit into that church. Prior to this time mission was defined by the Vatican's Sacred Congregation for the Propagation of the Faith and was understood as preaching the gospel among non-Christians or planting the church where the institutional Catholic Church had a weak presence. A number of documents that emerged from this council deeply reshaped Catholic mission thinking since that time: Dogmatic Constitution on the Church (LG: *Lumen Gentium* or "A Light to the Nations" [1964], dealing with ecclesiology), Decree of the Missionary Activity of the Church (AG: *Ad Gentes* or "To the Nations" [1965], dealing with the mission of the church), Pastoral Constitution of the Church in the Modern World (GS: *Gaudium et Spes* or "Joy and Hope" [1965], dealing with the church's social responsibility), the Declaration on the Relation of the Church to non-Christian Religions (NA: *Nostra Aetate* or "In Our Age" [1965], dealing with non-Christian religions).[22] In the decree on mission we read that the church is "missionary by its very nature," and that mission "pertains to the whole church" (AG, 9, 23). Interestingly, it is in the document on the church, and not the decree on mission, that we find the most consistent understanding of the centrality of mission for the church.

Since Vatican II the Roman Catholic mission tradition has been officially articulated in various papal documents, in documents that come from congregations and commissions appointed by the Vatican to treat various topics, and in documents that flow from various bishops' conferences. Perhaps the two most important documents defining mission since Vatican II are *Evangelii Nuntiandi* (EN), an apostolic exhortation issued by Paul VI in 1975, and *Redemptoris Missio* (RM), an encyclical written by John Paul II in 1990. Other important documents issuing from the Roman Magisterium are *Dominus Iesus* (2000) and *Doctrinal Notes on Some Aspects of Evangelization* (2007). While the Roman Catholic tradition is broad and deep, these documents give expression to central themes in their mission theology.

Contemporary Roman Catholic mission theology revolves around a number of themes: trinitarian mission, proclamation, liberation, dialogue, inculturation, holistic mission and mission to modern culture.[23] The first theme is that mission originates in the mission of God. *Ad Gentes* roots the missionary nature of the church in the mission of the triune God. For *Evangelii Nuntiandi*, evangelization finds its source in the call to the church to continue the mission of Jesus in making known the reign of God. This is what gives the church mission as its deepest identity. "Evangelizing is in fact the grace and vocation proper to the Church, her deepest identity. She exists in order to evangelize, that is to say, in order to preach and teach, to be the channel of the gift of grace, to reconcile sinners with God" (EN, 14).

Proclamation is central to the mission of the church: "Proclamation is the

---

[22]The council produced three kinds of documents: constitutions, decrees and declarations. It seems that those with the highest-ranking authority are the four constitutions, then the nine decrees, and finally the three declarations, although subsequent reception has not always made such distinctions.

[23]Stephen Bevans and John Nyquist mention the first five of these in "Roman Catholic Missions," in *Evangelical Dictionary of World Missions*, ed. A. Scott Moreau (Grand Rapids: Baker Books, 2000), p. 840.

permanent priority of mission. The Church cannot elude Christ's explicit mandate, nor deprive men and women of the 'Good News' about their being loved and saved by God. . . . All forms of missionary activity are directed to this proclamation" (RM, 44). Two themes are important: proclamation is christocentric, and proclamation is the task of the whole people of God. "There is a new awareness that *missionary activity is a matter for all Christians*" (RM, 2).

Since the Roman Catholic Church is the dominant one in Latin America, it was inevitable that the growing interest in liberation there would mean that this would be also an increasingly important theme in mission theology. This is, for example, a major theme in *Evangelii Nuntiandi* that gives expression to the theme of liberation in the Roman Catholic tradition. The good news proclaims a salvation that is a liberation from everything that oppresses humankind, but above all from sin and Satan so that humankind can know God. There is resistance to reducing liberation to its political, social, cultural or economic dimensions but also a desire to maintain "the primacy of [the church's] spiritual vocation" (EN, 34).

"Inter-religious dialogue is a part of the Church's evangelizing mission" (RM, 55). Six years previously, in 1984, the Pontifical Council for Dialogue (PCD) released an important statement entitled "Mission and Dialogue," in which dialogue was seen as integral to evangelization. This affirmation of dialogue as an important element of mission is based on Vatican II, which had offered a much more positive account of non-Christian religions than had been in vogue previously. In 1991 the Pontifical Council for Dialogue issued another statement on the relationship between proclamation and dialogue. It affirmed both dialogue and proclamation as essential but distinct aspects of the church's mission but makes clear that non-Christian religions are not on a par with Christianity. In a Roman Catholic approach to other religions an inclusivist position is prevalent. It is clearly affirmed that salvation is only through Jesus Christ; however, that affirmation is held along with two other factors: salvation is possible outside explicit faith in Christ, and other religions can be a channel of that salvation (LG, 16).

The word "inculturation" was not used at Vatican II but was introduced by John Paul II and since has become widespread in Roman Catholic mission thinking. In fact, John Paul could say, "From the beginning of my pontificate I have considered the dialogue of the church with the cultures of our time to be a vital area, of which the issue at stake is the destiny of our world at the end of this twentieth century."[24] As the church encounters each culture, it is important that it become involved in the lengthy process of inculturation. It is a mutual process: on the one hand, the culture benefits as the church transmits the values of the gospel to the culture; on the other hand, the church is enriched by the insights of diverse cultures. There are two sides to inculturation. On the one side, the church must be faithful to the Christian faith and thus critique culture. Since culture is affected by sin, it needs to be "healed, ennobled and perfected" by the gospel (LG, 17; EN, 19). The other side involves taking the good elements of each culture and renewing them from within. While both sides find expression, compared to evangelical approaches to contextualization what stands out is the stress on preserving favorable elements of culture rather than challenging sinful distortion, on the compatibility of the gospel with much of culture rather than its tension, on affirmation rather than critique.

Mission is described in increasingly holistic terms from Vatican II through the various descriptions of mission in the papal documents. *Redemptoris Missio* states that "mission is a single but complex reality" (RM, 41) and then goes on to define mission broadly: it is the witness of the individual and the Christian community, including a concern for the poor, generosity, justice, peace and human rights; it is proclamation of Christ as Savior; it is concerned with the total and radical conversion of believers to the gospel; it is the formation of communities that are a sign of the presence of God in the world, which certainly includes a concern for unity; it is transformation of culture by the gospel; it involves interreligious dialogue with "our brothers and sisters of other religions" (RM, 55); it is promoting integral development and liberation; and it is charity toward the poor.

One area that is receiving increasing attention is the evangelization of or mission to the culture of modernity.[25] A number of things have spurred this

---

[24]John Paul II, "Lettre Autographe du Pape Jean Paul II de Fondation du Conseil Pontifical de la Culture" (May 20, 1982) (my translation) (www.vatican.va/holy_father/john_paul_ii/letters /1982/documents/hf_jp-ii_let_19820520_foundation-letter_fr.html).

[25]See William Jenkinson and Helene O'Sullivan, eds., *Trends in Mission: Toward the 3rd Millennium* (Maryknoll, NY: Orbis Books, 1991), pp. 118-57 (five essays under heading "Modernity"); Hervé Carrier, *Evangelizing the Culture of Modernity* (Maryknoll, NY: Orbis Books, 1993).

interest: the Vatican II document *Gaudium et Spes*, the renewed interest in inculturation as part of church's mission, the pope's call for the reevangelization or new evangelization of the church in Western culture where the vast majority of Catholics no longer practice their faith because they are domesticated by the culture, and the phenomenon of globalization and consumerism as a global culture that impacts the whole world in terms of growing poverty and ecological damage. Catholic social teaching, both in official pronouncements and in scholarship, has developed a rich critique of modern Western culture and especially of secularization, pluralism, individualism, globalization and consumerism.

Eastern Orthodox tradition. Writing on Eastern Orthodox mission theology, James Stamoolis acknowledges that these churches "are not generally thought of as missionary churches."[26] That perception along with ignorance of the Eastern Orthodox Church often results in its scant treatment in much missiological discourse. It appears to Western churches that the Orthodox churches withdrew from missionally engaging their culture, focusing instead on their internal life, especially liturgy, prayer and doctrine. Bosch says that it is thus common to "pass an altogether negative verdict on the missionary endeavors of the Orthodox churches" and to even hold the view that there is "no such thing as mission in Orthodoxy."[27] The Orthodox bishops Anastasios Yannoutlatos and Kallistos Ware have acknowledged a problem. Yannoutlatos has said that the Great Commission has become "the forgotten commandment" in Orthodoxy, and Ware comments, "We Orthodox are still too inward looking; we should realize we have a message that many people will listen to gladly."[28]

Is this negative judgment because Western mission thinkers have absolutized their own view of mission and judged Orthodoxy by it? Is it because foreign mission has left a distaste in the mouth of the Orthodox because they associate it with Roman Catholic and Protestant proselytizing of their

---

[26]James J. Stamoolis, "Orthodox Theology of Mission," in Moreau, *Evangelical Dictionary of World Missions*, p. 714. See also David Neff, "The Fullness and the Center: Bishop Kallistos Ware on Evangelism, Evangelicals, and the Orthodox Church," *Christianity Today* 55, no. 7 (July 6, 2011): 38-41 (www.christianitytoday.com/ct/2011/july/fullnesscenter.html).

[27]Bosch, *Transforming Mission*, p. 206.

[28]James A. Scherer and Stephen B. Bevans, eds., *New Directions in Mission and Evangelization 1: Basic Statements, 1974-1991* (Maryknoll, NY: Orbis Books, 1992), p. xiv.

members? Is it because the Orthodox churches have lived out their existence under oppressive regimes such as atheistic communism in Eastern
Europe and the Soviet Union as well as under the Islamic regimes, first in
the Ottoman Turkish Empire and then the Islamic nations in the Middle
East, that rendered them unable to carry out missionary activities? Perhaps
these latter circumstances have become both a liability and an asset that
offer resources to contribute to an ecumenical paradigm of mission: a liability in that mission as intention has suffered and remained underde-
veloped, but an asset in that they have been able to develop mission as a
dimension of the church.

However one judges the past, it is the case that since the 1950s a renewed
interest has emerged that has partially coincided with Orthodox involvement
with the WCC and CWME beginning in Mexico City (1963). Orthodox del-
egations interacted both critically and appreciatively with the developing
ecumenical theology of mission, mining their own tradition for resources
to construct their unique vision of the church's mission. Indeed, in reading
Go Forth in Peace: Orthodox Perspectives on Mission, a series of articles in
response to ecumenical meetings and documents on mission, one sees two-
way traffic: there is much in common with the Ecumenical tradition, but at
the same time there has been a unique Orthodox contribution. Both traditions have been enriched in the dialogue.

When Bishop Ware was asked what is the center of the Christian message,
he replied,

> I would answer, "I believe in a God who loves humankind so intensely, so
> totally, that he chose himself to become human. Therefore, I believe in Jesus
> Christ as fully and truly God, but also totally and unreservedly one of us, fully
> human." And I would say to you, "The love of God is so great that Christ died
> for us on the cross. But love is stronger than death, and so the death of Jesus
> was followed by his resurrection. I am a Christian because I believe in the
> great love of God that led him to become incarnate, to die, and to rise again."[29]

In those words are several themes that repeatedly appear in an Orthodox
view of mission. Mission springs from the love of God for the world. In the
Orthodox tradition, love as the theological starting point for mission shapes

---

[29]Ware, "The Fullness and the Center," p. 41.

the christological emphasis on incarnation, cross and resurrection. The Eastern Orthodox Church does not play down the cross, but in comparison to Western traditions what is striking is the Orthodox stress on incarnation and resurrection. Incarnation and resurrection affirm the creation and life within it. The bodily incarnation of Jesus demonstrates the love of God for his world, and the bodily resurrection affirms the goodness of creation. Even when dealing with the cross, it is love that is accented. Ware comments on the legal imagery of the substitutionary atonement in Western theology: "I don't care so much for the idea of satisfaction. Satisfaction is not a scriptural word. The legal imagery, I think, should always be combined with an emphasis upon the transfiguring power of love. The motive for the Incarnation was not God's justice or his glory, but his love. That was the supreme motive. 'God so loved the world.' That is what we should start from."[30] Finally, this love of God revealed in Christ works itself out in a consistent trinitarian basis for mission. It is the love of the triune God that leads to the sending of Christ. It is the life of loving communion within the Trinity that is the goal of Christ's mission: "Mission does not aim primarily at the propagation or transmission of intellectual convictions, doctrines, moral commands, etc., but at the transmission of the life of communion that exists in God."[31]

Orthodox mission holds mission and ecclesiology closely together. Ion Bria says that it is "ecclesiology which determines missiology."[32] Like other traditions, the Orthodox tradition affirms the missionary nature of the

> IN THE ORTHODOX TRADITION, LOVE AS THE THEOLOGICAL STARTING POINT FOR MISSION SHAPES THE CHRISTOLOGICAL EMPHASIS ON INCARNATION, CROSS AND RESURRECTION.

church: "The proclamation of the kingdom of God lies at the very heart of the church's vocation in the world. Mission belongs to the very nature of the church . . . for without mission there is no church."[33] However, after an affirmation of the sentness or apostolic nature of the church, it is made clear

---

[30]Ibid.

[31]Ion Bria, ed., *Go Forth in Peace: Orthodox Perspectives on Mission* (Geneva: World Council of Churches, 1986), p. 3.

[32]Ion Bria, *Martyria/Mission: The Witness of the Orthodox Churches Today* (Geneva: World Council of Churches, 1980), p. 8.

[33]Bria, *Go Forth in Peace*, p. 11; see also pp. 17-23.

that "mission is not related exclusively to the 'apostolicity,' but to all the *notae*
of the church, including unity, holiness and catholicity."[34] It is especially in
the unity of the church that the Orthodox tradition sees its mission. Disunity
"is a scandal and an impediment to the united witness of the church."[35]
Stamoolis can even say that for some in the Orthodox tradition, when the
unity of the church was broken in 1054, "the Orthodox Church saw its
mission altered from evangelism to a search for Christian unity."[36] It is not
only unity, but also love. The church "is mission in its very being . . . pulsating
with God's all-embracing love and unity. The church, as the presence of the
kingdom of God in the world illuminates in one single reality the glory of
God and the eschatological destiny of creation."[37] Here is an important stress
of the Eastern Orthodox understanding of mission: the church is to embody
the message it proclaims. The church is the goal of mission and is itself an
expression of mission. As John Meyendorff succinctly puts it, "*Mission, in its
ultimate theological meaning, is an expression of the Church itself.*"[38]

The Orthodox emphasis on witness through liturgy calls for special attention. Ware states this position clearly: "To me, the most important missionary witness that we have is the Divine Liturgy, the Eucharistic worship
of the Orthodox Church. This is the life-giving source from which everything else proceeds. And therefore, to those who show an interest in Orthodoxy, I say, 'Come and see. Come to the liturgy.' The first thing is that
they should have an experience of Orthodoxy—or for that matter, of Christianity—as a worshiping community."[39] Orthodoxy criticizes the individualistic approach to worship that obscures the cosmic and eschatological
dimensions of salvation. The liturgy is a proclamation of the love of God for
the whole world; the kingdom of God is the horizon, the raison d'être, and
the goal of worship. At the end of the liturgy is the sending "Go in peace," in
which liturgy is transposed into another form—the liturgy after the liturgy.

---

[34]Ibid., p. 12.
[35]Ibid., p. 70.
[36]James J. Stamoolis, *Eastern Orthodox Mission Theology Today* (Maryknoll, NY: Orbis Books,
    1986), p. 110.
[37]"Final Report of CWME Consultation of Eastern Orthodox and Oriental Orthodox Churches,
    Neapolis, 1988," in Scherer and Bevans, *New Directions*, p. 236.
[38]John Meyendorff, "The Orthodox Church and Mission: Past and Present Perspectives," *St.
    Vladimir's Theological Quarterly* 16, no. 2 (1972): 63.
[39]Ware, "The Fullness and the Center," p. 40.

The church continues its worship in its immersion in the life of society. All of human life is sacred, lived in God's presence.

And so the eschatological and cosmic horizon of worship then shapes a holistic mission. "In the Bible, religious life was never limited to the temple or isolated from daily life. . . . The teaching of Jesus on the kingdom of God is a clear reference to God's loving lordship over all human history. We cannot limit our witness to a supposedly private area of life. The lordship of Christ is to be proclaimed to all realms of life."[40] Mission is to announce the good news of forgiveness and hope in a new heaven and new earth, denounce powers and structural injustice, console widows, orphans and the needy, to bring good news in the areas of science and technology. This view of mission has come a long way from the time under communism, when, says Bishop Ware, the church reduced its social mission to charity and did not challenge the unjust structures of communism. The cosmic and eschatological horizon of the kingdom, the love of God for the world, and the strong affirmation of creation in the incarnation and resurrection come into their own here in holistic mission.

Pentecostal tradition. To include a section on the mission theology of the Pentecostal (or Charismatic) tradition might surprise some readers. Many would see Pentecostalism as simply one (perhaps exotic) species of evangelicalism. Organizations such as the National Association of Evangelicals (NAE) and the World Evangelical Fellowship (WEF) have incorporated Pentecostals into their numbers. Indeed, many statisticians simply lump the two traditions together. Moreover, many Pentecostals would identify themselves as evangelicals, but with a difference.

Yet, according to Donald Dayton, there are very good reasons to study a Pentecostal theology of mission "as *Pentecostalism*, without the assumptions created by assuming it to be a part of a larger genus called 'evangelicalism.'" Dayton continues, "The usual connotations of 'evangelical' often serve only to obscure both the real nature of Pentecostalism . . . and the gifts they offer to us." Dayton would rather speak of a "third force" and see the Pentecostal movement "as a corrective to the classical traditions of Christian faith."[41]

---

[40]Bria, *Go Forth in Peace*, p. 77.
[41]Donald Dayton, "The Holy Spirit and Christian Expansion in the Twentieth Century," *Missiology* 16, no. 4 (1988): 402-3.

Indeed, there is a unique Pentecostal contribution to mission thought that can offer some correctives that would be obscured by folding them into the evangelical camp.

But there are a couple of other reasons as well. The most obvious is the sheer size of Pentecostalism; the Evangelical tradition is now dwarfed by the Pentecostal family of believers. There are more than twice as many Pentecostals. In the introductory chapter we briefly noted the explosive global growth of Pentecostalism. Today Pentecostals make up over 25 percent of all

> TODAY PENTECOSTALS MAKE UP OVER 25 PERCENT OF ALL CHRISTIANS AND SLIGHTLY LESS THAN 10 PERCENT OF THE ENTIRE POPULATION OF THE WORLD.

Christians and slightly less than 10 percent of the entire population of the world, and the growth continues at a remarkable rate. Beyond its numerical weight, the Pentecostal tradition brings a welcome (and sometimes not so welcome but necessary) critique to Western-oriented theologies shaped by the Enlightenment. This is in part due to the fact that Western Pentecostalism has grown up in the twentieth century and is the first postmodern theological tradition. But, more importantly, it is the result of the numerical dominance of third-world Pentecostals in Latin America, Africa and Asia. Even though there is a strong presence of non-Western Christians in the Roman Catholic, Ecumenical and Evangelical traditions, for various reasons they do not seem to have the same enriching and critical impact made by non-Western Pentecostals.

"Westerners who minister in Latin America, China, the Philippines, Africa or the South Seas consistently report that most Christian experience reflects a much stronger supernatural awareness than is characteristic of even charistmatic and Pentecostal circles in the West. . . . With only some hyperbole, we might say that although some of the world's new Christian communities are Roman Catholic, some Anglican, some Baptist, some Presbyterian and many independent, almost all are Pentecostal in a broad sense of the term."

Mark A. Noll, *The New Shape of World Christianity*, p. 34

This last comment raises the difficult question of how to categorize the growing group of third-world Christians that appears to the Western church to manifest marks associated with Pentecostalism. Wonsuk Ma uses the term "Pentecostal-charismatic" as an overarching category and distinguishes between three groups: classic denominational Pentecostals, Charismatic Pentecostals within other denominations, indigenous or Neo-Charismatic Pentecostals outside the West.[42] He recognizes the problems of lumping together such diverse cultural strands. In the 2001 *World Christian Encyclopedia* David Barrett uses the term "Independent," which, though understandable, hardly seems adequate. But what holds these groups together? Timothy Tennent asks, "What distinctive features might be found in movements as diverse as the Asian house church network, the African Initiated Churches of the apostolic variety, the Fourth Watch in the Philippines, the City Harvest Church in Singapore, the Fill the Gap Healing Centers in South Africa, the Meiti in India, the Cooneyites of Australia, the Igreja ev Pente of Brazil, and the Han house churches of China?"[43] He concludes that we simply need to wait and let these groups define themselves, yet he recognizes that whatever nomenclature we employ, we find here "a fourth branch of Christianity" along with Protestantism, Roman Catholicism and Orthodoxy. While Ma recognizes these difficulties, he sees common characteristics, continues with the language of "Pentecostal," and offers this definition: "Segments of Christianity which believe and experience the dynamic work of the Holy Spirit, including supernatural demonstrations of God's power and spiritual gifts, with consequent dynamic and participatory worship and zeal for evangelism."[44] Recognizing that this does not solve all the problems, especially the remarkable diversity and cultural distinctiveness, I will take my starting point in Ma's categorization, and briefly enumerate what this tradition offers the growing ecumenical paradigm of mission.

The traditional nexus that gave rise to the Pentecostal movement reveals important themes for a Pentecostal mission theology today: proclamation,

---

[42]Wonsuk Ma, "'When the Poor Are Fired Up': The Role of Pneumatology in Pentecostal-charismatic Mission," *Transformation* 24, no. 1 (2007): 32.

[43]Timothy Tennent, *Invitation to World Missions: A Trinitarian Missiology for the Twenty-first Century* (Grand Rapids: Kregel, 2010), p. 41.

[44]Wonsuk Ma, "Asian Pentecostalism: A Religion Whose Only Limit Is the Sky," *Journal of Beliefs and Values* 25, no. 2 (2004): 192.

eschatological urgency, Holy Spirit.[45] Put succinctly: the time is short, and so we must proclaim the gospel in the power of the Spirit. Not surprisingly, the most characteristic feature of Pentecostal mission thinking and the most important gift to the ecumenical church is its emphasis on the Spirit. The influence in this regard can be seen in, for example, the most recent ecumenical affirmation on mission and evangelism, "Together Towards Life," where the Spirit is mentioned 120 times in twenty-eight pages! The Anglican Roland Allen played something of a formative role for Pentecostal mission in his work on the Spirit and mission in Acts. Early in the century he said, "Missionary work as an expression of the Holy Spirit has received such slight and casual attention that it might also escape the notice of the hasty reader."[46] Paul Pomerville says that an "inordinate 'silence on the Holy Spirit' is part of the Protestant mission heritage. The Pentecostal Movement addresses that silence in a significant way."[47] The Spirit equips the church for world evangelism—that is, to proclaim the gospel and plant churches. Pentecostalism shares with evangelicalism a commitment to priority of proclamation, but it has not lacked voices calling for a broader kingdom vision that nourishes a more holistic approach. A commitment to compassion and justice is especially true of Pentecostalism in the third world.

> NOT SURPRISINGLY, THE MOST CHARACTERISTIC FEATURE OF PENTECOSTAL MISSION THINKING AND THE MOST IMPORTANT GIFT TO THE ECUMENICAL CHURCH IS ITS EMPHASIS ON THE SPIRIT.

The Pentecostal urgency for mission comes from a sense that time is short, which is fed by a premillennial eschatology.

Pentecostals have been more about doing and less about thinking, interested in mission that is more "acted out" than "codified."[48] This certainly has had its downside, as the lack of a vigorous theology can lead to imbalance. It must be noted, however, that the past three decades have seen a growing literature in the Pentecostal tradition articulating a more sophisticated missiology. But there is an upside to an emphasis on doing as well. At a number

[45]Byron D. Klaus, "Pentecostalism and Mission," *Missiology* 35, no. 1 (2007): 41-43.
[46]Roland Allen, *The Ministry of the Spirit: Selected Writings of Roland Allen* (Grand Rapids: Eerdmans, 1960), p. 21.
[47]Pomerville, *Third Force in Missions*, p. 3.
[48]Klaus, "Pentecostalism and Mission," p. 41.

of levels it has challenged the rationalism of the Enlightenment that is characteristic of other confessional traditions. Pomerville believes that in Protestantism the Holy Spirit has been tied to the written word, and thus the power of the Spirit in experience has been neglected.[49] The emphasis on an experience of the Spirit, on orthopraxis, and simply on doing has much that is biblical about it. Moreover, it has introduced the importance of obedience and living for the very practice of theology. Harvey Cox believes that there is something important in emphasizing experience over theology:

> As a theologian I have grown accustomed to studying religious movements by reading what their theologians wrote and trying to grasp the central ideas and the most salient doctrines. But I soon found out that with Pentecostalism this approach did not help much. As one Pentecostal scholar put it, in his faith, "the experience of God has absolute primacy over dogma and doctrine." Therefore the only theology that can give an account of this experience, he says, is "a mature theology where central expression is the testimony." I think he is right.[50]

It is not only the rationalism of the Enlightenment that Pentecostalism challenges; it is also the naturalism. Neuza Itioka rightly observes that naturalism has crippled the church's mission: "Certainly one of the most important issues worldwide missions must face in the 1990s is how to confront the destructive supernatural forces that oppose the missionary enterprise. For too long the western church has tended toward an intellectual expression of its faith, failing to face realistically the supernatural manifestations it must confront."[51] Exorcisms and healings have been prominent in large numbers of conversions. Moreover, the issues of spiritual warfare and the importance of prayer for mission are frequent in Pentecostal writing.

Pentecostalism has been able to actually accomplish a number of things that find expression within most mission theologies. Evangelism as the task of every member is something more characteristic of Pentecostal practice than other traditions. Evangelization of the urban poor is also something that Pentecostals have carried out. Perhaps this comes as no surprise when

---

[49]Pomerville, *Third Force in Missions*, pp. 79-104.
[50]Quoted in Klaus, "Pentecostalism and Mission," p. 46.
[51]Neuza Itioka, "Recovering the Biblical Worldview for Effective Mission," in Anderson, Phillips and Coote, *Mission in the 1990s*, p. 35.

we observe the demographic of world Pentecostalism, which stands in contrast to other confessional families. Statistics reveal a church that is "more urban than rural, more female than male, more Third World (66 percent) than Western, more impoverished (87 percent) than affluent, more family oriented than individualistic, and, on average younger than eighteen."[52] Walter Hollenweger tells us that Pentecostalism "is a church *of* the poor," not just for the poor. As the poor, he says, they are not dependent on the power centers of the West.[53] This certainly is one of the features of Pentecostalism that enables it to be effective. As poor, female and young, they do not have the same stake in the status quo and thus are not guardians of the old order. This position on the margins offers a better place to offer a witness to the structural injustice of the social, cultural and political powers.

One final emphasis should be noted. The exuberant and participatory worship of Pentecostalism has been an important factor in mission. Gary McGee notes, "Pentecostal spirituality has been a major factor behind church growth, enhanced by enthusiastic worship."[54] A vibrant form of worship that includes dance, emotional fervor, shouting, crying, spoken prayer and tongues has an attraction among the urban poor and tribal peoples where Pentecostalism has thrived. It also appeals to many others who have felt burdened by the heavy weight of rationalism in Western worship.

The success and growth of Pentecostalism raise many questions and issues for the tradition of mission theology. But the mission theology of other traditions put their own questions to Pentecostalism as well. How can an emphasis on word and proclamation incorporate a more holistic emphasis? As noted above, the third-world setting and ongoing scholarly work have already moved Pentecostalism well down this track. For example, Donald Miller and Tetsunao Yamamori speak of "progressive Pentecostalism" and document the social breadth of Pentecostal mission in mercy ministry, emergency services, education, counseling, medical help, eco-

---

[52]Grant McClung Jr., "Pentecostal/Charismatic Contribution to World Evangelization," in Anderson, Phillips and Coote, *Mission in the 1990s*, p. 65.

[53]Walter Hollenweger, "From Azusa Street to the Toronto Phenomenon," in *Pentecostal Movements as an Ecumenical Challenge*, ed. Jürgen Moltmann and Karl-Josef Kuschel (Concilium 1996/3; London: SCM Press; Maryknoll, NY: Orbis Books, 1996), p. 12.

[54]Gary B. McGee, "Pentecostal Strategies for Global Mission: A Historical Assessment," in *Called and Empowered: Global Mission in Pentecostal Perspective*, ed. Murray A. Dempster, Byron D. Klaus and Douglas Petersen (Peabody, MA: Hendrickson, 1991), p. 206.

nomic development, arts and policy change.[55] Moreover, some also speak
not only of word and works but also of wonders.[56] The growth of Pentecostalism in almost every country of the world has raised the question of the
relationship of gospel to culture. Byron Klaus says that traditionally the
Pentecostal position, when contrasted with other positions, such as Christ
against culture or Christ transforms culture, has been "gospel oblivious to
culture."[57] However, ecumenical discussion, scholarship and reflection
from the third world are changing this situation. Like evangelicalism, the
Pentecostal tradition in the West has been highly individualistic. Sin and
salvation have been understood primarily in individual terms. Again, it is
the communal cultures of the third world that challenge this. A further
question is how the rich reflection on the Holy Spirit can be incorporated
into a fuller trinitarian basis for mission. And finally, there is the question
of how to maintain a vibrant and expectant eschatology that is not captive
to the extreme eschatologization of mission in the early part of the twentieth century.

CONCLUSION

A new ecumenical era of mission is unfolding today in which the various
traditions share much in common but also have their various contributions
to make. We have looked primarily at its theological expression. Clearly, no
tradition lives up to its best theology. Alongside of faithful missiology we
often see sharp decline and syncretism of the church. The challenge of the
future will be for a prayerful, gospel-centered, Spirit-filled church to more
and more embody the best theological insights of the new ecumenical paradigm of mission.

FURTHER READING

Bosch, David J. *Transforming Mission: Paradigm Shifts in Theology of Mission.*
Maryknoll, NY: Orbis, 1991, pp. 349-519.

---

[55]Donald E. Miller and Tetsunao Yamamori, *Global Pentecostalism: The New Face of Christian Social Engagement* (Los Angeles: University of California Press, 2007).
[56]Ronald Sider, ed., "Words, Works, and Wonders: Papers from an International Dialogue between the Pentecostal/Charismatic Renewal and Evangelical Social Action," *Transformation* 5, no. 4 (1988).
[57]Klaus, "Pentecostalism and Mission," p. 49.

Bria, Ion, ed. *Go Forth in Peace: Orthodox Perspectives on Mission.* Geneva: World Council of Churches, 1986.

Klaus, Byron D. "Pentecostalism and Mission," *Missiology* 35, no. 1 (2007): 39-54.

Scherer, James A., and Stephen B. Bevans, eds. *New Directions in Mission and Evangelization 1. Basic Statements 1974-1991.* Maryknoll, NY: Orbis, 1992.

Moreau, Scott, ed., *Evangelical Dictionary of World Missions* (Grand Rapids: Baker, 2000): Paul E. Pierson, "Ecumenical Movement," pp. 300-303; Gary R. Corwin, "Evangelical Missions Conferences," pp. 335-36; Gary B. McGee, "Evangelical Movement," pp. 337-40; Edward Rommen, "Evangelical Theology," pp. 340-41; Bradley Nassif, "Orthodox Mission Movements," pp. 713-14; Gary B. McGee, "Pentecostal Missions," pp. 738-39; Gary B. McGee, "Pentecostal Movement," pp. 739-42; Stephen B. Bevans and John Nyquist, "Roman Catholic Missions," pp. 837-41.

Discussion Questions

1. Much of the mission theology emerging around an ecumenical paradigm is a corrective to the modern missionary movement. What do you find helpful in this theological response?

2. What tradition of mission do you find most helpful in enriching and critiquing your own view of mission?

3. How do you think the growing Pentecostal movement will affect mission theology and practice?

Essay Topics

1. Choose any three of the elements of an emerging ecumenical paradigm of mission and discuss it. What historical factors have shaped this response? How would you evaluate this response?

2. Analyze one of the mission traditions (ecumenical, evangelical, Roman Catholic, Orthodox or Pentecostal) in terms of its insights and weaknesses.

5

A Survey of the Global Church

CB

CHRISTIANITY IS A GLOBAL PHENOMENON. According to the Bible, the church is one people, the new humankind created in Christ Jesus. It is a multinational and multicultural community that spans the globe. Together they share a mission as a people sent into the whole world. In this chapter we will survey the global Christian church with a view to understanding the issues facing it in its mission in various parts of the world.

MISSION AND GLOBAL CHRISTIANITY?

It would be reasonable to question including a survey of global Christianity in an introduction to mission. Do these two areas of study constitute one discipline? Or is this simply a remnant of a colonial view of mission? That is, anything that has to do with the Christian church "overseas" or outside the West is mission. Or does mission studies treat the phenomenon of non-Western Christianity because it is neglected by other theological disciplines? Every area of theology should engage the insights of the non-Western church, but since much of the theological curriculum seems to be blind to the theology, church history and biblical scholarship emanating from the Southern hemisphere, it is incumbent on mission scholars who are aware of this rich fruit to display it for the rest of the theological academy. Perhaps there is something in this, but neither of these reasons is sufficient to include a chapter on world Christianity in an introductory book on mission. Rather, the approach of this chapter is to consider the church in other parts of the world in terms of the challenges that it faces in its mission to be, do and speak good news in its context.

"It is utterly scandalous for so many Christian scholars in older Christendom to know so much about heretical movements in the second and third centuries, when so few of them know anything about Christian movements in areas of the younger churches."

John Mbiti, "Theological Impotence and
the Universality of Church," p. 17

Some Initial Statistics

It is no longer true—if it ever was—that Christianity is a Western religion.[1] While the missions task of the church is far from done, the Christian church is now present in every part of the world. Kenneth Hylson-Smith writes, "The global expansion of Christianity during the final century of the second millennium of the Christian era eclipsed anything that had previously taken place within the span of any single century. The increase in the number of believers worldwide, and the enhanced impact the faith had on political, economic and social, as well as religious affairs, in great tracts of the world was without precedence."[2] Hylson-Smith is countering many pundits who have declared the Christian church to be in interminable decline and so have written its eulogy. And so his rosy picture of the church probably is too optimistic. Yet his counterbalance is important: the church has indeed made gains in the twentieth century and continues to thrive in many parts of the world.

> IT IS NO LONGER TRUE—
> IF IT EVER WAS—THAT
> CHRISTIANITY IS A
> WESTERN RELIGION.

Today there are just over 2.3 billion people who profess to be Christians existing on every continent. This is compared to about 1.6 billion Muslims, almost a billion Hindus, and just under a half billion Buddhists. Thus, throughout the twentieth century the

---

[1]The subtitle of Kwame Bediako's book indicates that Christianity originally was not a Western religion: *Christianity in Africa: The Renewal of a Non-Western Religion* (Maryknoll, NY: Orbis Books, 1995).

[2]Kenneth Hylson-Smith, *To the Ends of the Earth: The Globalization of Christianity* (London: Paternoster, 2007), p. 95.

Christian church has numbered about one-third of the total population of the world, a figure that has increased from about 23% in 1800. The annual growth rate of the Christian church is about 1.3%, which is slightly lower than the Muslim rate of 1.8% and the Hindu rate of 1.4%. And so, into the foreseeable future the Christian faith will remain the largest religious body in the world.

As to the makeup of the global Christian church, the Roman Catholic communion remains the largest body at about 1.2 billion adherents. Protestants number about 500 million, Orthodox 280 million, and Anglicans 90 million. A new category of "Independents" is the third-largest Christian group at 360 million, a group of non-Western "Pentecostals" whose diversity makes it difficult to categorize.

THE GLOBAL SHIFT TO THE SOUTH

Yet these statistics do not capture the remarkable changes taking place in the global church. The most important change in the world church today is the global shift to the South and the East. John Parratt claims that the "greatest single change that has come upon the Christian faith during the last century has been the demographic shift in its focus away from its traditional centres in Europe and North America. There it has been in deep decline for three centuries. . . . By contrast the growth of Christianity in the 'South' or 'Third World' has, within the last hundred years or so, witnessed a phenomenal growth." He touches on statistics in various regions and concludes, "While simple data never tell the whole story, it is evident that Christianity can no longer be regarded as a 'Western' religion; it is a global one of which the Western church is only a small fraction."[3]

> THE MOST IMPORTANT CHANGE IN THE WORLD CHURCH TODAY IS THE GLOBAL SHIFT TO THE SOUTH AND THE EAST.

Perhaps more than anyone it has been Philip Jenkins who made this fact headline news, startling many people, including, sadly, many Christians. He detailed the shift southward in his bestselling and widely read *The Next Christendom: The Coming of Global Christianity*. "We are currently living through

---

[3]John Parratt, introduction to *An Introduction to Third World Theologies*, ed. John Parratt (Cambridge: Cambridge University Press, 2004), p. 1.

one of the transforming moments in the history of religion worldwide," he writes. "Over the past century . . . the center of gravity in the Christian world has shifted inexorably southward, to Africa, Asia, and Latin America."[4] He looks to the future and says, "Christianity should enjoy a worldwide boom in the new century, but the vast majority of believers will be neither white nor European, nor Euro-American." In fact, by 2025 Africa and Latin America will be in competition for the title "the most Christian continent," and these two continents together will account for one half of the world's Christians.[5]

⬦⬦⬦

"The Christian church has experienced a larger geographical redistribu-tion in the last fifty years than in any comparable period in its history, with the exception of the very earliest years of church history. Some of this change comes from the general growth of world population, but much also arises from remarkable rates of evangelization in parts of Asia, Africa, Latin America, and the islands of the South Pacific—but also from a nearly unprecedented relative decline of Christian adher-ence in Europe."

Mark A. Noll, *The New Shape of World Christianity*, p. 21

⬦⬦⬦

How can we characterize these Southern churches? While there has been spectacular growth among Pentecostal and independent churches, it is still the Roman Catholic and mainstream Protestant churches that remain the largest, albeit transformed in their new cultural context. The growth of the church in the South means that there are now differences from the church in the West. For example, the church is now present among the least-reached peoples of the earth, among the poorest in the world, in difficult situations of deprivation, and in places of persecution. These Southern churches are also more likely to be theologically and ethically conservative, "much more committed in terms of belief and practice."[6] Worship displays characteristics

---

[4]Philip Jenkins, *The Next Christendom: The Coming of Global Christianity* (Oxford: Oxford Univer-sity Press, 2002), pp. 1-2.
[5]Ibid., pp. 2-3.
[6]Ibid., p. 94.

of their culture that are quite different from the West. And, finally, the church outside the West is "far more enthusiastic, much more centrally concerned with the immediate workings of the supernatural, through prophecy, visions, ecstatic utterances, and healing."[7]

Understanding the growing church in the South is especially important because it will be that church that provides leadership for the global church in the twenty-first century. Andrew Walls says,

> We have seen that in the twenty-first century Christianity has been revealed as an increasingly non-Western religion. Christianity is in recession in Western countries, and in Europe has dwindled out of recognition within the lifetime of people of my own age. The implication is that Africa and Asia and Latin America and the Pacific seem set to be the principal theaters of Christian activity in its latest phase. What happens there will determine what the Christianity of the twenty-first and twenty-second centuries will be like. What happens in Europe, and even in North America, will matter less and less.[8]

And so we will survey the global church with special attention to Africa, Asia and Latin America.

SUB-SAHARAN AFRICA

The growing church in Sub-Saharan Africa. In Sub-Saharan Africa Christians made up less than 10% of the population in 1900 but have grown today to over 60%—close to a half billion people. The Roman Catholic, Anglican, mainline and evangelical Protestant churches have thrived. But it is the growth of the Pentecostal churches, such as the Redeemed Church in Nigeria, and African Indigenous Churches (AICs)[9] that have been remarkable. Today there are perhaps ten thousand AICs, with over one-

> IN SUB-SAHARAN AFRICA CHRISTIANS MADE UP LESS THAN 10% OF THE POPULATION IN 1900 BUT HAVE GROWN TODAY TO OVER 60%—CLOSE TO A HALF BILLION PEOPLE.

---

[7]Ibid., p. 107.
[8]Andrew Walls, "Christian Scholarship and the Demographic Transformation of the Church," in *Theological Literacy for the Twenty-First Century*, ed. Rodney Lawrence Petersen, with Nancy M. Rourke (Grand Rapids: Eerdmans, 2002), p. 173.
[9]"AICs" can stand for "African Independent Churches," "African Initiated Churches" and "African Indigenous Churches."

third of African Christians belonging to one of these churches. Of these churches, 90 percent are made up of one hundred or fewer members. But there are also massive churches, such as the Kimbaguist Church, formed in the Democratic Republic of the Congo, and the Cherubim and Seraphim Church, which originated in Nigeria, whose members number in the millions.

The AICs arose in reaction to the Westernized Christianity that was imported to Africa. And so these churches are a contextualized expression of Christianity in African culture exhibiting many aspects of the African religious heritage. Direct revelation, such as dreams, visions and auditory messages, are an integral part of their faith. Healing plays an important role in the formation and the ongoing ministry of these churches. There is an emphasis on spiritual power—the power to heal, power in prayer to impact everyday life. AICs draw on a deep sense of community characteristic of Africa and adopt much of its social structures and tribal forms. Many of these churches are open to polygamy or at least are ambiguous about it. Rites of passage at times of transition—birth, puberty, marriage, first child, death—are prominent. The liturgies of these churches are highly colorful, emotional, energetic and symbolic. There is mystery in the sacraments. Dancing, symbolic gestures from African traditional religions, colorful robes and jubilant songs characterize the worship. There also has been a close connection between the translation of the Old Testament and the emergence of AICs. The world of the Old Testament is recognizable to Africans. There they find such familiar phenomena as prophets, sacrifices, priests, direct revelation, evil spirits, witches (cf. 1 Sam 28:3-25), polygamy and tribal social arrangements.

These churches have drawn varying judgments. Some take a wholly negative stance, seeing AICs as dangerously syncretistic with paganism. Others are quite positive, believing that AICs are a faithful expression of African Christianity in which Christian content has been poured into African cultural forms. And still others believe that AICs are ambiguous, combining both syncretism and faithfulness, as is the case in all other contextual expressions of Christianity.

Concern about the orthodoxy of AICs arises for a number of reasons. Most criticism is tied to the general fear that AICs have absorbed too much of the paganism of traditional African religions. For example, noisy and bizarre worship, untrained and charismatic leadership, rituals that interact with the spiritual world, and an emphasis on direct revelation rather than Bible seem to reflect pagan religion. Yet contextualization is an ongoing process in African culture, as it is everywhere else. No cultural expression of the Christian faith has achieved full faithfulness, and so it remains a journey. But often these churches are criticized not by biblical standards but rather by criteria rooted in a Western Enlightenment expression of the gospel.

"Outside the ranks of scholars and church bureaucrats, few commentators have paid serious attention to these trends, to what I will describe as the creation of a new Christendom, which for better or worse may play a critical role in world affairs. . . . For whatever reason, Southern churches remain almost invisible to Northern observers."

Philip Jenkins, *The Next Christendom*, p. 4

Dean Gilliland offers a helpful fourfold categorization of AICs.[10] The first is Evangelical-Pentecostal. These churches had a connection with European or American mission organizations but have broken away. They have kept much of theology and practice of their origin but are concerned to Africanize them. The second is Indigenous-Pentecostal. These churches also have some connection with Western church but are more committed to Africanizing all aspects of Christian life. They are characterized by direct revelation and by charismatic leaders and by an illiterate use of Bible. The third is Revelational-Indigenous. These churches are rooted in direct revelation that comes to the leader in the founding and continues in the ongoing life of the church. In fact, direct revelation can have more authority than the Bible. These churches have a highly ritualistic worship, place high priority on healing, and lean heavily on the Old Testament. The fourth is Indigenous-Syncretistic. These churches have appropriated so much of traditional religion that their claim to be Christian is in doubt. The pastor is more like a shaman or diviner, there is a magical use of

---

[10]Dean S. Gilliland, "How 'Christian' Are African Independent Churches?" *Missiology* 14, no. 3 (1986): 259-72.

crosses and Bibles, and the name of Jesus is invoked in magical way.

In this classification of AICs the tension at the heart of contextualization in all cultural settings is evident. On one side, there is the danger of irrelevance. The Western-mission and traditional churches are in danger of not touching the African heart. On the other side, there is the danger of syncretism. The more these AICs embrace their African traditional culture, the greater danger of syncretism.

AICs are important because they "have realised that in order to get in tune with true Christianity, they ought to set aside the Western interpretation, which in too many instances stifled Christianity, and get back to African culture which is quite akin to original Christianity."[11] Contextualization is absolutely necessary if the good news is to be an answer to the cry of the African heart, and if dualism and paganism are to be swept away. Moreover, a faithful expression of African Christianity can make an important contribution to the world church. Desmond Tutu holds that it is only "when African theology is true to itself that it will go on to speak relevantly to the contemporary African—surely its primary task—and also, incidentally make its valuable contribution to the rich Christian heritage which belongs to all of us."[12]

The African church is maturing in many ways. While the gospel has long reached the poor and uneducated, it is also making great inroads among the educated. There is a vision for church planting in Africa and a growing missionary vision for the unreached. There is a growth of contextual African theologies and well-educated African theologians. And although there is continuing need on all these fronts, all of this constitutes good news. It may well be true in the future that as the African church goes, so goes the global church.

> IT MAY WELL BE TRUE IN THE FUTURE THAT AS THE AFRICAN CHURCH GOES, SO GOES THE GLOBAL CHURCH.

Challenges facing the Sub-Saharan African church. Many challenges

---

[11]Kofi Osare Opoku, "The Relevance of African Culture to Christianity," *Mid-Stream* 13, nos. 3-4 (1974): 155.

[12]Desmond M. Tutu, "Black Theology/African Theology—Soul Mates or Antagonists?" *Journal of Religious Thought* 32, no. 2 (1975): 33.

still face the African church. The first involves the numerous social, economic and political problems in Africa facing the church. The AIDS epidemic has hit Africa particularly hard: 68% of the world's cases of AIDS are in Africa; 22 million are infected, about 5% of Africa's population; 1.5 million die annually; and the disease has left 11.6 million orphans.[13] Africa continues to face deepening poverty and massive debt because of unjust global economic structures, inappropriate aid programs, political corruption and growing slums that accompany rapid urbanization. As a result, Africa faces enormous challenges in healthcare, in education (40 percent of African children are not in school), and in a "brain drain" to the West. The question for the African church is urgent: what is the church's mission in the social, political and economic life of the nation?

A second challenge is in the ongoing struggle in relating the gospel to traditional African culture. This problem is a legacy of Western missionaries who simply condemned, for example, drums and "medicine men" without understanding the deeper cultural roots. Traditional African culture remains powerful. Questions of ancestor reverence, fetishism, spiritual power, "soul travel,"[14] and much more must be addressed by the gospel. The need for authentic contextualization and faithful African theology is urgent. Walls rightly observes that the "framework of theology inherited from the West, and still the staple of seminaries, cannot cope: it is not big enough for the universe that most Africans live in."[15] This is an urgent issue: it is the only way the gospel can deeply touch the hearts of the African people. But Africans' reflection on this issue has the potential not only to equip their own churches but also to enrich the whole Christian church, not least the church in the West. Africans are acutely aware of a spiritual world that has long been suppressed in the West by an

> AFRICANS ARE ACUTELY AWARE OF A SPIRITUAL WORLD THAT HAS LONG BEEN SUPPRESSED IN THE WEST BY AN ENLIGHTENMENT WORLDVIEW. AFRICAN THEOLOGY MIGHT WAKE UP THE WEST TO THE VERY WORLD OF THE BIBLE.

---

[13]"Worldwide HIV and AIDS Statistics" (www.avert.org/statindx.htm). The statistics are from the end of 2011.

[14]Jan Boer, "Opening the Reformed World to the Powers," *Perspectives* 9, no. 2 (1994): 16-18.

[15]Walls, "Christian Scholarship," p. 179.

Enlightenment worldview. African theology might wake up the West to the very world of the Bible.

A third challenge arises from the rapid growth of the church in Africa. There is a burning need for theological training, made difficult by a number of factors: lack of funds, lack of education in lower ages, a Western-oriented education and curriculum, and the need for African theologians and theologies. Groups such as NetACT, out of Stellenbosch University, are attempting to meet this need. Moreover, the rapid growth has often meant superficial discipleship. Consequently, we are already seeing nominal Christianity. There is an urgent need for unity. In Africa there are fifteen thousand denominations (second only to the West), a situation exacerbated by tribal structures and power issues that fragment body of Christ.

A fourth challenge concerns the ongoing evangelization of Africa. In spite of a large number of Christians, there are many unreached peoples in most countries. For example, even though Kenya is over 80 percent Christian, Operation World lists a number of least-reached and unreached peoples, including the pastoral and animistic people living in the north and the west, the Muslim tribes in the northeast, the mixed Muslim-traditional people of the coastal hills, and more.[16] Similar observations could be made on other African nations. Thus, missionary vision and effective practice are needed. The problem that remains from Western missions is that often Africans were disempowered from the beginning; mission was considered to be the white man's job. Moreover, there are few funds and little training. It is true that Africans have been the primary evangelists of Africa itself, and that a missions initiative continues to grow, but there remains a need for a bigger vision.

Finally, Africa faces the threat of violence because of its tribal past and also because of the encounter with Islam. The fault line between the Muslim north and the "Christian" south is moving south. Islam is growing rapidly in Africa, and this opens up the potential for violence. The African situation raises the urgent question of what is involved in a faithful missionary encounter with the world's religions.

---

[16]Jason Mandryk, Operation World: The Definitive Prayer Guide to Every Nation (7th ed.; Colorado Springs, CO: Biblica Publishing, 2010), p. 504.

ASIA

Good news about the church in Asia. In 1900 there were about 22 million Christians living in Asia, just over 2% of the population. Today there are over 360 million Christians, comprising over 8% of the population. But the growth has been uneven. While the church in most Asian countries is growing, in many countries Christians make up a tiny fraction of the population. Nevertheless, there is much to be thankful for. When Mao Zedong began to expel missionaries from China in 1949, there were about 4.5 million Christians in the country. That number has burgeoned, and today, although estimates vary, there could be as many as 100 million.[17] "The growth of the Church in China since 1977," says Jason Mandryk, "has no parallels in history."[18] In regard to South Korea, Patrick Johnstone put it nicely: it "is a land of Christian superlatives—the largest Christian gathering ever held, the world's largest congregations of Pentecostals, Presbyterians, and Methodists, the largest theological seminaries and the largest non-Western missionary-sending nation! All this in a land that only opened up for the gospel just over a century ago."[19] Christianity in Indonesia is growing faster than any other religion there, even though 85% percent of its population is Muslim; Christians now make up about 10% of the population. The Philippines is over 90% Christian and has emerged as a major player in missions, with over three thousand cross-cultural missionaries, predominantly from the Evangelical and Pentecostal wing of the church. Mandryk tells us that "some of the greatest growth in the past decade or two" has been not only in China but also in "India, Nepal, Iran, Bangladesh, Cambodia, Vietnam, and, although unverifiable, North Korea."[20] Add to this the growing missionary vision in a number of countries, most notably South Korea, China, India and the Philippines, and we can rejoice at what God is doing in Asia.

---

[17]Rodney Stark, Byron R. Johnson and F. Carson Mencken, "Counting China's Christians," *First Things* 213 (May 2011): 14-16. They note that estimates range from 16 million to 200 million, and that the standard estimate is 130 million. They believe that in 2011 there were about 70 million.

[18]Mandryk, *Operation World*, p. 161.

[19]Patrick Johnstone and Jason Mandryk, with Robyn Johnstone, *Operation World: 21st Century Edition* (6th ed.; Carlisle: Paternoster, 2005), p. 42.

[20]Mandryk, *Operation World*, p. 59.

"We may well decide that, as regards Christian history, [the twentieth century] was the most remarkable hundred years of any except the first. When it began, Christianity appeared to most people, whether well disposed or not, to be both *a* Western religion and *the* Western religion. The great majority of people in the West professed it, and the overwhelming majority of those who professed it lived in Europe or North America. When the century ended, the majority of professed Christians were living in Africa, Asia, Latin America, or the Pacific region. Every year, it now seems, there are fewer Christians in the West, and more in the rest of the world. Christianity is now entering a new phase of its existence, as a non-Western religion; a fact which must inevitably have implications for its expression, its ways of thinking, its theology."

Andrew F. Walls, "Mission History as the
Substructure of Mission Theology," p. 367

Challenges facing the Asian church. Among the many challenges facing the missional church in Asia, perhaps the most evident is the enormous population of Asia and the small percentage of Christians. About 55% of the world's population lives in Asia, and only a little more than 8% is Christian. Over 85% of the population is unevangelized. The three largest non-Christian religions are rooted in Asia: 1.1 billion Muslims, 950 million Hindus, 920 million Buddhists. There are 680 million Asians who have no formal religious affiliation. There are thirty-two Asian countries that are less than 10% Christian, and twelve that are less than 2%. In the world there are more than 16,000 ethno-linguistic peoples in the world, and over 7,000 that are unreached. About 75% (over 5,000) of the unreached people groups are found in Asia.[21] The influential country of Japan remains hard soil for the gospel.

> ABOUT 55% OF THE WORLD'S POPULATION LIVES IN ASIA, AND ONLY A LITTLE MORE THAN 8% IS CHRISTIAN. OVER 85% OF THE POPULATION IS UNEVANGELIZED.

[21]Ibid., p. 69.

The unfinished task of missions is especially clear in this region.

The religious pluralism of Asia constitutes an enormous challenge. We have just noted the sizable populations of Muslims, Hindus and Buddhists. All three religious communities not only make up a high percentage of the population but are also experiencing resurgence in growth and vitality. Some, but not all, are extreme—Hindu groups in India and Nepal, Muslims in Malaysia and Indonesia, Buddhists in Sri Lanka, Myanmar and Tibet— and this means opposition for Christians. An important agenda for the Asian church is to reflect on what Scripture teaches in terms of a missionary encounter with religious pluralism, on interreligious dialogue and on a theology of religions. Religious opposition comes not only from the world's religions but also from totalitarian political regimes such as those in North Korea, Myanmar, Laos, Vietnam and China. Moreover, the context of religious pluralism will also set the agenda for an authentic and faithful Asian theology.

The church in Asia also faces an urban challenge. Asia has seven of the ten largest cities in the world and over two hundred megacities. Over the next three decades population growth will be enormous. Over 90% of all population growth will take place in the cities of the Southern hemisphere, with 80% of that growth occurring in Asia and Africa. The Asian urban slums also constitute an opportunity. In South Asia 60% of the population lives in slums, and the numbers are expected to climb. Poverty is rampant, existing alongside of extreme wealth within the church. Drug trafficking, the sex trade and AIDS bring further misery to the urban slums. Urban mission will be an urgent task for the Asian church. At the same time, it also raises the importance of holistic mission—a church that understands its calling to evangelize, seek justice and practice mercy.

LATIN AMERICA

Today the church in Latin America is made up of two groups: Roman Catholics and Evangélicos (who, as we will see, comprise three subgroups), with Roman Catholics being by far the greatest in number. A brief look at these groups paints the picture of the church in Latin America.

Roman Catholics. Latin America was "evangelized" by the Catholic countries of Portugal and Spain in the sixteenth century. But the conquest approach adopted by these colonial powers meant that the faith often did not take deep root. Today just over 75% of the population is Catholic, yet less than 15% ever attends church. The Catholic Church has been hemorrhaging for decades, losing members to the Pentecostal and evangelical churches as well as to spiritism and secularism. In fact, in the last few decades more Catholics have left the church for Protestantism than at the time of the Reformation in the sixteenth century. But there has also been renewal in the Catholic Church as a result of the changes in Vatican II. The council of Latin American bishops (CELAM) that met in Medellín, Colombia, in 1968 took on board the changes of Vatican II. And there has also been renewal through the Charismatic movement, which has grown since the 1970s.

The context of Latin American Catholicism can be understood only by reflecting on the ferment of the last half-century. Poverty is rampant in Latin America, dominating the lives of 80 percent of the population. This poverty is the result of corrupt and unjust political regimes within the region as well as global economic structures that produce a new form of economic colonialism and burdensome debt. This is not the only place in the world where this situation exists, but the problem is exacerbated by the perception that the Roman Catholic Church is part of the problem. Some of the ecclesial hierarchy supports the corrupt regimes and participates in the system as one of the pillars of society in which there is an unequal distribution of power and money. They uphold the status quo because they benefit from it.

It is this context that explains the rise of liberation theology, which has reacted against blatant injustice that is held in place by unjust political and economic structures. Liberation theology developed in the womb of the Roman Catholic Church. Some of the influential pioneers were theologians who participated in Medellín, such as Juan Luis Segundo and Gustavo Guttiérrez. It understands salvation primarily in terms of liberation from economic, political and social oppression. Theological reflection within the liberationist tradition finds sources in both Scripture and Marxism. As is often the case, certain parts of Scripture hold the fascination of a group. Liberation thinkers have reflected deeply on the exodus, the message of the prophets and the Gospel of Luke—events and texts that prominently feature themes of economic, political and social justice. The exegetical tradition of liberation theology has been very fruitful opening up numerous insights into the gospel. Liberation theologians have further employed Marxist tools of social analysis, including a hermeneutic that calls for commitment to action for justice as the proper location for a true interpretation of Scripture. Liberation thinkers call the church to a preferential option for the poor, a place in God's mission that takes a stance of solidarity with the poor. The Marxist influence now appears to be waning, but questions about the compatibility with Marxist social analysis remain. Although it is clear that liberation theology has opened up new vistas in Scripture that are important for the global church, how much has the utilization of Marxism corrupted those insights? Further, has there been a reduction of salvation to social, economic and political liberation? Has the heart of salvation—liberation from sin to know God in Christ—been lost? Many of these problems have been addressed by liberation theologians over the past few decades, making many forms of liberation theology more faithful to the gospel. But these questions will continue to be debated. Latin American evangelicals such as René Padilla and Samuel Escobar have helped us to see the importance of this contextual theology for the West. In the Latin American context of grinding poverty upheld by unjust structures, a message that does not address these realities is something less than the full-orbed gospel of Scripture.

> IN THE LATIN AMERICAN CONTEXT OF GRINDING POVERTY UPHELD BY UNJUST STRUCTURES, A MESSAGE THAT DOES NOT ADDRESS THESE REALITIES IS SOMETHING LESS THAN THE FULL-ORBED GOSPEL OF SCRIPTURE.

This situation of poverty upheld by unjust structures and the emergence of liberation theology, with its call for the church to take its social location among the poor, is also the context in which base ecclesial communities (BECs) have developed. The Argentinian Baptist René Padilla says of these BECs, "They may well become the most powerful challenge to the church of Jesus Christ everywhere else in the next few years."[22]

BECs came into existence in the 1960s as small house churches of the poor. The shortage of priests to lead congregations and administer the

---

[22]C. René Padilla, "A New Ecclesiology in Latin America," *International Bulletin of Missionary Research* 11, no. 4 (1987): 162.

Eucharist, along with an imagination fired by evangelical and Pentecostal churches, led many Roman Catholic congregations to appoint lay
leaders. Together, they began to seriously study the Scriptures, attempting to grasp the message and its importance for the poverty that
enveloped them. Thus, liberation theology often went hand in hand with
these BECs. These churches were also impacted by the Charismatic renewal in the 1970s. Their worship was vital and aimed at equipping the
church to challenge the injustice that they faced daily. These communities have grown rapidly. Today it is estimated that there are 150,000
BECs in Brazil alone.

Both liberation theology and BECs present a challenge to the Roman
Catholic Church and thus have sparked a conservative backlash and an attempt to reestablish the power of the ecclesial hierarchy. This backlash has
come with the appointment of conservative bishops and priests to key positions and with the threat and practice of excommunication for leaders who
fail to conform.

Another important revival movement within the Roman Catholic Church
is the Charismatic renewal. The numbers have grown significantly to about
85 million, over 15 percent of the population of Latin America. When this is
coupled with Pentecostalism, Pentecostal-Charismatic growth and influence
in Latin America are seen to be quite significant.

Evangélicos. The term "Evangélicos" refers to all Protestants living in
Latin America. They are made up of three groups: mainline Protestants
(such as Lutherans, Anglicans, Presbyterians), evangelicals, Pentecostals.
Up until about fifty years ago Evangélicos hardly appeared on the demographic map. However, in the last half century there has been dramatic
growth, especially among Pentecostals, who account for over 80% of that
growth. Although past claims of growth were exaggerated, it seems that
the numbers we have today are more realistic. In 1940 about 1 million
Evangélicos lived in Latin America, with a negligible Pentecostal presence.
Today Evangélicos number well over 90 million, about 17% of the total
population of Latin America. Of that number, about 75% is Pentecostal. If
the Charismatic renewal in the Roman Catholic Church and the Pentecostal churches are taken together, they make up a significant portion of
Latin American Christianity, perhaps one-third. The number of Pentecostal-

Charismatics in Latin America comprises close to one-third of Pentecostal numbers worldwide.

‹‹‹

"In the last one hundred years, the course of evangelical Christianity has been accelerated and complicated by two notable developments: first, the rise of Pentecostal or charismatic expressions of the faith and, second, the rise of indigenous Christian churches. . . . Fuelled by Pentecostal and independent movements, Christians with more-or-less evangelical commitments are found almost everywhere on the globe. Evangelicalism has become a world religion of great consequence."

Mark A. Noll, *The New Shape of World Christianity*, pp. 42-43

‹‹‹

Pentecostalism is not without its problems, however. One of the largest and fastest-growing groups is a church in Brazil, the Universal Church of the Kingdom of God (IURD, from the Portuguese *Igreja Universal do Reino de Deus*). This group represents a problematic expression of Christianity that exists in many parts of the world in Pentecostalism. They are a "health and wealth" church that adheres to a radical prosperity gospel. Their stress on collective exorcisms, healing and sensational miracles is shaped by this vision. Moreover, they have developed a highly contentious relationship with Roman Catholics, denying their status as Christians and pursuing an aggressive proselytizing policy. The polemical character of Pentecostalism is directed not only at Catholics; it also occurs among Pentecostals themselves. Charismatic and authoritarian leaders compete for adherents, giving rise to numerous splits. A further problem in Latin American Pentecostalism is that often a shallow faith results from inadequate discipleship or catechetical formation. This breeds nominalism, defection and syncretism. Finally, an extreme individualism hampers much of the theology and mission of many Pentecostal churches, a situation made even more regrettable by the desperate need for analysis of sinful structures in Latin America.

Nevertheless, there is much to be thankful for. There is a wide spectrum of Pentecostals and Charismatics in Latin America, and much of it is a vital and orthodox expression of the Christian faith. Pentecostalism is primarily an urban phenomenon of the poor. Samuel Escobar has commented wittily, "Liberation theology opted for the poor but the poor opted for Pentecostalism."[23] Amidst dire economic need and burgeoning cities, Latin American Pentecostal churches are having an impact as they engage in "mission from below," mission from a position of weakness and poverty. One of the ways is through the renewal of the family that challenges male desertion and violence, making care and financial responsibility priorities. Another remarkable development is the political influence of Pentecostals in Brazil, Guatemala, Chile and Nicaragua.[24] There remains quite a diversity of political philosophies, ranging from right to left, from activistic to quietistic. And there are questions as to how much the gospel and Christian social ethics have been brought to bear on this political witness. Nevertheless, it is significant that a tradition rooted in an otherworldly dualism has mounted a political witness. Clearly, there is much need to develop a deepening understanding of the relationship of the gospel to the public square.

Challenges facing the Latin American church. A number of challenges face the Latin American church as it seeks to be faithful to its missional calling. Issues of politics, poverty and the gospel are urgent in this context. Inequitable global economic structures and unjust political and social structures within Latin America, the widespread poverty, the growing political power among Pentecostals, the influence of liberation theology and BECs—all of these feed a growing need for the Latin American church to address mission in an ecumenical way. The various confessional groups have important insights, and there is a need for mutual enrichment and correction as they work together. There is theological potential, not only to equip the

[23]J. F. Martinez, "Latin American Theology, Protestant," in *Global Dictionary of Theology: A Resource for the Worldwide Church*, ed. William A. Dyrness and Veli-Matti Kärkkäinen (Downers Grove, IL: IVP Academic, 2008), p. 475.
[24]Pew Research Religion and Public Life Project, "Overview: Pentecostalism in Latin America", October 5, 2006 (http://www.pewforum.org/2006/10/05/Overview-Pentecostalism-in-Latin-America.aspx).

church in Latin America but also to offer insight to the church everywhere else in the world on how to deal with the critical issue of poverty.

This highlights the need for ecclesial unity and more attention to ecumenical efforts. The tension between the Roman Catholic Church and Pentecostals despite recent encouraging initiatives, the divisions within Roman Catholicism itself over how to respond to liberation theology and BECs, and splits within Pentecostalism as the bitter fruit of powerful leaders and strong personalities contesting with one another—all of these situations cry out for the church to struggle toward a more united expression of the Christian faith. Escobar laments that recent developments "have brought about a seriously divided Christianity that could find itself engaged in religious infighting that will prevent the Churches from playing a significant social and political role in the new century."[25]

There is, moreover, an urgent need for well-trained leaders. Within the Pentecostal church the level of education for most pastors is abysmal. This accounts for further problems, such as an easy capitulation to a "prosperity" gospel, as well as poor discipleship that leads to shallow Christian commitment and less-than-holy living.

The church faces other challenges in the context of the Latin American culture. The monumental scale of the drug trade there is well known. The resulting financial windfall is enormous and has corrupted politicians, police and the judicial system. The drug trade has also bred horrific violence as traffickers go to great lengths to protect their huge profits. Prisons are full, and many lives have been destroyed. The widespread poverty of the area feeds the problem. How is the church to address this problem and be a living witness?

The remarkable story of Julio Ruibal in Cali, Colombia, offers an instructive example.[26] Cali had a notorious reputation of the cocaine capital of the world. By rousing the citywide church to united prayer, renewal and peaceful resistance of the drug trade that enveloped Cali, Ruibal faced vig-

[25]Samuel Escobar, "Christianity in Latin America: Changing Churches in a Changing Continent," in *Introducing World Christianity*, ed. Charles E. Farhadian (Malden, MA: Wiley-Blackwell, 2012), p. 171.

[26]This story is told in the video *Transformations 1*, produced by the Sentinel Group (www.youtube .com/watch?v=Dyrho_hoz5s); see also Mark Wingfield, "Martyrdom of Columbian [*sic*] Pastor Sparked Intensive Awakening," *The Baptist Standard*, September 22, 1999 (www.baptiststandard .com/1999/9_22/pages/cities_martyr.html).

orous opposition from the drug lords who benefited from the lucrative drug trade. He was martyred in 1995, but the result was even more dramatic renewal within the church, increased corporate prayer, tremendous growth of the church, and a covenant to unity made by the pastors of all the churches in Cali. A result was that within nine months all seven of the drug lords fell, and the crime rate dropped dramatically.

Finally, Latin America faces an urban future, and so urban mission will be a priority. Latin America is over 75 percent urban, with 114 cities over a half million people. Mexico City and Sao Paulo are two of the world's largest cities. Like so many places in the South, the cities are growing, and the church must attend to faithful and contextualized witness.

By 2025 Africa and Latin America will account for over half of the world's Christians. Thus, Escobar is correct when he says that there is in "Latin American Christianity the potential to play a significant role in the twenty-first century."[27] How well the church responds to these issues will determine its impact on the global church. Walls predicts that the "development of theological and ethical thinking and action in Africa and Asia and Latin America will determine mainstream Christianity"; the quality of theological scholarship, therefore, not only will be vital for Latin Americans, Africans and Asians, but also "will help to determine the shape and quality of world Christianity."[28]

THE MIDDLE EAST AND NORTH AFRICA

The history of the Christian community in the Middle East and North Africa has been variously described by scholars as "barely surviving"[29] and as "hanging on."[30] This part of the world is where the Christian faith began two millennia ago. It is the place of many readily recognizable figures in early church history, such as Augustine, Tertullian, Cyprian, Athanasius and Jerome. It is a place where the Christian faith grew and thrived for six hundred years. But in the seventh century Muslim armies overran the region, and it became an Islamic empire. Christians were tolerated, and they

[27]Escobar, "Christianity in Latin America," p. 183.
[28]Walls, "Christian Scholarship," p. 173.
[29]Douglas Jacobsen, *The World's Christians: Who They Are, Where They Are, and How They Got There* (Malden, MA: Wiley-Blackwell, 2011), p. 67.
[30]Martin Marty, *The Christian World: A Global History* (New York: Modern Library, 2007), p. 35.

took on the identity of *dhimmi*, an inferior but protected people who lived under the Islam state. However, it came at great cost: it was illegal to convert to Christianity, Christians paid an extra tax (*jizya*), and marriage and inheritance laws were designed to hinder Christian growth. Growth was possible only by birth (and the Christian community in these areas has a declining birth rate) and by taking members from one Christian community for another one ("sheep stealing"). Thus began a hemorrhaging of Christians to Islam (conversion) and out of the region (emigration) that continues to this day.

Before the Muslim invasion virtually the whole population considered themselves to be Christian. By 1000 Muslim pressure had cut this number in half. Three or four centuries later, during the time of the Crusades, this number was cut in half again to 25% of the population. A slow attrition left the Christian population at 15% in 1900, but today that has dwindled to 5% of the total population. There are now about 18 million Christians (1% of the global Christian community) dispersed among 330 million Muslims.[31] The rise of radical Islam has put even more pressure on the Christian community today.

The numbers of Christians are distributed unevenly, ranging from 12% of the population in Egypt (about half of all Christians in the Middle East and North Africa) to the persecuted and disappearing church in Iraq of perhaps fewer than 400,000. The eight oil-exporting nations (OPEC) have virtually no native Christians; the church is made up primarily of foreign workers. Christians accounted for 16% of the population in Palestine in 1900, but the Palestine-Israel tensions that continue unabated have led to a dramatic decrease to about 2-3% of the population. Throughout the region over half of the Christians are Coptic Orthodox, with Armenian Orthodox, Greek Orthodox and Roman Catholics making up about 40% of the rest. There are about a million Protestants and a quarter million Pentecostals.

The prevalence of Orthodox Christianity (over 80 percent) raises the issue of the close tie of nation, ethnicity and religion. The various parts of the Orthodox Church are closely tied to ethnic identity. One is born and baptized into the church, and often the level of commitment to the gospel

---

[31]Jacobsen, *The World's Christians*, pp. 68-69.

is secondary to loyalty to an ethnic community. This has sometimes been the reason for survival in a hostile environment, but it is is hardly the basis for a faithful Christian witness. Of course, this is not the whole story; there is a faithful Christian presence.

How do Christians live in such an unrelentingly hostile environment? The victory of the radical Islamic government in Egypt in early 2013, for example, highlights the question of how the Coptic Church is to live out its faith in Egypt under persistent persecution. According to Douglas Jacobsen, the leaders of the Coptic Church in Egypt offer two seemingly opposing options. A monk who took the name "Matthew the Poor" (1919-2006) sold his business and set off for a solitary life of holiness in the desert. He suggests that the right path is a life of total submission and humility before God as one adopts a posture of peace and nonretaliation. Following the Sermon on the Mount means turning the other cheek and even accepting martyrdom as the way to deal with persecution. Pope Shenouda III (1923-2012), head of the Coptic Church for forty years, suggested the way of Coptic nationalism. He saw Matthew's option as the way of weakness and in fact unrealistic for most Copts. He opted for a collective political defense of the rights of the Coptic Church and implemented a program to socialize all Copts into the church and strengthen Coptic identity as a basis for political clout. These two options raise fascinating issues about how the church is to live in a hostile environment. But it seems clear that the option of Shenouda III is barely possible only when there is a degree of freedom and a somewhat substantial minority. This has been the case in Egypt, but that has changed. Moreover, it certainly is not the situation in

> PERHAPS MISSION IN THE MIDDLE EAST AND NORTH AFRICA IS BEST UNDERSTOOD IN TERMS OF "PRESENCE AND WITNESS."

most countries of the Middle East and North Africa. Perhaps mission in the Middle East and North Africa is best understood in terms of "presence and witness," as the Middle East Council of Churches has expressed it.[32]

There have also been attempts at interreligious dialogue with Muslims and ecumenical efforts among a bitterly divided Christian church. Clearly, both are necessary in this cultural context.

---

[32]Michael Marten, "Middle East," in *The Routledge Encyclopedia of Missions and Missionaries*, ed. Jonathan J. Bonk (New York: Routledge, 2010), p. 246.

The question of the basis for this dialogue and for ecumenical endeavors is a pressing issue.

Heather Sharkey concludes her summary of Middle Eastern and North African Christianity with these words: "Today, churches in the Middle East function as vibrant centers of worship and social activity. Yet full of life as they are, the reality is that Christian populations are unlikely to grow or even hold their numbers in coming years.... The future of Christianity in the Middle East and North Africa holds uncertainties.... Middle Eastern Christians must find ways to survive in the region where Christianity was born."[33] One hopes and prays that they are vibrant centers of worship rooted in the gospel, and that perhaps again, as it was in the early church that thrived in the same region, persecution might mean growth and not attrition.

THE PACIFIC

The Pacific Islands are made up of three large cultural regions—Melanesia, Micronesia, Polynesia—that encompass thousands of islands in the South Pacific.[34] This region covers 20 million square miles, and the islands in this area are home to 34 million people. The relatively small size and the lack of international influence have meant that this area is often bypassed in discussions of global Christianity.

The peoples of these islands were evangelized by Protestant and Catholic missionaries in the nineteenth century. From the standpoint of a reception of the Christian faith, the missionary endeavor in this place has to be judged as quite a success. Today, 90 percent of islanders identify themselves as Christian. The two largest groups are Roman Catholic and Protestant, but there is a substantial presence of Pentecostals, Charismatics and, in one region, Mormons. Evangelization took place in the midst of a colonial approach to missions, and so all the blessings and problems of that period of missionary expansion can be found in the stories of these islands. Western missionaries, often with a sense of cultural superiority,

---

[33]Heather J. Sharkey, "Middle Eastern and North African Christianity: Persisting in the Lands of Islam," in Farhadian, *Introducing World Christianity*, pp. 18-19.

[34]Often Australia and New Zealand are included in the Pacific or Oceania region. However, these are more properly included in the West because they share a European culture. Thus, they will be treated under "The West" below.

> WESTERN MISSIONARIES, OFTEN
> WITH A SENSE OF CULTURAL
> SUPERIORITY, BROUGHT THE
> GOSPEL TO TRIBAL PEOPLES
> WHOSE COMMUNAL LIFE WAS
> SHAPED BY PRIMAL RELIGION.
> THIS ENCOUNTER HAS SHAPED
> PACIFIC CHRISTIANITY.

brought the gospel to tribal peoples whose communal life was shaped by primal religion. This encounter has shaped Pacific Christianity.

European missionaries were schooled by their culture to think in terms of individual conversion, but they found a tribal people who made collective decisions. It took a while to figure out that if conversion was to take place, it would be a communal or collective conversion, and that there must first be the agreement of the chiefs. We can get a glimpse of this communal conversion, and also of contextualization in evangelism, in the book *Peace Child*, where Canadian missionary Don Richardson uses a cultural practice of a "peace child"—when a child from one tribe is taken into the another—to bring about peace between warring tribes. Here conversion comes as a group. Of course, this is not the only place where conversion has been communal. In fact, this is the primary way most have come to Christ through history and in the world today. Mark Noll notes that third-world Christianity poses this question to all theology: "What is the unit of salvation?" He continues, "Protestant evangelicals usually think that salvation is one by one by one, as individuals come to develop a 'personal relationship with Christ.' But much of the emerging Christian world has not experienced conversion individually. Conversion, instead, has taken place by families, villages or even lineages extending back in time."[35]

Perhaps today the Pacific Islands is the only place where one can still find something of an older Christendom structure in practice. This is because the tribal cultures of the islands closely link land, people, culture, community, politics and religion. To accept the gospel means to embrace a new religious center for their corporate lives. Immediately the gospel was embraced, not on the terms of the European Enlightenment model, but within this tribal intermeshing of religion with the rest of a tightly knit communal

---

[35]Mark Noll, *The New Shape of World Christianity: How American Experience Reflects Global Faith* (Downers Grove, IL: IVP Academic, 2009), p. 34.

life. This had many tremendous benefits as some of the more egregious practices of cannibalism, slavery, tribal warfare, infanticide and witchcraft were gradually eliminated.

The form of Christendom that the church has taken in the Pacific today raises many questions. A prime example is evident especially in Fiji, where major tensions exist between a nation united and defined by Christian identity and a more pluralistic approach. Indigenous Fijians make up just over 50% of the population. There is also a large group of Indo-Fijians (about 40%) who were brought from India to the islands by the British to work the sugar plantations. These peoples are mostly Hindu (75%) and also Muslim (15%). There is tension as the indigenous Fijians who are Methodist expect their culture to be shaped by Christianity. But the Indo-Fijians will not adopt the Christian faith. This tension has led to ethnic prejudice against the non-Christian minority, legal privilege for Christian majority, political tensions, several political coups by Christians when Indo-Fijians gained political power, and even violence—all in the name of Christ! This illustrates the problem of Christendom and pluralism. It remains a problem on Fiji and may well spread to other islands. It has been held in check to this point only by the cultural and religious homogeneity still found for the most part on other Pacific Islands.

A couple of problems that are especially acute face the church in the Pacific. First, since the missionaries simply tried to replace tribal culture and primal religion with a European version of the Christian faith, there has not been a depth of contextualization and discipleship. Nominalism is a growing problem. This is especially problematic among the youth, who make up about 40 percent of the population. Combine this problem with the second one—the encroaching power of economic globalization that threatens their way of life—and there is potential for widespread defection from the Christian faith. Globalization is challenging the seemingly isolated and tribal-Christian life of many islands. Unemployment is increasing in step with a move away from a subsistence and agrarian economy and as the glow of Western consumerism and education captures the imagination. There is widespread emigration to Australia and New Zealand, where Christianity is in deep decline. The future of Christianity in this region remains quite uncertain.

Eastern Europe

There are at least three very different situations in which the missional church can find itself with respect to the state and its cultural context. All three bring possibilities and dangers for a faithful witness to the gospel. First, sometimes the state and cultural arrangement will favor the Christian church, giving it an established position. In this Christendom situation Christians are given the opportunity to shape the public life of culture according to the light of the gospel. The dangers are that they will not maintain a critical stance toward culture, and that they will become co-ercive and not uphold the rights of those with whom they disagree. Chris-tendom is the situation historically of the Orthodox and Catholic churches in Eastern Europe up until the beginning of the twentieth century. It is also the vision being pursued today by many churches seeking to recover their power after communism.

A second situation is when the state is hostile to the Christian faith and actively opposes the church. The church is limited in its ability to con-tribute to the public life of culture but can offer a forgiving and uncompro-mising witness to Christ in its life and worship. The danger is that the church may withdraw and confine its witness to the private realm or take a posture of fearful compliance and collaboration with the authorities. This was the situation of the church throughout much of the twentieth century under communism.

And finally, the church may find itself in a culture that simply ignores the Christian faith while allowing it to flourish as an individual and inner phe-nomenon confined to the private realm. This freedom offers the church numerous opportunities to carry out its mission in various ways, but the danger is, of course, that it might meekly conform to the place assigned to it by the culture and reduce the gospel to a private religious teaching. This is the danger facing the church in many parts of Eastern Europe today.

Perhaps the church in Eastern Europe is the only church to face all three of these situations in one century. For centuries, up until early in the twen-tieth century, Christendom prevailed. Both the Orthodox and the Catholic churches were the nationally established churches. For the next seven dec-ades it found itself under a hostile communist regime that employed nu-merous strategies and instruments to eliminate all religion from society.

With the fall of communism, there has been not only an attempt to recreate the Christendom of the past but also a situation in which the capitalistic culture of the West has made large gains and many churches find themselves in a situation where the Christian faith is simply ignored. This history has much to teach the church in other parts of the world.

The churches of Russia and Eastern Europe cannot be understood apart from their experiencing the ordeal of communist oppression. But contrary to reports of the press, blinkered as it is by secular bias, the church played a large role in toppling the communist regime. During the communist era the church failed in numerous ways: it took a posture of violent opposition and reacted by fighting back against the state, it took a posture of resig-

> THE CHURCHES OF RUSSIA
> AND EASTERN EUROPE CANNOT
> BE UNDERSTOOD APART FROM
> THEIR EXPERIENCING THE
> ORDEAL OF COMMUNIST
> OPPRESSION.

nation and withdrew from the social scene, and it took a posture of compromise and accommodated itself to the prevailing ideology.[36] There remains the need even today for healing between those who collaborated and those who did not and so suffered. Yet, even in the midst of failure during the communist era there was also much faithfulness—suffering, peaceful resistance, loving critique, worship, obedient living. And while there were other factors involved in the fall of communism, the faithfulness of the church played a large role.

The question is how the church has fared in the quarter of a century since and how that experience under communism is shaping the church today. In a word, it is ambiguous. On the one hand, positively, growth and renewal have occurred. Douglas Jacobsen writes,

> Since 1900, the main story of Christianity in the 21 nations that make up Eastern Europe has been one of revival. After decades of Communist domination that was decidedly biased against religion, the post-Communist era has been a time of religious recovery and advancement. Churches have been rebuilt, membership has increased, attendance at worship is up, and Christians are feeling more optimistic about the future than they have for generations.[37]

---

[36]Peter Kuzmič, "Christianity in Eastern Europe: A Story of Pain, Glory, Persecution, and Freedom," in Farhadian, *Introducing World Christianity*, pp. 85-86.
[37]Jacobsen, *The World's Christians*, p. 88.

Indeed, there is evidence to support this claim. Throughout the region there is a spiritual hunger arising out of the religious void created by the dominance of a materialist worldview. The churches certainly are blessed with a degree of freedom in many places. The Orthodox Church has experienced a resurgence. Eastern Europe is the center of Orthodoxy, with about three-fourths of all Orthodox believers residing there. Russia illustrates recent Orthodox revitalization. Just before the fall of communism there were 2,500 churches, but today there are more than 17,000 churches. In 1991 27% of the population identified themselves as Christians, but today that number is 60%. Twice as many people now attend church at least once a year. Similar growth can be found in other nations. A large number of Catholics and a growing evangelical and Pentecostal presence can be found in various countries of Eastern Europe as well. All the churches share a common challenge after communism: "reconstructing their identities and redefining their mission in a new era of freedom."[38]

But there is also evidence of a more negative assessment that suggests the church in Eastern Europe is in trouble and faces enormous challenges. For example, while it is good that many more people in these countries identify themselves as Christians, believe in God, and attend church a few times a year, this is hardly the kind of statistic that would invite confidence in a flourishing church. In fact, only 10-15% of the population of Eastern Europe attends church on a weekly basis. In Russia only 5% of the population attends church monthly, and 2% weekly.

There are many reasons for indifference to Christianity, but perhaps some of it can be attributed to the appreciation of the consumer culture of the West that now afflicts more people in Eastern Europe. Although there is still vitality in the Polish church where one-third attend services weekly,[39] the numbers have dropped significantly as Poland his grown in wealth. Just after the fall of communism in 1991, Pope John Paul II visited Poland and warned the church, "Don't let yourselves be caught up by the civilization of desire and consumption."[40] But it seems that many have not listened. Ukraine is

---

[38]Ibid., p. 89.

[39]Philip Jenkins, *God's Continent: Christianity, Islam, and Europe's Religious Crisis* (New York: Oxford University Press, 2009), p. 57.

[40]Stephen Engelberg, "Pope Calls on Poland to Reject Western Europe's Secular Ways," *The New York Times*, June 8, 1991.

another place that is infatuated with the capitalist and consumer culture of the West. The omnipresence of Western culture through media and the processes of globalization certainly have made inroads into a culture disappointed by communist promises.

Another challenge facing the church in Eastern Europe is the problem of nationalism and an established church. *Symphonia* is the Orthodox term that describes the ideal relationship between church and state, a situation in which both are bound together in inextricable unity. But there are enormous dangers in such a relationship that are being realized in the last two decades.

> SYMPHONIA IS THE ORTHODOX TERM THAT DESCRIBES THE IDEAL RELATIONSHIP BETWEEN CHURCH AND STATE, A SITUATION IN WHICH BOTH ARE BOUND TOGETHER IN INEXTRICABLE UNITY. BUT THERE ARE ENORMOUS DANGERS IN SUCH A RELATIONSHIP.

In many parts of Eastern Europe the churches are attempting to reassert themselves and recover the power that they held before the communist era. While the Roman Catholic Church has attempted to recover and even expand its power especially in Central Europe, it is the Orthodox Church that has been most aggressive. The patriarch of the Russian Orthodox Church has made it clear that it is his goal to promote the *symphonia* between church and state.

The most obvious problem for the *symphonia* is that it will often compromise the witness of the church. A cozy relationship with the state causes the church to lose the critical stance that is so important for its witness. It becomes simply one more partner in the nationalist aspirations of the country. It is the national agenda, rather than the kingdom of God, that defines the identity of the church. An established church is more often than not a compromised church lacking any prophetic critique in its life or words. It is evidence of an ecclesiastical nationalism, "the idea that a given people, united by faith and culture, constitute a nation."[41]

But the inextricable unity of church and state may carry more sinister implications as well. As a church agitates to regain lost power in a country, it

---

[41]Pedro Ramet, "Autocephaly and National Identity in Church-State Relations in Eastern Christianity: An Introduction," in *Eastern Christianity and Politics in the Twentieth Century*, ed. Pedro Ramet (Durham, NC: Duke University Press, 1988), p. 19.

can lead to bitter division among churches. Political power becomes more important than unity in the gospel. In Serbia, Romania, Greece and Russia there is copious evidence of the suppression and even active oppression of non-Orthodox expressions of the Christian faith—Roman and Greek Catholics, Protestants, Pentecostals. Orthodoxy is regarded as inseparable from Russian identity or Serbian identity or Romanian identity. And so it becomes a matter of national disloyalty not to belong to the Orthodox Church, and it makes other churches worthy targets of disdain, opposition and even violence. The state backs the national church with laws that discriminate against other Christian confessions. Peter Kuzmič says, "Today's search for a modern equivalent of a 'symphony' between secular and spiritual authorities . . . should also be politically and theologically questioned, as it is based on anti-democratic ethno-religious homogenization of their nations and leads to marginalization, as well as occasional legally induced discrimination of religious minorities, including well-established Protestant churches."[42]

Worst of all, this enmeshment of nation, culture and church has broken out into terrible violence. The lamentable history of Serbia shows that this is not simply a theoretical danger. At the end of communism there was a move to tie Serbian national identity closely to the Serbian Orthodox Church. Thus, Bosnian Muslims and Croatian Catholics represented a threat to the Serbian nation. This resulted in years of ethnic cleansing to rid the land of Muslims and Catholics. As in Rwanda and other places of ethnic cleansing where the church was present and often complicit, blame certainly cannot be laid entirely at the feet of the church. However, it is distressing to hear a Serbian Orthodox bishop advise his people to "disregard the Gospel of Christ and turn to the Old Testament which reads: An eye for an eye, and a tooth for a tooth!" and to also hear that few Serbian Orthodox are ashamed about what took place. "To their way of thinking, the life of the nation—and by extension the life of the Orthodox faith—was at risk, so the leaders who orchestrated Serbian attacks of Bosnian Muslims and Croatian Catholics were simply doing what had to be done."[43] This situation, and others like it—for example, in Western Ukraine between Orthodox and Eastern-rite Catholics—again illustrates what often happens when the church identifies

---

[42]Kuzmič, "Christianity in Eastern Europe," p. 82.
[43]Jacobsen, *The World's Christians*, pp. 96-97.

itself more with nationalist aspirations than the kingdom of God.

Learning what it means to embody the gospel faithfully in public life is another issue facing the church. Many painful and difficult transitions, both political and economic, have followed in the wake of communism. Corruption, injustice, social unrest, widespread poverty, a mentality of dependence and authoritarian leaders have created an unstable and difficult situation. The churches have not been able to provide critique or leadership. And so, says Kuzmič, "Developing a spirituality for transformative social engagement remains one of the priority tasks of the churches if they are to be credible and effective instruments of the Kingdom of God among the broken kingdoms of the post-communist world."[44]

THE WEST

While the church in the global South continues to grow, the church in Europe is "thin, but alive."[45] To make sense of Christianity in the West—Western Europe and European-derived cultures such as North America, Australia and New Zealand—we have to account for three observations.

First, the church in the West is in decline. This is clear from noting that in many different surveys church attendance is in dramatic decline, that increasing numbers claim to be nonreligious and do not believe in God, that belief and practice of Western people have been overtaken by a secular humanist worldview often as much in Christian circles as without, that to the degree Christianity is flourishing it does so in non-Western immigrant churches or as a private and inward spirituality with little impact on the public square. Furthermore, in many ways academic theology has capitulated to the Enlightenment, not only in liberal circles, where this is more obvious, but also in evangelical circles. This leaves the church vulnerable to the spirits of the age.

Yet there are two seemingly contrary observations to set against all the evidence of decline. The first is that the majority of people living in the West still claim the title "Christian." Over three hundred million people in Europe claim to be Christian—over 75 percent of the population. Yet only about one-fourth of the population ever attends church, and when we set

[44]Kuzmič, "Christianity in Eastern Europe," p. 87.
[45]Jacobsen, *The World's Christians*, p. 132.

the bar slightly higher by asking about those who attend weekly and pray, the number plummets. The number is greater in the Catholic South as compared to the Protestant North, yet in all cases there is significant decline. About a quarter of a billion people, over three-quarters of the American population, call themselves "Christian." Yet only about 40% attends church weekly, and many believe this number to be inflated. Tom Flynn says that "despite the rhetoric, active religious participation remains a minority interest in American life."[46] Although 72% of Canadians identify

Mark Noll begins his survey of "the new shape of world Christianity" with these observations:

- This past Sunday more Christian believers attended worship in China than in all of Europe.

- This past Sunday more Anglicans attended church in Kenya, South Africa, Tanzania and Uganda than did Anglicans in Britain and Canada and Episcopalians in the United States combined.

- This past Sunday more Presbyterians attended worship in Ghana than in Scotland.

- This past Sunday there were more members of Brazil's Pentecostal Assemblies of God at worship than the combined number in the two largest U.S. Pentecostal denominations.

- This past Sunday the churches with the largest attendance in England and France had mostly black congregations, and half of the churchgoers in London were African or African-Caribbean.

- This past Sunday the largest congregation in Europe was in Kiev pastored by a Nigerian Pentecostal.

- This past Sunday there were more Roman Catholics at worship in the Philippines than in any single country of Europe.

Mark A. Noll, *The New Shape of World Christianity*, pp. 20-21

[46]Tom Flynn, "True Churchgoing Revealed," *Free Inquiry* 18, no. 4 (1998) (www.secular humanism.org/index.php?section=library&page=frontlines_18_4).

themselves as Christian, only 20% attend church weekly; 70% of Australians are labeled Christian, but only about 12% worship weekly; over 50% of New Zealanders identify themselves as Christian, and the weekly attendance is similar to Australia.

The second observation that seems to jostle with the decline of the church in the West is that the United States does not seem to follow the same patterns as Europe, Australia, New Zealand and Canada. In certain senses, the Christian faith appears to be more viable and alive in the United States than in other Western nations. More people attend church, the numbers of missionaries sent to foreign places is still the highest, about 30 percent of the population identify themselves as evangelical, the word "God" is still mentioned by political leaders, there are more Christian educational institutions, Christian publishing is much more plentiful, and often church renewal movements in various forms begin in the United States and spread elsewhere. More could be said, but this is enough to show that the United States seems to have a different trajectory than the rest of the West.

The question is how to explain these contrary observations. As to the first, an answer might be sought in the history of the West. The West is the product of a long story in which two living religions—the Christian and humanist faith—have cohabited and interacted with one another in various ways. Today we speak of the West in terms of being "secularized." By that I mean that since the eighteenth-century Enlightenment the humanist worldview has triumphed and has now become the dominant cultural worldview. How is it that the Christian faith, which through most of the history was the dominant culturally formative worldview, has now been reduced to a shadow of its former self? How can we explain the triumph of secular humanism in the West? Much ink has been spilled to probe this question, so here I will make only a few observations.

Secularization often is explained in terms of two mistakes the church made in the centuries leading up to the eighteenth-century Enlightenment. First, the religious wars between differing confessional Christians fractured Europe and soaked the soil with Christians' blood, and this at a time when the new science seemed to be unifying Europe. Second, the church opposed the insights of the scientific revolution, setting the Christian faith over against advancing science. No doubt these two historical events played a large role. But more must be said.

The Christian faith was vulnerable to the powerful forces of humanism that were unleashed in the eighteenth century because of its Christendom

---

"The charismatic or Pentecostal character of much of the world's new Christianity poses a yet further question. It is one that has never been completely settled in traditional Western churches, but it is absolutely front and center for most of the newer Christian regions of the world: how much are the supernatural events that fill the pages of Scripture to be considered normative examples for what happens right now."

Mark A. Noll, *The New Shape of World Christianity*, p. 36

---

history. There is no doubt that Christendom had a very positive and powerful affect on the West. Jürgen Habermas affirms this, for example, when he says that freedom, social solidarity, individual morality of conscience, human rights and democracy are "the direct heir of the Judaic ethic of justice and the Christian ethic of love. This legacy, substantially unchanged, has been the object of continual critical appropriation and reinterpretation. To this day, there is no alternative to it. . . . We continue to draw on the substance of this heritage. Everything else is just idle postmodern talk."[47] Yet even with Christendom's positive impact, it has left the Christian church in the West vulnerable to the powerful winds of secular humanism. This is because the church, as part of a so-called Christian culture, lost its sense that there must be a missionary encounter with culture

> EVEN WITH CHRISTENDOM'S POSITIVE IMPACT, IT HAS LEFT THE CHRISTIAN CHURCH IN THE WEST VULNERABLE TO THE POWERFUL WINDS OF SECULAR HUMANISM.

---

[47]Jürgen Habermas, "A Conversation about God and the World," in *Time of Transitions*, ed. and trans. Ciaran Cronin (Cambridge: Polity Press, 2006), pp. 150-51. See the misquotation, or inaccurate paraphrase, of Habermas in Philip Jenkins, "Europe's Christian Comeback," *Foreign Policy*, June 12, 2007 (www.foreignpolicy.com/articles/2007/06/11/europes_christian_comeback).

that is prophetically critical of culture. Thus, it was not critical of humanism as it rose to power in the West. Instead, as it had done for over a thousand years, it quietly took its place in society, and in this case it was the private place assigned to it by the Enlightenment faith.

This explains, on the one hand, the deep decline in the West. The Christendom background of Europe also begins to explain why so many identify themselves as Christians, continue with the rite of baptism, attend church on Christian holidays, and manifest other Christian trappings yet call themselves "nonreligious" and can believe and live in ways that bear little resemblance to biblical Christianity. This history may be a cautionary tale to places like the Pacific and Eastern Europe that either practice or want to revive a Christendom model.

Perhaps this also begins to partially explain the anomaly of the United States. The United States was born in the midst of the Enlightenment, with many of its founders deeply rooted in Enlightenment deism. The United States is not laden with the same long history of Christendom. Apart from early local instances there has been no nationally established church. But there were other factors in American history, such as the Great Awakenings. At the time of independence (1776) only about 5 percent of the people were church members, but this steadily increased from that time, reaching 60 percent in 1970.[48] "The dramatic rise after 1776 is to be attributed almost solely to the Second Great Awakening."[49] The Second Great Awakening (1787-1825) built on the First Great Awakening (1726-1760). This is certainly something that was important for understanding the vitality and persistence of the Christian faith in the United States, but it does not explain everything. After all, this Great Awakening also took place in Britain (where it was known as the Evangelical Revival).

The thesis of Martin Marty as to how secularism took hold differently in various parts of the West may offer some insight into the unique situation of

---

[48]W. Richie Hogg, "The Role of American Protestantism in World Mission," in *American Missions in Bicentennial Perspective: Papers Presented at the Fourth Annual Meeting of the American Society of Missiology at Trinity Evangelical Divinity School, Deerfield, Illinois, June 18-20, 1976*, ed. R. Pierce Beaver (Pasadena, CA: William Carey Library, 1977), p. 361.

[49]David Bosch, *Transforming Mission: Paradigm Shifts in Theology of Mission* (Maryknoll, NY: Orbis Books, 1991), p. 279.

the United States.[50] Marty argues that during the nineteenth century the process of secularization has taken three paths in the West. The first he calls "utter secularity" or "maximal secularity." Here the Christian faith is viewed as the enemy of the secular humanist worldview and must be attacked, destroyed and replaced. This particular brand of secularity is what we find on the European continent. The second path is "mere secularity." This particular humanist vision is simply to ignore Christian claims, allowing them to die a slow death by simply paying them no mind. The United Kingdom, Canada, Australia and New Zealand would embody this particular version of secularism. The final route secularization has taken is "controlled secularity" or "ambiguous secularity." According to this vision, many, perhaps even the majority, continue to adhere to the traditional Christian religion but subtly transform it in significant ways to fit the secular vision. Controlled secularity is the way of life found in the United States. Thus, in the United States the accommodation of the gospel to secular humanism, especially its success in relegating the gospel to the individual and private realms, has been more complete.

Yet decline is not the only story. "Thin, but alive" does describe the situation. There is life that is evident in a multitude of ways: the growth and vitality of Evangelical and Pentecostal traditions, various kinds of renewal within in mainline Protestantism and Roman Catholicism, and perhaps most interestingly the growth of churches from the global South, which often are the largest worshiping congregation in various Western cities. This is the case in, for example, London, Paris and Amsterdam, where the largest and most vital congregations are made up of people from Africa or the Caribbean.

We can note only briefly some of the challenges facing the church in the West: growing religious pluralism; the powerful religious forces of humanism, which have taken at least three forms—postmodernity, economic modernity, consumerism; the deep syncretism of the church, with its humanist culture; lack of ecclesial unity, especially the United States, where a capitalistic approach to marketing religion is often the norm; decreasing interest in cross-cultural missions; the troubled state of Enlightenment-shaped theological education; the hemorrhaging of the younger generation from the church; a privatized and individualized form of religion that has

---

[50]Martin E. Marty, *The Modern Schism: Three Paths to the Secular* (New York: Harper & Row, 1969).

little engagement with the public square; comfortable lives arising from a consumer culture that leads to lethargy and apathy; the need to harness the remarkable power of technology used for communication, marketing, entertainment, and more. There will be opportunity to address some of these issues again in a later chapter on a missiology of Western culture.

CONCLUSION

This brief survey shows that, while each context is different, there are a number of issues facing many of the churches in all parts of the world: evangelism, justice and mercy, a witness in public life, a faithful contextual theology, religious pluralism, the encroaching power of Western culture especially in cities, the need for ecclesial unity, and unreached peoples who have no church in their midst. Several of these issues will be addressed in the chapters that follow.

FURTHER READING

Barrett, David B., George Kurian and Todd M. Johnson. *World Christian Encyclopedia: A Comparative Survey of Churches and Religions in the Modern World.* Second edition. New York: Oxford University Press, 2001.

Farhadian, Charles E., ed. *Introducing World Christianity.* Chichester, UK: Wiley-Blackwell, 2012.

Jacobsen, Douglas. *The World's Christians: Who They Are, Where They Are, and How They Got There.* Chichester, UK: Wiley-Blackwell, 2011.

Jenkins, Philip. *The Next Christendom: The Coming of Global Christianity.* New York: Oxford University Press, 2002.

Johnstone, Patrick. *The Future of the Global Church: History, Trends and Possibilities.* Downers Grove, IL: InterVarsity Press, 2011.

DISCUSSION QUESTIONS

1. What are the advantages and disadvantages of studying world Christianity in a mission class?

2. Is the shift of the center of Christianity to the global South a well-known phenomenon in your own Christian circles? How can it be better communicated, and why is this important?

3. Discuss what we can learn from the church in one or more of the following regions: Africa, Asia, Latin America, the Middle East, the Pacific
or Eastern Europe.

ESSAY TOPICS

1. Discuss the pros and cons of treating the subject of global Christianity
in a mission course.

2. Describe and evaluate the current situation in the African, Latin
American or Asian church.

3. Consider the question of whether the church has a viable future in the
United States. How would you approach this question? Why has Christianity in the United States not followed the patterns of other Western
countries?

☙

PART THREE

Current Issues
in Mission Today

6

Holistic Mission

Witness in Life, Word and Deed

CB

J UST OVER THIRTY YEARS AGO David Bosch commented that the "evangelical and ecumenical approaches to mission have to a large extent dominated the theory and practice of mission in recent decades."[1] They represented "two missiological models contending for supremacy" throughout much of the twentieth century.[2] While much water has gone under the bridge since those comments were made, the emphases of these two traditions still play a vital role in shaping the mission scene today. Bosch longed for a convergence that would bring mission practice and theology more in line with Scripture. And there were many others like him who simply did not fit either paradigm but stood at the boundaries finding themselves both at home and at odds with both positions.

In order to understand mission today, we must survey an important thread of the historical interaction between these two traditions of mission: the struggle over whether the center of mission is verbal proclamation of the gospel or social action for justice and mercy. This chapter begins with that history and then attends to both dimensions of the church's mission, evangelism and social action. The final section addresses the calling of believers in society, the most important place where word and deed witness to the kingdom.

---

[1]David Bosch, *Witness to the World: The Christian Mission in Theological Perspective* (Atlanta: John Knox, 1980), pp. 39-40.
[2]Ibid., p. 201.

OUR LEGACY: A SPLIT BETWEEN WORD AND DEED

As the nineteenth century drew to a close and the twentieth century dawned, a rift emerged in the church that would have profound implications for mission. Two different traditions—the fundamentalist revivalist and the liberal social gospel—developed in sharp contrast to one another. Through the course of the twentieth century the revivalist stream would merge into the Evangelical tradition, and the social gospel stream into the Ecumenical tradition. These early traditions developed in counterpoint to one another and cultivated sharply divergent understandings of mission. The revivalist tradition emphasized evangelism while the social gospel tradition stressed sociopolitical action for mercy and justice. Word and deed were torn asunder. Richard Lovelace describes this division: "The broad river of classical evangelicalism divided into a delta, with shallower streams emphasizing the ecumenism and social renewal on the left and confessional orthodoxy and evangelism on the right."[3]

> THE REVIVALIST TRADITION EMPHASIZED EVANGELISM WHILE THE SOCIAL GOSPEL TRADITION STRESSED SOCIOPOLITICAL ACTION FOR MERCY AND JUSTICE. WORD AND DEED WERE TORN ASUNDER.

The Evangelical tradition. Between 1865 and 1930 a "great reversal" took place in the Evangelical church that reduced the missional calling of the church to the verbal proclamation of the gospel.[4] At least three factors contributed to this narrowing of mission: premillennialism, individualism, and a reaction to the social gospel.

By the middle of the nineteenth century the majority of the Protestant Church was characterized by an optimistic postmillennialism. That changed dramatically at the turn of the century when the revivalist side of the church shifted to a more pessimistic premillennialism. This would spell doom for social concern in that tradition of the church. Timothy Weber observes that although "not all premillennialists accepted the extreme position on the futility of reform activities, one must finally conclude that premillennialism

---

[3]Richard Lovelace, "Completing an Awakening," *The Christian Century* 98, no. 9 (1981): 298.
[4]The term "great reversal" was coined by Timothy Smith in *Revivalism and Social Reform: American Protestantism on the Eve of the Civil War* (New York: Harper & Row, 1957); see David O. Moberg, *The Great Reversal: Evangelism versus Social Concern* (Philadelphia: Lippincott, 1972).

generally broke the spirit of social concern which had played such a prominent role in earlier evangelicalism."[5]

~~~

"It is evident that missions claim the kingship of God over the whole of life. Jesus Christ is Lord of everything. The whole of life ought to be subjected to the royal authority of Him who has redeemed us by His precious blood."

J. H. Bavinck, *Impact of Christianity on Non-Christian World*, p. 30

~~~

There were at least two reasons for this. First, the kingdom was viewed primarily as future, which emptied the present of significance. And to the degree the kingdom was viewed as present, it was considered to be merely a spiritual or inward reality of the heart that had no social or political implications. Second, history was viewed pessimistically. The world was getting progressively worse and would finally culminate in destruction. So why would one bother to polish the brass knobs on a sinking ship?

A second reason for a loss of social concern was individualism. Sin was viewed primarily in personal terms, with little attention given to how it manifested itself in social, economic or political structures. Correspondingly, salvation was a matter of rescuing individuals from a dark world. The nineteenth-century evangelist Dwight L. Moody exemplifies this: "I looked at this world as a wrecked vessel. God has given me a lifeboat, and said to me 'Moody, save all you can. God will come in judgment and burn up this world. . . . If you have any friends on this wreck unsaved, you had better lose no time in getting them off.'"[6]

The third reason was reaction to the social gospel movement. The social gospel movement became entangled with the Western progress myth, and its theology was deeply compromised. Revivalists viewed this as a betrayal of the gospel, and so there was a reaction on many fronts. One can see a

---

[5]Timothy Weber, *Living in the Shadow of the Second Coming: American Premillennialism 1875-1925* (Oxford: Oxford University Press, 1979), p. 183.
[6]Quoted in George Marsden, *Fundamentalism and American Culture: The Shaping of Twentieth-Century Evangelicalism: 1870-1925* (New York: Oxford University Press, 1980), p. 26.

direct counterpoint in their reaction to the social gospel. The social gospel tradition (SGT) held an optimistic view of history in which the kingdom was an immanent and present process whereby human beings could transform society through education and reform programs. In response, the revivalist tradition (RT) held a pessimistic view of history in which the kingdom was only future and human social action futile. The SGT emphasized a gradual coming of the kingdom as a continuous incremental process within history (equated with progress), while the RT stressed discontinuity with history in which the kingdom comes suddenly with the return of Jesus. While the SGT held sin to be embedded in the structures of society, the RT reduced it to individual disobedience. Salvation for the SGT was corporate and social renewal in the present, while for the RT it was individual conversion that meant eternal life in the future. The SGT stressed the horizontal dimensions of salvation (relations among humankind), while the RT emphasized the vertical (relations between God and humankind). If the SGT agenda was to change society, for the RT it was to save souls. Thus, reaction led to imbalance.

A turning point came in the middle of the century when a number of fundamentalists (as they called themselves because they maintained the fundamentals of the faith that the liberal tradition had abandoned) or new evangelicals (as others referred to themselves) challenged their own community to recover the holistic dimensions of the gospel. Evangelical theologian Carl Henry (1913-2003) challenged the church: "Whereas once the redemptive gospel was a world-changing message, now it has narrowed to a world-resisting message. . . . Fundamentalism in revolting against the Social Gospel seemed also to revolt against the Christian social imperative. . . . It does not challenge the injustices of totalitarianisms, the secularisms of modern education, the evils of racial hatred, the wrongs of current labor-management relations, and inadequate bases of international dealings. It has ceased to challenge Caesar and Rome."[7]

A new social conscience began to develop in which social concern was

---

[7]Carl F. H. Henry, *The Uneasy Conscience of Fundamentalism* (Grand Rapids: Eerdmans, 1947), pp. 30, 33, 45, quoted in Rodger C. Bassham, *Mission Theology, 1948-1975: Years of Worldwide Creative Tension—Ecumenical, Evangelical, and Roman Catholic* (Pasadena, CA: William Carey Library, 1979), p. 176.

recognized to be part of the church's mission. The either-or relationship of the early twentieth century gave way to a both/and relationship. The question was how to relate the two. Some saw social activity as a consequence of evangelism: social concern results from changed lives as one accepts the gospel. Others saw it as a bridge to evangelism: social concern can break down prejudice and suspicion so that one can share the gospel. And finally others saw social concern and evangelism as equal partners, like two wings of a bird or two blades of scissors. However, Harvie Conn rightly observes, "The fact remains that we are far from a holistic solution that integrates the two components. . . . Formerly, the emphasis was on either soul or body, church or society, evangelism or social action. Two abstractions do not make a whole. But two are better than one."[8]

"The gospel is more than merely a message of grace for lost sinners. The gospel of Jesus Christ presents norms for the reordering of all human relationships; it contains the seed of a new society. It gives us a new conception of the state and it grants light upon social problems and upon the principles of science. The work of Jesus Christ cannot be split; we cannot share His redeeming grace without giving obedience to His royal word. It is not possible to be a Christian at home and to surrender the world about us to the destructive influence of sin. Whoever belongs to Him belongs to Him in the complete greatness of His work. Thus it is plain that mission should never be confined to a part of the message. . . . The work of Jesus Christ is an indivisible unity."

J. H. Bavinck, *The Impact of Christianity on the Non-Christian World*, p. 19

If evangelism and social action are two equal partners the question arises as to which is primary. The Lausanne Covenant (1974) affirmed that both evangelism and sociopolitical involvement are part of Christian duty but

---

[8]Harvie Conn, *Evangelism: Doing Justice and Preaching Grace* (Grand Rapids: Zondervan, 1982), p. 62.

232 INTRODUCING CHRISTIAN MISSION TODAY

insists, "In the Church's mission of sacrificial service evangelism is primary."[9] And so although Christians seldom will have to choose between healing bodies and saving souls in their mission, "If we must choose, then we have to say that the supreme and ultimate need of all humankind is the saving grace of Jesus Christ, and that therefore a person's eternal, spiritual salvation is of greater importance than his or her temporal well-being."[10]

Not all evangelicals took this stance. Already at the Lausanne conference a group of some two hundred radical evangelicals, calling themselves the Radical Discipleship group, used strong language to denounce the dichotomy of word and deed. "There is no biblical dichotomy between the word spoken and the word made visible in the lives of God's people. Men will look as they listen and what they see must be one with what they hear. . . . We must repudiate as demonic the attempt to drive a wedge between evangelism and social action."[11]

This statement, and Conn's above, point to the underlying problem. The original split between the fundamental and liberal traditions was born of a shared dualism. When the imbalance was recognized, the two parts were artificially joined together. Two dimensions of the church's mission—word and deed—were abstracted from their original context of the full-orbed mission of the church. Each was given a life of its own. This forced a choice about which of the two has priority, and that was given to the word because (in keeping with a deeper dualism) the eternal had priority over the temporal.

> TWO DIMENSIONS OF THE CHURCH'S MISSION—WORD AND DEED—WERE ABSTRACTED FROM THEIR ORIGINAL CONTEXT OF THE FULL-ORBED MISSION OF THE CHURCH. EACH WAS GIVEN A LIFE OF ITS OWN.

At a conference of the World Evangelical Fellowship in Wheaton (1983)

---

[9]Lausanne Covenant, paragraph 6 (www.lausanne.org/en/documents/lausanne-covenant.html).
[10]*Evangelism and Social Responsibility: An Evangelical Commitment* (Lausanne Occasional Papers 21; Lausanne Committee for World Evangelization and the World Evangelical Fellowship, 1982), paragraph D (www.lausanne.org/en/documents/lops/79-lop-21.html).
[11]"A Response to Lausanne: Theological Implications of Radical Discipleship," in *Evangelization*, ed. Gerald H. Anderson and Thomas F. Stransky (Mission Trends 2; Grand Rapids: Eerdmans, 1975), pp. 249-50.

for "the first time in an official statement emanating from an international evangelical conference the perennial dichotomy was overcome." It did not ascribe priority to evangelism and said that the "mission of the church includes both proclamation of the Gospel and its demonstration." It also stated that "evil is not only in the human heart but also in social structures."[12]

While these signs and others like it are encouraging, it remains the case that in many places of the Evangelical church this history, which separated word from deed, continues to have a formative influence. In popular evangelicalism[13] there often remains a deep dichotomy between eternity and time, kingdom and history, salvation and social action, church and society, soul and body, spiritual and physical, heaven and earth, word and deed, with the former given priority in each case. A fundamental dualism continues to percolate below the surface of much evangelical thought and action.

The Ecumenical tradition. Gerald Anderson observes a shift in mission within the Ecumenical tradition in the early twentieth century that was fueled by the fundamentalist-modernist controversy. Three of the changes that he specifies are relevant for our subject: the accent in mission shifted from the individual to society; mission became concerned less with preaching the gospel and more with transformation; and salvation was considered primarily in terms of the present world rather than the world to come.[14]

Following this path, we can identify three tendencies or characteristics of the social gospel movement that would continue to have influence in the Ecumenical tradition. First, the social gospel was primarily this-worldly and naturalistic. The postmillennialism of the previous century was sheared of its transcendence, and the kingdom often merged with social progress. Salvation was equated with well-being brought about by Western technological progress. A second tendency was toward anthropocentrism. Mission was a project of human effort, technique, and an assortment of social programs designed to bring about human aspirations and dreams. A final character-

---

[12]David Bosch, *Transforming Mission: Paradigm Shifts in Theology of Mission* (Maryknoll, NY: Orbis Books, 1991), p. 407; the quotation is from the Wheaton Statement, paragraph 26.

[13]I make a distinction between academic and popular evangelicalism. While much of the dualism that I speak of has been overcome among many scholars and the literature of evangelicalism, my experience of speaking widely to evangelical audiences convinces me that at the "popular level of the pew" these dualisms remain.

[14]Gerald Anderson, "American Protestants in Pursuit of Mission: 1886-1986," *International Missionary Bulletin* 12, no. 3 (1988): 105.

istic was the turn to the social at the expense of the individual. Sin was found exclusively in social structures, salvation reduced to a change in society, and mission limited to social action.

"It is notorious that the times and places from which successful evangelistic campaigns and mass conversions have been reported have often been marked by flagrant evils such as racism, militant sectarianism, and blind support of oppressive economic and political systems. How are we to evaluate a form of evangelism that produces baptized, communicant, Bible-reading, and zealous Christians who are committed to church growth but uncommitted to radical obedience to the plain teaching of the Bible on the issue of human dignity and social justice? And how can we defend a form of evangelism that has nothing to say about the big issues of public righteousness and talks only of questions of personal and domestic behaviour? Can we agree that the big ethical issues are secondary matters, which can be attended to after conversion?"

Lesslie Newbigin, *The Open Secret*, pp. 134-35

In the early twentieth century social action was carried out in charitable acts of mercy. But a new emphasis on structural sin shifted attention to issues of justice that sought to address the underlying problems. Here an important distinction can be made between relieving human need and removing the causes of human need, between ministering to victims of injustice and addressing the underlying structures of injustice, between short-term treatment of symptoms and long-term treatment of the disease, between mercy and justice. The social gospel opened up the eyes of the church to the deep structural dimensions of sin. The proverb "Give a man a fish, and you'll feed him for a day; teach a man to fish, and you'll feed him for a lifetime" captures this insight. Giving a man a fish is a

> THE SOCIAL GOSPEL OPENED UP THE EYES OF THE CHURCH TO THE DEEP STRUCTURAL DIMENSIONS OF SIN.

short-term treatment of the symptoms. To teach him to fish is to deal with the deeper disease.

In 1928 the International Missionary Council in Jerusalem gave institutional status to what is known as the "comprehensive approach," which aimed to serve the whole human being in every aspect of life and relationships. In turn, the comprehensive approach was revamped and expanded in the developmental approach. The root disease is ignorance and underdevelopment. The solution is education and socioeconomic, technological development. The church must become involved in education: for example, diseases and deaths can be prevented by better hygiene and medicine, and hunger can be alleviated by better farming methods and by agricultural training. Development meant especially technological and socioeconomic progress, and a full-scale plan of development was envisioned to enable undeveloped countries to catch up with the developed West. Sin and salvation are replaced by ignorance and education or by underdevelopment and development.

The developmental model was criticized quite severely within a couple decades of its emergence. The 1960s, 1970s and 1980s were declared to be the development decades by the United Nations. At the beginning of these decades the poorest billion people were thirty times poorer than the richest billion people, but by the end of these decades the poorest billion were sixty times poorer. Clearly, development was not working: the richer were getting richer, and the poor were getting poorer. Some in poorer countries argued that the problem was that underlying the whole process of development were unjust economic and political structures. The problem was not underdevelopment but structural injustice at an international level. What was needed was not development but liberation—liberation from structures that maintained the status quo and often disguised the injustice with terminology of development. Liberation was the new order of the day.

Liberation from underlying structural injustice remains an important emphasis today. However, in the last three decades the urgency of a variety of global crises has led to new concerns and emphases. The phrase "justice, peace and the integrity of creation" captures many of the issues that dominate the social agenda in the Ecumenical tradition today. The phrase calls attention to things that threaten human life: economic injustice, racism, ecological destruction, war and violence. Justice, peace and stewardship of the nonhuman creation provide a vision for the church's mission.

The urgency of these planet-threatening crises combined with a growing pluralistic ideology has obscured evangelism over the last three or four decades in the Ecumenical tradition. Although some voices within the Ecumenical tradition have protested the eclipse of evangelism, generally the development of the tradition has been otherwise. The Ecumenical tradition has often been shaped by a "diluted gospel"[15] domesticated by a compromise with pluralism, naturalism, scientism, technicism and the progress vision of modern humanism.

While social responsibility and involvement still hold a clear priority in an Ecumenical vision of mission, that is not the only story. In some recent official documents of the World Council of Churches the evangelistic mandate to proclaim the gospel has been affirmed (we noted three of these documents in a previous chapter). The most recent, *Together Towards Life: Mission and Evangelism in Changing Landscapes* (2012), makes a strong statement on the importance of verbal proclamation. Perhaps there is growing convergence between the Evangelical and Ecumenical traditions, as Bosch claimed a quarter century ago,[16] prompted not least by the growing third-world church and its participation in the Ecumenical meetings. Nevertheless, while one is thankful for the insights that this tradition offers on issues of justice and mercy, a fresh recognition of the importance of evangelism is sorely needed.

Toward a solution. A solution for the unbiblical dichotomy that underlies both traditions can come only by way of a return to the gospel and mission in the way of Jesus. As I have observed in earlier parts of this book, the gospel that Jesus preaches is a gospel of the kingdom: in Jesus God is decisively acting in love and power to restore the whole creation and the entirety of human life to again live under his rule. The mission of the church

---

[15]The language is that of Bosch, *Witness to the World*, p. 212. While he characterizes the gospel of the Ecumenical tradition as "diluted," he terms that of the Evangelical tradition "emaciated" (p. 202).

[16]David Bosch speaks of an "era of convergence" (ibid., p. 464) between ecumenicals and evangelicals beginning in 1974. The years 1966-1973 he calls "the period of confrontation" (ibid., p. 462) in "'Evangelicals' and 'Ecumenicals': A Growing Relationship?" *The Ecumenical Review* 40, nos. 3-4 (1988): 458-72.

is to make known this salvation and to invite others to share in it by faith in Jesus the Lord Christ. We make this known in our words and our deeds, but both are grounded in the deeper reality of the kingdom of God present in the life of the Christian community as a gift of the Spirit. Both parties in the dispute over word and deed need to be challenged to "recover a fuller sense of the prior reality, the givenness, the ontological priority of the new reality which the work of Christ has brought into being. . . . The central reality is neither word nor act but the total life of a community enabled by the Spirit to live in Christ, sharing his passion and the power of the resurrection."[17] We ought to see evangelism and social action not as "separate components or parts of mission, but dimensions of the one, indivisible mission of the Church."[18]

Certainly, the church is following Jesus when both words and deeds are recognized as essential dimensions of the mission of kingdom witness. His deeds were powerful demonstrations that the kingdom had dawned, and his words announced its arrival. His words explained his deeds, and his deeds validated his words. But both were rooted in the deeper reality of the kingdom at work in the whole life of the community—a new work of the Spirit in Jesus to renew the world. The mission of the church is to *be* the witness, to *do* the witness, and to *say* the witness.[19]

THE CHURCH IS FOLLOWING JESUS WHEN BOTH WORDS AND DEEDS ARE RECOGNIZED AS ESSENTIAL DIMENSIONS OF THE MISSION OF KINGDOM WITNESS.

AUTHENTIC EVANGELISM

The meaning of evangelism is contested.[20] So it is important to make some initial comments. Evangelism is an indispensible dimension of the mission of the church; it is essential and cannot be replaced by deeds or presence or

---

[17]Lesslie Newbigin, *The Gospel in a Pluralist Society* (Grand Rapids: Eerdmans, 1989), pp. 136-37.
[18]David Bosch, "In Search of a New Evangelical Understanding," in *In Word and Deed: Evangelism and Social Responsibility*, ed. Bruce Nicholls (Grand Rapids: Eerdmans, 1985), p. 81.
[19]Darrell Guder, *Be My Witnesses: The Church's Mission, Message and Messengers* (Grand Rapids: Eerdmans, 1985), p. 91.
[20]For example, Frances Adeney sketches seven contemporary theologies of evangelism (*Graceful Evangelism: Christian Witness in a Complex World* [Grand Rapids: Baker Academic, 2010], pp. 78-95). And there are many more.

by any other aspect of the church's mission. To abandon it is disobedience, a "guilty silence."[21] Yet evangelism is only one dimension of the church's mission, not the whole of it. While the words "evangelism" and "evangelization" sometimes are used as synonyms for the broad witness and mission of the church, I reserve the word to describe more narrowly a verbal witness to the gospel that invites people to believe and follow Jesus. Since there is much confusion surrounding the meaning and practice of evangelism, it is important to take a more careful look.

Evangelism is the proclamation of the kingdom of God in Jesus. Mortimer Arias records his journey to explore the nature of evangelism. He registers a number of "findings" of what he discovered. His first two are important for our purposes.

> The gospel in the Gospels—Jesus' good news—is none other than "the good news of the kingdom."
>
> The kingdom-of-God theme has practically disappeared from evangelistic preaching and has been ignored by traditional "evangelism." The evangelistic message has been centered in personal salvation, individual conversion, and incorporation into the church. The kingdom of God . . . as content of proclamation has been virtually absent.[22]

Lesslie Newbigin makes a similar observation:

> If I am not mistaken, our current evangelism hardly ever uses the category of the Kingdom of God. And yet the original preaching of the Gospel on the lips of Jesus was—precisely—the announcement of the coming of that Kingdom. I believe that we may recover a true evangelism for our day if we return to that original language (translated into the idiom of our own time and place) as the basic category for our proclamation of the Gospel.[23]

And finally, Bryan Stone agrees:

> To speak of Jesus' own way of evangelizing, therefore, is impossible apart from its reference to the reign of God. It serves not just as a single or important doctrine that he held but rather is "the orienting concern" that guides his

---

[21]John R. W. Stott, *Our Guilty Silence* (Downers Grove, IL: InterVarsity Press, 1967).
[22]Mortimer Arias, *Announcing the Reign of God: Evangelization and the Subversive Memory of Jesus* (Philadelphia: Fortress, 1984), p. xv.
[23]Lesslie Newbigin, *The Good Shepherd: Meditations on the Christian Ministry in Today's World* (Grand Rapids: Eerdmans, 1977), p. 67.

thought and activity. His invitation to followers was an invitation to accept this reign as reality, to order their lives together around it, and to serve as a sign and foretaste of it together in the world.[24]

While the theme of kingdom has received growing attention, it still does not function centrally in discussions and, even more so, in the practice of evangelism.

The eclipse of the kingdom of God in contemporary evangelism is no minor loss. It has led to a diluted understanding and practice of evangelism, which in turn has weakened the church. First, it truncates the gospel, reducing it to an otherworldly, future and individual salvation: on what basis does God allow you to enter heaven? But the kingdom of God is a message about the comprehensive rule of God: it is not otherworldly but rather is about the restoration of human life in this world; it is not only about life in the future but also about God's

> THE ECLIPSE OF THE KINGDOM OF GOD IN CONTEMPORARY EVANGELISM IS NO MINOR LOSS. IT HAS LED TO A DILUTED UNDERSTANDING AND PRACTICE OF EVANGELISM, WHICH IN TURN HAS WEAKENED THE CHURCH.

saving power in the present; it is not only personal conversion but also about God's rule over the whole of human life. Evangelism that lacks the central component of the kingdom of God invites listeners to embrace an emaciated gospel and from the start socializes new converts into a misunderstanding of the nature of the Christian faith. It profoundly weakens robust discipleship from the beginning.

Second, the kingdom of God is prophetic: it is in conflict with and confronts the idolatrous powers at work in the world. A reduced gospel allows evangelism to offer a way that lives comfortably with powers of injustice. This kind of evangelistic practice does not follow the practice of Jesus, who invites his hearers to a costly and radical discipleship. Rather, it peddles

---

[24]Bryan Stone, *Evangelism After Christendom: The Theology and Practice of Christian Witness* (Grand Rapids: Brazos, 2007), p. 86. The words "reign" and "kingdom" are used to point to the same reality. Stone goes on to ask whether the theme of "God's reign" in the preaching of Jesus is replaced by the "person of Jesus" in the preaching of the early church. He concludes, "The reign of God does not disappear or get 'replaced'; it is instead impressed upon their worship, their economic practices, their fellowship, their crossing of social boundaries, and their joy and boldness; it shows up daily in the patterns and practices of their new life together" (ibid., p. 109).

cheap grace. Such evangelism weakens the church from the outset. Bosch speaks of "an evangelism which couches conversion only in micro-ethical terms" but neglects politics, racism and structural injustice. He continues, "All of this is a far cry from authentic evangelism. It led to a conversion to the predominant *culture*, not to the Christ of the gospels."[25] Similarly, Stone says that our evangelism is distorted "when it is reduced to 'getting right with Jesus' as a private spiritual affair." Rather, he insists, the gospel of Scripture has social, political, and subversive dimensions of a new order. "Anything less can never be a full 'offer' of the Christ."[26]

◇◇◇

"We may, then, summarize evangelism as that dimension and activity of the church's mission which, by word and deed and in light of particular conditions and a particular context, offers every person and community, everywhere, a valid opportunity to be directly challenged to a radical reorientation of their lives, a reorientation which involves such things as deliverance from slavery to the world and its powers; embracing Christ as Savior and Lord; becoming a living member of his community, the church; being enlisted into his service of reconciliation, peace, and justice on earth; and being committed to God's purpose of placing all things under the rule of Christ."

D. J. Bosch, *Transforming Mission*, p. 420

◇◇◇

The Ecumenical tradition has recognized that many evangelical approaches to evangelism follow the pattern described above: they are individualistic, they stress an otherworldly future, and they demand no costly or sacrificial conflict with the powers of injustice. And so the Gospels' theme of the kingdom of God is eagerly seized to correct such views. However, another problem emerges precisely at this point. Often in these circles the kingdom is detached from the person of Jesus and becomes merely a program of action for justice and peace. The personal dimension is lost. Yet in the Gospels the kingdom has a face and a name: Jesus. Proclaiming the

---

[25]Bosch, *Transforming Mission*, p. 417.
[26]Stone, *Evangelism after Christendom*, p. 110.

kingdom is a challenge and an invitation to each person to follow Jesus, to commit themselves to him in trust, love and obedience. If an evangelical stress on the individual proclaims a personal relationship with Jesus without a kingdom, an ecumenical emphasis on society

> IF AN EVANGELICAL STRESS ON THE INDIVIDUAL PROCLAIMS A PERSONAL RELATIONSHIP WITH JESUS WITHOUT A KINGDOM, AN ECUMENICAL EMPHASIS ON SOCIETY OFFERS A KINGDOM WITHOUT THE PERSON OF JESUS.

offers a kingdom without the person of Jesus. Evangelism shaped by the kingdom of God in the way of Jesus will keep both clearly in view.

It must be admitted that the kingdom of God is not an image easily understood in our time. In some circles it carries oppressive overtones, while in others it is simply irrelevant and unfamiliar. And so we need to translate its content into our own idiom and context. How might the all-encompassing, challenging message of the gospel be communicated in a faithful way today? This is an urgent question.[27]

"The affirmation that Jesus is *Lumen Gentium*, the light of the nations, is in danger of being mere words unless its value is being tested in actual encounters of the gospel with all nations, so that the gospel comes back to us in the idiom of other cultures with power to question our understanding of it. In this sense the foreign missionary is an enduring necessity in the life of the universal Church, but of course, the missionary journeys have to be multidirectional and not—as in the former period—only from west to east and from north to south."

Lesslie Newbigin, *A Word in Season*, p. 115

Evangelism must be contextual and therefore both relevant and challenging. Evangelism must also be contextual. This means that it is a matter

---

[27]In his excellent book *The Best Kept Secret of Christian Mission: Promoting the Gospel with More Than Our Lips* (Grand Rapids: Zondervan, 2010), John Dickson adds an appendix, "A Modern Retelling of the Gospel" (pp. 211-18), in which he fleshes out a number of ways to communicate the gospel in today's idiom. Dickson says, "I am simply illustrating what it might look like in a modern context to explain what the New Testament calls 'the gospel'" (ibid., p. 211).

of both accommodation and confrontation, of both relevance and challenge. It is disturbing to note that the word "contextual" in popular parlance is often understood to refer only to the task of making the gospel familiar or relevant. And indeed this is important; the gospel must be addressed to real needs and heard as good news. Yet the other side of contextual evangelism is that it confronts and challenges idols and invites one to radical conversion to Christ. Stone quotes a pastor who claims that in evangelism the "Christian Church needs to be even friendlier than Disneyland" and then refers to Søren Kierkegaard's attack on such accommodation as nauseating. He goes on to critique such an approach. We may well reach more people that way, but our evangelism will be "a pale reflection of consumer preferences and a market-driven accommodation to felt-needs" in which the "offensive and scandalous dimensions of the gospel will have been softened, disguised, forgotten, or placed on the back burner"; and when this happens, the "subversive nature of the gospel will then have been itself subverted, and that which is unprecedented and radical about the church will have been compromised in favor of mere ratings."[28] Authentic evangelism that is contextual will be both relevant and challenging, accommodating and confronting.[29]

This opens up a very difficult issue that we will explore in the next chapter. If one attempts to use the categories and address the needs of a certain culture, the question is how to do so in a way that does not capitulate to the idolatry of that culture. If I look for a familiar term to communicate the significance of Jesus in India and decide on "avatar" (god incarnate), then have I not allowed a Hindu worldview to overtake the gospel? If I invite people to rest in Jesus in the midst of a harried urban world, have I not given approval to the idolatries that produce such busyness in the first place? Does the gospel not challenge the Hindu and the Western humanist worldviews?

We will return to this problem in the next chapter, but at this point it is essential to be clear that evangelism must both speak in relevant ways and challenge the hearer to repentance and conversion. A biblical example is the

---

[28]Stone, *Evangelism After Christendom*, pp. 14-15.
[29]Mortimer Arias captures the two sides in the title of his article "Contextual Evangelism in Latin America: Between Accommodation and Confrontation," in *The Study of Evangelism: Exploring a Missional Practice of the Church*, ed. Paul W. Chilcote and Laceye C. Warner (Grand Rapids: Eerdmans, 2008), pp. 384-404.

Gospel of John. He employs the terminology of *logos* ("In the beginning was the Word [*logos*] . . ."), which would have evoked different images in the minds of his hearers. Some would have heard an ethereal rational principle of reason that ordered the cosmos, others a created intermediate being linking God to creation, others the preexistent wisdom of God, and still others simply Genesis 1. But John challenges all of these at a deep level when he invites his readers to believe that the incarnate Jesus is the origin and source of order in the world. John's communication is relevant: he hears the religious longing to understand the source of order so that one's life can be conformed to it. Thus, he connects with the heart-cry of his readers. "The employment of the Logos concept in the prologue to the Fourth Gospel is the supreme example within Christian history of the communication of the gospel in terms understood and appreciated by the nations."[30] His communication is also challenging: he calls for repentance from a worldview that offers a distorted answer. "John thus embraces a familiar term that resonates with both Jewish and Hellenistic cultures. . . . But he proceeds to melt it down and recast it with new meaning that explodes the symbolic worlds of his contemporaries."[31]

Hendrik Kraemer offers much wisdom in what it means to communicate the gospel. He says, "There is the obligation to strive for the presentation of the Christian truth in terms and modes of expression that make its challenge intelligible and related to the peculiar quality of reality in which they live." This requires self-denial and love to "find ways to tune this presentation to the peculiar sound-waves of these peculiar human hearts." This will require "the presentation of the Christian truth against the background of the universal human problems of aspiration, frustration, misery and sin, because these men and women must be for us in the first place human beings, fellowmen, and not non-Christians."[32]

---

[30]George R. Beasley-Murray, *John* (Word Biblical Commentary 36; Waco, TX: Word, 1987), p. 10. See George E. Ladd, *The Pattern of New Testament Truth* (Grand Rapids: Eerdmans, 1968), where he discusses the way the gospel is translated by John and Paul from a Hebrew to a Greek world in their missionary situation to communicate the gospel. See also Dean Flemming, *Contextualization in the New Testament: Patterns for Theology and Mission* (Downers Grove, IL: InterVarsity Press, 2005).

[31]Flemming, *Contextualization*, p. 260.

[32]Hendrik Kraemer, *The Christian Message in a Non-Christian World* (London: Edinburgh House Press, 1938), p. 303.

Authentic evangelism requires that a church be in tune with the heartfelt needs of its neighbors but also fully aware of the cultural idolatries that drive human life today. Evangelism is an invitation and challenge to find a new and liberating way of life in following Jesus.

Evangelism requires that we be present in the lives of people in an attractive way. To communicate the gospel in ways that are in tune with people's heartfelt needs will require time spent with them. Before we can communicate the gospel, verbally we must truly be present. Evangelism is not shouting from a distance. It is being present in people's situations and sharing our lives with them. Only then do we earn the privilege to speak to them about Jesus. The terms "friendship evangelism" and "relational evangelism" also capture something of the importance of this relational element, so important for loving communication.

> EVANGELISM IS NOT SHOUTING FROM A DISTANCE. IT IS BEING PRESENT IN PEOPLE'S SITUATIONS AND SHARING OUR LIVES WITH THEM. ONLY THEN DO WE EARN THE PRIVILEGE TO SPEAK TO THEM ABOUT JESUS.

Clearly, the more evangelism is relational, the more it will be important to adorn the gospel with an attractive approach. Radical humility, love, kindness, respect and gentleness will go a long way toward embodying the message that we seek to present. Untiring and genuine interest in people, their needs and dreams, as well as a sympathetic listening ear will clothe the gospel in the love of Christ.

What might it mean to communicate the gospel in an effective and appealing way in a postmodern society? Certainly, a posture of humility and listening will attractively adorn the gospel, a dialogical rather than a dogmatic approach. In the complexity of our world it is important to avoid offering cheap and easy answers to difficult questions. We need to see our dialogue partners as friends and potential strugglers. Our communication of the gospel should be winsome, with respect and compassion. And an especially effective way to communicate the gospel in a postmodern culture is through stories—listening to others' stories and telling ours.

The communication of the gospel should be organically connected to everyday life. Too much evangelism seems to be a matter of memorizing and practicing a canned methodological approach. We learn various evangelistic methods, strategies and techniques. This seems to make evangelism more propaganda or slick sales pitch than good news. We zero in on the decision of our listener. Conversion then seems to be something that can be programmed and managed in the style of a military campaign or marketing promotion.

Yet if the gospel is a message about the kingdom of God and God's rule over all of life, and if the gospel is a message that is relevant to all human needs and questions, then evangelism should be something that connects organically to and flows naturally out of the daily experiences of our lives. Kraemer offers wise words:

> One of the fundamental laws of all presentation of the Christian truth everywhere in the world is that this truth is vitally related to all spheres and problems of life, the most common and trivial as well as the most elevated. . . . The radically religious view of life as embodied in Biblical realism is of the same vital significance to man's relation to his friend or fellow-villager, or to the way in which he spends his money or works his fields or accepts his material successes or adversities, as to the nurture of his spiritual life or to his religious needs and experiences in the more restricted sense of the word.[33]

If we understand the global economic crisis, for example, as a problem of communal greed and corporate idolatry that make economic growth a central cultural goal, then the gospel cannot be kept out of our discussions about economic issues today. If we see that the breakdown of education stems from the lack of a compelling narrative to give it meaning, and we believe that only the Bible can offer that kind of narrative, then our participation in education cannot help but refer to the gospel. If our struggles with death, sickness and loss are buttressed by the hope and comfort of the good news of Christ's work, then we are unlikely to be silent when unbelieving neighbors and friends struggle with their pain. If we live in the experience of God's grace and forgiveness in our sin and waywardness, our words to those caught in addiction and self-destructive behavior will humbly and sympathetically point to the source of our forgiveness and renewal. In these cases we can "chatter the gospel" naturally pointing to Christ and the gospel as good news.

---

[33]Ibid., p. 304.

This will demand that the church grow in its understanding of the all-encompassing scope of the gospel and its relation to the whole spectrum of their lives. It will mean living over against the practical atheism of our culture that disconnects much of human life from God. If the whole of our lives are being formed by the gospel and the biblical story, then there will be opportunity for an organic evangelism that verbally expresses the hope of the gospel.

"The pure verbal preaching of the story of Jesus crucified and risen would lose its power if those who heard it could not trace it back to some kind of community in which the message was being validated in a common way of life which is recognizable as embodying at least a hint and a foretaste of the blessedness for which all men long and which the Gospel promises. . . . It is in the life of a new kind of community that the saving power of the Gospel is known and tasted, and such a community—in however embryonic form—will always be the *locus* of that miracle by which the paradigm shift which we call conversion takes place."

Lesslie Newbigin, *The Open Secret*, p. 304

Our evangelistic words must flow from a community whose life demonstrates the truth of the gospel. Words can be cheap. In fact, we live in a world of information overload whereby a glut of words on the market devalues verbal communication. Moreover, our consumer society offers a wide choice of worldviews that leaves many paralyzed. If we announce, "Good news: the kingdom of God has arrived, and there is a new renewing power at work in the world because of the death and resurrection of Jesus Christ," our neighbors have every right to ask, "Where is this new power at work?" Our evangelistic words will be heard only if they are authenticated by the lives of the Christian community. The gospel gains its power from a community that embodies something of the life that the gospel promises (cf. Acts 4:32-35). "Insofar as evangelism is the heart of this mission, this very people constitutes both the public invitation and that to which the invitation points."[34]

---

[34]Stone, *Evangelism after Christendom*, p. 15; see also pp. 171-275.

Friedrich Nietzsche once chastised the church for its lack of joy, vibrancy and delight in creational life and left us with these sobering words: "They would have to sing better songs for me to learn to have faith in their Redeemer: and his disciples would have to look more redeemed!"[35]

A community that lives as an attractive contrast community over against the idolatries of the age will call forth questions: What is the source of this new life? Why do you live this way? This presents us with evangelistic opportunities to point to the gospel. We must, as the Scripture says, "Always be prepared to give an answer to everyone who asks you to give the reason for the hope that you have. But do this with gentleness and respect" (1 Pet 3:15).

And so Newbigin issues a sharp warning to a church whose life is not producing questions:

> The preaching of the gospel can never be irrelevant. But if the Church which preaches it is not living corporately a life which corresponds with it, is living in comfortable cohabitation with the powers of this age, is failing to challenge the powers of darkness and to manifest in its life the power of the living Lord to help and to heal, then by its life it closes the doors which its preaching would open. That does not mean that the preaching is void, because there is no limit to the power of the word of God. But it means that the Church comes under severe judgment from him who will ask of us not about our confession but about our commitment to doing his will.[36]

MERCY AND JUSTICE

Distressing statistics and the church's calling. In the first chapter we saw some statistics that indicate the staggering social and economic need of our day. Our world is ravaged by economic injustice, by disregard for basic human rights especially evident in neglect of the poor and vulnerable, by the scandal of millions of homeless and displaced refugees, by sex trafficking and a billion-dollar pornography "industry," by wars, terrorism, violence and escalating military spending, by a blatant disregard for the environment and natural resources, and by hunger, illiteracy and increasing poverty. Statistics hardly begin to tell the story of the misery of billions in our world.

---

[35]Friedrich Nietzsche, *Thus Spoke Zarathustra: A Book for None and All*, trans. Walter Kaufman (New York: Penguin Books, 1978), p. 92.
[36]Newbigin, *Gospel in a Pluralist Society*, p. 140.

The call for justice, peace and the integrity of creation surely is a timely one in our day. But what is the calling of the church in all this?

The church's mission is to participate in God's mission to restore the whole creation and all of human life. If the scope of salvation is as broad as creation, our participation must be equally broad. The gospel is a gospel of the kingdom—the restoration of God's rule over the world. The church is a sign, foretaste and instrument of the kingdom of God in the world, a community that says with its life, words and deeds, "Jesus is Lord over all." Central to the kingdom of Jesus is a life of self-giving love for the sake of others. All of this commits the church to the justice and mercy of the kingdom. But what does that look like?

> THE CHURCH'S MISSION IS TO PARTICIPATE IN GOD'S MISSION TO RESTORE THE WHOLE CREATION AND ALL OF HUMAN LIFE. IF THE SCOPE OF SALVATION IS AS BROAD AS CREATION, OUR PARTICIPATION MUST BE EQUALLY BROAD.

Justice, mercy and the calling of the church. In order to understand the church's role in seeking justice and mercy, it is important to understand the relationship of the church to the kingdom proclaimed in the gospel. The relationship between church and kingdom can be articulated in three statements: the church is the place where the eschatological kingship of God in Jesus Christ becomes visible; the church has to serve the kingdom by proclaiming the message that Jesus is Lord; the church is engaged in the struggle of Christ's kingdom in this world against the destructive powers of darkness revealed in unbelief, powers of injustice and suppression of the poor, the powers of materialism, selfishness, discrimination, atheism, racism, and more.[37]

The first priority of the church, as the place where the kingdom life is present, is to itself be a model of the justice and mercy of the kingdom in its own life. There is a welcome growing emphasis on this communal witness that issues from the Anabaptist wing of the church. John Howard Yoder has emphasized the corporate witness of the Christian community in every culture to be both a "pulpit and paradigm" of the new humanity.[38] Along

---

[37]Reformed Ecumenical Synod, *The Church and Its Social Calling* (Grand Rapids: Reformed Ecumenical Synod, 1980), pp. 18-19.

[38]John Howard Yoder, *For the Nations: Essays in Public and Evangelical* (Grand Rapids: Eerdmans, 1997), p. 41.

similar lines, the Reformed missiologist Harvie Conn refers to the church as an "advance copy of the new world order it preaches" as its members give their allegiance to Christ and embark "on a great campaign to banish war and poverty and injustice, to set up a life where love and service and justice have taken the place of selfishness and power."[39] The church is a preview of the kingdom, actual footage of the world coming designed to interest viewers in it.

The book of Acts certainly gives support to such a view. The church in Jerusalem is a community that shares together and holds everything in

---

"It is a disastrous misunderstanding to think that we can enjoy salvation through Jesus Christ and at the same time regard action for justice in the world as a sort of optional extra—or even as an inferior substitute for the work of passing on the good news of salvation. Action for social justice *is* salvation in action. Of course it is true that no action of ours can do more than produce a *little* more justice in the world."

Lesslie Newbigin, *The Good Shepherd*, p. 109

---

common, and "the Lord added to their number daily those who were being saved" (Acts 2:47). We are told that the apostles testified to the resurrection of Jesus with great power (Acts 4:33). But this statement is set in the midst of a description of a church living a life of radical sharing. It is a community where God's grace is powerfully at work such that there are no needy among them (Acts 4:32-35).

But this life of justice and mercy in the church will spill over into a struggle for the life of the kingdom within its host culture. The church is not only the place but also the instrument of the kingdom. This is evident in the witness in the first centuries of the church. Deeds of

> THE CHURCH IS NOT ONLY THE PLACE BUT ALSO THE INSTRUMENT OF THE KINGDOM.

---

[39]Harvie Conn, *Evangelism: Doing Justice and Preaching Grace* (Grand Rapids: Zondervan, 1982), p. 56.

mercy and justice, as an expression of self-giving love, were a powerful witness to the truth of the gospel. Indeed, loving deeds toward the needy were a primary reason the early church grew in the first three centuries. "Pagan and Christian writers are unanimous that not only did Christian scripture stress love and charity as the central duties of faith, but that these were sustained in everyday behavior."[40] It was because of this powerful witness that many deacons lost their lives both in martyrdom and by contracting deadly diseases while caring for the sick. It was also because of this powerful witness that when Emperor Julian (331-363) attempted to revive pagan religion in the Roman Empire after its "conversion" to Christianity, he saw the church's love and charity as the main reason the Christian church was so popular and attempted to imitate it.[41] As Pope Benedict XVI succinctly explains in his first encyclical,

> In one of his letters, [Julian] wrote that the sole aspect of Christianity which had impressed him was the Church's charitable activity. He thus considered it essential for his new pagan religion that, alongside the system of the Church's charity, an equivalent activity of its own be established. According to him, this was the reason for the popularity of the "Galileans." They needed now to be imitated and outdone.[42]

Benedict goes on to say what every Christian tradition should affirm: "For the Church, charity is not a kind of welfare activity which could equally well be left to others, but is a part of her nature, an indispensable expression of her very being."[43]

Is the church today ready to hear this challenge? In spite of voices that claim that the church is on the margins (which has some truth), people who claim Christ in some way control one-third of the world's wealth. We spend an enormous amount of money on buildings while 20 percent of our Christian family goes to bed hungry every night. Deacons, who were meant to lead the church in stewardship and justice, often become simply financial officers who oversee a self-concerned budget. Our right to enjoy our private

---

[40]Rodney Stark, "Epidemics, Networks, and the Rise of Christianity," *Semeia* 56 (1991): 169.
[41]Ibid., p. 167.
[42]Pope Benedict XVI, *Deus Caritas Est*, paragraph 24 (first encyclical, dated December 25, 2005, released January 25, 2006).
[43]Pope Benedict XVI, *Deus Caritas Est*, paragraph 25a.

property and a consumer lifestyle sometimes seems to have as much grip on Christians as those outside the church. What would the church today look like if it took seriously the call to be a model of justice and mercy in its own ranks as well as an instrument in broader society?

The nature of social action. Two theological pitfalls continue to subvert the true nature of social concern in the mission of the church. The first is to identify the kingdom with history and to see it fully present in the historical process. We are then in danger of an uncritical triumphalism: it is our efforts, programs and activity that will usher in the kingdom of God. Yet the "mission of the church is not to accomplish God's eschatological reign. The church does not bring in the kingdom. It does not establish God's reign over society"; rather, the "church in this period of history between the cross and return of Christ witnesses to an accomplished fact . . . and lives in the hope of its final realization in the second coming of Jesus Christ."[44] The kingdom will arrive fully only when Christ returns, and until that day our efforts will bear the character of witness.

"*Being* is tightly bound to *doing*. 'Let your light shine before others,' Jesus says, 'so that they may see your good works and give glory to your Father in heaven' (Mt 5:16). Here 'good works' probably embrace all the ways that God's people witness to the kingdom in everyday life, in both word and deed, in interpersonal relationships and through acts of justice and compassion. Such good deeds are both public and missional. Their ultimate purpose is to lead those who 'see' them to offer glory to God. . . . Through the quality of their character and loving behavior, God's people are to attract others to the worship of the true and living God."

Dean Flemming, *Reclaiming the Full Mission of God*, pp. 98-99

The other danger is to separate the kingdom from history and to see it as entirely future or perhaps present only within the individual person. Instead of the activism of the former position, this breeds a quietism, even a de-

---

[44]Robert E. Webber, *Ancient-Future Evangelism: Making Your Church a Faith-Forming Community* (Grand Rapids: Baker Books, 2003), p. 154.

featism, that sanctions the unjust status quo. It sanctions selfish withdrawal from the painful social, economic and political issues that face us today. Such a path is starkly inconsistent with the mission of Jesus.

If we avoid these extremes of quietist withdrawal and activist triumphalism, what is the goal and purpose of our deeds of mercy and justice? What are we really doing with our deeds? And what do we hope to achieve? Our best efforts will, after all, only be a drop in the bucket. Three things can be said. First, our deeds bear the character of witness to the presence and power of the kingdom of God that has broken into history. Our deeds are hope in action or an enacted prayer that God's kingdom might come fully. Like the mighty acts of Jesus, they are signs or windows that enable people to see something of the nature of the kingdom of God.

As a witness to the kingdom, they are, second, an expression of our love for a world caught in the destructive clutches of sin. In John 13 Jesus shows us that the very nature of life in the kingdom of God is a matter of self-giving, self-sacrificing love for the sake of others. When he washes the disciples' feet, it is not simply a lesson in humility but rather a picture of the self-emptying, loving service that is characteristic of the true intent of human life. Newbigin writes,

> The works of mercy, of healing, of liberation—all are part of the breaking in of a new reality. They are parts of it and therefore signs of it. . . . Jesus' deeds of love were not part of a contrived programme with some ulterior purpose: they were the overflowing of the love which filled his whole being. Just so, the Church's deeds of love ought to be—not contrived signs but natural and spontaneous signs of the new reality in which we have been made sharers through Christ.[45]

And so, if love is the key, there are at least three goals: to offer merciful relief, to seek justice, and to hope for conversion. To see our neighbor in misery and need and be unconcerned about easing that suffering (mercy) or dismantling the structures that feed it (justice) surely lacks love. "If anyone has material possessions and sees a brother or sister in need but has no pity on them, how can the love of God be in that person? Dear children, let us not love with words or speech but with actions and in truth" (1 Jn 3:17-

---

[45]Newbigin, *Good Shepherd*, p. 93.

18). But love longs for that person to be reconciled to God in Jesus Christ and to know the salvation of the kingdom. Mission aims not only at changing the conditions that have created slums but also the person in the slums. We want to see people converted to Jesus Christ.

> MISSION AIMS NOT ONLY AT CHANGING THE CONDITIONS THAT HAVE CREATED SLUMS BUT ALSO THE PERSON IN THE SLUMS.

But, third, we hope that our actions may produce more justice in the world. There is much talk of transformation: is it the goal of the mission of the church to transform the structures of society? Surely, love will seek more just economic structures that ease the plight of hunger and through which the poor, weak and vulnerable are protected. Certainly, Jesus did not avoid confrontation with the structural evil of his day that brought suffering, and so neither can we. But we recognize the provisional nature of the kingdom; it will not come fully until Christ returns. And so such endeavors for peace and justice will always be proximate and penultimate, a mitigation of the injustice and violence of our world that is born of love for a suffering world. Ultimately, a faithful witness to Christ and sharing in his love for the world remain the mission of the church. Nevertheless, we can rejoice when through a faithful and loving witness God's saving work spills over the boundaries of the church and has a salting effect (Mt 5:13) on society. We celebrate partial victories and provisional evidences of justice and peace because that may well mean a measure of relief from suffering. But our ultimate goal remains a loving witness to Jesus Christ and his liberating kingdom.

Social action and the local congregation. The church, if is to offer a faithful witness to the gospel, must be seen as a community that gives itself for the sake of the other, a community that is deeply involved in the needs and concerns of its neighborhood. This will require leadership that constantly challenges the selfish introversion that seems to be the default mode of congregations. The congregation, if it is to take up its social calling, must be equipped with faithful deacons who lead and challenge the church to self-giving service for the sake of its neighbors.

Moreover, if congregations are to be seen as communities committed to mercy and justice, then these deeds must be recognizable as actions that flow from a community that believes and embodies the gospel. There is a danger that various kinds of denominational and interdenominational organizations, committees and programs will assume total responsibility for the work of mercy and justice. This seems to be the most efficient way. Yet, this may cause the local congregation to lose its self-understanding of being a missional body that seeks justice and mercy in its own place. It may also blur the proper character of these efforts for mercy and justice as signs of the kingdom in the eyes of others if they are cut off from the Christian community in that particular place.

> With the development of powerful denominational structures, nationwide agencies for evangelism and social action, it can happen that these things are no longer seen as the direct responsibility of the local congregation except insofar as they are called on to support them financially. But if the local congregation is not perceived in its own neighborhood as the place from which the good news overflows in good action, the programs for social and political action launched by the national agencies are apt to lose their integral relation to the good news and come to be seen as part of a moral crusade rather than the gospel.[46]

This is not to say that these agencies have no place; rather, their task is to coordinate the efforts of local congregations and to enable, equip and train their members so that their involvement in the needs of their community are recognizable as arising from a body that has its source in the gospel.

CALLING OF BELIEVERS IN SOCIETY

The importance of the laity in society. Adding congregational initiatives for social action for justice and mercy in the community to evangelism is important but insufficient. Holistic mission means much more: all our callings in life must bear witness to the lordship of Jesus.

Ian Barns reflects on the life and work of Lesslie Newbigin:

> For Newbigin it was lay Christians, in the context of their daily occupations and professions, that played a crucial role in communicating the public truth of the gospel in our culture. Because of this he was particularly concerned for the effective and ongoing equipping and support of lay Christians in their daily lives. Notwithstanding the various impressive "Christians at work" ini-

---

[46]Newbigin, *Gospel in a Pluralist Society*, p. 229.

tiatives around the world, I don't think that this challenge has really been taken on board by pastors, theologians, Christian educators and Christian leaders in the professions. . . . Many Christians in professional occupations are godly, honest and caring people in their personal dealings with others, but they default to being technocratic humanists at a cognitive level. Given the enormous societal upheavals that are about to befall the planet, the human community will desperately need Christian community organisers, food producers, doctors, engineers, peacemakers, counsellors, inventors (to name just a few) inspired by the love of Christ and the public vision of God's peaceable universal kingdom.[47]

Five observations on this insightful quotation highlight the importance of this topic. First, the laity plays a crucial role in the mission of the church in their witness to the public truth of the gospel. They do so in the context of

---

"I do not believe that the role of the Church in a secular society is primarily exercised in the corporate action of the churches as organized bodies in the political or cultural fields. . . . On the contrary, I believe that it is through the action of Christian lay people, playing their roles as citizens, workers, managers, legislators, etc., not wearing the label 'Christian' but deeply involved in the secular world in the faith that God is at work there in a way which is not that of the 'Christendom' pattern."

Lesslie Newbigin, "Baptism, the Church and Koinonia," p. 127

---

their everyday callings, jobs and occupations. This is where the primary witness to the Lordship of Christ over all of human affairs must be given. A verbal witness to the gospel takes place as the members of the church are trained to live as agents of the kingdom in their various sectors of public life. As they begin to understand how the gospel and the lordship of Christ impact their workplace, a missionary encounter takes place. Newbigin observes,

> Here is the place where the real interface between the Church and the world, between the new creation and the old, takes place. Here is where there ought

---

[47]Ian Barns, "Some Reflections on Lesslie Newbigin's Challenge to Bear Witness to the Gospel as 'Public Truth'" (www.fost.org.uk/bigincont.htm).

to be a discernible difference in behavior between those who live the old story and those who live by the story the Bible tells. It ought at many points to lead to differences in behavior, to dissent from current practice, to questioning. And this, of course, will be the place where the counterquestions arise. The Christian will be asked, "Why do you do this? Why do you behave like this?" Here is where the true evangelistic dialogue begins.[48]

Therefore, second, congregations must find ways to effectively support and equip the laity in their various callings. But alas, third, this challenge of training the laity for their callings has not been taken on board by most congregations. There have been some fine general initiatives, but it is not a widespread dimension of the church's mission. In fact, it is quite rare to find this as a primary focus of the mission of the local congregation. And so, fourth, most Christians, even though they are godly and well-meaning believers, are deeply shaped by the technocratic humanist story of Western culture in their callings. Yet, fifth, believers committed to the gospel and who carry out their callings in the public square are desperately needed at a time when there are enormous global crises threatening our existence. After all, the most important contribution the church can make in the face of the momentous issues and problems of our day is to nourish its people so they can live out the gospel in their various callings.

> THE MOST IMPORTANT CONTRIBUTION THE CHURCH CAN MAKE IN THE FACE OF THE MOMENTOUS ISSUES AND PROBLEMS OF OUR DAY IS TO NOURISH ITS PEOPLE SO THEY CAN LIVE OUT THE GOSPEL IN THEIR VARIOUS CALLINGS.

The problem of dualism. And yet, as Newbigin says, "It is very rare to find this kind of situation because the churches have so largely accepted the relegation to the private sector, leaving the public sector to be controlled by another story."[49] Christopher Wright also attributes the failure of a strong Christian mission in the public square to a "dichotomized life."[50] It seems clear that if Christians are to recover the importance of their daily callings

---

[48]Lesslie Newbigin, *A Word in Season: Perspectives on Christian World* Mission (Grand Rapids: Eerdmans, 1994), p. 156.

[49]Ibid.

[50]Christopher J. H. Wright, *The Mission of God's People: A Biblical Theology of the Church's Mission* (Grand Rapids: Zondervan, 2010), p. 223.

for the mission of the church, they will need to eradicate this dichotomy.

A return to the gospel must be the starting point. The good news that Jesus preached was a gospel of the kingdom. That is, in the person and work of Jesus Christ God is restoring his rule over the whole creation and every aspect of human life. This means that the gospel is first of all restorative and comprehensive: all of human life is being restored by the Spirit in Christ.

When the gospel is understood in this way, we realize that salvation is a matter of creation restored. This drives us back to recover a more robust doctrine of creation, which often has been lacking in the evangelical community. And in the early chapters of Genesis we discover that the first indication of what it means to be human is the call, as creatures made in God's image, to develop and care for the creation in a cultural and societal way (Gen 1:26-28; 2:15). Thus, our cultural callings are central, not marginal, to who we are as human beings. Yet, as we see in the early chapters of Genesis, the rebellion of humankind twisted and disfigured this process (Gen 3–11). And corporate human idolatry continues today in each cultural situation to mar the healthy and prosperous development that God intended. Structural evil defaces what God originally meant for blessing. The salvation of the kingdom is a matter of recovering also precisely this cultural and societal dimension of human life.

The church must be defined in terms of the coming kingdom proclaimed in the gospel. The church is a sign, preview and instrument of the kingdom of God. If the kingdom involves a comprehensive restoration, the church is to be a preview of that restoration, including cultural and societal renewal, which is coming fully at the end of the age. Moreover, it is to be an instrument in God's hand to struggle for the justice, reconciliation, righteousness and peace of the kingdom today. Thus, is it a sign of the new world that is breaking in by the work of the Spirit.

> IF THE KINGDOM INVOLVES A COMPREHENSIVE RESTORATION, THE CHURCH IS TO BE A PREVIEW OF THAT RESTORATION.

Yet, often when we use the word "church," we are thinking not of a community of the kingdom but rather of a congregation gathered to carry out various "religious" activities, such as prayer, worship, reading Scripture, and so on. And the Bible certainly does use the word "church" (in Greek *ekklēsia*) to describe the local congregation gathered for certain "religious" activities. But the Bible also uses the word "church" to describe the new humankind of the kingdom begun in Christ. That is, "church" refers to the new people of God in the totality of their lives as the reconstitution of humankind in Jesus Christ.[51] And so God's people represent Christ as members of his body wherever they are and whatever they are doing, not just when gathered together.

Thus, the church is to be a people whose whole life shows the comprehensive renewing work of Christ, a community that witnesses to the lordship of Jesus over the whole spectrum of human life. "The church is placed in the world not as a passive observer of God's action in and with the world; rather, she is called to 'involvement,' or engagement with the world—with the whole of human life in all its dimensions."[52] So the mission of the church cannot possibly ignore or marginalize the callings of Christians in the public square if it is to be faithful. This is where God is at work, and this is where his people live the large majority of their lives.

There is no dichotomy or dualism between aspects of human life that matter or are more directly related to God and those that are not. All of human life arises from creation; all of human life has been devastated by human rebellion; all of human life, including the social and cultural dimensions, is being restored in Jesus and by the work of his Spirit. The church is the community called to make known this comprehensive restoration in its words and deeds, but also across the whole spectrum of the cultural and social lives of its members. A dualistic approach in which we live out certain areas of our lives, such as prayer and individual ethics, faithfully within the biblical story under the lordship of Christ and yet live out other areas in the public square under the idolatrous cultural story is nothing less than an abandonment of our calling as Christians. It is that serious!

The importance of the local congregation. Defining the church as the new humankind does not take away from the significance of the church gathered as a local congregation. Indeed, if the church is to be faithful in this

---

[51]For Paul's use of *ekklēsia* in these ways, see Herman Ridderbos, *Paul: An Outline of His Theology*, trans. John Richard de Witt (Grand Rapids: Eerdmans, 1975), pp. 328-30.
[52]G. C. Berkouwer, *The Church: Studies in Dogmatics*, trans. James E. Davison (Grand Rapids: Eerdmans, 1976), pp. 395-96.

calling, it will be essential for the local congregation to play a central role in supporting, training and equipping the people of God for their callings.

There are at least four ways that the local congregation can take up this calling. First, the local congregation must be a fellowship that nourishes the life of Christ through word and sacrament. Living out the gospel in the midst of the public square is not first of all a matter of strategy and planning; rather, it is manifesting the very life of Christ in the midst of the world. This can happen only if this life is being constantly nurtured with the gospel in word, sacrament, prayer and liturgy.[53] This will require a recovery of the gospel as good news that Jesus is Savior and Lord of all of human life—a gospel that is much broader than the individualistic gospel at work in many congregations.

> Being saved to serve, Christ-confessors must sense keenly that Sunday's worship is unto Monday's work. Worship, which opens the door to a new week, is not a retreat from reality, but a rallying-point, a launching-pad, a spring-board which sends believers forth upon their way as "living letters known and read of all men." The preaching and teaching ministries of the church must shape and mold the Christian community to challenge the "principalities and powers" of this world as it carries out its reconciling mission in society.[54]

And so, second, each local congregation must have leadership that is equipped to enable the laity in their callings. Folk who live out their callings in the difficult situations of the public square need pastors who understand the painful tension of being faithful in a place where powerful spiritual forces work in opposition to the gospel. Yet, so much theological training does not equip pastors for this calling. Too many leaders are blissfully unaware that this is their task, and so the ministry of the local congregation does not have the horizon of the public square in view in its ministry.

Third, the local congregation must be a people who support members in their callings. This certainly will mean prayer and encouragement. And yet

---

[53]Mark Glanville introduced a "lay liturgy" at Willoughby Christian Reformed Church in which people from different sectors of society were interviewed about their job during the worship service and how they serve Christ in that capacity. The interview was followed by a responsive reading in which the congregation blessed and sent that person into their vocation to witness to Christ's lordship with a reminder that it is a call on all of us. It ended with a prayer for faithfulness.

[54]Reformed Ecumenical Synod, *The Church and Its Social Calling*, p. 24.

it is rare to hear prayers on Sunday morning for church members in their daily callings. And precious little encouragement focuses on the difficulty in swimming upstream against the idolatrous current of culture. Beyond prayer and verbal encouragement, it may well mean financial support for the person who loses work because of their faithfulness. If the modern church were to practice this, it would be following in the footsteps of the early church, which generously cared for its members who suffered because they were faithful in the face of powers that opposed them (e.g., Acts 4:32-35). And, finally, support will mean insight into and teaching about the gospel and culture that would equip the members for their task. In this regard, worldview studies has a plethora of resources to equip pastors and leaders to offer the insight needed by its members.

Fourth, the local congregation will need to construct creative structures that equip their members for their callings. This may be small groups formed

"No human societies cohere except on the basis of some kind of common beliefs and customs. No society can permit these beliefs and practices to be threatened beyond a certain point without reacting in self-defense. The idea that we ought to be able to expect some kind of neutral secular political order, which presupposes no religious or ideological beliefs, and which holds the ring impartially for a plurality of religions to compete with one another, has no adequate foundation. The New Testament makes it plain that Christ's followers must expect suffering as the normal badge of their discipleship, and also as one of the characteristic forms of their witness."

Lesslie Newbigin, *Trinitarian Faith and Today's Mission*, p. 42

to study culture or worldview. It may be Christians gathered to tell their stories of their callings or to share their struggles in living out the gospel in their occupations. A particularly helpful structure is what has been called "frontier groups." These are groups of believers, often across various congregations, who work in the same sector of public life. They meet together to seek and share insight in light of Scripture, to encourage and pray for one another, and to thrash out the controversial and difficult issues of their business or profession in the light of the gospel.

Suffering and spirituality. The church, if it is to recover this vital aspect of its mission, will need also to attend closely to two important threads of biblical teaching: faithfulness means suffering, and faithfulness requires a robust spirituality. Western Christians have long lived in a culture in which their numerical dominance and social power give them the sense that their mission in the public square was a matter of transforming the culture. However that may be—and it certainly is a hot topic for discussion—today the church is just as likely to suffer as to transform. This is not to say that the church has lost all cultural power; it does, after all, control a large portion of the world's wealth. Nevertheless, the public doctrine that controls Western culture is far more resistant, and growingly so, to the Christian faith than in years past.

Christopher Wright makes this point in three steps: we are called to be different; we are called to resist idolatry; we are called to suffer. This is precisely the logic of the New Testament. Human societies and cultures cohere on the basis of foundational beliefs and a shared story rooted in idolatry. When a dissenting group within that culture challenges the public doctrine and reigning story, the powers quite naturally lash back; they cannot allow those beliefs to be challenged beyond a certain point if the cultural community is to hold together. Being different, resisting the idolatry of the dominant story, will mean suffering for Christians as they pursue their callings in culture.

The businessperson who challenges the idolatry of the profit motive, the scholar who challenges the modern or postmodern secularist assumptions of scholarship, the healthcare professional who resists the humanist underpinnings of the healthcare "industry," the person working in politics who demurs from the operative liberal ideology—all will find that living faithfully in the biblical story under the lordship of Jesus Christ demands that a price be paid for obedience. Truly, faithfulness means suffering: "Everyone who wants to live a godly life in Christ Jesus will be persecuted" (2 Tim 3:12).

Newbigin tells the story of a young teacher in India who, as the representative of his extended family, trained to be a teacher. In his first year his Christian faith met head-on the pluralistic powers of public education.

When he refused to succumb, he was fired, losing years of education and the investment of his entire family. In the days after, Newbigin baptized more people in that town than he had before. "The costly witness of a village boy who was willing to lose his teaching certificate rather than compromise his faith so shook the whole institution that I was soon baptizing students within the college campus."[55] This event convinced him of three things: the incompatibility of the gospel with the dominant doctrine shaping public institutions, the cost of faithful witness, and the power of a costly witness to draw others to Christ.

How can believers be fortified for this task of a costly witness? We have noted the importance of a supportive and nurturing congregation. It will also be important to develop a robust spirituality, both communal and individual. In the final analysis, an effective and faithful missionary encounter will depend on a life that is constantly renewed in communion with God in a life of praise, thanksgiving and petition. It is only as the life of Christ flows to us by the Spirit as we abide in him that it is possible to bear the painful tension of challenging the destructive spiritual powers at work in culture. N. T. Wright believes, "All Christians, particularly those involved at the leading edge of the church's mission to bring healing and renewal to the world, should be people of prayer, invoking the Spirit of Jesus daily and hourly as they go about their tasks, lest they be betrayed into the arrogance of their own agendas or into the cowardice of relativism."[56]

Further Reading

Dickson, John. *The Best Kept Secret of Christian Mission: Preaching the Gospel with More Than Our Lips*. Grand Rapids: Zondervan, 2010.

Goheen, Michael W. "The Missional Calling of Believers in the World: Lesslie Newbigin's Contribution," in *A Scandalous Prophet: The Way of Mission After Newbigin,* edited by Thomas F. Foust et al., pp. 37-54. Grand Rapids: Eerdmans, 2002.

Newbigin, Lesslie. *The Gospel in a Pluralist Society*. Grand Rapids: Eerdmans, 1989, pp. 128-40.

---

[55]Lesslie Newbigin, *Unfinished Agenda: An Autobiography* (Geneva: World Council of Churches, 1985), p. 120.
[56]N. T. Wright, *New Tasks for a Renewed Church* (London: Hodder & Stoughton, 1992), p. 86.

Stone, Bryan. *Evangelism After Christendom: The Theology and Practice of Christian Witness*. Grand Rapids: Brazos Press, 2007.

Webber, Robert E. *Ancient-Future Evangelism: Making Your Church a Faith-Forming Community*. Grand Rapids: Baker, 2003.

DISCUSSION QUESTIONS

1. From your experience, to what extent and in what ways do the evangelical and ecumenical theologies of mission still dominate thinking about mission for Christians in the pews?

2. How would your church answer this question: Which is more important, evangelism or mercy and justice?

3. Evaluate the description of authentic evangelism in this chapter. What do you find most helpful, and what is less so? Discuss this in light of some of your own evangelistic experiences and observations.

ESSAY TOPICS

1. Trace the twentieth-century debate between the ecumenical and evangelical traditions surrounding word and deed. What can we learn from it? How would you resolve it? Does it still affect our understanding of mission today?

2. How is introducing the theme of the kingdom of God into evangelism helpful? What are some ways to translate that theme into the twenty-first century?

3. Lesslie Newbigin argues that it is in the calling of the laity that the most important missional encounter with our culture takes place. Do you agree? Why or why not? What is hindering the church from making this a priority?

7

Faithful Contextualization

Church, Gospel and Culture(s)

ᏧᏋ

FOR MUCH OF CHURCH HISTORY the church for the most part embodied the gospel in one macrocultural context: Europe. When cross-cultural missions exploded from Europe with the Roman Catholics in the sixteenth century and the Protestants in the eighteenth century, they faced a new situation perhaps known only by missionary monks in the medieval period. How did the gospel relate to these new cultural contexts? What made this issue especially problematic, then but still today, was the assumption that Western culture was superior and Christian and, therefore, that non-Western cultures were inferior and pagan. In fact the word "cultures" (plural) was not used until the late nineteenth century, and then rarely. It has only come to prominence in the twentieth century. Instead, the word "civilization" (singular) was used. Western culture was the standard of what civilization should be. Bolstered by a theory of cultural evolution, Western people believed that their civilization was the culmination of evolutionary human development, and others had to catch up. The West stood atop a hierarchical ladder, and all other cultures of the world were assigned a place on the lower rungs according to how they approximated the Western standard. Moreover, the gospel found its natural home in the Christian West in distinction from the pagan nations of the non-West.

Today the church has been planted in every culture of the world, and the gospel now takes many cultural forms. Confidence in the moral superiority of the West or its Christian character is greatly diminished. The legacy of the modern missionary movement has left us with many issues surrounding the topic of gospel and culture in every part of the world. The problem is more urgent than ever: What is the relationship between gospel and culture(s)? What is faithful contextualization?

THE URGENCY OF THE ISSUE

This issue is critical for every church in each cultural setting as well as for the global church as a whole. It is not an exotic item of interest for cross-cultural missionaries or mission students who want to translate and communicate the gospel in understandable ways in a foreign setting. The issue arises from the very nature of the gospel itself. The gospel inevitably will take cultural form. It is not a matter of whether the gospel is shaped by culture; the only question is whether the contextualization of the gospel is faithful or unfaithful.

> IT IS NOT A MATTER OF WHETHER THE GOSPEL IS SHAPED BY CULTURE; THE ONLY QUESTION IS WHETHER THE CONTEXTUALIZATION OF THE GOSPEL IS FAITHFUL OR UNFAITHFUL.

Contextualization is essential to the gospel, and this makes it a pressing missional problem for the church everywhere in the world. It is an issue that necessarily arises as we attempt to live and communicate the gospel. The gospel is good news. God has revealed and accomplished the goal of cosmic history in the life, death and resurrection of Jesus Christ. The gospel has universal validity and so must be communicated to all. Thus, it must be communicated in every culture, and as it is embraced and a Christian community is formed, it must be embodied in a way of life. And so the relation of that gospel to culture is a concern facing the church in mission everywhere and not just for the one who wants to communicate the gospel in a new cultural place.

"A society which accepts the crucifixion and resurrection of Jesus as its ultimate standards of reference will have to be a society whose whole style of life, and not only its words, conveys something of that radical dissent from the world which is manifested in the Cross, and at the same time something of that affirmation of the world which is made possible by the resurrection."

Lesslie Newbigin, "Stewardship, Mission, and Development," p. 6.

Jesus made provision for the communication of the gospel by choosing and forming a community to bear the gospel in every nation to the ends of the earth. The significance of this initial act of Jesus stands in contrast to Islam. In Islam, provision is made for the communication of the prophet Mohammed's message by committing the revelation to writing. The Koran is the apostle and bearer of the message. By contrast, Jesus did not write a book; he formed a community. To be sure, the Bible plays an authoritative role in unfolding God's story of redemption. Nevertheless, Jesus formed a community to be primary bearer of the gospel. Not only is a book the bearer of the message in Islam, but also one must learn Arabic in order to embrace its message. It cannot be translated into another language or culture for fear that the message will be altered and contaminated. Conversion to Islam is cultural as well as religious: to be Muslim, one must welcome the culture of the Koran. In contrast, the church is sent to the ends of the earth to embody and communicate the gospel within each culture of the world. The nature of the gospel and of the church's mission requires that it be translated into the idiom of many cultures. The question of the relationship of this one gospel to the various cultures into which it has come is the issue of contextualization.

Here are some issues to consider. A Nepali pastor once said to me, "We are building a church. The older members of the congregation want a European architectural structure because that is what they believe a Christian church building is. The younger members of the congregation want an indigenous structure—one that looks more like a Buddhist temple. The older members believe the younger members are compromising the gospel with Buddhist culture. The younger members believe the older members are holding on to alien [Western] forms of the gospel. What should we do?" Or another: I showed to some mission students a video on African Independent Churches in which a woman performs a ceremony with animal entrails that arose out the animistic religion. It is offered as a Christian ceremony. A sharp disagreement arose among them: some believed this to be syncretistic—paganism with a Christian veneer—while others argued that we cannot judge so easily any cultural expression of the gospel that is not our own. Perhaps those ceremonies had been filled with Christian meaning. What should be done with these older animistic ceremonies? Should they be abandoned or just modified? Missionaries of the nineteenth and twentieth centuries struggled to know what to do with drums that were associated with erotic pagan rituals, and the *sangoma* (medicine man), who played a key role in African society.

This issue is not confined to the non-Western church. There is a divide in the Western church, for example, about how to relate to the new winds of postmodernism that are blowing in our culture. Many contemporary authors argue for a postmodern expression of the gospel to make it relevant. Others warn that this capitulates to our entertainment and marketing culture. What is a faithful embodiment of the gospel in postmodern culture?

And, very importantly, the issue is not just about worship or church or evangelism. It is an issue that permeates every aspect of our daily lives. Consider these examples, all taken from true stories. How is the businessperson to be faithful to the gospel in a cultural context where much injustice arises because business is driven by profit motive? How is a PhD student in a postmodern university setting to be faithful to the gospel while doing scholarship when the academic context takes for granted many idolatrous assumptions taken from its cultural setting? How is the Christian teacher to be faithful to the gospel in the public school system when the humanist story shapes the curricular content in ways that are opposed to the biblical story? How does the Christian who works in a psychiatric hospital embody the gospel faithfully when the entire industry is built on a faulty humanistic understanding of the human person?

Such questions multiply at every point in life. If mission is faithfully embodying the gospel in the midst of every cultural setting, and every culture is based on a set of beliefs that are to some degree contrary to the gospel, the question of living out the gospel in culture is an urgent one. Contextualization is a pervasive and vital issue.

"The gospel gives rise to a new plausibility structure, a radically different vision of things from those that shape all human cultures apart from the gospel. The Church, therefore, as the bearer of the gospel, inhabits a plausibility structure which is at variance with, and which calls in question, those that govern all human cultures without exception."

Lesslie Newbigin, *The Gospel in a Pluralist Society*, p. 9

THE GOSPEL AND CULTURES: ETHNOCENTRISM AND RELATIVISM

Martin Luther is reported to have once said, "The gospel is like a caged lion; it does not need to be defended, just released." The issue of contextualization is a missional problem because a wrong relationship between the gospel and culture can hold the gospel captive in two ways. Or, to put it differently, there are two sets of bars that can imprison the gospel and tame its power.

The first set of bars is concerned with the gospel and the many cultures (plural) of the world: the problem of ethnocentrism and relativism. Ethnocentrism is where one cultural expression of the gospel is considered normative for all others. The gospel and its cultural form are not distinguished. This was the problem of much of the missionary movement in the last couple of centuries. A Western form of the gospel was considered normative for all the cultures to which missionaries went. This is the complaint of the young Nepalis: why should Western architecture be normative for a worship building? This is the complaint of many Africans: why should Western humanism, rationalism and individualism cast their shadow over ceremonies that express power encounters between Christ and the demonic world?

Relativism is the opposite problem. This is the situation where no cultural expression can be judged good or bad by Scripture or by the church from another culture. Since any judgment of another culture will be by someone who stands in his or her own cultural setting, there is no standard by which to judge others. Chung Hyun Kyung, a Korean professor, invoked the spirit of her Korean ancestors as the Holy Spirit at the World Council of Churches meeting in Canberra (1991). She said that it is through the cries of those ancestor spirits that Koreans are able to hear the voice of the Holy Spirit. Many evangelical and Eastern Orthodox participants responded that this was syncretism. Others said that we cannot judge this practice as unfaithful because we do so from within our own cultural context. When there is no criterion for judging faithful and unfaithful embodiments of the gospel, we have relativism. Relativism arose in the middle part of the twentieth century partially from an acute bad conscience of Westerners who had imposed their culture on others. Any cultural manifestation of the gospel was equally good.

Both ethnocentrism and relativism inhibit the faithful embodiment and communication of the gospel. The crucial question is this: How can the church be faithful to one gospel (without falling into ethnocentrism) and embrace plural expressions (without falling into relativism)? How can the gospel be authoritative (and not one cultural expression) while taking on different forms in various cultures?

HOW CAN THE CHURCH BE FAITHFUL TO ONE GOSPEL (WITHOUT FALLING INTO ETHNOCENTRISM) AND EMBRACE PLURAL EXPRESSIONS (WITHOUT FALLING INTO RELATIVISM)?

THE GOSPEL AND CULTURE: SYNCRETISM AND IRRELEVANCE

A closely related set of issues arises from the relationship of the gospel to various aspects of a single, particular culture—the problem of syncretism and irrelevance. Syncretism comes from the attempt to make the gospel relevant to the culture. Syncretism takes place when the gospel is absorbed into idolatrous forms, structures and categories of the culture and is consequently compromised. Older Nepalis believed that this is what would happen if the church were to utilize Buddhist architecture. This is what many believed about the animistic ceremony of the African Independent Church and about the Korean professor's prayer. This is what may happen with younger churches as they embrace postmodernity or with their detractors as they hold on to modernity. This is also the problem faced by the businessperson who submits to unjust economic practices, or by the PhD student who simply conforms to the secular academic mores of the university, or when psychiatric workers are uncritical of the humanistic shape of their work.

The other side of the problem is irrelevance. This results from the attempt to be faithful to the gospel by holding on to older or foreign forms of the gospel. Many younger evangelicals nourished in a postmodern world believe that traditional evangelicalism holds an irrelevant form of the Christian faith shaped by modernity. It is an older form of the gospel. The conviction of some in churches in the third world is that forms of worship, theology and confessions, ethical and social practices—in fact, the total package of Christianity handed on to them—have come from the West and are therefore irrelevant to their situation. They are alien forms of the gospel. Thus, the gospel is not good news familiar to the cultural contemporaries of the church in that setting.

HOW CAN WE BE
FAITHFUL TO THE
GOSPEL (WITHOUT
BEING IRRELEVANT)
AND RELEVANT TO THE
CULTURE (WITHOUT
BEING SYNCRETISTIC)?

Both syncretism and irrelevance inhibit a faithful embodiment and communication of the good news. Syncretism compromises the gospel while irrelevance makes it unrecognizable as good news. The crucial question is this: How can we be faithful to the gospel (without being irrelevant) and relevant to the culture (without being syncretistic)? Ethnocentrism and relativism, syncretism and irrelevance—all are bars that imprison the gospel and weaken the church's mission.

A BRIEF HISTORY OF CONTEXTUALIZATION

The model of John's Gospel. Lamin Sanneh says of the gospel in the early church that "in straddling the Jewish-Gentile worlds, [it] was born in a cross-cultural milieu, with translation as its birthmark."[1] The translation of the gospel into Greco-Roman culture already happened within the canon of the New Testament. Dean Flemming has given us a marvelous study that shows how the dynamic of contextualization is at the heart of the New Testament. He understands contextualization to be "the dynamic and comprehensive process by which the gospel is incarnated within a concrete historical or cultural situation. This happens in such a way that the gospel both comes to authentic expression in the local context and at the same time prophetically transforms the context. Contextualization seeks to enable the people of God to live out the gospel in obedience to Christ within their own cultures and circumstances."[2]

Perhaps the elaboration of one example will be instructive: a comparison of the Synoptic Gospels (Matthew, Mark, Luke) with John. In the Synoptic Gospels the kingdom of God is the primary category of Jesus' ministry. This is to be expected: the kingdom of God was a popular and readily recognizable category of eschatological expectation among the Jews to whom Jesus directed his message. Yet, when we read John's Gospel, mention of the

---

[1]Quoted in Max L. Stackhouse, *Apologia: Contextualization, Globalization, and Mission in Theological Education* (Grand Rapids: Eerdmans, 1988), p. 58.
[2]Dean Flemming, *Contextualization in the New Testament: Patterns for Theology and Mission* (Downers Grove, IL: InterVarsity Press, 2005), p. 19.

kingdom of God virtually disappears. "John sings the gospel in a new key."[3] Now we hear language that seems to reflect the dualism of pagan culture: light and darkness, heaven and earth, above and below, spirit and flesh, truth and falsehood, life and death. Paul likewise employs this language, although in different ways. This language had been taken up in various ways by different pagan and Jewish groups within the Roman Empire. To adopt such language certainly is understandable: it would be familiar to and evoke various images among its hearers. But it also seems to put John and Paul in danger of allowing the gospel to be swallowed up by pagan or Jewish worldviews contrary to the gospel.

In the writings of John and Paul do we have a gospel domesticated by pagan culture, or do we have a faithful translation and contextualization of the gospel into a new cultural setting? The opening words of John's Gospel are instructive: "In the beginning was the *logos* [word]" (Jn 1:1). Roman citizens living in a world shaped by Greek culture knew what that meant: in the beginning was the spiritual, rational principle that permeated the universe, giving and maintaining order. All humans possessed a spark of it (reason) that enabled them to understand that order. For Jews, it might have evoked the creative word in Genesis 1 or the preexistent wisdom of God, or for those who had fused the Old Testament with Greek philosophy, a created intermediate being between God and the world that was the mediating principle in creation. As John continues, all these options are both fulfilled and contradicted: "The *logos* [word] became *sarx* [flesh]" (Jn 1:14). That which gave and maintained the order of the world was a personal Creator who had become flesh in the man Jesus.

This contradicted and challenged the whole classical worldview that held as fundamental a separation between the visible and invisible spheres of the world. The *logos* (word) belonged to the invisible, and the *sarx* (flesh) to the visible. But here in John was a confusion of basic categories, a challenge to the very structure and idolatry of the Greek worldview. It also challenges a Jewish syncretistic view that there is a created intermediary being. Moreover, for the Jew whose ear is tuned to the Old Testament, Jesus is God the Creator, the wisdom of God in human flesh. The hearer now had three choices. First,

---

[3]Ibid., p. 257.

reject the gospel as nonsense: the spiritual *logos* simply cannot become material flesh; the God of Genesis 1 cannot become human. A second possibility was repentance: turn from Greek dualism or Jewish syncretism or Judaism to understand and live in the world from the new starting point of the gospel. Or, third, one might want to ask to hear more in order to clarify such a confusing message.

John has not compromised the gospel and capitulated to the pagan worldview. He has employed the terminology but challenged the very worldview that is given expression in those categories. Hendrik Kraemer calls this "subversive fulfillment."[4] J. H. Bavinck calls this *"possessio."*[5] Both authors are pointing to the same thing. All evangelistic language must be at home and at odds with the culture. John is first of all at home in classical culture: he employs a familiar cultural category and touches on a deeply felt need. His point of contact is the heart longing for one of the burning religious desires of humankind: to know the source and origin of the world order. He identifies with this need and offers good news. Thus, his communication is relevant and fulfills a deepest need of that culture. George R. Beasley-Murray rightly comments, "John's employment of the concept to introduce the story of Jesus was a master-stroke of communication to the world of his day."[6]

Yet John is also at odds with the culture of his day: he challenges rationalistic idolatry, Jewish-Hellenistic syncretism, and a Judaism that has rejected Christ. John explodes all the worldviews of his contemporaries. The origin of order is not an impersonal invisible principle or an intermediary being but rather God himself, who has come among us in the man Jesus. John subverts or challenges all views that try to understand the true source of order and meaning in the world apart from Jesus. John takes familiar terms and notions, hears in them the religious cry for order, and fills them with new meaning. Jesus is the Creator—the source of order in the world. John both fulfills and subverts. As Lesslie Newbigin puts it,

---

[4]Hendrik Kraemer, "Continuity and Discontinuity," in *The Madras Series*, vol. 1, *The Authority of Faith* (New York: International Missionary Council, 1939), p. 4.

[5]J. H. Bavinck, *An Introduction to the Science of Missions* (Philadelphia: Presbyterian & Reformed, 1960), pp. 178-79.

[6]George R. Beasley-Murray, *John* (Word Biblical Commentary 36; Waco, TX: Word, 1987), p. lxvi.

I suppose that the boldest and most brilliant essay in the communication of the gospel to a particular culture in all Christian history is the gospel according to John. Here the language and thought-forms of that Hellenistic world are so employed that Gnostics in all ages have thought that the book was written especially for them. And yet nowhere in Scripture is the absolute contradiction between the word of God and human culture stated with more terrible clarity.[7]

This is an approach to contextualization that can serve us well not just for initial missionary communication. All cultural forms, and not just language, can be transformed and filled with new meaning by the gospel. Political structures, economic systems, educational institutions, family forms, artistic expressions, as well as all other customs, practices and institutions express something of the creational good

> ALL CULTURAL FORMS, AND NOT JUST LANGUAGE, CAN BE TRANSFORMED AND FILLED WITH NEW MEANING BY THE GOSPEL.

(which can be embraced) as well as idolatrous distortion (which is to be rejected). John offers an approach to cultural forms that can move us beyond the problems of ethnocentrism and relativism, and syncretism and irrelevance.

This approach to contextualization is not peculiar to John. This is also the way that the rest of the New Testament approaches the problem of gospel and culture. For example, this is the way Paul goes about communicating the gospel as well as instructing churches in his letters how to live out the gospel in the context of the pagan cultures in which they found themselves. Flemming presents a compelling picture of Paul's practice of contextualization as he employed the cultural categories of Greco-Roman culture in evangelism, in theology, in biblical interpretation and in social and cultural practices.[8]

The experience of Christian missions. By its very nature, the gospel is translatable; that is, the gospel will always take on some cultural form.

---

[7]Lesslie Newbigin, *Foolishness to the Greeks: The Gospel and Western Culture* (Grand Rapids: Eerdmans, 1986), p. 53. Newbigin here uses the term "Gnostic" broadly and is not supporting the now discredited theory of Bultmann that the Gospel of John had Gnostics in view.
[8]Flemming, *Contextualization*, pp. 56-233.

During the first three centuries of the church's existence the gospel found a home in a number of cultural contexts, and there was a plurality of expressions of the gospel: Jewish, Greek, barbarian, Thracian, Egyptian and Roman expressions of the gospel in the apostolic church, and Syriac, Greek, Roman, Coptic, Armenian, Ethiopian and Maronite in the postapostolic church.[9] As the European church gained in power during the medieval period, the move was toward an embodiment of the gospel in one macrocultural setting. Yet because of the very translatable nature of the gospel, varied cultural

"The question of the relation of gospel to culture is one of the most vigorously debated subjects in contemporary missiology. But one has to ask whether the way in which the question is posed does not imply already an unacknowledged and disastrous dualism. . . . The question of gospel and culture is sometimes discussed as though it were a matter of the meeting of two quite different things: a disembodied message and a historically conditioned pattern of social life."

Lesslie Newbigin, *The Gospel in a Pluralist Society,* p. 188

expressions remained, for two reasons. First, the church remained for many centuries in other cultural settings. Philip Jenkins tells us that "for most of its history, Christianity was a tricontinental religion, with powerful representation in Europe, Africa, and Asia, and this was true into the fourteenth century."[10] The "Orientializing of Christianity" by the Nestorian church in Persia (fifth century on) and then as it spread by its missionaries to China (seventh to ninth centuries) and other Asian countries is an example.[11]Moreover, Europe itself was not culturally unified, and various cultural expressions of the gospel remained evident. For example, the Christian ruler of England Alfred the Great (849-899) translated the Latin

---

[9]David Bosch, *Transforming Mission: Paradigm Shifts in the Theology of Mission* (Maryknoll, NY: Orbis Books, 1991), p. 448; Dale T. Irvin and Scott W. Sunquist, *History of the World Christian Movement,* vol. 1, *Earliest Christianity to 1453* (Maryknoll, NY: Orbis Books, 2001), pp. 47-97.

[10]Philip Jenkins, *The Lost History of Christianity: The Thousand-Year Golden Age of the Church in the Middle East, Africa, and Asia—And How It Died* (New York: HarperCollins, 2008), p. 3.

[11]Samuel Hugh Moffett, "The Earliest Asian Christianity," *Missiology* 3, no. 4 (1975): 415.

liturgy into the Anglo-Saxon language—"a strategic action which would foster new indigenous theology that wasn't possible in Latin."[12] The second reason for varied cultural expressions of the gospel was that those who traveled to new places for missionary purposes understood the need to contextualize the gospel. For example, Patrick (387-493) planted a thoroughly contextualized church in Ireland employing Celtic poetry, music and art in worship and creating monastic communities that fit Celtic agricultural life better than cathedrals and parishes.[13] The missionaries who went from Ireland in the following centuries utilized similar methods as they encountered new cultural settings. However, the Roman church exerted increasing cultural power and strived toward an official uniformity. Many of the churches outside of Europe died or became very weak. It is understandable, given the growing power of the church in one macrocultural context and lacking an official plurality of cultural expressions of the gospel, that contextualization simply would not be an issue in the consciousness of many for many centuries.

In the fifteenth and sixteenth centuries the age of discovery opened up a new opportunity for a fresh advance in Christian missions outside Europe. The dominant powers at the time were Portugal and Spain, so the early missionary movement was Roman Catholic. Thus, the missionary initiative of the Roman Catholic Church opened up the issue of gospel and cultures afresh. It was especially Jesuit cross-cultural missionaries who raised the issue as they encountered many new cultures. They sought to indigenize the faith in those non-Western cultures with various experiments that adopted cultural customs, employed vernacular languages, and utilized the religious concepts and books of the people. For example, Matteo Ricci employed the Confucian name for "High God" (*Shangti*) to refer to the God of the Bible. He built on the continuity between the monotheistic character of *Shangti* and Yahweh. The Spanish Dominican and Franciscan orders vigorously op-

---

[12]Todd M. Johnson, "Contextualization: A New-Old Idea; Illustrations from the Life of an Italian Jesuit in 17th-Century India," *International Journal of Frontier Missions* 4 (1987): 10.

[13]Patrick's contextualization was a matter not only of relevance but also of challenge. "But if it is significant that he made himself at home in the 'pagan' vernacular, it is no less significant that this very instance is an example of his unwillingness to compromise with overt pagan practices" (William Henry Scott, "St. Patrick's Missionary Methods," *International Review of Mission* 50, no. 198 [1961]: 145).

posed Ricci because they saw this as a contamination of Christianity by Confucian paganism. The Dominican strategy was to coin a neologism, *T'ienzhu*, meaning "Lord of Heaven," to protect Christian orthodoxy. Unfortunately, after a protracted battle for over a century, the Roman Catholic Church finally sided with the Dominicans and suppressed the creative efforts of the Jesuits. Jesuit missionaries were recalled, and further experiments in contextualization lost urgency. In the nineteenth century the issues were raised once again by Protestant missions in the modern missionary movement. It is helpful to note what it was in both Roman Catholic and Protestant cross-cultural missionary experience that pressed questions of gospel and culture.

First, the initial communication of the gospel raised issues of gospel and culture. Imagine going to a Hindu culture that has never heard the gospel. How do you proclaim Jesus to the people? You must use the terms of the culture, and so which do you choose when asked who this person Jesus really is? One may believe the term *swami* to be biblical, since it means "lord." The trouble is that there are 330 million *swami*s, and so this is hardly good news. How about the term *avatar*? This refers to a descent of the god in bodily form to put down evil and establish the unfaltering rule of righteousness. Yet an *avatar* is taken up into the cyclical worldview of Hinduism, and an *avatar* makes no claim to finality in history. Why not just tell the historical narrative of the gospel? But his would be to reduce the gospel to *maya*, the illusory and transient material world of passing events that the Hindu believes to be unimportant. Other terms might appear initially promising: *kadavul* (transcendent god), *satguru* (teacher), *chit* (second member of triad of ultimate reality) or *adipurushan* (primal man). The problem is that all these terms "necessarily describe Jesus in terms of a model which embodies an interpretation of the world significantly different from the interpretation which arises when Jesus is accepted as Lord absolutely."[14] It would seem that if one adopts one of these terms, the gospel is compromised; there is a syncretistic accommodation to Hindu culture. Yet if one does not, the gospel is incomprehensible and thus certainly cannot be good news for its hearers. In either case, the good news is not communicated. This

---

[14]Lesslie Newbigin, "Christ and the Cultures," *Scottish Journal of Theology* 31, no. 1 (1978): 2-3.

experience has been multiplied thousands of times over in many cultural settings. Thus, for cross-cultural missionaries the problem of the initial communication of the gospel opened up the issue of gospel and culture.

"It is not possible to describe the life of a people without at every point coming across religion as the invisible background. Can the gospel take the place of the old religion? Can it maintain the unity of life while laying new foundations? An old native once said to a missionary in one of the islands of the Indian Archipelago: 'We know concerning everything exactly how we should do it, but when we follow you, we know nothing any more. If we accept your book, how shall we then build our houses? How shall we sow our fields and bury our dead?' That is the embarrassment every heathen has to face when he begins to appreciate the meaning of the gospel."

J. H. Bavink, *The Impact of Christianity on the Non-Christian World*, p. 21

Second, the translation of the Bible raised issues of gospel and culture. Missionaries who translated the Bible into Korean disagreed over whether to translate "God" as *Hananim* (the Supreme Being of indigenous Korean religion) or transliterate "Jehovah" into Korean or coin a new word as the Dominicans had done in China. To use the indigenous name for God seemed to compromise the Christian faith with pagan culture, but other terms were foreign and incomprehensible. Bible translators to the Tzeltal people in Mexico realized that there was no word for "king" or "kingdom," which are central to the gospel. The available expressions were "head of a clan," "president of a municipality" and "large-ranch owner." None of these faithfully communicates the idea of kingdom, and it would seem that to choose any of them would be to significantly alter the notion of king. What would a translator working in Balinese society, where the viper is the snake of paradise, do with the text in which Jesus refers to the Pharisees as a "brood of vipers"? This is hardly a rebuke in Bali! Or what would a missionary do in West Africa with the story of the publican beating his breast, when this gesture indicates taking pride in one's accomplishments in that culture?[15] The closest translators could get to "Jesus came into the world to save sinners" (1 Tim 1:15) in Tamil in their first translation was "Christ Jesus came into the world to give free board and lodging for rascals"![16] How does one translate the word "sin" into the shame-based Japanese culture, where the closest word means something like "imprudent"?[17] Every Bible translator has many stories of the problems raised by translation. Words are shaped by the cultural worldview, which is to some degree incompatible with the gospel. The whole process of Bible translation continues to raise fresh questions of gospel and culture.

> THE WHOLE PROCESS
> OF BIBLE TRANSLATION
> CONTINUES TO RAISE
> FRESH QUESTIONS OF
> GOSPEL AND CULTURE.

Third, the problem of what to do with certain social, cultural and moral practices after people became Christians raised the question of the relation of gospel to culture. A good example is polygamy in Africa. The following story by Walter Trobisch enables us to get a feel for the problem.[18] On a trip to Africa he visited a church, and after the service he talked with a boy whose father, Omodo, was a polygamist married to three women. The children of all three wives had been baptized, and all three wives had been baptized but only the first took Communion. Omodo had not been baptized. Trobisch went to visit the man. He found out that Omodo had taken the second wife at the prompting of his first wife (ironically, the only one who could take Communion) so that she could help with the work in the compound. It had been a costly sacrifice because of the high bride price. He had taken the third wife because her first husband, Omodo's brother, had died and she needed protection. The next brother in line who should have married her according to African custom was an elder in the church, and so he could not fulfill his obligation. The only way that Omodo could now be baptized and become a church member was if he

---

[15]Some of the examples in this paragraph are taken from Paul Hiebert, *Anthropological Insights for Missionaries* (Grand Rapids: Baker Books, 1985).

[16]Lesslie Newbigin, *Sin and Salvation* (London: SCM Press, 1956), p. 8.

[17]Harvie Conn, "Contextual Theologies: The Problem of Agendas," *Westminster Theological Journal* 52 (1990): 52.

[18]Walter Trobisch, "Congregational Responsibility for the Christian Individual," in *Readings in Missionary Anthropology II*, ed. William A. Smalley (Pasadena, CA: William Carey Library, 1978), pp. 233-35. I have shortened the story with some paraphrase.

divorced his last two wives. But the Bible forbade divorce, and besides, it would have put two vulnerable and now unmarried women in a socially difficult, even dangerous situation. The more Trobisch probed the situation, the more complex it became. Polygamy was woven into the warp and woof of African culture and this could not easily be eliminated. He was left pondering this question: what would he have done if he were a pastor in Omodo's town? Indeed, many missionaries in Africa have continued to ponder the issue of polygamy years later, wondering what should have been done.

Problems of social practice are not limited to such "exotic" practices as polygamy. Every custom and institution is shaped to some degree by the beliefs of the culture. As local customs and institutions clashed with the way missionaries were used to organizing their familial, political, economic and social lives, it raised the issue of what faithful contextualization would look like across the whole range of human life.

Fourth, the issue of the form of worship and liturgy raised questions of gospel and culture. For example, what was to be done with the drums in Africa? For many, drums were associated with erotic rituals in animistic paganism. Should drums be banned from Christian worship? Is that like burning the magic books in Acts 19:17-20? If so, what instruments should replace them in the middle of the African jungle—pipe organs? Too often in nineteenth- and twentieth-century missions the missionaries condemned such practices, yet these questions were raised.

Finally, as churches began to grow, questions surrounding theology arose and called for new reflection. In Africa missionaries faced the issue of the powers in traditional religion, a subject that Western theologies had not addressed. In Latin American issues of structural economic injustice were prominent, and yet theologies of the wealthy Western church were blind to such concerns. In Asia the intensely religious environment raised theological issues different from those faced by Western theologians in a secular setting. Unfortunately, missionaries often were in the grip of assumptions that could not allow a full contextual theologizing. For example, Korean Presbyterians were required to accept the Westminster Confession of Faith, a document written in 1640s with the use of Aristotelian categories that addressed issues of seventeenth century. How could it address issues in Korean culture? Harvie Conn comments on this missionary practice:

Our creedal formulations, structured to respond to a sixteenth-century cultural setting and its problems, lose their historical character as contextual confessions of faith and become cultural universals, having comprehensive validity in all times and settings. . . . The Reformation is completed, and we in the West wait for the churches of the Third World to accept as their statements of faith those shaped by a Western church three centuries ago in a *corpus Christianum*. . . . We have diminished their historical, cultural character. The creed as a missionary document framed in the uniqueness of an historical moment has too often been remythologized by white paternalism into a universal Essence for all times.[19]

The issue of contextual theology, as seen for example in the growing theologies in the third world (and it must be stated emphatically that all theologies are contextual, not just those of the third-world variety), is urgent. Only as a theology is contextual will Christians be able to own the faith and challenge the idolatrous spirits of their time. In other words, faithfulness is dependent upon it. Newbigin writes,

> ONLY AS A THEOLOGY IS CONTEXTUAL WILL CHRISTIANS BE ABLE TO OWN THE FAITH AND CHALLENGE THE IDOLATROUS SPIRITS OF THEIR TIME.

The responsibility of the church [is] to declare to each generation what is the faith, to expose and combat errors destructive of the faith, to expel from her body doctrines which pervert the faith, and to lead her members into a full and vivid apprehension of the faith. . . . This is always a fresh task in every generation, for thought is never still. The words in which the Church states its message in one generation have changed their meaning by the time the next has grown up. No verbal statement can be produced which relieves the Church of the responsibility continually to re-think and re-state its message. No appeal [to creeds and confessions] can alter the fact that the Church has to state in every new generation [and every new culture] how it interprets the historic faith, and how it relates it to the new thought and experience of its time. . . . Nothing can remove from the Church the responsibility for stating now what is the faith. It belongs to the essence of a living Church that it should be able and willing to do so.[20]

---

[19]Harvie Conn, "The Missionary Task of Theology: A Love/Hate Relationship?" *Westminster Theological Journal* 45 (1983): 17.
[20]Lesslie Newbigin, *The Reunion of the Church: A Defence of the South India Scheme* (London: SCM Press, 1948), pp. 137-38.

Thus, all of these attempts by cross-cultural missionaries to communicate the gospel and nurture faithfulness in newly formed Christian communities in new settings raised the issue of gospel and culture(s) afresh. Missionaries often responded with confidence in their Christian Western culture. Nevertheless, many missionaries sensed the problems and looked for new paths. The mission experience was awakening the Western church from its monocultural slumber.

This experience of new cultures led to the practices of indigenization (Protestants) and accommodation or adaptation (Catholics). Missionaries recognized the importance of the translation of the gospel into the varied cultures of humankind. Foreign cultures were taken more seriously. Yet, indigenization or accommodation is still far from ideal. We must appreciate that this was a big step forward, that missionaries were children of their time, and that they were usually much more culturally sensitive than their contemporaries. Nevertheless, their practice must be critiqued.

The problem was that colonialism enveloped the missionary enterprise. Western culture was considered to be superior; Western Christianity was considered to be suprahistorical and universally valid. Thus, indigenization was characterized by the following four elements. First, the Western expression of the gospel was considered normative, and the need was for that expression, not the gospel itself, to be accommodated to foreign cultures. Second, indigenization took place only in the younger churches. The West was exempt because the gospel supposedly was already faithfully indigenized there. Third, indigenization was a once-for-all process. It involved only the initial insertion of the gospel into a new cultural setting. The process was already successfully completed in the West—a fait accompli. When it was finally completed in a third-world country, then it was a finished task there too. And finally, indigenization was a concession to cultures outside the West. It was a pedagogical or strategic tool to communicate the gospel. Thus, it was peripheral and not essential to the gospel; it was necessary merely for evangelistic and missionary purposes.

Contextualization Today

Today, living in a different time, we are more awake to the issue of gospel and culture. A number of factors have led us to this place. First, the shattering of colonialism and imperialism has led to a more critical stance toward Western culture and more appreciation of non-Western cultures. Further, the growth and maturity of the third-world church has led to new cultural translations of the gospel that provide a critique of long-standing Western expressions. Moreover, the weakening of the Western church and the growing awareness that it is more culturally captive than could be imagined a hundred years ago have challenged the assumption that Western Christianity is normative. Finally, postmodernity and a global culture, where technology has made us much more aware of difference, have enabled Christians to gain a critical distance on the modern scientific worldview that has shaped us for centuries. Many unexamined assumptions that arise from this worldview and have shaped the modern missionary enterprise, including a notion of truth as supracultural ideas, are now called into question.

"The reference to mutual correction is the crucial one. All our reading of the Bible and all our Christian discipleship are necessarily shaped by the cultures which have formed us. . . . The only way in which the gospel can challenge our culturally conditioned interpretation of it is through the witness of those who read the Bible with minds shaped by other cultures. We have to listen to others. This mutual correction is sometimes unwelcome, but it is necessary and it is fruitful."

Lesslie Newbigin, *The Gospel in a Pluralist Society*, p. 196

Signs of renewed interest in the question of gospel and culture are evident in all ecclesial traditions. Since Vatican II (1962-1965) Roman Catholicism has wrestled with the issue favoring the word "inculturation." In the evangelical tradition the Willowbank Consultation on Gospel and Culture (1978) manifested a vital interest in the subject, making it a prominent topic since then. Since the Bangkok Conference of the Commission of World Mission and Evangelism of the World Council of Churches (1973) and the Nairobi meeting of the World Council of Churches (1975), it has been a vital item on the agenda in the ecumenical tradition.

There is much debate on every aspect of the issue of contextualization, and a number of models of contextualization have been advanced. But perhaps there are at least six general points of consensus among these differing and contradictory models.

- No single expression of the gospel stands above history and culture and therefore is universally normative. The gospel must be at home in and at odds with all cultures.

> NO SINGLE EXPRESSION OF THE GOSPEL STANDS ABOVE HISTORY AND CULTURE AND THEREFORE IS UNIVERSALLY NORMATIVE. THE GOSPEL MUST BE AT HOME IN AND AT ODDS WITH ALL CULTURES.

- Contextualization is a process that is concerned with every part of life. Craig Ott, Stephen Strauss and Timothy Tennent rightly tell us, "Scripture should penetrate every aspect of society and transform every part of culture. . . . Contextualization must be comprehensive."[21] Flemming concurs, saying that contextualization "must take place at many levels: evangelism, preaching, Bible translation, hermeneutics, theologizing, discipleship, Christian ethics and social involvement, worship, church structures and leadership, and theological education among them. In short, it has to do with the mission of the church in the broadest sense."[22]

- Contextualization is an issue for all churches—the West as well as other parts of the world. Contextualization is a concern not only for the younger non-Western churches but also for the older churches of the West. Indeed, perhaps it is in the West that the problem is more acute, suffering from centuries of neglect.

- Contextualization is an ongoing process. It is not something that takes place at the point of the introduction of the gospel to culture and then achieves its goal. Two things keep it as a continuing concern: culture continues to change, and no church ever completes the task and reaches full faithfulness.

- Contextualization is constitutive of the gospel. And so the issue facing us is not one of making a decision for or against contextualizing the gospel,

---

[21]Craig Ott, Stephen J. Strauss and Timothy C. Tennent, *Encountering Theology of Mission: Biblical Foundations, Historical Developments, and Contemporary Issues* (Grand Rapids: Baker Academic, 2010), pp. 284-85.
[22]Flemming, *Contextualization*, p. 20.

but rather of being faithful to it in our theory and practice of contextualization. "One might say that *every* perception of Christian truth and practice is contextual. The question is not whether we will contextualize the gospel. The question is whether we will do good contextualization or bad contextualization."[23]

- It is the gospel that must be contextualized, not a theological system or religious teaching.

Models of Contextualization

Despite some agreement on certain issues, a wide divergence of understandings and models of contextualization remains. Stephen Bevans has helpfully mapped out six of these models.[24] We will briefly examine two of them—the translation and anthropological models—because they stand at opposite ends of the spectrum, and a brief analysis can highlight some of the issues involved in contextualization.

The translation model is characteristic of evangelical and traditional Roman Catholic circles. It employs the analogy or metaphor of the translation of literature from one language to another. At the heart of this model is the translation of an unchanging message into various cultures. The gospel has priority and must be inserted into culture. The gospel is somehow supracultural; there is a gospel "core" that stands above culture that is "wrapped" in cultural expression. The gospel is the essential "kernel," which is encased in a disposable, nonessential cultural husk. Contextualization takes place as the pure gospel is separated from its culturally bound mode of expression and then contextualized within another cultural husk.

This model can be commended for taking the gospel message with utmost seriousness; the word of God is universally true and cannot be absorbed into any human culture. It is especially appropriate for situations of primary evangelism when translating the message of the gospel from one culture to another. There is a problem, though, with the view of revelation: it is primarily propositional and informational. Revelation is considered to be truths or doctrines that transcend culture and history. This is indebted to

[23]Ott, Strauss and Tennent, *Encountering Theology*, p. 266.
[24]Stephen B. Bevans, *Models of Contextual Theology* (rev. ed.; Maryknoll, NY: Orbis Books, 1992).

the Greek view, which sees truth as unchanging ideas, as opposed to a biblical view, which sees truth as bound up in events within history. One also wonders if the kernel/husk or core/wrapping image is plausible. Can the gospel be so easily separated from its cultural form?

Newbigin writes of his missionary experience in India: "My Christianity was syncretistic, but so was theirs. Yet neither of us could discover that without the challenge of the other. Such is the situation in cross-cultural mission. . . . So the missionary, if he is at all awake, finds himself, as I did, in a new situation. He becomes, as a bearer of the gospel, a critic of his own culture. He finds there the Archimedean point. He sees his own culture with the Christian eyes of a foreigner, and the foreigner can see what the native cannot see."

Lesslie Newbigin, *A Word in Season*, p. 68

The anthropological model stands in stark contrast to the translation model. It starts with the primacy of culture rather than the gospel. Revelation is considered to be the personal, loving and sustaining presence of God in every culture. Culture provides a twofold context and starting point: first, a dialogue with culture uncovers the needs and problems that must be addressed by the gospel; second, one looks for areas of culture where God is already revealing himself as opportunities to express the gospel. The missionary is more like a "treasure hunter" than a "pearl merchant."[25] Pearl merchants have something to give, whereas treasure hunters come empty-handed looking for the treasure already present in various cultures of the world. One may discover, for example, a strong communal solidarity in Asian or African culture as a way to express an understanding of the community called to embody the gospel.

This model has a number of things to commend it: it recognizes that God has not left himself without a witness in any culture of the world; it recognizes that good news can be heard only when one understand the needs and concerns of people; it will open up a plurality of genuine cultural responses

---

[25]See Robert T. Rush, "From Pearl Merchant to Treasure Hunter: The Missionary Yesterday and Today," *Catholic Mind* 76 (September 1978): 6-10.

to the gospel. But there also are serious problems. The gospel is an announcement of news of something that happened. This is not something that can be discovered but rather must be proclaimed. Moreover, it does not account sufficiently for the sin and idolatry of culture.

Contrasting these two models, we begin to see that each is stressing something important while at the same time neglecting other important emphases:

- The translation model is a redemption-centered approach (culture is fallen and in need of a message to redeem it), while the anthropological model is creation-centered (culture is good and the scene of God's work).

- The translation model is the good news of Jesus that comes from outside, while the anthropological model stresses its relevance and expression from within culture.

- The translation model stresses redemptive or special revelation, while the anthropological model stresses creation or general revelation.

- The translation model fears syncretism and tends toward irrelevance with an ahistorical gospel, while the anthropological model fears irrelevance and tends toward syncretism with an uncritical acceptance of cultural categories.

- The translation model stresses the message to be contextualized, while the anthropological model stresses the culture into which the message is to be contextualized.

MACROCONTEXTUAL DIFFERENCES

Contextualization faces different issues in various parts of the world. The different histories and acute problems of each place give a different color to the whole process. We can observe four macrocontexts that shape contextualization differently. In the African church we find the problem of cultural estrangement created by the suppression of their cultural memory and identity by European racism and ethnocentrism in the colonial period. The crucial issue is to recover and faithfully embody the gospel in the traditional culture of Africa. In a situation where so much of pagan animism has gone underground because it was simply dismissed by Western missionaries, an authentic encounter is essential. It is complicated, of course, by the advent of Western culture in globalization and the incursion of Islamic culture from the north. Nevertheless, for the health of the African church this is an urgent need.

In the Latin American church there is widespread poverty and misery upheld by unjust social, economic, political and ecclesial structures, both national and international. The need in contextualization is for an analysis of culture and of the processes of social change that will contribute to a quest for justice. In a situation of dire poverty and injustice, where so many have turned to Marxism and revolution for answers, a church that simply upholds the status quo will be rightly dismissed.

The Asian church exists as a small minority in the midst of ancient and powerful religious traditions that stand as comprehensive visions of life and thus give foundational shape to the culture. The need of contextualization in that context is to relate the gospel to the comprehensive cultural expressions of these vital religious traditions. The church must find a way to locate the insights and reject the idolatry in each area of life. Syncretism or withdrawing into isolation is a real danger.

The Western church has long embraced a symbiotic relationship between the gospel and culture. Whereas the problem in Africa, Asia and Latin America is that the gospel often is viewed as foreign to culture, the problem in the West is that the gospel has been at home for so long that it is captive to the unrecognized idols of culture. The need is to recover the countercultural dimensions of the gospel while using power responsibly in the service of the gospel in democratic cultures that afford this opportunity. Moreover, a missionary encounter with Western culture is essential for the global church because this culture itself is in the process of being globalized.

> WHEREAS THE PROBLEM IN AFRICA, ASIA AND LATIN AMERICA IS THAT THE GOSPEL OFTEN IS VIEWED AS FOREIGN TO CULTURE, THE PROBLEM IN THE WEST IS THAT THE GOSPEL HAS BEEN AT HOME FOR SO LONG THAT IT IS CAPTIVE TO THE UNRECOGNIZED IDOLS OF CULTURE.

FAITHFUL CONTEXTUALIZATION

In this last section I offer for consideration five elements of a faithful approach to contextualization.

The church at the crossroads between gospel and culture. Often the issue of contextualization is considered from the standpoint of the relationship between gospel and culture, as if these were two discrete entities that need to be related. The gospel is a universally valid message that announces what God has done for the world. Yet it is never an abstract, disembodied message. It is always incarnated and expressed, in word or life, in some cultural idiom. And culture is a whole way of living together built up by a human community that is passed along from one generation to another. So neither is culture an abstract entity; it is an embodied way of life.

The gospel calls for faithful living in all of life. Yet each culture shapes all of human life by a different set of beliefs. The church is part of the cultural community and the people of God. As such, it indwells two irreconcilable stories. How does one solve this painful tension? The Christian community finds itself at the crossroads between the gospel and culture, the place where two incompatible ways of life meet and encounter one another. Contextualization is not the theoretical exercise of relating two entities, gospel and culture; rather, it is the concrete daily task of finding ways to faithfully live out the gospel across the whole spectrum of human life in the midst of a culture shaped by a different set of religious beliefs. The very nature of the gospel as a comprehensive call to an all-embracing obedience, and the very nature of human life as culturally embodied, mean that this is an unavoidable and ongoing process. There is a missionary encounter between two ways of life that meet in the very life of the Christian community. The struggle is to find a faithful way embodied and expressed, as it always is, within the culture.

Andrew Walls has expressed the unbearable tension of belonging to two communities in terms of two principles. The first is the "indigenizing" principle. Since it is impossible to separate the individual from the network of his or her social relationships, it is necessary to live out the whole of one's life as a member of one's own society. The church seeks to be at home, and this includes a place where its faith can settle. Thus, the indigenizing principle requires the church's people to live faithfully and fully as members of their own culture, implicated in the network of institutions, practices and patterns of life of their context. In tension with this principle is a second one, equally inspired by the gospel. This is the "pilgrim" principle, which warns the Christian that "to be faithful to Christ will put him out of step with his society; for that society never existed . . . which could absorb the word of Christ painlessly into its system."[26] One is part of culture and therefore at home; one is called by the gospel, which demands a different pattern of life, and therefore at odds.

The first commitment is to the gospel and the biblical story. In resolving this struggle, the church's first commitment and loyalty must be to the

"We would . . . prefer to use the term *possessio*, to take possession. . . . Within the framework of the non-Christian life, customs and practices serve idolatrous tendencies and drive a person away from God. The Christian life takes them in hand and turns them in an entirely new direction; they acquire an entirely different content. Even though in external form there is much that resembles past practices, in reality everything has become new, the old has in essence passed away and the new has come. . . . [Christ] fills each thing, each word and each practice with a new meaning and gives it new direction. Such is neither 'adaptation' nor accommodation; it is in essence the legitimate taking possession of something by him to whom all power is given in heaven and on earth."

J. H. Bavinck, *The Science of Missions*, pp. 178-79

gospel—to faithfully embody and live it out in every department of human life. Here, properly understanding the nature of the gospel is critical. In the humanist tradition that shaped Western culture it was assumed that ultimately reliable truth was to be found in ideas that transcend culture and history. These ideas are first of all in the mind of God, given expression in Scripture, and arranged in our theology. The gospel, then, becomes a timeless idea that stands above culture and history to be applied to our context. This is part of the problem that has plagued the Western missionary enterprise.

---

[26]Andrew Walls, "The Gospel as Prisoner and Liberator of Culture," in *The Missionary Movement in Christian History: Studies in the Transmission of Faith* (Maryknoll, NY: Orbis Books, 1996), p. 8.

The biblical notion of truth is different. Truth is found in the mighty acts of God in history to give meaning to history. These deeds of God are directed to the restoration of creation. There is an underlying unity that leads to Jesus Christ. It is supremely in Jesus—his life, death and resurrection—that truth can be found. Here the kingdom of God as the goal of universal history is revealed and accomplished. These mighty deeds of God in history are given authoritative interpretation in Scripture. The gospel reveals the story told in the Bible as the true story of the whole world. Thus, truth is historical (in God's mighty acts), personal (especially revealed in Jesus Christ) and narratival (expressed in a story that is true for all). Contextualization is not about applying universal ideas to new contexts but rather finding ways to faithfully translate and indwell this story of the renewal of creation in the various cultural contexts of the world.

This story carries divine authority; it is God's word. So in authentic contextualization the cultural story and its lived expression must be evaluated from the standpoint of Scripture, not the other way around. The Bible gives us the truth, and each culture must be understood and evaluated in its light. We do not have two sources of truth to be coordinated in a negotiated settlement but rather a true story that must find faithful expression in each culture of the world. So, authentic contextualization means that the church unapologetically takes a committed stance within the biblical story and from within that story attempts to understand culture.

> IN AUTHENTIC CONTEXTUALIZATION THE CULTURAL STORY AND ITS LIVED EXPRESSION MUST BE EVALUATED FROM THE STANDPOINT OF SCRIPTURE, NOT THE OTHER WAY AROUND.

A missionary encounter with culture. Faithful contextualization requires that the church understand its cultural context. It is especially important to understand the religious roots that shape a culture. There is a collective and communal commitment to a way of life rooted in fundamentally religious beliefs. Our secular blinders often have kept us from understanding this: all cultures are communally embodied ways of life shaped and nourished by religious beliefs that are collectively held. All religious beliefs apart from the gospel will be idolatrous, serving some aspect of creation rather than the Creator. Faithful contextualization requires that the church understand well those religious beliefs and how they shape the various dimensions of culture.

It is equally important to recognize God's common grace in upholding cultures. The various practices, institutions, customs and systems of culture are not totally corrupt because of core idolatry. In fact, God continues to uphold his creation. There is much justice, stewardship and truth in all the cultures of the world. In some cultures, most notably the West, the good in culture is the result not only of God's common grace, but also of the influence and salting effect of the gospel in its history with a culture.

When we understand that every culture is shaped by idolatrous core beliefs but at the same time is a place where much good is still to be found, it will be clear that viewing culture though the lens of the gospel will involve both affirmation and critique, embrace and rejection, a yes and a no. Every aspect, institution and custom of culture will manifest something of God's creational design but at the same time will be distorted by sinful idolatry. Whether it be a political or economic system, a family structure, a standard of ethics, a way of knowledge, language or any other part of culture, both that which is creationally good and that which has been polluted and twisted by idolatry will be present. A missionary encounter with culture will be a matter of growing discernment and wisdom—learning how not to be conformed to the world but rather to be transformed in the renewing of the mind, learning what is creationally good and how it has been distorted, learning how to say yes and no.

"A culture operates as both binoculars and blinkers, helping you see some things and keeping you from seeing others. So we shall need to be consciously critical of whatever form of the Christian tradition—in our case, the evangelical tradition—we have inherited. . . . Being unaware of our own blind spots, we shall be tempted to ascribe to those expressions of the Gospel in the theology, liturgy, and behavior patterns which we know best a finality, fullness and universality which may only be claimed for the Gospel itself, and for the Christ of whom it speaks."

J. I. Packer, "The Gospel: Its Content and Communication," p. 101

Discernment by way of a threefold dialogue. A Chinese proverb says, "If you want to know about water, don't ask a fish." The fish swims in the water as its natural environment all day and cannot discern when the water is polluted. We all have our blind spots because the idols of our own culture are so familiar to us and we have long accommodated ourselves to them. We even wear our cultural prejudices as spectacles when we read Scripture. So how is it possible for the church to get any kind of distance on its own culture to critique it? There is no "transcultural theology" or "metatheology"[27] or "super-cultural theology"[28] that stands above culture and is universally true for all.

> THERE IS NO "TRANSCULTURAL THEOLOGY" OR "METATHEOLOGY" OR "SUPER-CULTURAL THEOLOGY" THAT STANDS ABOVE CULTURE AND IS UNIVERSALLY TRUE FOR ALL.

All theology is expressed in a certain language with certain cultural categories addressing specific issues. Only the Scriptures can carry universal authority. Every human voice and life that answers the gospel will do so in a particular cultural form. We may not exalt any human tradition to the place of Scripture. That is the ethnocentric pitfall.

The only way we can avoid syncretism and relativism is in dialogue with the whole church around the Scriptures. Paul tells us that the love of Christ revealed in the gospel is so wide and long and high and deep that it is only "together with all God's people" that we will be able to grasp it (Eph 3:18-19). This is not only together with other members of our own congregation or denomination, as important as that is. We do need to labor together with our brothers and sisters with whom we share the life of Christ in a particular place. However, believers together in one place will share many of the same blind spots and prejudices. Our dialogue must be broader.

Rather, a threefold dialogue will enable us to have the kind of critical distance that we need in order to properly judge our culture. First, faithfulness will require a dialogue that is cross-confessional. We need to hear from those in other branches of the Christian family who see things quite differently than we do as they stand within a different theological history.

[27]Hiebert, *Anthropological Insights*, pp. 217-19.
[28]Clemens Sedmak, *Doing Local Theology: A Guide for Artisans of a New Humanity* (Maryknoll, NY: Orbis Books, 2002), p. 79.

We have already noted in a previous chapter, for example, how much of the Western church has been awakened to the importance of the Spirit to mission because of our Pentecostal brothers and sisters. Second, the dialogue should be cross-cultural. Churches in other parts of the world will have a much better eye for the idols that shape us, and vice versa. Our cultures give us prejudices: although a culture helps us see certain things, it blinds us to others. The global church has been awakened to the communal dimensions of the faith because of the African church and to the gospel and structural injustice because of the theological work of Latin Americans. As Paul Hiebert puts it, the church is a kind of "universal hermeneutical community, in which Christians and theologians from different lands check one another's cultural biases."[29] Third, the dialogue needs to be cross-historical. There is much to learn in the way the people of God have struggled to be faithful in different eras of history. The currents that shaped them often will be quite different from the currents shaping us. Only as the church in various parts of the world takes a posture of humility will dialogue produce mutual enrichment and mutual critique.

The ongoing process of contextualization. The task will never be complete. There never comes a time when we can say, "Now the gospel is faithfully contextualized." This is not only because of our sinful imperfection but also because culture is constantly changing. The process of contextualization is an ongoing process. Christopher Wright describes contextualization as a "constant missiological task" from biblical times to the present, which is ever at work determining "the fine lines between cultural relevance and theological syncretism."[30]

As the church continues to struggle to live faithfully in the biblical story, encountering its culture with appreciation and critique, its life will be one of challenging relevance. It will challenge a death-dealing way of life that comes from serving idols, and the good news will be relevant to our contemporaries. It must be stressed that it is not a matter of whether we will contextualize the gospel in our lives; it is only a matter of whether we will

---

[29]Paul Hiebert, "Missiological Implications of an Epistemological Shift," *Theological Students Fellowship Bulletin* 8 (May 1985): 16.
[30]Christopher J. H. Wright, *The Mission of God: Unlocking the Bible's Grand Narrative* (Downers Grove, IL: InterVarsity Press, 2006), p. 447.

do so faithfully and offer with the witness of our lives, deeds and words the authentic good news of Jesus in ways that make clear that it is, in fact, good news.

FURTHER READING

Bevans, Stephen B. *Models of Contextual Theology*. Revised and expanded edition. Maryknoll, NY: Orbis, 1992.

Bosch, David. *Transforming Mission: Paradigm Shifts in Theology of Mission*. Maryknoll, NY: Orbis, 1991, pp. 420-57.

Conn, Harvie M. *Eternal Word and Changing Worlds: Theology, Anthropology, and Mission in Trialogue*. Grand Rapids: Zondervan, 1984.

Flemming, Dean. *Contextualization in the New Testament: Patterns for Theology and Mission*. Downers Grove, IL: IVP Academic, 2005.

Newbigin, Lesslie. "Christ and Cultures." *Scottish Journal of Theology* 31 (1978): 1-22.

DISCUSSION QUESTIONS

1. Discuss some of the examples shared in this chapter: How would you respond to the Nepali pastor? Do you think the practice of the woman in the African Independent Church was syncretistic or not? What would you have done with drums or the *sangoma* in Africa if you had been a missionary in the nineteenth century? Was invoking the spirit of Korean ancestors syncretistic?

2. Discuss the dilemma of living faithfully in the West today by considering some of the examples in this chapter: the PhD student, the businessperson, the Christian teacher in the public school. Tell stories from your own experience to illustrate this dilemma.

3. Consider and explain the various ways Western Christians might feel the tension between gospel and culture.

ESSAY TOPICS

1. Explain the issues of contextualization in terms of ethnocentrism and relativism as well as syncretism and irrelevance. Give examples to illustrate the problems.

2. Explain why the Gospel of John has been so important to mission thinkers reflecting on the problem of gospel and culture. Illustrate John's mode of gospel communication and why this is important for contextualization.

3. Evaluate the model of faithful contextualization offered in this text.

8

Toward a Missiology of
Western Culture

CB

THROUGHOUT THE NINETEENTH and early twentieth centuries, when the missionary movement had momentum, mission was understood as taking place in non-Western cultures. There was little critical reflection on Western culture, where the gospel had been at home for centuries. But it was precisely the missionary movement that would change that through what mission advocates in the nineteenth century called the "blessed reflex" or "reflexive action."[1] They argued that the missionary impulse would result in a reflex action that would rebound back on the sending church in the West, which in turn would reap some benefits of this missionary activity. These benefits were never spelled out, and this theme gradually disappeared at the end of the nineteenth century as mission became increasingly woven together with colonialism. Today the dynamic of reflexive action is becoming increasingly evident.

This process was initially evident with particular missionaries whose cross-cultural experience gave them critical distance and new eyes for a fresh look at the church in Western culture. They were able to see how the religious beliefs of Western culture compromised the gospel and the witness of the church. But the dynamic is now taking place at a global level. The growth and maturing of the churches in the majority world now provide a critique and a challenge to the Western church. It can see itself and its culture with new eyes. Moreover, it can rethink its identity and stance toward their culture. In this new situation a missiology of Western culture can develop.

---

[1]I owe the insights regarding "blessed reflex" and "reflexive action" to Wilbert Shenk in private correspondence.

AN URGENT TASK

Lesslie Newbigin believed that developing a missiology of Western culture is "the most urgent task facing the universal church at this time,"[2] and that therefore "there is no higher priority for the research work of missiologists than the question of what would be involved in a genuinely missionary encounter between the gospel and this modern Western culture."[3] Several factors support such a strong claim. First, Western culture is the most powerful global force in our world today. It has reached far beyond its lands of origin and is now the shared culture of the urban centers of the world. Second, Western culture has a long association with the Christian faith that has made it almost immune to critique. The countercultural thrust of the gospel has been eclipsed, and the church has accommodated itself to the idols that permeate the West. Third, Western culture is perhaps the most powerful cultural force we have seen in human history. The breathtaking advances in technology have given these cultural powers un-precedented access to people's lives. The "acids of modernity" have had a destructive impact on the Christian faith in the West, and there is no reason to think that the same thing will not happen in non-Western churches. Fourth, even though the Western church has slipped in terms of its global influence, it still maintains a significant leadership role in the global mission of the church. It seems that "'modern' Western culture will continue to strengthen its grip on the life of human communities every-where and—therefore—Christian churches that have so long accepted a syncretistic co-existence with the 'modern' worldview will continue to bear the prime responsibility for articulating the Christian message for this particular culture. That remains a task which calls for the best intel-lectual and spiritual energies we can bring to it."[4] In this chapter I will sketch the contours of a missiology of Western culture.

---

[2]Lesslie Newbigin, "Culture of Modernity," in *Dictionary of Mission: Theology, History, Perspectives*, ed. Karl Müller et al. (Maryknoll, NY: Orbis Books, 1997), p. 98.

[3]Lesslie Newbigin, *Foolishness to the Greeks: The Gospel and Western Culture* (Grand Rapids: Eerdmans, 1986), p. 3.

[4]Lesslie Newbigin, "The Christian Message versus 'Modern' Culture," in *Mission in the 1990s*, ed. Gerald H. Anderson, James M. Phillips and Robert T. Coote (Grand Rapids: Eerdmans; New Haven: Overseas Ministries Study Center, 1991), p. 26.

Missionary Encounter with Culture: The Faithful Posture of the Church

The faithful posture that the church must take within any cultural context is that of a missionary encounter. When the Christian community faithfully embodies the gospel, a missionary encounter occurs between the gospel and the reigning public doctrine that shapes the society. Insofar as the church is faithful to the gospel, then, there will be three aspects to this missionary encounter. First, the foundational beliefs shared by a cultural community will be challenged. A missionary encounter is about a clash of ultimate and comprehensive stories: the biblical story and the cultural story. A missionary encounter requires that the church live fully in the biblical story and interpret its culture in the light of that story. Second, the church will challenge the idolatrous cultural story and offer the gospel as a counterstory, as a credible alternative way of life. Finally, the lives and words of those in a Christian community will be a call for radical conversion, an invitation to understand and live in the world in the light of the gospel.

Ian Barns captures the heart of a missionary encounter when he says that the "purpose is not to make a 'space' for Christianity *within* a wide pluralism, but to recover the alternative universalist counter claims of Christianity based on the . . . life, death and resurrection of Jesus."[5] All three adjectives are important: "alternative" because the gospel's claims present another way of understanding and living in the world; "universalist" because the call of the gospel is valid for all people and claims the whole of human life; and "counter" because the gospel challenges the story of modernity, calling for repentance and conversion.

A missionary encounter with culture does not mean an anticultural stance[6] nor a polemical opposition that simply seeks to displace a public doctrine of culture with a Christian one. There is much about Western culture that is good, and so there will be dialogical engagement with culture that embraces the creational good while rejecting the idolatrous distortion.

Yet the church in the West is not well positioned to assume this posture of a missionary encounter. First, the church does not have a critical distance on its

---

[5]Ian Barns, "Christianity in a Pluralist Society: A Dialogue with Lesslie Newbigin," *St. Mark's Review* 158 (winter 1994): 29.
[6]See Michael W. Goheen, "Is Lesslie Newbigin's Model of Contextualization Anticultural?" *Mission Studies* 19, no. 2 (2002): 136-58.

own culture. The church is a fish that takes its cultural water for granted. Second, the myth of a Christian culture continues to set the mind of the Western church at ease. This myth assumes that the West is, or once was, a Christian culture. If the culture is Christian, there is no need to analyze its assumptions or develop a counter-cultural instinct. Third, the myth of a neutral secular or pluralistic society is powerful. A neutral culture poses no danger to the gospel but supposedly offers a level playing field for all faith commitments. However, this recog-

> THE MYTH OF A
> CHRISTIAN CULTURE
> CONTINUES TO SET THE
> MIND OF THE WESTERN
> CHURCH AT EASE.

nizes neither the deeply religious foundational beliefs of the West nor the threat that they pose to the public witness of the faith. "The idea that we ought to be able to expect some kind of neutral secular political order, which presupposes no religious or ideological beliefs, and which holds the ring impartially for a plurality of religions to compete with one another, has no adequate foundation."[7] The humanistic faith of the West is a powerful *religious* faith that brooks no rivals. But it has a smiling face: it offers peace, privilege, prosperity and a place in the sun to those who will accept its terms for life in the public square. In this way it domesticates all other religious claims and simply relegates them to a private sphere with the promise of tolerance.

"As a young missionary, I used to spend an evening each week at the Ramakrishna Mission, studying with the monks the Hindu Upanishads and the Christian Gospels. The great hall of the monastery was lined with pictures of the great religious figures of history, among them Jesus. Each year on Christmas Day, worship was offered before the picture of Jesus. It was clear to me as a missionary that this was an example of syncretism: Jesus had simply been co-opted into the Hindu worldview. It was only slowly that I began to see that my own Christianity had this same character, that I too had, in measure, co-opted Jesus into the world-view of my culture."

Lesslie Newbigin, *Mission and the Crisis of Western Culture*, pp. 1-2

---

[7]Lesslie Newbigin, *Trinitarian Doctrine for Today's Mission* (1963; repr., Carlisle: Paternoster, 1998), p. 46.

What might be needed for the Western church to recover its faithful missionary posture? Wilbert Shenk proposes two urgent tasks. The first is to nurture an inward mission consciousness. The church must develop a deep consciousness of its own foundational missional identity, "a people living out their fundamental role and purpose, mission."[8] The second is to foster an outward mission consciousness. The church must also "become self-critically aware of the 'kingdom of the Western world,' which is counterposed to the reign of God," recognizing that "wherever 'this gospel of the kingdom of God' is proclaimed, deep tension with the world appears."[9]

Shenk's agenda suggests three important tasks: a theological task that faithfully articulates the gospel of the kingdom; an ecclesiological task that explores the missional identity of the church; and a cultural task that probes the story and fundamental assumptions of Western culture. The theological task is significant because the authority and the power of the gospel have been narrowed and muted as it has accommodated itself to the more ultimate religious beliefs of Western culture. The ecclesiological task demands our attention because the church has turned its gaze inward and neglected its missional identity. And to the degree that the church has looked outward, its mission has been narrowed in conformity with a pared-down gospel. The cultural task is important because the Western church has not fostered a critical attitude toward its culture and thus has allowed itself to be shaped more by the cultural story than by the biblical story. Newbigin observes,

> The peaceful co-existence of Christianity with post-Enlightenment culture . . . has endured so long that it is hard for the Church now to recover the standpoint for a genuinely missionary approach to our "modern" culture. . . . The Church has lived so long as a permitted and even privileged minority, accepting relegation to the private sphere in a culture whose public life is controlled by a totally different vision of reality, that it has almost lost the power to address a radical challenge to that vision and therefore to "modern Western civilization" as a whole.[10]

[8]Wilbert R. Shenk, *Write the Vision: The Church Renewed* (Valley Forge, PA: Trinity Press International, 1995), p. 87.
[9]Ibid., p. 94.
[10]Lesslie Newbigin, *The Other Side of 1984: Questions for the Churches* (Geneva: WCC, 1983), pp. 22-23.

If the church is to renew its missionary encounter with its culture, these three tasks are urgent.

THE THEOLOGICAL TASK: LIBERATING THE GOSPEL

The question is whether or not the Western church has gotten itself into a situation "where the biblical message has been so thoroughly adapted to fit into our modern Western culture that we are unable to hear the radical challenge, the call for radical conversion which it presents in our culture."[11] If this is true—and I believe it is—then it will cripple the Western church in its missionary calling in and to Western culture. Taking hold of the authentic good news of Jesus Christ will be the first item on our agenda. This involves at least five interrelated threads.

First, we must take hold of the gospel as public truth. The good news is an announcement of what God has done, is doing, and will do in Jesus Christ for the renewal of the creation and human life. It is a claim made with universal intent: the gospel is true and therefore universally valid for all peoples and all of human life. Two battlefronts must be engaged. On the one hand, the relativism of our pluralistic culture threatens any claim to truth. Those in the liberal wing of the church often have allowed the gospel to be accommodated to this relativism. The gospel is considered to be the tribal story of Israel or the story of one particular religious tradition that possesses no validity beyond those who inhabit it. On the other hand, believers in the more conservative wing of the church often have allowed the gospel to be accommodated to the continuing influence of Enlightenment thought. In an admirable attempt to protect the truth of the gospel they have reduced it to unchanging ideas that transcend history. In contrast to both of these traditions, the truth of the Bible is found in a person and in events in which God has acted. It is especially in the life, death and resurrection of Jesus Christ that we understand the truth about the world. What God has accomplished in these events has universal significance and validity.

This can be clarified further in the second point: we must take hold of the

> FIRST, WE MUST TAKE HOLD OF THE GOSPEL AS PUBLIC TRUTH.

---

[11]Lesslie Newbigin, "The Bible and Our Contemporary Mission," *Clergy Review* 69, no. 1 (1984): 11.

gospel as a true story. Western culture has been shaped by at least two different traditions: the biblical tradition and the rationalistic-humanist tradition. What distinguishes these two is where ultimately reliable truth is said to be found. In the rationalistic-humanist tradition truth is found in unchanging ideas that transcend history. In the biblical tradition truth is found in the mighty acts of God that constitute an unfolding narrative that is moving toward a goal. This story is found in the Bible and claims to be universal history. It offers an answer to the origin and destiny of the whole world and offers a clue to the meaning of world history and human life within it.

In order to be faithful to its missionary calling, the church must understand the Bible as one true story, which provides the context to understand the meaning of our whole lives—personal, social, cultural. Only in its canonical whole can it address our culture. If the story of the Bible is fragmented into bits (historical-critical, devotional, systematic-theological, moral), it can easily be absorbed into the reigning story of culture. Thus, holding to the Bible as one comprehensive story in contrast to the comprehensive worldview of a culture is a matter of life and death. Interestingly, Australian sociologist John Carroll, who does not profess to be a Christian, says that the "waning of Christianity as practised in the West is easy to explain. The Christian churches have comprehensively failed in their one central task—to retell their foundation story in a way that might speak to the times."[12]

This leads to the third element: we must take hold of the gospel in its comprehensive scope. If the Bible is indeed universal history, then it makes a comprehensive claim on our lives—individual and communal, social and cultural—and on the lives of all peoples. It claims to understand and narrate the world as it really is. Thus, the way we understand all of human life depends on what we believe to be the true story of the world. The gospel is not a message that can be slotted into a little private religious realm of life that concerns the future, or the moral

> THE GOSPEL IS NOT A MESSAGE THAT CAN BE SLOTTED INTO A LITTLE PRIVATE RELIGIOUS REALM OF LIFE.

---

[12]John Carroll, *The Existential Jesus* (Brunswick, VIC: Scribe Publications, 2008), p. 7.

and "religious" life of humankind, or the interior or church life of humankind. It demands that we conform the whole of our lives to its message.

A missionary encounter occurs when the church believes the Bible to be the true story of the world and embodies its comprehensive claims as a countercultural community in the midst of the dominant cultural story. Richard Bauckham helpfully formulates the comprehensive authority of the biblical story.

> The Bible's total story is a metanarrative. That is, it sketches in narrative form the meaning of all reality. To accept the authority of this story is to enter it and to inhabit it. It is to live in the world as the world is portrayed in this story. It is to let this story define our identity and our relationship to God and to others. It is to read the narratives of our own lives and of the societies in which we live as narratives that take their meaning from this metanarrative that overarches them all. To accept this metanarrative as the one within which we live is to see the world differently and to live within it differently from the way we would if we inhabited another metanarrative or framework of universal meaning.[13]

Since both the biblical and the cultural stories make comprehensive and absolute claims, only one story can be *the* basic and foundational story for life. The Western church is in a state of syncretism to the degree that it has allowed the biblical story to be accommodated into the more comprehensive cultural story in much of its public life.

"The gospel must necessarily clash with contemporary culture. It must challenge the whole 'fiduciary framework' within which our culture operates. It must call unequivocally for radical conversion, a conversion of the mind so that things are seen differently, and a conversion of the will so that things are done differently. It must decline altogether the futile attempt to commend the biblical vision of how things are by seeking to adjust it to the assumptions of our culture."

Lesslie Newbigin, *The Other Side of 1984*, p. 53

---

[13]Richard Bauckham, *God and the Crisis of Freedom: Biblical and Contemporary Perspectives* (Louisville: Westminster John Knox, 2002), pp. 64-65.

The fourth element is the restorative nature of the gospel. The good news is an announcement, not that we will be taken out of this world to an otherworldly heaven, but that God will restore our lives as part of this good creation. The notion of an otherworldly salvation has been particularly damaging to the church's mission. N. T. Wright comments, "As long as we see salvation in terms of going to heaven when we die the main work of the church is bound to be seen in terms of saving souls for that future. But when we see salvation, as the New Testament sees it, in terms of God's promised new heavens and new earth and of our promised resurrection to share in that new and gloriously embodied reality . . . then the main work of the church here and now demands to be rethought in consequence."[14] It is precisely when we get the restorative nature of the gospel straight—a vision of the goal of cosmic restoration that has broken into the present—that "we will rediscover the historical basis for the full-orbed mission of the church."[15] A community that understands the comprehensive and restorative nature of the gospel cannot see any part of its life outside its mission to witness to the lordship of Jesus Christ over all of human life.

N. T. Wright says that it is "the Christian claim that every square inch of the world, every split second of time, belongs to Jesus, by right of the creation and by right of redeeming love."[16] And so Wright can speak of our mission in terms of moving from worship straight into tasks such as humanizing and harmonizing beauty in architecture, work in office and shop, shaping public life, campaigning for decent libraries and sporting facilities, discussing town planning, running playgroups for children of single working moms, organizing credit unions for the poor, and creative and healthy farming methods, among other things, and then repeat the refrain three times: "This is not an extra to the church's mission. It is central."[17] Wright's comment on farming and caring for soil echoes Newbigin's thought when he says, "A farmer who farms his land well but neglects to say his prayers will be certainly condemned by Christians as failing in his duty. But

---

[14]N. T. Wright, *Surprised by Hope: Rethinking Heaven, the Resurrection, and the Mission of the Church* (New York: HarperCollins, 2006), p. 197.
[15]Ibid., pp. 200-201.
[16]N. T. Wright, *Bringing the Church to the World: Renewing the Church to Confront the Paganism Entrenched in Western Culture* (Minneapolis: Bethany House, 1992), p. 150.
[17]Wright, *Surprised by Hope*, pp. 265-66.

a farmer who says his prayers, and allows weeds, bad drainage, or soil erosion to spoil his land, is failing in his primary duty as a churchman. His primary ministry in the total life of the Body of Christ is to care rightly for the land entrusted to him. If he fails there, he fails in his primary Christian task."[18] For Newbigin, Bauckham, Wright and many others, the nature of the church's mission is rooted in an understanding of the gospel of the kingdom as the comprehensive restoration of creation and human life.

Finally, we must take hold of the gospel as a present power. If we take our starting point in the gospel that Jesus himself proclaimed, we see that it is the good news that God's kingdom is breaking into history. This is not simply new religious doctrine; it is an announcement about what God is doing: God is acting in love and in power in Jesus by the Spirit to bring this about. When Jesus is challenged by Pharisees regarding his remarkable claims, he pointed to the power of God in the Spirit at work in him as proof that the kingdom has come (Mt 12:28). Paul certainly believed that the gospel was the power of God (Rom 1:16; 1 Cor 1:18, 24; 2:4). A missionary encounter will require that the church be equipped with a message that has the power to confront the commanding and powerful idolatrous story that shapes our culture.

THE ECCLESIOLOGICAL TASK: UNDERSTANDING OUR MISSIONAL IDENTITY

Recovering our missional identity. The word "missional" is being used in a different way when used as an adjective to describe the nature of the church. At its best, the word "missional" describes not a specific activity of the church, but the very identity of the church as it takes up its role in God's story in the context of its culture and participates in his mission to the world. This means at least two things: the church is a distinctive people, and it is oriented to the world. These two things can be captured in the phrase "an alternative community for the sake of the world."

> AT ITS BEST, THE WORD "MISSIONAL" DESCRIBES NOT A SPECIFIC ACTIVITY OF THE CHURCH, BUT THE VERY IDENTITY OF THE CHURCH AS IT TAKES UP ITS ROLE IN GOD'S STORY.

---

[18] Lesslie Newbigin, "The Christian Layman in the World and in the Church," *National Christian Council Review* 72 (1952): 186.

The Western church too often has been an introverted body primarily concerned with its own internal affairs and institutional life. This has come from a misunderstanding of salvation that reduces God's work of grace to what is done in and for us, blinded to the fact that it is also what God does through us for the sake of the world. When salvation is considered merely as a gift that we enjoy, the church is reduced to being a community concerned with "individual salvation" and "pastoral care."[19] It is an institution that channels grace to its members for their own eternal benefit. In the consumer culture of the West this can be further corrupted to reimaging the church into a vendor of religious goods and services. N. T. Wright uses a comical image: to assume that salvation is just for us "is as though the postman were to imagine that all the letters in his bag were intended for him." Indeed, to assume that the salvation of the covenant is just a gift to be enjoyed is to "betray the purpose for which the covenant was made."[20]

◇◇

"If the gospel is to challenge the public life of our society, if Christians are to occupy the 'high ground' which they vacated in the noontime of 'modernity' . . . it will only be by movements that begin with the local congregation in which the reality of the new creation is present, known, and experienced, and from which men and women will go into every sector of public life to claim it for Christ, to unmask the illusions which have remained hidden and to expose all areas of public life to the illumination of the gospel. But that will only happen as and when local congregations renounce an introverted concern for their own life, and recognize that they exist for the sake of those who are not members, as sign, instrument, and foretaste of God's redeeming grace for the whole life of society."

Lesslie Newbigin, *The Gospel in a Pluralist Society*, pp. 232-33

◇◇

---

[19]David J. Bosch, *Believing in the Future: Toward a Missiology of Western Culture* (Valley Forge, PA: Trinity Press International, 1995), p. 30.
[20]N. T. Wright, *What Saint Paul Really Said: Was Paul of Tarsus the Real Founder of Christianity?* (Grand Rapids: Eerdmans, 1997), p. 108.

The church is called to be oriented to the world; it exists for the sake of others. Cross-cultural missionaries of the past few centuries were sent with a task that was not first of all for themselves but rather for the sake of those to whom they were sent. Thus, to describe the church as "missional" is to define the entire Christian community as a body sent to the world and existing not for itself but rather to bring good news to the world.

There is, moreover, a growing recognition within the Western church of how it has been so deeply compromised by the idols of its culture. If the church embodies the coming kingdom of God in the midst of the world, its members will be critical participants in their cultural setting. This involves two sides: solidarity and challenge. A missionary who understands his or her purpose to be an agent of God's mission among the people to whom he or she is sent will embody both sides. This will mean that missionaries know that they must not capitulate to the spiritual currents of the host culture: it is God's story that gives meaning to why they are there as missionaries. The church today in the West has far too often found its identity and role in the story of the dominant culture in which it exists.

Thus, a recovery of our "missional" nature means that we are to be oriented to the world and to remain true to our identity as a participant in God's mission. It is only as the church is a faithful embodiment of the kingdom in the midst of the surrounding culture but set over against that culture's idolatry that its life and words will bear compelling and appealing testimony to the good news that in Jesus Christ a new world has come and is coming. The challenge is for the church to take up this role and leave behind its self-interested preoccupation and its sinful accommodation to its cultural story.

Ecclesiology has an important role to play in the recovery of this role and identity: "When we, the church, are confused about who we are and whose we are, we can become anything and anyone's."[21] Ecclesiology is about understanding our identity, *who* we are, and why God has chosen us, *whose* we are. If we do not develop our self-understanding in terms of the role that we have been called to play in the biblical drama, we will find ourselves shaped by the story of the dominant culture. To comprehend who

---

[21]John G. Stackhouse Jr., preface to *Evangelical Ecclesiology: Reality or Illusion?* ed. John G. Stackhouse Jr. (Grand Rapids: Baker Academic, 2003), p. 9.

we are means grappling with the role of God's people in the biblical story.[22] Wilbert Shenk writes, "The Bible does not offer a definition of the church or provide us with a doctrinal basis for understanding it. Instead, the Bible relies on images and narrative to disclose the meaning of the church."[23] Deepened theological reflection on the nature and calling of the church will be an ongoing priority.

Recovering the countercultural dimensions of our mission. An important task for fostering a missional identity is to recover the countercultural dimensions of the gospel and the church's mission. The lengthy period of Christendom has led the church to surrender "the vital critical relationship to its culture that is indispensable to a sense of mission."[24] Today the "legacy of Christendom has hobbled the church in responding to the vigorous challenges of

> IT IS ESSENTIAL THAT THE CHURCH RECOVER A REDEMPTIVE TENSION WITH CULTURE.

modern culture to faith."[25] It is essential that the church recover a redemptive tension with culture. Hendrik Kraemer puts it well: "The deeper the consciousness of the tension and the urge to take this yoke upon itself are felt, the healthier the Church is. The more oblivious of this tension the Church is, the more well established and at home in this world it feels, the more it is in deadly danger of being the salt that has lost its savour."[26]

There are two sides to the Christian community's stance in its cultural context. The first side is solidarity and participation. The gospel speaks an affirmative word, a "yes" to human culture. But to speak only these words would be to assume a chameleon-like existence within its culture. "Christianity at rock bottom radically conflicts with American culture, even subverts it. . . . The practicing Christian should look like a Martian. He or she will never feel fully at home in the commodity kingdom. If the Christian

---

[22]See Michael W. Goheen, *A Light to the Nations: The Missional Church and the Biblical Story* (Grand Rapids: Baker Academic, 2011).

[23]Wilbert Shenk, foreword to *Images of the Church in Mission*, by John Driver (Scottsdale, PA: Herald Press, 1997), p. 9.

[24]Shenk, *Write the Vision*, p. 34.

[25]Ibid., p. 3.

[26]Hendrick Kraemer, *The Communication of the Christian Faith* (Philadelphia: Westminster, 1956), p. 36.

does feel at home, something is drastically wrong."[27] Therefore, with equal force, we must emphasize the second side: separation and rejection. Since idolatrous religious beliefs shape every aspect of Western culture, the Christian community must also say no and reject the development that has taken place in the West. It is precisely the second side—faithful cultural engagement—that must be stressed in Western culture.[28]

The reason is that the church in the West exists as "an advanced case of syncretism."[29] Brian Walsh and Sylvia Keesmat say that the "ethical crisis at the turn of the millennium is that Christians by and large accept the empire [of economic globalization and consumerism] as normal."[30] Wendell Berry concurs: "Despite protests to the contrary, modern Christianity has become willy-nilly the religion of the state and the economic status quo."[31] Thus, it is precisely the countercultural side of the gospel that must be recovered. Walsh and Keesmat speak of the need for an "ethic of secession"—secession from the empire of consumerism into the kingdom of Christ.[32]

"Neither in practice nor in thought is religion separate from the rest of life. In practice all the life of society is permeated by beliefs which western Europeans would call religious, and in thought what we call religion is a whole worldview, a way of understanding the whole of human experience. The sharp line which modern Western culture has drawn between religious affairs and secular affairs is itself one of the most significant peculiarities of our culture and would be incomprehensible to the vast majority of people who have not been brought into contact with this culture."

Lesslie Newbigin, *The Gospel in a Pluralist Society*, p. 172

---

[27]John F. Kavanaugh, *Following Christ in a Consumer Society: The Spirituality of Cultural Resistance* (rev. ed.; Maryknoll, NY: Orbis Books, 1991), p. 127.

[28]Konrad Raiser, "Gospel and Cultures," *International Review of Mission* 83, no. 331 (October 1994): 623-29.

[29]Newbigin, *The Other Side of 1984*, p. 23.

[30]Brian J. Walsh and Sylvia C. Keesmat, *Colossians Remixed: Subverting the Empire* (Downers Grove, IL: InterVarsity Press, 2004), p. 168.

[31]Wendell Berry, "Christianity and the Survival of Creation," in *Sex, Economy, Freedom and Community: Eight Essays* (New York: Pantheon Books, 1993), p. 114.

[32]Walsh and Keesmat, *Colossians Remixed*, pp. 147-68.

The need for recovering the antithetical dimensions of the gospel has not gone unnoticed. The long history of a close symbiotic relationship between the Christian faith and Western culture has allowed Christians to be deeply involved participants in cultural development and major players in the public square. The problem has been that in the process an antithetical stance has been downplayed. Liberation and Anabaptist approaches to mission in the public square have received new life as they stress an antithetical stance. This raises new questions about what authentic participation in the public square might look like.

The comprehensive scope of mission and authentic engagement of the public square. In order to be a faithful missional church, we must recover the comprehensive scope of mission, especially its calling in the public square. The question is this: how do we witness to Christ's lordship and comprehensive salvation? David Bosch distinguishes five different traditions or models of missional engagement with the cultural and political powers: Constantinian, Pietist, Reformist, Liberationist, Anabaptist.[33] He dismisses the first two as sub-Christian. In Constantinianism the church simply finds its small place as part of the broader culture and thus loses sight of its prophetic-critical calling. It ends up supporting the status quo.

The Pietist tradition, which has been strong in evangelical circles, often is individualistic, otherworldly and dualistic. Sin is reduced to the individual person. Salvation is about the individual going to heaven and has little to do with this creation. Life is divided into secular and sacred activities, activities that belong to our spiritual inheritance (sacred), and activities that belong to our earthly life (secular). What really matters for the Christian are sacred ones—prayer, worship, Bible reading, individual morality, and so forth. Mission is about evangelism only. This tradition does not see the gospel as a transforming power in all culture and therefore limits the mission of the church. Bosch describes this Pietistic temptation of "withdrawing from public life altogether":

---

[33]David Bosch, "God's Reign and the Rulers of This World: Missiological Reflections on Church-State Relationships," in *The Good News of the Kingdom: Mission Theology for the Third Millennium*, ed. Charles van Engen, Dean S. Gilliland and Paul Pierson (Maryknoll, NY: Orbis Books, 1993), pp. 89-95.

As our concern over rampant secularization increases, we may in fashioning a missiology of Western culture easily be seduced into concentrating on the "religious" aspect only, leaving the rest to the secular powers, not least because these powers exert massive pressures on the church to limit itself to the soul of the individual. This is, after all, in keeping with the Enlightenment worldview: religion is a private affair, its truth claims are relative and have no place in the public sphere of "facts."[34]

In contrast, Bosch believes that the Liberation, Anabaptist and Reformist models engage the full breadth of culture, though in different ways. These different approaches are perhaps more complimentary than it appears on the surface, and they emphasize different yet important dimensions of the church's cultural task. All three traditions acknowledge that the gospel of the kingdom is as broad as human life, and therefore the church's mission must have an equally comprehensive scope.

Yet there remain differences among these three traditions on how the church ought to engage its culture. A Liberationist approach arises out of a keen sense of the oppressive nature of economic, political and social structures, and the resulting poverty. The Christian church is to side with those who are marginalized and impoverished by these structures. Salvation involves liberation from an oppressive order. The church's mission, then, is to participate in God's liberating work to free the victims of these unjust systems. This involvement in God's liberating mission comes from the ground up. The church that is either poor itself or identifies with the struggle of the poor is the agent of liberation. A Liberationist approach stresses the evil of these unjust systems and demands all-out war on them. One must take sides in the struggle—for or against the poor, for or against the unjust status quo. There is also no room for compromise or neutrality. Liberation comes only by way of direct confrontation with the oppressive powers and through a revolutionary overturning of these unjust institutions.

The Anabaptist approach is rapidly gaining ground in North America.[35] In elaborating this position, it is common to divide church history into

---

[34]Bosch, *Believing in the Future*, p. 34.

[35]See, for example, Stanley Hauerwas and William H. Willimon, *Resident Aliens: A Provocative Christian Assessment of Culture and Ministry for People Who Know That Something Is Wrong* (Nashville: Abingdon, 1989); Douglas John Hall, *The End of Christendom and the Future of Christianity* (Valley Forge, PA: Trinity Press International, 1997).

three eras: the early church, Christendom beginning with Constantine, and the present. There have been two major shifts that account for this division. The first major shift was the establishment of the church under the Roman emperor Constantine, when the church received a privileged position in the empire. The whole Christendom experiment is viewed quite negatively. The church was thoroughly compromised in its partnership in the culture. Although historical Christendom is over, its pattern has continued throughout the West in a functional Christendom in which the church continues to enjoy a degree of power as a result of its privileged place in culture. The second shift is the disestablishment of the church today. The church is again being pushed to the margins of society. This disestablishment is seen as a positive development, for now the church can recover its identity as shaped by the biblical story rather than the cultural story.

> THE ANABAPTIST APPROACH IS RAPIDLY GAINING GROUND IN NORTH AMERICA.

Three important features characterize the Anabaptist view of the church's missional calling. First, it is anti-Christendom. It sees Christendom as a period that deeply compromised the church's calling in culture. Second, it emphasizes the communal dimensions of the missionary witness of the church. There is a reaction against a reduction of mission to the calling of individuals in culture characteristic of Christendom. It stands against a neglect of the church as a community that embodies the life of the kingdom together. The Anabaptist model emphasizes that "the primary task of the church is simply to *be* the church, the *true* community of committed believers which, by its very existence and example, becomes a challenge to society and the state."[36] Third, the critical or negative side of the church's relationship to its culture dominates. The concern is that the church of Christendom has domesticated itself and been uncritical of the idolatrous powers of culture. "The church is understood to be an implicit or latent *critical factor* in society. . . . The church is critical of the status quo, indeed *very* critical of it."[37]

---

[36]Bosch, "God's Reign," p. 92.
[37]Ibid.

"How is it possible," Newbigin asks, "that the gospel should be credible, that people should come to believe that the power which has the last word in human affairs is represented by a man hanging on a cross? I am suggesting that the only answer, the only hermeneutic of the gospel, is a congregation of men and women who believe it and live by it."

Lesslie Newbigin, *The Gospel in a Pluralist Society*, p. 227

It is not surprising that this approach is getting a wide hearing in North America. The individualistic approach to mission calls forth a biblical emphasis on community. A church deeply compromised by culture requires a new emphasis on its countercultural identity. These renewed emphases are badly needed. The question is whether or not this way of understanding the church's mission offers resources to the believers in their callings in the public life of society. The church in the West is not as marginalized as the early church; in fact, it holds a great deal of cultural power. This cannot simply be dismissed as Christendom. The question is how cultural power is to be used in a faithful way. Rightly emphasizing the communal dimensions will open new perspectives but not offer insight for the callings of believers in their day-to-day living. Rightly calling attention to the critical and antithetical side of the church's involvement in culture will not aid the people of God in their necessary participation in their cultural callings—the place, in fact, where they spend most of their week.

The Reformist approach is a third way of understanding the church's cultural calling. The Reformist tradition wants to cast a vision that will equip Christians as they hold cultural power to carry out their callings in the world faithfully. It rejects the Christendom stance, which supports the status quo; it realizes the depth of idolatry in culture and how it has polluted all cultural institutions, structures and systems. Yet it also believes that the Anabaptist and Liberationist traditions have not adequately come to terms with the callings of individual believers in society and how to use power responsibly in light of the gospel. A Reformist approach recognizes the creational good in various cultural structures and is concerned that revolution may sweep away what justice and good there is, constructing even more evil structures in its place. It is concerned to work within cultural structures toward their renewal. It may be just as radical as the Anabaptist and Liberationist model, but it is a radicalism of loving involvement and critical participation.

There are dangers. The most obvious is the ever-present and oft-realized danger of domestication and compromise. There is pressure and temptation to play by the cultural rules of the game and thereby imbibe the idolatry. Both the Anabaptist and Liberationist traditions criticize a Reformist position for this very thing. They believe that compromise is inevitable and therefore urge the church to take a position on the margins. For example, the Kairos Document,[38] a Liberationist document out of South Africa, is hard on the Reformist position (calling it "church theology") because it believes that one will ultimately side with the oppressor.

A second danger is a nostalgic tendency for a triumphalistic return to Christendom. One sometimes hears Reformist language of "building God's kingdom," with the understanding that our cultural endeavors may largely usher in God's kingdom and Christianize society. However, these dangers are not necessarily inherent in the Reformist tradition. And since the church still wields a great deal of cultural power, there is a need to draw on this tradition's resources to equip the church today for its engagement in public life of culture in a way that is not Constantinian.

Each of these traditions has important biblical emphases that need to be affirmed. Moreover, Bosch is correct that since they share important foundational beliefs, they are closer to each other than is sometimes thought. And, finally, while all emphasize themes that are relevant in all contexts, certain models are more appropriate for differing situations.

The differing stances that the church took toward its cultural situation are evidenced in the biblical books of Romans and Revelation. Dean Flemming offers a helpful analysis comparing Romans 13 and Revelation 13: they represent different contexts under the Roman Empire, calling for different responses. While the contexts differ, the key is that in both situations the church is called to witness to God's kingdom: "Both, in fact, engage their

---

[38]The Kairos Document (1985) is a theological statement from a black Liberationist tradition that challenged the injustices of the apartheid system in South Africa during the state of emergency in 1985. It critiques "state theology" (Christendom) and "church theology" (Reformist), and calls for a "prophetic theology" (Liberationist) (available at www.sahistory.org.za/archive/challenge-church-theological-comment-political-crisis-south-africa-kairos-document-1985).

public worlds with a missional goal, but they do so from alternative angles." The book of Romans seems to "encourage Christians to positively participate in the life of society in redemptive ways."[39] As James Dunn puts it, "Good citizenship was also a missionary strategy which commended the gospel to those of good will."[40] Flemming observes, "Christians were to live out their calling within the existing structures of Greco-Roman society while displaying a visible internal difference";

> ROMANS 13 AND REVELATION 13: THEY REPRESENT DIFFERENT CONTEXTS UNDER THE ROMAN EMPIRE, CALLING FOR DIFFERENT RESPONSES.

they were to live within those institutions with a "cross-shaped difference" that would lead to transformation from within.[41] On the other hand, Revelation takes a more sectarian stance because of the demonic depths that idolatry has reached. Thus, Revelation "launches a countercultural critique" and calls the church to a "prophetic and costly witness." In Romans and Revelation "we discover two different but complementary theological visions. Each spotlights one side of the church's relationship to the Empire; each shows sensitivity to the particular needs of the communities they address."[42]

A concern about the burgeoning Anabaptist and Liberationist traditions, which are much more in the tradition of Revelation than Romans, is that the church in the West is not yet marginalized and persecuted to the same extent as the church in Revelation. The church continues to exercise cultural power. Further, the structures of Western culture perhaps have not reached the same demonic depth. We recognize that the church is gradually being marginalized, and that global economic structures are increasingly unjust and oppressive, and so it is clear that the book of Revelation has rich resources for a church that sees this trend.[43] However, much of the Romans situation still prevails, and so the church must ask how it might participate redemptively in the structures of our culture.

---

[39]Dean Flemming, *Contextualization in the New Testament: Patterns for Theology and Mission* (Downers Grove, IL: InterVarsity Press, 2005), pp. 289-90.
[40]James D. G. Dunn, *The Theology of Paul the Apostle* (Grand Rapids: Eerdmans, 1998), pp. 679-80.
[41]Flemming, *Contextualization*, p. 149.
[42]Ibid., pp. 290-91.
[43]See ibid., pp. 266-95. See also Richard Bauckham, *Bible and Mission: Christian Witness in a Postmodern World* (Grand Rapids: Baker Academic, 2003), pp. 83-112.

The calling of believers in culture will be the primary way the church must carry out its mission in Western culture: "A missionary encounter with the West will have to be primarily a ministry of the laity."[44] The hindrance is that there has been "deep-seated and persistent failure of the churches to recognize that the primary witness to the sovereignty of Christ must be given, and can only be given, in the ordinary secular work of lay men and women in business, in politics, in professional work, as farmer, factory workers and so on."[45]

Our changing situation will mean that the church will have to continue to struggle with the shape of its mission in the public square. Since the church's calling in culture means participation, the Reformist tradition can offer insight into how to use its cultural power under the sign of the cross; since the church's calling in culture also means resistance, the Liberationist and Anabaptist traditions can offer wisdom in how to oppose cultural idolatry. Loving our neighbor means both positive involvement and negative resistance that takes both communal and individual form. If the church is to be faithful in its engagement with the public life of Western culture it will be urgent to appropriate the insights of the various traditions in fresh and creative ways.

THE CULTURAL TASK: A MISSIONARY ANALYSIS
OF WESTERN CULTURE

There has been a "whole mass of missiological writing . . . that has sought to explore the problems of contextualization in all the cultures of humankind"; but curiously and regretfully, "it has largely ignored the culture that is the most widespread, powerful and persuasive among all contemporary cultures—namely . . . modern Western culture."[46] Indeed, mission studies have a long and rich tradition of studying cultures in light of the gospel for the missionary task. For the cross-cultural missionary, it is essential to carefully analyze culture. It is a matter of life and death, since a domesticated gospel would undermine the missionary enterprise. This is especially urgent in the

[44]Bosch, *Believing in the Future*, p. 59.
[45]Lesslie Newbigin, "The Work of the Holy Spirit in the Life of the Asian Churches," in *A Decisive Hour for the Christian World Mission*, ed. Norman Goodall et al. (London: SCM Press, 1960), p. 28.
[46]Newbigin, *Foolishness to the Greeks*, pp. 2-3.

West, not only because an uncritical attitude toward culture has led to accommodation, but also because of the power and scope of this culture. And yet surprisingly, it has been the West that has been neglected.

Religious core of culture. The first necessary step in a missionary analysis of Western culture is to unmask the secular bias of our culture and expose its religious core. There is an assumption that we have moved from being a religious society in the Middle Ages to being a secular society in the modern period, that medieval culture was a biased culture based on religious faith, whereas modern culture is a neutral culture based on secular reason. Armed with this faulty assumption, anthropologists and sociologists have studied culture blind to its religious nature. Religion has been reduced to one more human activity dealing with god(s), afterlife, spiritual and moral issues along with the associated practices. Analysts who take this path are full participants in the Western story and are simply blinded to the religious nature of the story that they have embraced.

> THE FIRST NECESSARY STEP IN A MISSIONARY ANALYSIS OF WESTERN CULTURE IS TO UNMASK THE SECULAR BIAS OF OUR CULTURE AND EXPOSE ITS RELIGIOUS CORE.

"Often in the West the inculturation process has been so 'successful' that Christianity has become nothing but the religious dimension of the culture—listening to the church, society hears only the sound of its own music. The West has often domesticated the gospel in its own culture while making it unnecessarily foreign to every other culture."

David J. Bosch, *Transforming Mission*, p. 466

This assumption has been challenged by a variety of people, including anthropologists, sociologists, cultural theologians, Christian worldview scholars, mission thinkers and Christians from the Southern hemisphere. Philip Jenkins asks what is the "greatest change" that Southern Christianity will bring to our understanding of God and the world, and answers that it is "likely to involve our Enlightenment-derived assumption that religion should be segregated into a separate sphere of life, distinct from everyday reality."[47]

To speak of religion in this comprehensive and radical way is based on a view of humankind taken from Scripture. Human beings are, at the deepest level, religious creatures made to serve God in the whole of their individual and corporate lives. If they refuse to center their lives in the living God, they are no less religious; rather, they serve some aspect of creational life to which they offer ultimate allegiance. The Bible calls this idolatry.

Four metaphors have been used to express the religious nature of culture. Newbigin speaks of religious beliefs that lie below the surface of culture that function like *tectonic plates* or a *foundation* that supports and gives shape to the observable patterns of culture. "Incomparably," he writes, "the most urgent missionary task for the next few decades is the mission to 'modernity'. . . . It calls for the use of sharp intellectual tools, to probe behind the unquestioned assumptions of modernity and uncover the hidden credo which supports them."[48] Lying beneath the surface of Western culture is an unquestioned and hidden credo, a religious confession of beliefs, that must be probed. This religious credo is a "set of beliefs, experiences, and practices that seek to grasp and express the ultimate nature of things, that which gives shape and meaning to life, that which claims final loyalty."[49]

Harvie Conn speaks of the religious *core* of culture. Religion is "not an area of life, one among many, but primarily a *direction* of life. . . . Religion, then, becomes the heart of culture's integrity, its central dynamic as an organism, the totalistic radical response of man-in-covenant to the revelation of God."[50] Religion is not simply an aspect of culture but a core power that animates, unifies, and directs the whole (see fig. 3.)

Egbert Schuurman, a philosopher of technology, using a third image, likens religious beliefs to a root that sends its death- or life-giving sap throughout all the branches of human culture. He believes that "religion is not just a typical

---

[47]Philip Jenkins, *The Next Christendom: The Coming of Global Christianity* (Oxford: Oxford University Press, 2002), p. 141.

[48]Lesslie Newbigin, "Gospel and Culture—But Which Culture?" *Missionalia* 17, no. 3 (1989): 214.

[49]Newbigin, *Foolishness to the Greeks*, p. 3.

[50]Harvie Conn, "Conversion and Culture: A Theological Perspective with Reference to Korea," in *Down to Earth: Studies in Christianity and Culture*, ed. John Stott and Robert Coote (Grand Rapids: Eerdmans, 1980), pp. 149-50.

function among others but is, rather, the *root* from which the different branches of life sprout and grow and from which they are continually nourished. Religion is of *radical* and *integral* importance to culture: it concerns the deepest root of human existence and integrates human life into a coherent whole."[51]

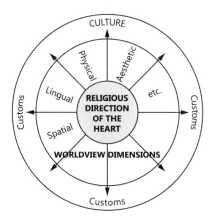

Figure 3. The religious core of culture

Finally, economist Bob Goudzwaard pictures religion in terms of the *chief end* of culture. He observes, "Every style of culture is in turn related to the religious question of how people view the ultimate meaning of their life and society."[52] He suggests that a culture will absolutize certain goals and then form itself around that goal.[53] For example, Western culture makes economic growth and material prosperity the goal of human life, and so all other cultural institutions and mechanisms are enlisted and unified to reach that goal. Goudzwaard compares culture to a beehive, in which the center of the hive is the production of eggs by the queen bee. Every other activity in the hive is directed to that end.[54]

These religious beliefs are socially and concretely embodied in institu-

---

[51]Egbert Schuurman, "The Challenge of Islam's Critique of Technology," in *Gospel and Globalization: Exploring the Religious Roots of a Globalized World*, ed. Michael W. Goheen and Erin G. Glanville (Vancouver: Regent College Press, 2009), p. 199.

[52]Bob Goudzwaard, *Capitalism and Progress: A Diagnosis of Western Society*, trans. Josina Van Nuis Zylstra (Toronto: Wedge Publishing; Grand Rapids: Eerdmans, 1979), p. 7.

[53]Ibid. See also Bob Goudzwaard, Mark Vander Vennen and David Van Heemst, *Hope in Troubled Times: A New Vision for Confronting Global Crises* (Grand Rapids: Baker Academic, 2007), pp. 31-45.

[54]Goudzwaard, *Capitalism and Progress*, pp. 87-88.

tions, customs, practices, systems, symbols, and so on. Sociologist James Davison Hunter argues that the modern worldview that shapes Western culture is not simply ideas but rather the "key ideas, values and characteristics of modernity mentioned above are 'carried' by specific institutions."[55] He notes three major spheres of human activity: economic, political, cultural. In the economic sphere it is industrial capitalism that is the carrier of modernity's religious beliefs; in the political, it is the modern state; in the cultural, it is especially the "knowledge sector"—the modern university, the media of mass communication, the arts, popular culture.

Western culture is a concrete pattern of life that is animated, unified and directed by a dominant religious vision of what it means to be human. Political systems, economic arrangements, family and marital life, patterns of thinking and emotional response, social relationships, and more are expressions of a deeper religious credo. A missional analysis of culture is concerned to uncover this creed and critique it in light of the gospel. What is the religious commitment of Western culture?

> WESTERN CULTURE IS A CONCRETE PATTERN OF LIFE THAT IS ANIMATED, UNIFIED AND DIRECTED BY A DOMINANT RELIGIOUS VISION OF WHAT IT MEANS TO BE HUMAN.

Telling the story that shapes us. In order to uncover this religious commitment, it is necessary to tell the story that shapes us. The philosopher Charles Taylor, in his book *A Secular Age*, examines the shift from 1500 to 2000 in which Western culture became secular. He emphasizes that telling a story to make his point is "indispensable": "To get straight where we are, we have to go back and tell the story properly. Our past is sedimented in our present, and we are doomed to misidentify ourselves, as long as we can't do justice to where we came from. That is why the narrative is not an optional extra, why I believe that I have to tell a story here."[56] I will identify the religious beliefs of Western culture by sketching the skeleton of a story.

[55]James Davison Hunter, "What Is Modernity? Historical Roots and Contemporary Features," in *Faith and Modernity*, ed. Philip Sampson, Vinay Samuel and Chris Sugden (Oxford: Regnum Books, 1994), p. 18. See also Hunter's *To Change the World: The Irony, Tragedy, and Possibility of Christianity in the Late Modern World* (Oxford: Oxford University Press, 2010).
[56]Charles Taylor, *A Secular Age* (Cambridge, MA: Belknap Press of Harvard University Press, 2007), p. 29.

Two creedal statements arise in the context of the Western story that might qualify as succinct confessions of faith. The first articulates the humanism that is at the heart of Western culture. Friedrich Nietzsche (1844-1900) asks, "Must we ourselves not become gods?" In "The Parable of the Madman" a madman makes the startling accusation that we have killed God. Nietzsche here refers to the eighteenth-century Enlightenment, when Western culture excluded God from public life. "How shall we comfort ourselves, the murderers of all murders?" the madman asks. He answers with another question: "Must we ourselves not become gods simply to appear worthy of it?"

If there is no God, then there is no Creator to give the meaning of human life, to order the creation, or to give universally valid standards of right and wrong, true and false, good and bad. Human beings must step in to this place of the Creator, define the purpose of life, construct order, and become the ultimate arbiter of right, true and good. If there is no God, moreover, then there is no Sovereign Ruler to give history meaning and guide it to its goal. Humankind now must take up that task. And, finally, if there is no God, then there is no Savior to liberate our world from evil. Again, human beings must take on that role and save themselves with their own resources. The humanist Corliss Lamont says that humanism "assigns us nothing less than the task of being our own savior and redeemer."[57]

The madman asks in disbelief, "Who gave us a sponge to wipe away the entire horizon?" The horizon offered by a story, shaped to some degree by the Bible, that had given meaning to human life in the West for centuries has been erased. Now in this spiritual vacuum Western humankind must "create a new narrative from which to make sense of things. People must design a different horizon than the one that has been wiped out."[58] In this story humankind plays the role of creator, ruler and savior.

We now live in a different story. There has been an "anthropocentric shift,"[59] and so we live in a "secular age" in which we no longer encounter God in the natural or social world: a mechanistic universe empties the

---

[57]Corliss Lamont, *The Philosophy of Humanism* (1949; 8th ed.; Amherst, NY: Humanist Press, 1997), p. 309.

[58]Goudzwaard, Vander Vennen and Van Heemst, *Hope in Troubled Times*, p. 37.

[59]Taylor, *Secular Age*, pp. 221-69.

natural world of God's purpose, action and presence; a secular society removes God's norms, meaning and presence from the human cultural and societal realm; a disenchanted world devoid of God and spiritual, religious and moral forces replaces an "enchanted" one in which God's purposeful action and presence are assumed; and the history of progress with humankind as the driving engine replaces God's providential rule and purpose in history.[60] Taylor calls this new world that Western people inhabit "exclusive humanism."[61]

A second creedal statement, made by Francis Bacon in the seventeenth century, makes clear that the humanism of the West is a rationalistic or scientific humanism: *scientia potestas est* ("knowledge is power"). Knowledge is power in two ways. First, as the scientific method enables human beings to know the laws of the nonhuman creation, these can be translated into technological control to dominate nature for our social use. Second, as scientific reason reveals the laws of the various social dimensions of life, we can fashion a more rational society.

Humanism finds its roots in religious choices going back to the Greeks. The humanism of Greece and Rome was preserved in a synthesis with medieval Christianity for close to a millennium. The fifteenth-century Renaissance was a hinge into the modern world as it purportedly "broke the shackles of tradition, religion and superstition with the hammer of a humanism forged in Greece and Rome."[62] Roman Catholic philosopher Romano Guardini helpfully formulates three compass points of the modern world that emerged at this time: nature, subject, culture.[63] The key to understanding all three of these concepts is "autonomy," which refers to an understanding of creation, human life and cultural development as existing apart from God and his authority. The nonhuman creation is removed from God's presence and rule and is made independent and thus becomes "nature."[64] Likewise, the person becomes a "subject" as human life is defined

---

[60]Ibid., pp. 2, 25-27.

[61]Ibid., pp. 19-21, 26-28.

[62]Philip Sampson, "The Rise of Postmodernity," in Sampson, Samuel and Sugden, *Faith and Modernity*, p. 33.

[63]Romano Guardini, *The World and the Person*, trans. Stella Lange (Chicago: Henry Regnery, 1965); originally published as *Welt und Person: Versuche zur christlichen Lehre vom Menschen* (Würzburg: Werkbund-Verlag, 1939).

[64]Ibid., p. 11.

apart from God's purpose and norms and instead bears "the law of existence within itself."[65] "Culture" is autonomous humankind's mastery of and domination over nature to shape it for their purposes.[66] It is this will to dominance that will lead to the idolatry of science, technology, economic growth and material abundance in the coming centuries.

The scientific revolution gave a method to the Western world that would enable it to realize its autonomy and control the world. At the beginning of the scientific revolution the Christian impetus was more culturally formative than the emerging humanism; by the end, humanism was the dominant faith, taking up science into its stream. Contributing to this triumph were two things: the reactionary opposition of the church to the original pioneers of science that seemed to indicate Christianity's irrelevance to the emerging scientific world; and the religious wars of the seventeenth century that seemed to prove that the Christian faith was an unworthy cultural faith that only produced violence while science could achieve unity. As the scientific revolution drew to a close, the "West had 'lost its faith'—and found a new one, in science and in man."[67]

During the eighteenth-century Enlightenment this historical faith matured, and the credo of modern humanism was forged. The dominating belief was a faith commitment to progress. Augustine's *City of God* had stamped upon Western culture a narrative shape to the world with the notion of the movement of history toward the city of God. The Enlightenment writers substituted the notion of progress for God's providential rule of history. Faith is placed in human ability to build a better world. Historian Ronald Wright refers to this as "secular religion."[68]

The impact of the Christian story also remains evident during the eighteenth century in the biblical images of paradise that shape the hopeful imagination of many writers during this time. And what is the primary characteristic of the good life in paradise? Theologian Lawrence Osborn correctly observes that for Enlightenment social and economic architects, "progress is identified with economic growth," and therefore "the economy

---

[65]Ibid., p. 9.
[66]Ibid., p. 11.
[67]Richard Tarnas, *The Passion of the Western Mind: Understanding the Ideas That Have Shaped Our World View* (New York: Ballantine, 1991), p. 320.
[68]Ronald Wright, *A Short History of Progress* (Toronto: House of Anansi Press, 1994), p. 4.

[is] the chief instrument in modernity's pursuit of happiness."[69] Material prosperity and the freedom to pursue and enjoy it—this is the secular paradise toward which the West is now directed.

> MATERIAL PROSPERITY AND THE FREEDOM TO PURSUE AND ENJOY IT—THIS IS THE SECULAR PARADISE TOWARD WHICH THE WEST IS NOW DIRECTED.

How does one get to this paradise? The medieval notion of providence is replaced by an understanding that humankind is now the primary agent in historical progress. The human capacity that can best get us to this materially abundant world is reason. Humankind "is capable, guided solely by the light of reason and experience, of perfecting the good life on earth."[70] Scientific reason liberated from religion, tradition and faith can be employed to control, predict and shape the world according to humankind's autonomous will.

This better world is realized, first, as scientific reason discerns the natural laws of the nonhuman creation and translates them into technological control. In this way humankind could be the "master and possessor of nature."[71] But, second, if scientific reason could discern the built-in laws of politics, society, economics, law and education, analogous to physical law, then those laws too could be controlled to produce a more rationally ordered society. These spheres of society are emptied of God, his norms and purpose, and instead carry a rationality internal to each sphere—maximum profit within the economic sphere, rights that give the greatest benefit to the most in the political sphere, and so on.[72] Forming a secular society according to human rationality can "alter human nature and create a heaven on earth."[73]

In this context Adam Smith (1723-1790) articulated his vision of progress toward a better world of material prosperity. He was first a moral philos-

[69]Lawrence Osborn, *Restoring the Vision: The Gospel and Modern Culture* (London: Mowbray, 1995), pp. 46, 57.
[70]Carl Becker, *The Heavenly City of the Eighteenth-Century Philosophers* (New Haven: Yale University Press, 1932), p. 31.
[71]René Descartes, *Discourse on Method*, trans. Donald A. Cress (3rd ed.; Indianapolis: Hackett, 1993), p. 3.
[72]Taylor, *Secular Age*, p. 2.
[73]John B. Bury, *The Idea of Progress: An Inquiry into Its Origin and Growth* (New York: Dover, 1932), p. 205.

opher, and one of his primary concerns in a situation of economic deprivation was to increase goods so that they could be distributed to the poor. For this to happen, it was necessary to corral two forces: division of labor and accumulation of capital. The market would be the mechanism that would coordinate these forces for the material betterment of humanity. Thus, the market, along with innovative technology, becomes a key to the prosperous future of humankind.

If the Enlightenment vision is true, then "the establishment of *new* social institutions is not a tedious, incidental task, but a dire necessity and a high ethical imperative. In that case, the narrow way to the lost paradise can only be the way of *social revolution.*"[74] The revolutions of the nineteenth and twentieth centuries—Industrial, French, American, Democratic, Marxist— sought to bring society into conformity with this Enlightenment faith.

The Industrial Revolution began to implement the Enlightenment economic vision of Adam Smith. But it did much more, however, than reorganize economic production: it shaped a new society around economic life, the world of industrial capitalism. About this emerging social form theologian David Wells says, "Capitalism has successfully reorganized the social structure for the purposes of manufacturing, production, and consumption. . . . In short, it has changed the shape of our world."[75]

Confidence in progress toward material abundance and a growing economy through technological innovation and a free market hit its high point by the end of the nineteenth century. Sociologist Morris Ginsberg observes that the "culminating point in the history of the belief in progress was reached toward the end of the nineteenth century. . . . It owed its wide prevalence to the optimism inspired by the triumphs of applied science, made visible in the striking advances made in the technical conveniences of life."[76]

Discerning the religious spirits today. We can discern three spirits at work in the West today that arose during the twentieth century: postmodernity, economic globalization, consumerism. The twentieth century landed some heavy body blows on confidence in human progress. Nu-

---

[74]Goudzwaard, *Capitalism and Progress*, pp. 50-51.
[75]David F. Wells, *God in the Wasteland: The Reality of Truth in a World of Fading Dreams* (Grand Rapids: Eerdmans, 1994), p. 8.
[76]Morris Ginsberg, *Essays in Sociology and Social Philosophy*, vol. 3, *Evolution and Progress* (London: Heinemann, 1961), p. 8.

merous problems and crises seemed to make clear that the story of progress was not working—among them environmental destruction, growing poverty, the nuclear threat, economic breakdown, social problems and psychological disorders. This widespread challenge to the Enlightenment faith is termed "postmodern." "There are those—and this is the core of postmodernist philosophical thought—who insist that we should in the name of human emancipation, abandon the Enlightenment project entirely."[77]

A postmodern spirit has challenged numerous dimensions of the Enlightenment story: its optimism that believed that human beings could construct a better and more prosperous world; its commitment to the centrality of universal reason in defining the nature of humanity; its confidence in the objectivity of knowledge; its faith that a single story could shape society; the injustices created by this story; and its naturalistic secularism. A new spirit pervades Western culture. A new generation no longer believes grand stories of progress. It does not trust reason to arrive at truth. It is suspicious of exclusive truth claims and tends toward a pluralistic embrace of many versions of the truth. It is suspicious of authority, and it is sensitive to the injustices of humanist story.

> EVEN WHILE A GROWING POSTMODERN SPIRIT PROTESTS THE ENLIGHTENMENT VISION, PROGRESS REMAINS RESILIENT IN ITS LIBERAL FORM AS THE WORKING FAITH OF WESTERN CIVILIZATION.

Nevertheless, even while a growing postmodern spirit protests the Enlightenment vision, progress remains resilient in its liberal form as the working faith of Western civilization. Historian and social critic Christopher Lasch analyzes this interesting phenomenon. He suggests that today "it is to Adam Smith and his immediate predecessors . . . that we should look for the inner meaning of progressive ideology."[78]

The concept of progress can be defended against intelligent criticism only by postulating an indefinite expansion of desires, a steady rise in the general standard of comfort, and the incorporation of the masses into the culture of

[77]David Harvey, *The Condition of Postmodernity: An Enquiry into the Origins of Cultural Change* (Oxford: Basil Blackwell, 1989), p. 14.
[78]Christopher Lasch, *The True and Only Heaven: Progress and Its Critics* (New York: Norton, 1991), p. 54.

abundance. It is only in this form that the idea of progress has survived the rigors of the twentieth century. More extravagant versions of the progressive faith . . . collapsed a long time ago; but the liberal version has proven surprisingly resistant to the shocks to easy optimism administered in rapid succession by twentieth-century events.[79]

Lasch further offers insight into the global spread of this worldview: "It remained only to complete the capitalist revolution by making the 'blessings of leisure' available to all."[80] Indeed, globalization is the spread of this new economic form of the modern worldview around the world. Economist Jane Collier comments on this development: "Precisely because the culture of economism is a quasi-religion, with a pretence of encompassing the totality of life and of bringing happiness and fulfilment, we find ourselves obliged from a Christian point of view to denounce it as dehumanizing idolatry."[81]

Economic globalization has generated great wealth, but that wealth has been spread unevenly. There is an "asymmetric globalization,"[82] whereby dire poverty exists alongside an excessive consumer culture in which one-fifth of the population accounts for one-half of consumption. Thus, the other side of the economic globalization coin is a consumer society in the West.

Sociologist Steven Miles believes that in the West "consumerism appears to have become part and parcel of the very fabric of modern life. . . . And the parallel with religion is not an accidental one. Consumerism is . . . arguably *the* religion of the late twentieth century."[83] During the twentieth century consumerism as a way of life has been designed as manufacturers devise products to break down or be unusable quickly (planned obsolescence) and as advertising instills dissatisfaction, new desires, the need to own something a little newer, a little better, a little sooner than is necessary (perceived obsolescence). Today consumerism is perhaps the most powerful spirit at work in the West, thoroughly pervading and shaping Western cultural life. It is a consumption of goods and experi-

---

[79]Ibid., p. 78.
[80]Ibid., pp. 78-79.
[81]Jane Collier, "Contemporary Culture and the Role of Economics," in *The Gospel and Contemporary Culture*, ed. Hugh Montefiore (London: Mowbray, 1992), p. 122.
[82]Joseph E. Stiglitz, *Making Globalization Work* (New York: Norton, 2006), p. 62.
[83]Steven Miles, *Consumerism: As a Way of Life* (Thousand Oaks, CA: Sage Publications, 1998), p. 1.

> TODAY CONSUMERISM
> IS PERHAPS THE MOST
> POWERFUL SPIRIT AT
> WORK IN THE WEST,
> THOROUGHLY
> PERVADING AND
> SHAPING WESTERN
> CULTURAL LIFE.

ences. Indeed, "consumer capitalism, both for good and for ill, is a pervasive and foundational reality of our day."[84]

The church committed to living out the good news of the kingdom of God in the midst of this kind of culture cannot remain content with the status quo. A consumer culture produces excessive consumption by some while others suffer want, threatens the environment as well as the well-being of those caught in its grip, and creates ungodly character.

A contrast community in the West. The church is called to offer the gospel in life, word and deed to a community in bondage to dehumanizing idolatry. The Western church can do this only as a contrast community. What would a contrast community look like in the twenty-first century?

The following list flows directly from what I believe to be, on the one hand, the most urgent spiritual currents of our culture that the church must challenge and fulfill in its own life. In other words, this list is highly contextual: this is what a church faithful to the gospel in this particular context might look like as an attractive alternative community in contrast to and in fulfillment of the religious currents of Western culture. What spiritual currents in our culture must we set our lives against? What do those spiritual currents reveal about the religious hunger of our contemporaries to which our lives can be good news? What areas of a contrast community need to be emphasized today? By way of illustration I briefly list eighteen characteristics of a contrast community in Western culture. It will be a community of

- self-giving love in a world of self-interest
- wisdom in a world of proliferating knowledge and information technology
- justice in a world of economic injustice
- creational care in a world of ecological destruction

---

[84]Rodney Clapp, "Why the Devil Takes VISA: A Christian Response to the Triumph of Consumerism," *Christianity Today* 40, no. 11 (October 7, 1996): 21 (available at www.ctlibrary.com /ct/1996/october7/6tb018.html).

- humility in a world of arrogant self-indulgent and self-centered behavior
- patience in a world of immediate gratification
- compassion in a world numbed by overexposure to violence and tragedy
- joy in a world dominated by a frantic and hedonistic pursuit of pleasure
- thanksgiving in a world of entitlement
- self-control and marital fidelity in world saturated by sex
- truth (in humility and boldness) in world of uncertainty
- living moment by moment in God's presence in a secular world
- generosity in world of consumption
- simplicity (of enough) in a world of excess
- forgiveness in a world of competition, violence, grudge and revenge
- praise in a world of narcissism
- hope in a world of despair and consumer satiation
- edifying communication in a world of destructive words
- commitment in a world of apathy

FURTHER READING

Bosch, David. *Believing in the Future: Toward a Missiology of Western Culture.* Valley Forge, PA: Trinity Press International, 1995.

Newbigin, Lesslie. *The Other Side of 1984: Questions for the Churches.* Geneva: World Council of Churches, 1983.

———. *Foolishness to the Greeks: The Gospel and Western Culture.* Grand Rapids: Eerdmans, 1986.

———. *The Gospel in a Pluralist Society.* Grand Rapids: Eerdmans, 1989.

Shenk, Wilbert. *Write the Vision: The Church Renewed.* Valley Forge, PA: Trinity Press International, 1995.

DISCUSSION QUESTIONS

1. What do you think of the idea of a "missiology of Western culture"? Explain how you agree or disagree with Newbigin that this is the most urgent task facing the church today.

2. Do you believe the Western church is in fact "an advanced case of syncretism"? Why or why not?

3. How might the theme of this chapter be communicated to the average
   Christian who does not study theology academically?

ESSAY TOPICS

1. Briefly summarize the theological or ecclesial or cultural task of a missiology of Western culture and explain its importance for shaping a
   faithful church in the West today.

2. Today there is much discussion of the nature of the gospel. Evaluate the
   way the gospel is described in this chapter. How does our view of the
   gospel affect our understanding and practice of mission?

3. Why is it so important to understand the religious nature of culture?
   What is hindering this today?

9

A Missionary Encounter
with World Religions

ೲ

J UST OVER A HALF CENTURY AGO Hendrik Kraemer predicted that the church was headed toward a real missionary encounter with the great non-Christian religions. "Up until now," he said, "the other great non-Christian religions and the Christian Church have, so to say, only met in passing. Notwithstanding brilliant individual efforts, a real meeting in openness and fairness has never taken place. The great meeting of the Christian Church as a whole with the great religions . . . is still awaiting us."[1] That time has come. And the factors precipitating such an encounter will only continue to intensify. This is one of the urgent issues facing the Christian church today.

AN URGENT ISSUE

At least four factors make the issue of a missionary encounter with the world's religions an urgent issue.

The expansion of plurality. The economic and technological processes of globalization have expanded exponentially in the latter half of the twentieth century and now unify the world. One consequence has been great migrations of peoples across the face of the earth. This global interdependence and massive migration mean that adherents of the great religions now live in close proximity to one another. Religious plurality has become a global phenomenon. Whereas in the past the church in the West could safely ignore the rival claims of the world religions because they were geographi-

---

[1]Hendrik Kraemer, *Religion and the Christian Faith* (Philadelphia: Westminster, 1956), p. 20.

cally remote, today the church increasingly lives in close proximity to and constant interaction with adherents of the world faiths. The vitality of these world religions has become more evident to the church in the West, as well as their dramatic worldwide resurgence in numbers and missionary zeal. The church can no longer afford to ignore or patronize other religions as it has done in the past.

> THE CHURCH CAN NO LONGER AFFORD TO IGNORE OR PATRONIZE OTHER RELIGIONS AS IT HAS DONE IN THE PAST.

The global South: A Christian minority amidst a sea of religious plurality. The church in the global South has grown throughout the twentieth century and now constitutes the numerical majority of the global Christian church. But in Asia, for example, the church makes up less than 9 percent of the population in a continent where the much larger religions of Islam, Hinduism and Buddhism are flourishing. Thus, the emerging church in the Southern hemisphere lives in the midst of powerful and ancient religious traditions, and its situation raises the urgent question of faithfulness in the context of religious pluralism. A faithful encounter with these religions is not a mere academic exercise; it is a matter of life and death.

Moreover, a different understanding of religion exists in the non-Western world. Religion in the post-Enlightenment West is considered to be one department of life concerned with things such as worship, prayer, sacred texts, ethical systems, beliefs about God and the afterlife. As such, it belongs to the private and personal realm. However, "the sharp line which modern Western culture has drawn between religious affairs and secular affairs is itself one of the most significant peculiarities of our culture and would be incomprehensible to the vast majority of people who have not been brought into contact with this culture."[2] In other cultures religion is a comprehensive vision that animates, directs and unifies all of human life. This understanding of religion, which is in fact closer to a biblical view, considerably complicates the issue of religious pluralism and a faithful Christian witness. Our religious differences have implications for the public life that we share together.

---

[2]Lesslie Newbigin, *The Gospel in a Pluralist Society* (Grand Rapids: Eerdmans, 1989), p. 172.

∞∞∞

"The Christian Church is, as never before since A.D. 312, challenged by the existence and vitality of the non-Christian religions, because the growing interdependence in every field of life in the world of today presses this upon us. A century ago we could ignore their existence. They seemed immaterial to the dominating curve of history, so patently embodied in the Western world. Today it is impossible to ignore them; and their development, good or evil, will affect all other parts of the world. Some small signs of this . . . are already visible."

Hendrik Kraemer, *Religion and the Christian Faith,* p. 23

∞∞∞

Ideology of religious pluralism. A third reason that makes this issue urgent is that the existence of religious plurality has collapsed into an ideology of religious pluralism. It is now common to celebrate religious plurality as an enriching situation and to dismiss the truth claims of any of the religious traditions.

Several dynamics have fostered this religious pluralism.[3] In Western culture religion has been relegated to the private realm of life. A prevailing relativistic spirit reduces religion to a matter of personal taste or individual preference rather than a comprehensive vision of life that makes truth claims about the world. Exacerbating this relativism is a second dynamic: the troublesome history of the relationship between the so-called Christian West and other parts of the world. Our imperialistic past and cultural arrogance have given way to an acute sense of guilt and embarrassment. Any claim to truth seems to immediately conjure up our coercive past.

Global crises and the fragile interdependence of the world. A fourth factor that makes the issue of a missionary encounter pressing is what may be considered to be a genuinely new element in our situation today. Religious tensions have heightened ecological, political, economic and military crises that threaten the very future of our planet. Indeed, a look at fault lines and places of conflict across the globe make it clear that they lie at the

---

[3]For an excellent analysis of religious pluralism, see Harold Netland, *Encountering Religious Pluralism: The Challenge to Christian Faith and Mission* (Downers Grove, IL: InterVarsity Press, 2001).

borders of people holding different religious beliefs. In such a situation a relativistic tolerance is perceived to be the only hope for peace and cooperation that will ensure a global future. Any claims to truth seem only to foster tension that imperils our fragile and interdependent planet.

Today religious pluralism constitutes one of the greatest challenges to the mission of the church. However, this is not the first time the church has had to carry out its mission in a pluralistic context. In fact, the church was born into a milieu in which there were many lords and many gods (see 1 Cor 8:5), and it has continued to face this challenge at many times in its history.[4] However, today the peculiar combination of factors briefly sketched here makes this issue particularly urgent. Calvin Shenk rightly says, "Religious plurality poses a problem for Christian churches and Christian theology. This is not a new question, but in recent years it has acquired a new significance and urgency. . . . No other issue presents more challenge than the issue of Christian faith and other faiths."[5]

THE PROPER POSTURE AMIDST RELIGIOUS PLURALISM— A MISSIONARY ENCOUNTER

In this context the urgent questions facing the church today are these: "What does it mean to be faithful to the gospel in the context of religious plurality? What is the proper posture that the church must take amidst the sea of differing religious commitments?" A faithful stance for the Christian church toward the world's great religions will be a missionary encounter. I spoke in a previous chapter about a missionary encounter, but here I will make a few more comments that are important for this subject.

A FAITHFUL STANCE FOR THE CHRISTIAN CHURCH TOWARD THE WORLD'S GREAT RELIGIONS WILL BE A MISSIONARY ENCOUNTER.

A "missionary encounter" is an encounter between ultimate and comprehensive religious commitments that shapes different ways of life. The word "encounter" advocates an unflinching commitment to ultimate and all-embracing claims and precludes the

[4]Robert Wilken, *Remembering the Christian Past* (Grand Rapids: Eerdmans, 1995), chapter 2.
[5]Calvin Shenk, *Who Do You Say That I Am? Christians Encounter Other Religions* (Scottdale, PA: Herald Press, 1997), p. 32.

accommodation of any religious vision into another more ultimate and comprehensive one. They can meet only by way of an encounter. The word "missionary" advocates an invitational and appealing approach and precludes a violent and coercive meeting. A missionary encounter with other religions rests on a twofold basis: the comprehensive scope of the gospel and an understanding of religion as a comprehensive vision and way of life.

The comprehensive scope of the gospel and the comprehensive scope of religion. The gospel is a message that in the life, death and resurrection of Jesus Christ God has revealed and accomplished the salvation of the whole world and all peoples. The claim of the gospel is one of universal validity; it is true for all people in all places and at all times. The claim is also one of comprehensive authority; it is true for all of life. The problem is that in Western culture religion has been reduced to practices and beliefs associated with the transcendent or to a private relationship of God to the immortal soul. Religion—privatized, individualized, spiritualized, confined to the future—is separated from most of life.

This view of religion has prevailed in Western culture as a result of the fact-value dichotomy that is the public doctrine of the West (see fig. 4). At the heart of the Western faith is a commitment to scientific reason as the final arbiter of truth. All truth claims must stand before this final judge. Those truth claims that can be validated by scientific reason are considered to be truth, public facts that we know. Those truth claims that cannot be so authenticated are merely opinions, private values that we believe.

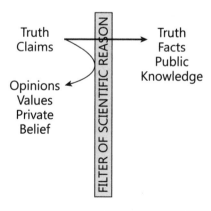

Figure 4. The fact-value dichotomy

Such a distorted view of religion is peculiar to Western culture. In other times and other cultures it is recognized that religion is an all-embracing vision of life. It is an ultimate set of beliefs that give direction and meaning to a whole way of life. We could call numerous witnesses both from the Christian church in other parts of the world and from missionaries who have lived long in other cultures who have new eyes to see the West. The African theologian Kofi Asare Opoku expresses what many Christians outside the West believe: "In African culture, religion and culture are inextricably bound up. Religion derives its profound meaning to the African from the fact that it touches him in the totality of his culture. Religion touches every aspect of life and there are no blank areas in life where man is supposed to fall on other resources. Life is religion and religion is life; and religion is not restricted to certain areas of life but pervades all of life."[6] J. H. Bavinck speaks for many missionaries when he says, "All elements [of culture] have their secret ties with the religious faith of the people as a whole. Nothing is to be found anywhere that can be called a no-man's land. Culture is religion made visible; it is religion actualized in the innumerable relations of daily life."[7]

⸺⸺⸺⸺⸺⸺⸺⸺⸺⸺⸺⸺⸺⸺⸺⸺⸺⸺⸺⸺⸺⸺⸺

"The so-called 'Asian Revolution' (one should also speak of the 'African Revolution') has marked effects in the field of religion, which face the younger churches and Christian missions with an uncharted future. The resurgence of the great religions in their habitat will have consequences—and not only unforeseeable consequences—for the position of the Christian churches. These religions evince more and more a missionary spirit, of a rather aggressive kind, and start movements for the conversion of Christians back to the religion (Hinduism or Buddhism) which they or their ancestors left to become Christians."

Hendrik Kraemer, *Religion and the Christian Faith*, p. 28

⸺⸺⸺⸺⸺⸺⸺⸺⸺⸺⸺⸺⸺⸺⸺⸺⸺⸺⸺⸺⸺⸺⸺

---

[6]Kofi Osare Opoku, "The Relevance of African Culture to Christianity," *Mid-Stream* 13, nos. 3-4 (1974): 156.

[7]J. H. Bavinck, *The Impact of Christianity on the Non-Christian World* (Grand Rapids: Eerdmans, 1949), p. 57.

If we are to speak properly about a missionary encounter with world religions, we must be clear about what we mean by "religion." If we start with the peculiar understanding of religion dominant in the West—an odd anomaly in history and in the rest of the world—we will distort the conversation from the start. Religion is made up of the following characteristics:

- Over against *dualism*, religion is comprehensive: religious commitment shapes all of life.

- Over against *individualism*, religion is a social and cultural phenomenon: religious commitments are held collectively and shape all of human society and culture.

- Over against *secularism*, religion is a matter of spiritual power: we are caught up in a spiritual battle for all of life.

A missionary encounter is a stance that takes this view of religions seriously. It emerges as a result of four interlocking realities: (1) religion is a comprehensive way of understanding and living in the world; (2) there is a plurality of religious visions of human life as we share life together in a common culture; (3) all religious visions claim to be true; (4) adherents of these religions want to live out their comprehensive commitments. Thus, faithfulness lies in the posture of a missionary encounter between these conflicting religious commitments

"In the history of mankind, however, religion almost always appears to be a social phenomenon. Man acts collectively, especially when he responds to what he considers the deepest realities of life. In his response he is conscious of the fact that he is not an individual but a member of a group. . . . Therefore we can say that, although there is a strictly personal element in religion, the great religions of the world have been and still are great social powers, whose influence can hardly be overestimated."

J. H. Bavinck, *The Church Between Temple and Mosque*, pp. 19-20

The word "encounter" means that there will be a clash between these religious visions that will take place in every sphere of life; the word "missionary" means that this clash will be noncoercive, nonviolent and gentle. It will be an uncompromising call to conversion but will offer the gospel in life, word and deed as an attractive and credible alternative in an invitational and appealing way.

ISLAM LIKEWISE REJECTS RELIGION AS A PRIVATIZED PHENOMENON.

A contrast with Islam clarifies the Christian notion of a missionary encounter. Islam likewise rejects religion as a privatized phenomenon. Khurshid Ahmad, for example, insists,

> Islam is not a religion in the common, distorted meaning of the word, confining its scope to the private life of man. It is a complete way of life, catering for all the fields of human existence. Islam provides guidance for all walks of life—individual and social, material and moral, economic and political, legal and cultural, national and international. The Qu'ran enjoins man to enter the fold of Islam without any reservation and to follow God's guidance in all fields of life.[8]

The encounter that ensues, however, is coercive. According to one Muslim leader, in the twentieth century Islam will seek to displace all rivals by force: "Islam is a comprehensive system that tends to annihilate all tyrannical and evil systems in the world and enforce its own program. . . . [Islam is] a revolutionary concept and ideology which seeks to change and revolutionize the world social order and reshape it according to its own concept and ideals."[9] Thus, there is a difference between Islam and Christianity. Lesslie Newbigin writes,

> What is unique about the Christian gospel is that those who are called to be its witnesses are committed to the public affirmation that it is true—true for all people at all times—and are at the same time forbidden to use coercion to enforce it. They are therefore required to be tolerant of denial . . . not in the sense that we must tolerate all beliefs because truth is unknowable and all have equal rights. The toleration which a Christian is required to exercise is not something which he must exercise *in spite of* his or her belief that the gospel is true, but precisely *because* of this belief. This marks one of the very important points of difference between Islam and Christianity.[10]

---

[8]Khurshid Ahmad, *Islam: Its Meaning and Message* (London: Islamic Foundation, 1975), p. 37.
[9]John L. Esposito, *Unholy War: Terror in the Name of Islam* (Oxford University Press, 2003) p. 55.
[10]Lesslie Newbigin, "A Light to the Nations: Theology in Politics," in *Faith and Power: Christianity and Islam in "Secular" Britain,* by Lesslie Newbigin, Lamin O. Sanneh and Jenny Taylor (London: SPCK, 1998), pp. 148-49.

"History obtains a remarkable value in Christianity: it is the framework within which God realizes His great plan of the salvation of the world. Historical facts are very important because they have a place in God's plan in relation to the world. . . . In history God has brought about His marvellous deeds of atonement and redemption. . . . This is what strikes many of the peoples of Asia and of the other mission fields of the world. Their own religions are mythical, vague, and nebulous. When they hear the gospel they are struck first of all by the fact of its historical reality."

J. H. Bavinck, *The Impact of Christianity on the Non-Christian World*, pp. 159-60

Two popular positions that preempt a missionary encounter. The two most common ways to study world religions today in the West are ideological pluralism and the study of comparative religions. Both, in fact, preempt a missionary encounter at the outset by setting the Christian faith within the context of the Western religious vision.

Today the majority of textbooks on world religions are written from the standpoint of comparative religions. It is also the most common way to teach a world religions course in universities and seminaries. The father of this approach, Friedrich Max Müller, defines comparative religions as "a science of religion based on an impartial and truly scientific comparison of all, or at all events, of the most important religions of mankind."[11] With the zeal of a missionary, Müller calls upon the scientific community to "take possession of this new territory in the name of science."[12] The assumption of this approach is that there is a neutral scientific standpoint from which one can objectively and neutrally assess all the religious options. A missionary encounter is eliminated at the outset by assuming the truth of one ultimate religious commitment and camouflaging it in the language of scientific neutrality.

The second position that precludes a missionary encounter is pluralism.

---

[11]Friedrich Max Müller, *Introduction to the Science of Religion* (London: Longmans Green, 1882), p. 26.
[12]Ibid., pp. 26-27.

This approach holds that all religions are equally true. Although religions are different, they are equally true paths to the same God. Christ is considered to be a partial and incomplete revelation of God alongside of the revelation of other religions. The pluralist assumes a neutral position from which to survey the equally true religions of the world.

Both positions preempt a missionary encounter, first by assuming the truth of their own religious position, and second by not taking seriously the comprehensive claims of other religions but rather tailoring all of them to fit into their own. Yet there is no neutral standpoint. Both positions simply stand alongside of other possible ones. Both make truth claims and hold a vision of the world. It is specious to assume the truth of their position rather than set them over against rival truth claims. They cannot pretend to be neutral among their committed rivals. It is only the widespread acceptance of the scientific humanist assumptions of Western culture that allows them to cloak the arrogance and dogmatism of their claims and permit them to go unrecognized.

In fact, what often distorts the discussion of world religions from the start is the assumption that religions are those ultimate commitments that are marginalized by Western secularism. Says Newbigin, "The things now called 'religions' have very little in common with each other except that they dissent from the reigning 'public doctrine'—the doctrine which denies the reality of anything that cannot be handled with the tools of modern science."[13]

The Western humanist story as one more religious vision. And so it is important to make clear what I argued in a previous chapter: religion is at the core of Western culture. J. H. Bavinck observes that one of the striking aspects of Western culture is that it is loosening ties with traditional religions, a process called "secularization." Yet he says, we "have forgotten that our culture, too, is . . . a religious phenomenon. . . . It is time for us to acknowledge frankly that our modern civilization . . . is based on certain presuppositions about man, his place in the world and his responsibility towards God, and that this implies a definite worldview." The more we are willing to probe the roots and worldview of our culture, the more we will see that "modern culture, too, is a religious phenomenon."[14]

---

[13]Lesslie Newbigin, "A Question to Ask; A Story to Tell," *Reform*, November 1990, p. 11.
[14]J. H. Bavinck, *The Church Between Temple and Mosque: A Study of the Relationship Between the Christian Faith and Other Religions* (Grand Rapids: Eerdmans, 1981), pp. 22-23.

Muslim scholar Ziauddin Sardar also argues that secularism is religious and comprehensive in scope. He accuses Western Christianity of becoming dualistic, as it has accommodated itself to secularism. Thus, he charges, *Western Christianity* has "become a handmaiden to secularism. . . . Christianity, it appears, always chooses as secularism wills." But, he correctly insists, *biblical* Christianity is not dualistic and ought to be an "antithesis to secularism."[15]

It is precisely their blindness to the religious nature of modern culture that hinders both pluralists and advocates of comparative study of religions from recognizing they are not neutral. This blindness also keeps us from gaining a proper perspective on how to study and live among plural religions in the West. As Christian believers, we take a position from within the truth of the gospel and encounter all religions from that standpoint. Those who reject the truth of the gospel will do the same. Only the truth in which they take their stand will differ. An encounter is unavoidable.

> AS CHRISTIAN BELIEVERS, WE TAKE A POSITION FROM WITHIN THE TRUTH OF THE GOSPEL AND ENCOUNTER ALL RELIGIONS FROM THAT STANDPOINT.

A CHALLENGE TO PLURALISM

We have begun to explore pluralism. But since this position has become orthodoxy in our day, and because it is pervasively present among those who profess Christ, it is important to deepen our investigation of pluralistic assumptions. Pluralism, in fact, stands apart from all other Christian positions in its denial of the gospel and of the uniqueness of God's revelation in Christ. Indeed, "it is highly questionable whether pluralism can be regarded as a valid option for Christian theology of religions."[16]

Reasons for the widespread popularity of "Christian" pluralism. How can a position that has departed so far from the Christian faith be so persuasive among those who identify themselves as Christians? There are at least three reasons. First, pluralists have inhaled deeply the prevailing rela-

---

[15]Ziauddin Sardar, "The Ethical Connection: Christian-Muslim Relations in the Postmodern Age," *Islam and Christian-Muslim Relations* 2, no. 1 (1991): 59.

[16]Christopher J. H. Wright, "Theology of Religions," in *Evangelical Dictionary of World Missions*, ed. A. Scott Moreau (Grand Rapids: Baker Books, 2000), p. 953.

tivistic air of the post-Enlightenment West. And the fear of absolute truth is aggravated by Christian guilt over centuries of imperialism in which the church has been implicated. Sadly, sometimes in the past a Christian stance for the truth of the gospel has gone hand in hand with an arrogant and coercive imperialism. Pluralists are now at pains to distance themselves from such a posture. Second, our proximity to adherents of other religious traditions has enabled us to see a certain piety and moral uprightness that sometimes we do not see even in other Christians. Surely, such riches, it is thought, cannot be the fruit of an erroneous religious tradition.

"Affirming the finality of Christ does not relieve us of the responsibility to explain the relationship between Christianity and other religions. Sadly, the evangelical world seems almost silent on this crucial issue."

Harvie Conn, "Do Other Religions Save?" p. 207

But it is the third reason that is most persuasive today: "Christian" pluralists feel the force of the urgent need for the unity of humankind facing the threats of ecological destruction and nuclear weapons. They embrace the more widespread fear that any exclusive truth claim for one religion will jeopardize the fragile unity and peace that are constantly endangered by religious strife. It seems to be much more humble to substitute justice or peace as a center to which all world religions can contribute.

A critique of pluralism. There are serious problems with the pluralist position as a Christian option. First and foremost, in pluralism the Christian faith has been made to conform to the controlling humanist story of the West rather than the other way around. When the gospel is tailored to fit the story of the post-Enlightenment West, the Christian faith has been deeply compromised at best, effectively abandoned at worst.

A second problem with pluralism is its arrogance. This may seem initially surprising because this is precisely the accusation that the pluralist levels at someone who holds the gospel to be true. And on the surface there is the appearance of humility and tolerance in pluralism. Yet a closer look reveals that pluralists too hold an exclusive center around which they invite all religions to gather. They too hold their position to be ultimately true and relativize all other standpoints in light of their claim. To say that they alone can truly see that real center toward which all religious traditions are blindly groping is supreme arrogance.

This can be seen in the tale of the blind men and the elephant. Each of the blind men grasps one part of the elephant and claims to know what the animal is like. One grasps the trunk and says that the elephants is like a snake; another the tail, declaring it to be like a rope; still another the tusk, claiming it is like a spear; and so on. It ends: "The blind men argued loud and long. Each of them was partly right, but all of them were wrong." But note carefully: this tale can be told only if there is someone who can truly see. The story is told by the king and his courtiers, who are able to see that the blind men are fumbling about with no more than a partial grasp on the whole. Pluralists cast themselves in the role of those who can see and religions in the role of the blind men groping after ultimate reality. But on what basis can pluralists see that the claims of other religions are simply partial? On what indisputable belief do they stand that enables them to see the whole truth for what it really is? In fact, pluralists simply offer one more claim to truth alongside others. For them to assume that they see clearly while others grope blindly is arrogance. The arrogance is concealed only by the fact that the pluralism's relativistic spirit of tolerance blends in with the reigning assumptions of our day.

> PLURALISTS SIMPLY OFFER ONE MORE CLAIM TO TRUTH ALONGSIDE OTHERS. FOR THEM TO ASSUME THAT THEY SEE CLEARLY WHILE OTHERS GROPE BLINDLY IS ARROGANCE.

A final problem with pluralism is that it substitutes impersonal and abstract ideas as the center around which all religions must gather. Some pluralists, such as John Hick, speak of God. But which God? God becomes an impersonal idea into which all religions can pour their own content. Some, such as Paul Knitter, speak of salvation. But what is it? Again, salvation becomes an abstract concept that can tolerate mutually contradictory viewpoints. Others look to notions of justice or peace, but again these concepts are not given meaning by a particular tradition and are left as empty and vague notions. The question can be raised as to whether such abstract concepts really suffice to gather and reconcile a deeply divided world more than the person and work of Jesus Christ.

A BRIEF SKETCH OF A THEOLOGY OF RELIGIONS

The great meeting of the church with the great religions of the world is indeed upon us. If the church is to be equipped for a missionary encounter, it must have a sound theology of religions that takes its confessional stance within the truth of the gospel. Gerald Anderson correctly says, "No issue is more important, more difficult, more controversial, or more decisive for the days ahead than the theology of religions. . . . This is *the* theological issue for mission in the 1990s and into the twenty-first century."[17]

Anderson points to two factors that have hindered a robust theology of religions. The first is theological neglect. Theology has been more concerned with intra-Christian relations and has not addressed this burning issue. Timothy Tennent comments that it is "quite astonishing that theological students in the West will spend countless hours learning about the writings of a few well-known, now deceased, German theologians whose global devotees are actually quite small and yet completely ignore over one billion living, breathing Muslims who represent one of the most formidable challenges to the Christian gospel today."[18] This theological neglect leaves the church and its leadership ill-equipped to deal with their growing pluralistic context. Second, the reigning pluralism, which is hardly distinguishable from nihilism in its denial of universally valid truth claims, has infected Christian theological reflection. There is a "rampant radical relativism" that abandons claims of the uniqueness of Christ and the truth of the gospel and thus accepts a parity of religions. Anderson certainly is correct: if the church is to be equipped for its encounter with religious pluralism, it will need a robust and biblical theology of religions. In this section I will offer only a brief sketch of what such a theology might look like.

Starting with the public truth of the gospel. In the seductive environment of pluralism the church humbly—yet boldly—confesses that salvation is

[17]Gerald H. Anderson, "Theology of Religions and Missiology," in *The Good News of the Kingdom: Mission Theology for the Third Millennium*, ed. Charles van Engen, Dean S. Gilliland and Paul Pierson (Maryknoll, NY: Orbis Books, 1983), p. 200.
[18]Timothy C. Tennent, *Invitation to World Missions: A Trinitarian Missiology for the Twenty-first Century* (Grand Rapids: Kregel, 2010), p. 192.

found in Christ alone. Carl Braaten rightly declares that the "question of whether there is the promise of salvation in the name of Jesus, and in no other name, is fast becoming a life-and-death issue facing contemporary Christianity. In the churches this issue will become the test of fidelity to the gospel, a matter of *status confessionis* more urgent than any other."[19]

> IN THE SEDUCTIVE ENVIRONMENT OF PLURALISM THE CHURCH HUMBLY—YET BOLDLY—CONFESSES THAT SALVATION IS FOUND IN CHRIST ALONE.

The starting point for a theology of religions must be the public truth of the gospel. To speak of the truth of the gospel is to say that in the person of Jesus Christ and in the events of his life, death, resurrection and ascension God has revealed and accomplished the goal of cosmic history. Since all communities and all people will find themselves somehow included in that final destiny, God's revelation in Christ is true for all people, all nations, all cultures. Perhaps the best word, therefore, to describe the uniqueness of Jesus and his work is "finality." In the biblical view all history is in some way a unity, with the incarnation of Jesus Christ at the center giving it meaning. In Jesus, especially in his death and resurrection, the fullest and final revelation of God and his will for the cosmos has been disclosed and achieved. God's revelation in Jesus Christ must be considered in terms of its historical finality.

Jesus stands at the center of a long biblical story, pointing to the goal of that story and looking back to the beginning of the world. The biblical narrative reveals the one true God, who creates the world and begins his redemptive work in Israel, for the sake of the whole creation and all nations, which culminates in the work in Jesus Christ. This is the context in which we hear the testimony of Scripture: "Salvation is found in no one else, for there is no other name given under heaven by which we must be saved" (Acts 4:12 TNIV); and "There is one God and one mediator between God and human beings, Christ Jesus, himself human, who gave himself as a ransom for all people" (1 Tim 2:5-6 TNIV). This is the context in which we can hear the testimony of Jesus when he says, "I am the way and the truth and the life. No one comes to the Father except through me" (Jn 14:6). These are not

---

[19]Carl E. Braaten, *No Other Gospel! Christianity among the World's Religions* (Minneapolis: Fortress, 1992), p. 89.

proof texts to be ripped from their context and used as clubs in the contemporary debate about individual salvation. No doubt they have implications for that discussion, yet these words testify to the finality of the work of Jesus in the midst of a cosmic story that claims to be the true story of the world.

There are two broadly defined positions that confess the finality of Christ: exclusivism and inclusivism. Exclusivism has been the traditional approach of the Christian church through history, and it is the view shaping this chapter. This use of the word "exclusive" is easily misconstrued.[20] Here it does not refer to a haughty sense of superiority that comes to mind when one thinks of an "exclusive club"; rather, it gives expression to the distinctive and particular truth claims that the Christian faith makes about Jesus Christ. The Christian faith assigns exclusivity to Jesus as the fullest revelation of God and his purpose for the world; there is no other revelation that rivals Jesus. The Christian faith assigns exclusivity to Jesus Christ as the only way of salvation for the world; there is no other path to salvation.

The affirmation that truth and salvation is found in Jesus Christ can be interpreted in different contexts. Often the salvation of the individual is the tacit backdrop for the texts quoted above. Then these words become proof texts lifted from their redemptive-historical context and made to answer questions of who will ultimately experience salvation. A better starting point is to recognize that the Bible is the unfolding story of God's redemptive work for the whole creation. The proper question is not "Who will be saved?" but rather "How will God accomplish a comprehensive salvation for the world and humankind?" This question then forms the narrative backdrop for the confession that salvation is found in Christ alone. The Bible is first of all cosmic history in which individuals find their place.

The question of the fate of those who have never heard the gospel is gaining attention today. Some maintain that explicit faith in the gospel is a necessary prerequisite for salvation. Others remain somewhat agnostic about those who have never heard, leaving it an open question to be answered at the final judgment.[21] Appeal is made to saints in the Old Tes-

---

[20]Timothy Tennent (*Invitation to World Missions*, p. 221) correctly urges us to be more attentive to our nomenclature and embrace more precise and descriptive terms for each position. He suggests a better label for exclusivism is "revelatory particularism." "Revelatory" stresses the importance of revelation, and "particularism" emphasizes the particularity and primacy of Jesus Christ.

[21]For a brief summary of the issue, see Christopher J. H. Wright, *Salvation Belongs to Our God:*

tament who were not part of God's covenant people—for example, Melchizedek, Job and Enoch. Tennent speaks of three nonnegotiables in a theology of religions: the uniqueness of Jesus Christ, the centrality of his death and resurrection, and the need for an explicit response of repentance and faith.[22] The question is whether the last of these, explicit response, is really a nonnegotiable. Here we encounter an important distinction between the ontological basis of Christ's work for salvation and the epistemological necessity of faith in Christ's work.[23] There is agreement that salvation is accomplished through the life, death and resurrection of Jesus (ontological basis), but disagreement as to whether faith is a requirement (epistemological necessity) to experience that salvation.

"Even for those who recognize the inspiration and authority of Scripture, and who take seriously the lordship of Christ, there are difficulties in describing and defining the relationship between the gospel and people of other faiths. In Scripture and in the history of Christian doctrine, there are two major streams or traditions regarding the relationship of God's redemptive activity in Jesus Christ and God's activity among people of other faiths. One tradition, while recognizing the uniqueness and universality of Jesus Christ, emphasizes the *continuity* of God's revealing and redeeming activity in Christ with God's activity among all people everywhere. . . . The other tradition emphasizes a radical *discontinuity* between the realm of Christian revelation, which is unique, and the whole range of non-Christian religious experience. . . . These two streams of teaching and tradition are hard to reconcile; they seem almost contradictory. Yet they are often found almost side-by-side in the New Testament."

Gerald Anderson, "Christian Mission in Our Pluralistic World," p. 38

Celebrating the Bible's Central Story (Downers Grove, IL: InterVarsity Press, 2007), pp. 157-71.

[22]Tennent, *Invitation to World Missions*, p. 219; idem, *Christianity at the Religious Roundtable: Evangelicalism in Conversation with Hinduism, Buddhism, and Islam* (Grand Rapids: Baker Academic, 2002), p. 17.

[23]"Ontological basis" refers to the fact that Christ has accomplished salvation whether or not one knows about it. "Epistemological necessity" refers to the requirement of knowing Christ and responding explicitly in faith to his work.

Among those who affirm an ontological basis in Christ but not the epistemological necessity, there are different approaches. Some simply refuse to go beyond what they believe the Bible clearly teaches and hold a cautious hope that some might be saved by responding to Christ in a way other than the proclamation of the gospel. Others hold a more confident optimism that it will not be few but many who will be saved apart from the response of faith.

Inclusivism is embraced by those who share with exclusivism a firm commitment to the centrality of Christ but at the same time are much more willing to acknowledge salvation for those who do not subjectively respond in faith. A helpful distinction can be made between strong (or hard) and weak (or soft) inclusivism.[24] The difference between these two positions involves whether or not salvation flows to adherents through other religions. A strong inclusivism sees the world religions positively as channels of God's saving revelation. A weak inclusivism rejects non-Christian religions as the means of salvation but recognizes the broad reach of God's saving grace nevertheless.

A strong inclusivism attempts to hold together "the operation of the grace of God in all the religions of the world working for salvation, and the uniqueness of the manifestation of the grace of God in Christ, who is the final way of salvation."[25] Christ is present and at work in the various religions, employing them as channels of salvation. God's saving power comes from Christ but is not confined to the historical Jesus of Nazareth. It may well flow through the religions of the world. "Inclusivists hold that while the source of salvific water is the same for all people, it comes to various people through different channels."[26] Salvation can be known by those who meet Christ not as Jesus of Nazareth, crucified and risen, revealed in the gospel, and made known by the church, but rather through a universal and saving revelation through other religions. This revelation is variously described as

---

[24]Also termed "negative" and "positive" inclusivism. See D. A. Carson, *The Gagging of God: Christianity Confronts Pluralism* (Grand Rapids: Zondervan, 1996), pp. 279-80; also Stanley Grenz, "Toward an Evangelical Theology of Religions," *Journal of Ecumenical Studies* 31, nos. 1-2 (1994): 53; R. Douglas Deivett, "Misgivings and Openness: A Dialog on Inclusivism between R. Douglas Deivett and Clark Pinnock; Some Misgivings about Evangelical Inclusivism," *Southern Baptist Journal of Theology* 2, no. 2 (1998): 27.

[25]Shenk, *Who Do You Say That I Am?* p. 43.

[26]John Sanders, *No Other Name: An Investigation into the Destiny of the Unevangelized* (Grand Rapids: Eerdmans, 1992), p. 226.

the work of the Spirit, or the cosmic Christ based on a Logos Christology (Jn 1:9; Eph 1:10; Col 1:15-20), or more traditionally as general revelation.

This position raises questions. The first set has to do with revelation. Is there confusion between creational or general revelation and redemptive revelation disclosed in the gospel? Have revelation and salvation collapsed into one another? Is there biblical evidence that revelation apart from a gospel centered in the historical Jesus brings salvation? The second set has to do with Christology. Has the historical particularity of Jesus of Nazareth been separated from the cosmic Christ of Ephesians and Colossians (Eph 1:10-23; Col 1:15-20)? Is Harvie Conn correct when he wonders if "the particularity of Jesus of Nazareth evaporates and Christ remains only as a universal Absolute"?[27] A final question is concerned with the view of sin at work in this position. Has this position taken seriously the biblical teaching on the radical power of sin (e.g., Rom 1:18-32)? Although language of idolatry, wrath and judgment sound harsh to our ears, it is the language of Scripture.

Revelation beyond the gospel. To affirm the truth of the gospel does not mean a denial of revelation outside the gospel; rather, the truth is most fully revealed in Jesus, and that is the criterion by which all other truth claims are assessed. Indeed, Scripture itself makes clear that God reveals himself beyond Scripture. Paul proclaims that God has not left himself without testimony, revealing his kindness by providing rain, crops, food and joy (Acts 14:17). Paul writes, "What may be known about God is plain to them, because God has made it plain to them. For since the creation of the world God's invisible qualities—his eternal power and divine nature—have been clearly seen, being understood from what has been made" (Rom 1:19-20). He further affirms, "Gentiles, who do not have the law, do by nature things required by the law," and this is because "the requirements of the law are

> TO AFFIRM THE TRUTH OF THE GOSPEL DOES NOT MEAN A DENIAL OF REVELATION OUTSIDE THE GOSPEL; RATHER, THE TRUTH IS MOST FULLY REVEALED IN JESUS, AND THAT IS THE CRITERION BY WHICH ALL OTHER TRUTH CLAIMS ARE ASSESSED.

---

[27]Harvie M. Conn, "Do Other Religions Save?" in *Through No Fault of Their Own? The Fate of Those Who Have Never Heard*, ed. William V. Crockett and James G. Sigountos (Grand Rapids: Baker Books, 1991), p. 200.

written on their hearts, their consciences also bearing witness, and their thoughts sometimes accusing them and at other times defending them" (Rom 2:14-15). So there is revelation beyond Christ and Scripture. The question remains as to how to understand and assess that revelation.

At no point does Scripture tell us that this revelation brings salvation. In fact, in the first chapter of Romans the opposite is clear: the affirmation of God's revelation in creation is found in the context of sin, darkness, idolatry, guilt, wrath and judgment. Human beings suppress the truth and exchange the knowledge of God for idolatry (Rom 1:18, 23, 25). Revelation in creation cannot be confused with God's grace revealed in Christ.

This is not to say, however, that creational revelation has only the negative role of establishing guilt. In fact, humankind is unable to suppress and eliminate the revelation of God. This is what makes humankind religious. Even though it does not bring salvation, some of that revelation "gets through" and has a positive effect. With a series of rhetorical questions, Johannes Verkuyl eloquently expresses the beneficial power of God's revelation in creation:

> Who could fail to see evidence of the clemency of God in the fact that the great religions have created forms of human community that have provided for a certain amount of regularity and order in the lives of whole peoples? Who could fail to recognize the presence of God's compassion in the humanizing of social relationships brought about by the great religious systems of the world? Who would dare to deny the workings of God's mercy in the development of ideas and the refinement of human thought inspired by these religions? Who would not view it as a proof of God's grace that the peoples of the world, though ignorant of the law of God, accept and do things that are in accordance with that law?[28]

Although revelation in creation does not bring salvation, it does have a beneficial effect in human society even through the various religions of humankind. Some refer to this as "common grace."

Religious consciousness and empirical religions. God's revelation in creation produces in humankind a religious consciousness that in turn gives rise to historical religions. Here I distinguish between the universal religious

---

[28]Johannes Verkuyl, "The Biblical Notion of the Kingdom: Test of Validity for Theology of Religion," in van Engen, Gilliland and Pierson, *Good News of the Kingdom*, p. 75.

consciousness and particular empirical religions.[29] Figure 5 illustrates this distinction, as well as several others that will follow.

A religious consciousness is constitutive of all human beings because they are created fundamentally as religious creatures made in God's image and

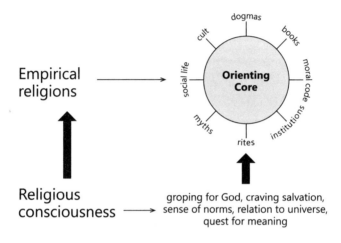

Figure 5. Religious consciousness and empirical religions

fashioned to answer God's revelation. They cannot escape his revelation and must give answer by their very human nature. "Man is 'incurably religious' because his relation to God belongs to the very essence of man himself. Man is only man as man before God."[30] This is John Calvin's notion of the *sensus divinitatus* (a basic sense of God's existence) that is the *semen religionis* (seed of religion). There is a basic religious sense that is oriented toward God's revelation that is the seed of religion.[31]

However, the answer to God's revelation is always distorted to some degree by sin. This is Calvin's corresponding notion of the human being as

[29]Bavinck, *Church Between Temple and Mosque*, pp. 25-34; Hendrik Kraemer, *The Christian Message in a Non-Christian World* (London: Edinburgh House Press, 1938), p. 112.

[30]Johannes Blauw, "The Biblical View of Man in His Religion," in *The Theology of the Christian Mission*, ed. Gerald H. Anderson (London: SCM Press, 1961), p. 32.

[31]John Calvin, *Institutes of the Christian Religion* 1.3.1 (trans. Ford Lewis Battles, ed. John T. McNeill [Philadelphia: Westminster, 1960], pp. 43-44).

a factory of idols: human nature is a "perpetual factory of idols."[32] In fact, "Each one of us, from his mother's womb, is wonderfully adept at devising idols." The source of this idolatry "lies in the fact that men are ungrateful to God and transfer His glory to another person or thing"[33] (cf. Rom 1:21-23, 25). As religious creatures, human beings give answer to God's revelation, but as sinful creatures, their answer is always idolatrous—truth distorted. It is a caricature in which truth is recognizable and present but at the same time disfigured.

There are two sides to the distortion of truth. First, human beings suppress or repress the truth in unrighteousness. Unable to completely hold down the truth, they express it in idolatry. So, second, they exchange the truth of God for an idol. Emil Brunner calls this the "fatal exchange"[34]—the exchange of the true knowledge of God for an idolatrous substitute.

Brunner uses a striking metaphor to illustrate how God's revelation is corrupted by human sin: "The sinful human being is a vessel in which the lees of sin transform the wine of knowledge of God into the vinegar of idolatry."[35] God's revelation is like sweet wine, but when poured into sinful humanity, this wine is transformed into idolatrous vinegar. Calvin speaks of the "confused knowledge of God" that comes from stifling the sparks of God's glory revealed in the creation; he continues, "Yet that seed remains which can in no wise be uprooted: that there is some sort of divinity; but this seed is so corrupted that by itself it produces only the worst fruits."[36] Thus, the religious consciousness bears the imprint of the truth of God's revelation answered by human beings made in God's image yet transformed into the vinegar of idolatry by the darkness of sin.

J. H. Bavinck gives an insightful description of the content of the religious consciousness in terms of five magnetic points. These are the deepest religious longings that shape human life. As religious creatures, human beings grope after God, crave salvation, search for their place in the universe, sense

---

[32]Calvin, *Institutes of the Christian Religion* 1.11.8 (p. 108).

[33]John Calvin, *The Acts of the Apostles 14-28*, vol. 7, trans. John W. Fraser (Grand Rapids: Eerdmans, 1995), p. 301.

[34]Emil Brunner, *The Letter to the Romans*, trans. H. A. Kennedy (London: Lutterworth, 1959), p. 19.

[35]Emil Brunner, *Reason and Revelation: The Christian Doctrine of Faith and Knowledge*, trans. Olive Wyon (Philadelphia: Westminster, 1946), p. 65.

[36]Calvin, *Institutes of the Christian Religion* 1.4.4 (pp. 50-51).

a moral standard or norm, and seek for meaning.[37] The historical religions of the world give concrete expression in their beliefs, practices and institutions to these basic religious impulses. Sin will always pollute and corrupt that response. And so can be found in all the religions of the world both an orientation toward God, salvation and truth, and a corrupted understanding of each of them.

"Most religions presuppose that human beings, and in some cases the cosmos at large, are presently in some kind of undesirable predicament. Furthermore, they presuppose that, in contrast to this predicament, an ultimately good and desirable state can be achieved—either through one's own individual efforts or through the benevolent assistance of one or more higher beings or powers. Given this common structure, three questions naturally emerge that can profitably be put to the various religious traditions: What is the nature of the religious ultimate? What is the nature of the human predicament? What is the nature of salvation (or enlightenment or liberation)? The three questions are clearly interrelated, for one's views on the human predicament and the religious ultimate will have profound implications for beliefs about salvation and how it is to be achieved."

Harold Netland, *Encountering Religious Pluralism*, pp. 182-83

It is this fundamentally religious nature of humankind expressed in the religious consciousness that gives rise to the various empirical religions of the world. The empirical religions are the historical answers that certain communities collectively give to God's creational revelation. We

> IT IS THIS FUNDAMENTALLY RELIGIOUS NATURE OF HUMANKIND EXPRESSED IN THE RELIGIOUS CONSCIOUSNESS THAT GIVES RISE TO THE VARIOUS EMPIRICAL RELIGIONS OF THE WORLD.

---

[37]Bavinck, *Church Between Temple and Mosque*, pp. 32-33. Bavinck expresses these magnetic points in terms of "I and the cosmos," "I and the norm," "I and the riddle of my existence," "I and salvation," "I and the Supreme Power."

might offer a crude equation to account for the phenomenon of empirical religion among all human cultures: God's revelation + a corrupted response + various historical circumstances = particular religion.

Each religion arises in the context of various historical circumstances. Islam arose as Mohammed responded to the corrupt religion of his day. A degenerate and superstitious polytheism calls forth his strict monotheism, and a morally decadent society of injustice, strife and murder finds a ready response in the strict moralism and legalism of Islam. Buddhism was the result of a search for enlightenment to provide deliverance from a transient world in the midst of a superstitious and irrelevant Hinduism. It was Buddha's particular experience with suffering that led him to express the four noble truths that answer this quest that would subsequently shape all the Buddhist traditions. All the empirical religions arise in the context of concrete historical circumstances that continue to shape that religious tradition. Yet beneath these journeys are people with a religious consciousness who search for God, thirst for salvation, hunger for meaning, and long for normativity. Particular historical circumstances shape the idolatrous response that they give.

To this point I have spoken only of a human response to creational revelation. It is possible that more than creational revelation shapes some religions. In the case of Mohammed, it seems that he was also influenced by some form of Christianity or by Judaism. So in this case, God's redemptive revelation recorded in Scripture would play a role in shaping Islam. Bavinck offers an additional intriguing, and more controversial, suggestion: God revealed himself in a special way to the various founders of the great religions of the world.

> In the night of the *bodhi*, when Buddha received his great, new insight concerning the world and life, God was touching him and struggling with him. God revealed Himself in that moment. Buddha responded to this revelation, and his answer to this day reveals God's hand and the result of human repression. In the "night of power" of which the ninety-seventh sura of the Koran speaks, the night when "the angels descended" and the Koran descended from Allah's throne, God dealt with Mohammed and touched him. God wrestled with him in that night, and God's hand is still noticeable in the answer of the prophet, but it is also the result of human repression. The great

moments in the history of religion are the moments when God wrestled with man in a very particular way.[38]

Orienting core and the various components of religions. When we consider the various historical religions of the world, a further distinction can be made between the various phenomena of the empirical religions and the orienting core of each religion. Each religion has many components: its dogmas, its religious books and myths, its moral codes and rites, its cultic and worship practices, its social structures and institutions, and so on. Comparative studies of world religions often begin by examining just these elements separately. What does this religion believe? What are its myths and religious books? What rites and worship practices define this religion? And so on.

But this way of proceeding never allows one to comprehend the spirit that pervades and unifies each religion. These elements are abstracted from the lifeblood of the whole religion. In fact, each religion is a total unity with a pulsating and orienting core. This central religious impulse throbs in every aspect of a religion and binds it together in organic unity. An orienting core is a directing religious motive that animates a religion and gives shape and meaning to all of its elements. It is like a heart that pumps its religious lifeblood into each part.

An orienting core is unique to each religion and arises out of the particular way each religion gropes after God, seeks salvation, wrestles with moral normativity, and so on. For example, the orienting core of Hinduism is the quest to escape from the endless and meaningless cycle of finite existence. The orienting core of Buddhism is the pursuit of deliverance from transient existence. The orienting core of Islam is to proclaim one transcendent God and to found a community ruled by God and his prophet. This particular driving center orients and unifies the various elements of an empirical religion. Again, figure 5 brings all these distinctions together and offers a schematic summary of a theology of religions.

A MISSIONARY APPROACH AND SUBVERSIVE FULFILLMENT

The way one formulates a theology of religions will in turn shape a missionary approach. If God is revealing himself to all people, the longings and cravings of the heart need to be heard; if God's revelation is repressed and

---

[38]Bavinck, *Church Between Temple and Mosque*, p. 125.

exchanged for idolatry, the expression of these longings needs critique. Thus, a missionary approach will involve both a sympathetic, insider approach to religions and a critical, outsider approach.

Sympathetic, insider approach. D. T. Niles once remarked that you do not really understand a religion until you are tempted by it. Until you can imaginatively step inside a religion and understand its drawing power, appreciate how it sees the world, and feel its attraction, Niles believed, you do not understand that religion. Clearly, if we are to love our neighbors from other religious traditions, we need to sympathetically enter their world. It is necessary to "feel" the fundamental religious longings, needs, aspirations and desires at heart of a religion.

> D. T. NILES ONCE REMARKED THAT YOU DO NOT REALLY UNDERSTAND A RELIGION UNTIL YOU ARE TEMPTED BY IT.

Bavinck's five elements of a religious consciousness are helpful here. For example, In Islam we hear a cry for a God who is holy, transcendent and just. We hear a longing for salvation from idolatry, immorality and injustice. We hear a desire for a fixed moral order to govern the whole of our lives. And we see the desire to give our lives for something that matters beyond the grave. And in Buddhism we hear a cry to be liberated from a suffering world, and in Hinduism the longing to find what will endure.

"The whole character of the missionary's message is determined by his attitude towards the non-Christian religion that he has to wrestle with. If we take our stand on the natural goodness and ability of human nature, we will try to build our work upon the foundations of human reason and the strivings of the human heart. But the Bible forbids us to do this. 'Their foolish heart was darkened,' the Scriptures say. . . . The only basis we can ground our message upon is the certainty that God was concerning Himself with these Gentiles before we met them. God was occupying Himself with them before we came to them."

J. H. Bavinck, *The Impact of Christianity on the Non-Christian World*, p. 109

A sympathetic and insider missionary approach also means that we discern the orienting, pulsating and throbbing core at heart of the religions. We hear from Muslims the longing for a community that lives out a just and upright existence because they have discovered the one true God, who orders life in godly way. If we do not hear this, we do not understand Muslims. We hear from Hindus that this finite world is meaningless; everything is futile and empty because it does not last. How can we escape this meaningless, finite reality? Is there something that will last that is worth pursuing? Again, if we do not sense this driving concern, we do not understand Hindus. We hear in the secular person shaped by consumerism, "I can't get no satisfaction, though I've tried and I've tried and I've tried." The elusive search for satisfaction, joy and fulfillment left unsatisfied by an endless parade of goods and experiences is a cry that we must hear if we want to understand our secular neighbors.

Finally, we will need to be able to affirm the good that we hear in the cries of their hearts. The kinds of gropings and cravings identified here are something that we would want to affirm. We want to serve a holy and transcendent God who orders a just and loving community. We too want to give our lives for something that will not be buried beneath the rubble of history but will finally last. We too long for salvation from the immorality, injustice and idolatry of our world that are destroying human life today. We too want our lives to matter, to find fulfillment, to be liberated from evil in the world. All of this should elicit from us compassionate and sympathetic affirmation.

God's common grace opposes the destructive power of sin in human life. Thus, we can see much that is good, right, just, beautiful and true in people who do not confess Christ and in their empirical religions. This forms not only a point of contact (something that I address in the next section) but also a basis on which we can work together toward a more just and equitable society.

Critical, outsider approach. At the same time, we must bring the light of the gospel to bear on all religious life outside the gospel. Because suppression and exchange of the truth always occur, sympathetic affirmation cannot be the only course of action. There will always be a fundamental distortion of the truth that comes from sin. The light of the gospel affirms the religious longing but challenges and critiques the form this longing takes.

Allah is not the God of Abraham, Isaac and Jacob, and the Father of our Lord Jesus Christ. There is in Allah a naked majesty that emphasizes the transcendence and omnipotence of God in such a way that Allah is a twisted version of Yahweh revealed in Jesus. The response of submission (from which the word "Islam" comes) does not measure up to the full covenantal response called for by, say, the book of Deuteronomy. The Christian notion of creation order or wisdom differs from that of the sharia law, which is not sufficiently rooted in the good creation. The Muslim community and its mission differ drastically from the church and its mission, and the Koran is a very different kind of book from the Bible.

> THE LIGHT OF THE GOSPEL AFFIRMS THE RELIGIOUS LONGING BUT CHALLENGES AND CRITIQUES THE FORM THIS LONGING TAKES.

Moreover, a critical, outsider approach will recognize that a spiritual battle is taking place for all of human life, and this includes, fundamentally, our religious convictions. Paul recognized demonic activity in the pagan religions at Corinth. Anthony Thiselton comments on 1 Corinthians 10:18-22 that Paul "acknowledges that the world, especially the world of Gentile religion and culture, embodies pockets of evil power that serve as foci for evil forces in relation to God and to God's people. This power is in the process of crumbling, but still retains the *impact and effect* of devilish powers that operate more forcefully in their *corporate, structural, or institutional effects* than any evil generated by any individual human person as such. *Evil systems have power.*"[39] Demonic power at work in the religious life of humankind is a theme already expressed in the writing of some early church fathers. We see, moreover, that it is the adherents of the highest religions that are most resistant to the Gospels.

Subversive fulfillment. If the sketch of religion offered thus far has validity, a missionary approach will both affirm and challenge each aspect of a religion. Can we integrate and bring these two emphases together? Kraemer offers a fruitful option that he calls "subversive fulfillment" or "contradictive fulfillment." Bavinck calls a very similar approach "*possessio.*"[40]

---

[39]Anthony Thiselton, *1 Corinthians: A Shorter Exegetical and Pastoral Commentary* (Grand Rapids: Eerdmans, 2006), p. 160.
[40]Hendrik Kraemer, "Continuity and Discontinuity," in *The Madras Series*, vol. 1, *The Authority*

We can illustrate this by examining a statement from the Jerusalem Missionary Council (1928).

> We recognize as part of the one Truth that sense of the Majesty of God and the consequent reverence in worship, which are conspicuous in Islam; the deep sympathy for the world's sorrow and the unselfish search for the way of escape, which are at the heart of Buddhism; the desire for contact with ultimate reality conceived as spiritual, which is prominent in Hinduism; the belief in a moral order of the universe and the consequent insistence on moral conduct, which are inculcated by Confucianism.[41]

Gerald Anderson, in his writings, consistently points out that "there are two major traditions regarding the relationship of God's redemptive activity in Jesus Christ and the people of other faiths." Both find their roots in Scripture. The first is the broad, inclusive tradition that emphasizes continuity between God's activity in Jesus and his activity among all peoples. The second is the narrow, particular and exclusivistic tradition that emphasizes radical discontinuity between God's unique revelation in Christ and the range of non-Christian religious experience.[42] If we were to look at how each tradition interprets the Jerusalem Missionary Council statement, we would see the following:

Table 9.1

	Continuity with Christianity	**Discontinuity with Christianity**
Islam	Majesty of God and reverent worship of God	Allah is not Yahweh, and worship of them differs also.
Buddhism	Sympathetic compassion for suffering and unselfish search to escape it	Both compassion and salvation are understood entirely differently from the Buddhist conceptions.
Hinduism	Desire for contact with the ultimate, spiritual reality	Brahman is impersonal; the biblical God is personal.
Confucianism	Universal moral order requiring human moral conduct	Moral order is an impersonal or social structure; in the Bible it is how God directs the creation and human life.

---

of the Faith (New York: International Missionary Council, 1939), p. 4; J. H. Bavinck, *An Introduction to the Science of Missions*, trans. David Hugh Freeman (Philadelphia: Presbyterian & Reformed, 1960), pp. 178-79.

[41]W. H. T. Gairdner, with W. A. Eddy, *The Christian Life and Message in Relation to Non-Christian Systems*, vol. 1, *Christianity and Islam* (Papers for the Jerusalem Meeting of the International Missionary Council; London: Oxford University Press, 1928), p. 491.

[42]Anderson, "Theology of Religions and Missiology," p. 205.

The Jerusalem Missionary Council statement recognizes that each religion has true insight that is in continuity with the "one Truth" revealed in Jesus Christ. Islam has a profound sense of the majesty of God, Buddhism a keen sympathy for the world's sorrow, Hinduism a strong desire for spiritual reality beyond the creation, and Confucianism a central acknowledgment of a moral order in the world that leads to moral conduct. Precisely here we see the religious consciousness come to expression in the great religions of the world—Islam's groping after God, Buddhism's and Hinduism's quest for salvation, and Confucianism's search for moral normativity. The statement rightly insists that these are part of the "one Truth" of the gospel. Continuity exists between the Christian faith and these world religions; the gospel *fulfills* each of these religious insights.

The statement is insufficient, however. Islam's insights about the transcendence of God, Buddhism's and Hinduism's understanding of salvation, and Confucianism's understanding of moral order do not fit easily into a biblical expression of God, salvation and moral order. These expressions of the nature of God, salvation and moral order are not just incomplete and in need of something to complete and fulfill them; rather, they are misunderstandings of God, salvation and morality. These conceptions are the "vinegar of idolatry" that has transformed the wine of God's revelation. Thus, the gospel challenges and subverts each of these notions as it offers Christ as the true answer to the religious longing. God is not simply a transcendent deity; rather, God has been revealed as the triune God centered in Jesus Christ. Salvation is not an escape from the world's sorrow or the physical world; rather, salvation is the renewal of world that removes sin (and not transiency) as the cause of the world's pain. Moral normativity is not an impersonal structure built into the creation or a social construction of a community; rather, it is the way God the Creator constantly orders the creation and human life by his word. The gospel both fulfills religious longing and subverts its twisted expression. It "possesses" the true religious insight, prying it loose from its idolatrous religious

> THE GOSPEL BOTH FULFILLS RELIGIOUS LONGING AND SUBVERTS ITS TWISTED EXPRESSION. IT "POSSESSES" THE TRUE RELIGIOUS INSIGHT, PRYING IT LOOSE FROM ITS IDOLATROUS RELIGIOUS FRAMEWORK AND OFFERING FULFILLMENT IN JESUS CHRIST.

framework and offering fulfillment in Jesus Christ.

This is what we see in the Gospel of John when he finds the religious longing of the Greeks and Jews. He shows Jesus as the Logos who answers that quest while extracting that concept from other religious frameworks. This is what we see in Paul as he employs terminology from Greek mystery religions and the pagan imperial cult and, as Dean Flemming puts it, "wrests the *form* from its Hellenistic thought world only to inject it with a new Christian meaning." Flemming points to words such as "transformation" (Rom 12:2; 2 Cor 3:18), "mystery" (Rom 16:25-26; 1 Cor 2:7; Eph 1:9, 3:3, 5; Col 1:26-27) and "libation" (Phil 2:17 NRSV) as examples of an extensive vocabulary from pagan religious practice.[43] Paul seizes on the religious longing embodied in these words and points to Christ as the fulfillment. Paul's constant practice as he encounters the religious world of his day is to use its terms freely to express forcefully the revelation in Christ as the answer to what these mystery religions were seeking. Kraemer writes, "Paul does not shun the use of terms and ideas so near to these mystery-religions, but he uses them here also to express in a clear way that to believe in Christ is to become a quite new moral and religious being as the old self has died, free from slavery to sin, and the new self has arisen, alive to God in Jesus Christ."[44] When Paul took an idea or practice from pagan religion or culture, says N. T. Wright, "he made sure it was well and truly baptized before it could join the family."[45]

It is precisely a biblical account of creational revelation and human sin that enables us to account for both. The continuity comes as a result of God's revelatory work that gets through and has a beneficial effect. The discontinuity comes because human beings suppress the truth and exchange it for an idolatrous lie. Kraemer brings these two together:

> In the religions, in the moral and cultural life of man outside the realm of God's self-disclosure in the Law, the Prophets, and Jesus Christ, there is evidence of a more or less positive answer to God's manifestation of His ever-

---

[43]Dean Flemming, *Contextualization in the New Testament: Patterns for Theology and Mission* (Downers Grove, IL: InterVarsity Press, 2005), p. 145. Flemming's book is a marvelous exposition of how subversive fulfillment is operative throughout the whole New Testament as the church pursues its mission.

[44]Kraemer, *Christian Message*, pp. 311-12.

[45]N. T. Wright, *What Saint Paul Really Said: Was Paul of Tarsus the Real Founder of Christianity?* (Grand Rapids: Eerdmans, 1997), p. 81.

lasting power and divinity, and of a more or less negative answer to it. The world outside the revelation is not exclusively the world of apostasy and rebellion. It is also the world in which the *humanum* is not annihilated and destroyed, but shows itself in deep longings for and gropings toward God.[46]

This groping after God constitutes a fundamental and universal religious consciousness in humankind that is not entirely erased by sin.

The Church's Mission in the Context of Religious Pluralism

What is the church's mission to adherents of the world religions in the midst of a religiously plural world? In this last section I will attend to one aspect of the church's mission: to communicate the gospel. Specifically, I will treat two important aspects: point of contact and dialogue.

The gospel is not religious teaching that can be added to a fine collection of doctrinal treasures in the world's religious storehouse. Nor is it religious teaching that completes and fulfills the incomplete teaching of the other religions. The gospel is the announcement of historical events— the life, death and resurrection of Jesus Christ—in which God has acted for the salvation of the world. Historical events can only be told with an invitation to believe. The very nature of the gospel as historical events requires that those who believe them make them known with an invitation to believe. Thus, evangelism—telling the story—remains an essential task for the Christian church in the midst of religious pluralism.

> THE GOSPEL IS NOT RELIGIOUS TEACHING THAT CAN BE ADDED TO A FINE COLLECTION OF DOCTRINAL TREASURES IN THE WORLD'S RELIGIOUS STOREHOUSE.

Point of contact. Faithfulness to our missionary calling to broadcast the gospel requires that we attend to the point of contact with adherents of other religions. A point of contact is that place which people from different religious traditions have in common that makes possible true communication. It is a common point that a Christian can use to make contact with another person and communicate good news that touches the person's real needs.

The first point of contact in communicating the gospel is our attitude and

---

[46]Kraemer, *Religion and the Christian Faith*, p. 311.

disposition. Our approach will make the gospel either attractive or unattractive. Taking a controversial stance or one of polemical confrontation can estrange our conversation partner. We could make a long list of characteristics that are important to Christlike communication: love, radical humility, openness, empathy, kindness, gentleness, vulnerability, an untiring and genuine interest in people—their needs, dreams, life situations.

Our communication will also need to present the gospel in ways that are understandable and offer good news where people need to hear it. We must scratch where they itch. Witnessing to the gospel will mean relevance, on the one hand, and challenge, on the other. What is that point of contact where we can present the gospel in a way that touches the heart yet calls for repentance? Again we return to the need to sensitively discern the religious needs and aspirations embodied in the great religions and in the individual hearts of our neighbors. The gospel answers those deep longings yet challenges the very way they are understood. True "points of contact in the real, deep sense of the word can only be found by antithesis. This means by discovering in the revealing light of Christ the fundamental misdirection that dominates all religious life *and at the same time* the groping for God which throbs in this misdirection and finds an unsuspected divine solution in Christ."[47] Yet, again, this antithetical way of proceeding is not to take up a negative and polemical stance but rather is a positive way of dealing with the very nature of human religion. It is faithfulness to the gospel and does not entail an adversarial attitude and disposition.

"Religion is by its very nature a communion, in which man answers and reacts to God's revelation. This definition implies that there is divine revelation, an act of self-disclosure on the part of God. It also implies that there is a human response to this self-disclosure, either in a negative or in a positive sense. Religion can be a profound and sincere seeking of God; it can also be a flight from God, an endeavor to escape from his presence, under the guise of love and obedient service. At bottom of it lies a relationship, an encounter."

J. H. Bavinck, *The Church Between Temple and Mosque*, p. 19

---

[47]Kraemer, *Christian Message*, p. 139.

But we may never forget that it is not only the so-called religious hungerings that provide fruitful points for witness; it is also the universal human problems that people face every day. We approach our neighbor not first of all as an adherent of another religion but rather as a fellow human being who lives in the same world that we live in and faces the same misery, frustration, pain, sorrow and temptation that we face. Since the gospel is concerned with renewal that is as wide as human life, the communication of the gospel must be related to all the varied spheres and problems of life, including the daily grind of life. We often think of our conversations as rising to the inspiring heights of ultimate religious issues. Yet it is precisely in the common and trivial details of our lives that we may find the gospel to be most relevant.

Dialogue. The word "dialogue" in relation to interfaith relations has become common. It has also raised large concerns among evangelicals in the way it has been understood in more liberal circles. Indeed, Tennent rightly comments, "For too long interreligious dialogue has been advanced and identified with a pluralist agenda that openly seeks to accommodate other world religions by discarding distinctive Christian doctrines such as the incarnation and the resurrection of Christ."[48] Fear of dialogue rests on concerns that a relativistic basis is at the foundation of it all: the truth of the gospel is surrendered and is considered to be one more religious view among many. Another concern is that dialogue may lead to syncretism, a blending of the religious traditions in a compromised synthesis. This danger seems to lurk where dialogue is understood to be the way to discovering truth or the way of salvation. And, finally, some evangelicals perceive that dialogue replaces witness and evangelism.

Indeed, many of these concerns are realized in certain Christian traditions that engage in interreligious dialogue. But there can be different kinds of dialogue based on very different worldviews. Indeed, "all too often ecumenical interfaith dialogue has been built on sub-Christian views of revelation, Christ, and man."[49] On the basis of the modern scientific worldview,

[48]Tennent, *Christianity at the Religious Roundtable*, pp. 239-40.
[49]David Hesselgrave, "Interreligious Dialogue—Biblical and Contemporary Perspectives," in *Theology and Mission: Papers and Responses Prepared for the Consultation on Theology and Mission, Trinity Evangelical Divinity School, School of World Mission and Evangelism, March 22-25, 1976,* ed. David Hesselgrave (Grand Rapids: Baker Books, 1978), p. 229.

dialogue has been understood as a dialectical movement that moves us ever closer to the truth. This view has great confidence in human rationality, and dialogue is the means by which autonomous reason is able to come closer to truth. On the basis of a postmodern reaction that often is skeptical of truth claims, dialogue is a matter of sharing our stories, none of which are truer than any another. The goal is mutual enrichment as we share with others the riches of our religious traditions. If modern dialogue is rationalistic, postmodern dialogue is relativistic. Neither of these ways of dialogue is consistent with the gospel.

Yet we need not reject dialogue out of hand. It is possible to understand dialogue within the story of the Bible.[50] In fact, there are good reasons to pursue such an understanding. In a pluralistic setting we live side by side with our neighbors of different faiths, and this requires ongoing conversation. Further, our Western sense of superiority of the past often has led to a stance of confrontational monologue that has hindered communication. It is essential that our posture be one of humility and vulnerability, and a listening ear will be important to repair perceptions of the past. Dialogue is also a recognized and familiar approach in our world, and so a contextualized witness will require that we employ methods that are broadly shared. Moreover, the threats to our global community are very real. While we affirm that true human unity can be found only in Jesus Christ, there is a place to seek proximate justice and peace based on common grace. Such efforts certainly will require mutual dialogue among those of different faiths. And, finally, we have much to learn: we will learn about our own faith and often be able to clear up misunderstandings and do away with caricatures of our fellow citizens.[51]

But in the end dialogue is an expression of our love for others. John Stott writes, "Dialogue is a token of genuine Christian love, because it indicates our steadfast resolve to rid our minds of prejudices and caricatures which we may entertain about other people; to struggle to listen through their ears and look through their eyes so as to grasp what prevents them from hearing the gospel and seeing Christ; to sympathize

---

[50]For a model and example from within the Evangelical tradition of how this might work, see Tennent, *Christianity at the Religious Roundtable.*
[51]Ibid., p. 241.

with them in all their doubts, fears, and hang-ups."[52] For these, and other reasons, dialogue may not be discarded. "The question for evangelicals is not *Shall we engage in dialogue?* but *In what kinds of dialogue should we engage?*"[53]

True Christian dialogue will be built on a trinitarian foundation. We dialogue on the basis of the Father's work in creation and history. This means that we share a common creation and common concerns with our neighbors of different faiths living in a common world. This will provide basis for dialogue. It is especially clear that we share a common cultural and social calling to develop and care for the creation. This shared task of building a culture and society should mean a constant dialogue among different religious traditions that seek a way to find peace and public justice to live together. This is not to discount religious difference—precisely the opposite. What is needed is a committed or principled pluralism that takes seriously the various religious commitments and how they shape the public square. Here witness and dialogue are held firmly together.

We dialogue also as a witness to Jesus Christ. We enter dialogue with different faith commitments whether we engage Muslims and Hindus or humanists of various sorts. Our fundamental identity is as witnesses of Jesus, and we must not downplay that identity. In fact, our "dialogue will be all the richer if both of us give ourselves as we are. For the Christian that giving must include witness."[54] It is not permissible to suspend our commitments or to hide or relativize the faith commitments that shape us. "As Christians we must be willing to do interreligious dialogue with a measure of risk. But the methods we adopt for that encounter cannot put at risk our commitment to Jesus Christ."[55] There is no neutrality in the public square, only faith stances. We may not shed

> THERE IS NO NEUTRALITY IN THE PUBLIC SQUARE, ONLY FAITH STANCES. WE MAY NOT SHED OURS AND CLOTHE OURSELVES WITH ANOTHER.

---

[52]John Stott, *Christian Mission in the Modern World* (Downers Grove, IL: InterVarsity Press, 1975), p. 81.

[53]Hesselgrave, "Interreligious Dialogue," p. 235.

[54]Willem A. Visser 't Hooft, *No Other Name: The Choice Between Syncretism and Christian Universalism* (Philadelphia: Westminster, 1963), p. 118.

[55]Conn, "Do Other Religions Save?" p. 205.

ours and clothe ourselves with another. And true adherents of other faith communities do not want us to disguise or camouflage our true faith. On many occasions perplexed and irritated Muslims (especially, and sometimes Hindus or Buddhists) wonder why Christians are so quick to set aside their Christian commitment for another, for a pluralist vision that is incompatible with their faith.

A distinction made by John Hick offers an example of a pluralist attempt to jettison our identity as witnesses of Christ and set aside our commitment to the gospel. He distinguishes between confessional dialogue and truth-seeking dialogue. Confessional dialogue is dialogue on the basis of a commitment to the truth of one's faith, and this Hick rejects. For him, this kind of dialogue will end either "in conversion or in a hardening of differences."[56] Instead, Hick calls for a shift to truth-seeking dialogue, in which adherents of the faiths engage in dialogue for a mutually enriched understanding of the Transcendent Being. But such a contrast is false. One cannot separate "confession" from "truth-seeking." A confession of faith will always be the starting point for seeking the truth. Hick does not seem to recognize this and accordingly substitutes his faith commitment for the truth. He seems to be unaware that his view is only one of many ways in which people grasp their experience; it is only one religious vision of life based among others. In fact, Hick has not eliminated the confessional stance at all; rather, he has assumed and imposed his own. It is true of Hick's view, no less than any other position, that "no standpoint is available to anyone except the point where they stand; that there is no platform from which one can claim to have an 'objective' view that supersedes all the 'subjective' faith-commitments of the world's faiths; that everyone must take their stand on the floor of the arena, on the same level with every other, and there engage in the real encounter of ultimate commitment with those who have also staked their lives on their vision of the truth."[57]

In fact, with his view of dialogue Hick has given up his claim to come to the table as a representative of the Christian faith. As Alister McGrath notes of such approaches, "It is not Christianity that is being related to other world

---

[56]John Hick, "Christian Theology and Inter-Religious Dialogue," *World Faiths* 103 (August 1977): 7.
[57]Lesslie Newbigin, *The Open Secret: An Introduction to the Theology of Mission* (Grand Rapids: Eerdmans, 1995), p. 168.

faiths; it is a little more than a parody and caricature of this living faith, grounded in the presuppositions and agenda of western liberalism rather than in the self revelation of God."[58]

Finally, dialogue will be on the basis of the work of the Spirit. It is the Spirit's work to convince the world of sin, righteousness and judgment (Jn 16:7-11). Conversion is not our work but rather that of the Holy Spirit. Our witness to Christ in the midst of dialogue may lead to the conversion of our neighbor, but it may also be the case that the Spirit will convert us more fully to the gospel (cf. Acts 10).

CONCLUSION

The issues raised in this chapter will only become more urgent. Mission advocate Max Warren said over a half century ago, "The impact of agnostic science will turn out to be child's play compared to the challenge to Christian theology of the faiths of other men."[59] We have seen the impact of unbelieving science on theology in devastating ways in the last four centuries. If Warren is even close to the truth, this will remain one of the most critical issues for the church in mission in the foreseeable future.

FURTHER READING

Bavinck, J. H. *The Church Between Temple and Mosque: A Study of the Relationship Between the Christian Faith and Other Religions.* Reprint. Grand Rapids: Eerdmans, 1981.

Bolt, John, ed. *The J. H. Bavinck Reader.* Grand Rapids: Eerdmans, 2013.

Kraemer, Hendrik. *Religion and the Christian Faith.* Philadelphia: Westminster, 1956.

Netland, Harold. *Encountering Religious Pluralism: The Challenge to Christian Faith and Mission.* Downers Grove, IL: IVP Academic, 2001.

Shenk, Calvin E. *Who Do You Say That I Am? Christians Encounter Other Religions.* Scottsdale, PA: Herald Press, 1997.

---

[58]Alister McGrath, "The Christian Church's Response to Pluralism," *Journal of the Evangelical Theological Society* 35, no. 4 (1992): 489.
[59]Quoted in Wilfred Cantwell Smith, *The Faith of Other Men* (New York: Harper & Row, 1962), pp. 120-21.

DISCUSSION QUESTIONS

1. Calvin Shenk suggests that there is no more urgent challenge to the Christian church today than the relation of the church to other religions. Explain why you agree or disagree with this.

2. What specific pressures might the church feel in a pluralistic environment? Tell some stories that illustrate these pressures.

3. How do you account for your Muslim or Hindu neighbor who seems more godly and upright than your Christian brother or sister?

ESSAY TOPICS

1. This chapter begins by suggesting that it is essential to start with the proper posture of a missionary encounter. What is a missionary encounter? Compare and evaluate other common ways of approaching the topic.

2. Pluralism is the majority view of Western people. Offer a critical analysis of pluralism from the standpoint of the gospel.

3. Gerald Anderson believes that a theology of religions is *the* theological issue of our time. Sketch and evaluate the theology of religions offered in this chapter.

10

Urban Mission

The New Frontier

☙

Harvie Conn predicts that if "we are to reach the world of the twenty-first century, we must reach its cities."[1] Likewise, James Scherer forecasts that "mission in the 21st century will be won or lost in the battle for the soul of big cities."[2] Roger Greenway and Timothy Monsma call cities the "new frontier" and exhort the church to recognize the importance of urban mission.

> The urbanization of Christian missions is an urgent and serious need. Cities determine the destiny of nations, and their influence on the everyday affairs of individuals is incalculable. As cities grow in number, size, and influence, it is incumbent on those responsible for world evangelization . . . to focus on cities. . . . Likewise, in the years ahead students of missions . . . will need to wrestle with urban issues if they are to be prepared for ministry in tomorrow's world.[3]

These are strong statements indeed. And rightly so as there is much to suggest that cities are indeed mission's new frontier. This chapter responds to these urgent calls and briefly focuses attention on the important issue of urban mission.

---

[1]Harvie Conn, "Urban Mission," in *Toward the 21st Century in Christian Mission*, ed. James M. Phillips and Robert T. Coote (Grand Rapids: Eerdmans, 1993), p. 334.

[2]James Scherer, *Gospel, Church, and Kingdom: Comparative Studies in World Mission Theology* (Minneapolis: Augsburg, 1987), p. 47.

[3]Roger S. Greenway and Timothy M. Monsma, *Cities: Missions' New Frontier* (Grand Rapids: Baker Books, 1989), p. xi.

OUR URBAN FUTURE—AND PRESENT

An older Urbana Student Missions Conference video, *God Is Building a City*, ends its presentation on urban mission abruptly with the words "You've got an urban future whether you like it or not!" And indeed, 180,000 people move to cities every day, 65 million per year. Indeed, we have an urban future—and that future is rapidly becoming the present—whether we like it or not. How can we characterize our urban world? Statistics are notoriously slippery because definitions differ, but perhaps some urban statistics can begin to paint some aspects of the picture. When we observe the statistics of our urban present, three things emerge: the phenomenal growth of cities both in terms of numbers and size; the growth of cities in the Southern hemisphere; and the enormous socioeconomic need in these cities.

> WE HAVE AN URBAN FUTURE—AND THAT FUTURE IS RAPIDLY BECOMING THE PRESENT—WHETHER WE LIKE IT OR NOT.

Phenomenal growth. The remarkable growth of cities can be tracked by seeing the exponential growth since 1800. When the modern missionary movement began, at the beginning of the nineteenth century, only 3% of population lived in cities. One hundred years later, in 1900, it had risen to 14%. By 1980 it was up to 40%, and as we moved into the new millennium, half of the world's population lived in cities. It is expected that by 2050 80% and by 2100 90% of the world's population will be urban. At the present rate of growth, the urban population will double in less than two decades. In 1950 there were 69 cities over one million—already a remarkable phenomenon in the history of humankind at that time—but by 2012 that number had expanded to 486. In the latter half of the twentieth century a new urban phenomenon emerged: the megacity, defined a city with more than 10 million people. In 1950 there were only two megacities, but by 2012 there were 27 megacities, with another 10 poised to cross that threshold. Sociologist J. John Palen is justified in saying that the "rapid transformation from a basically rural to a heavily urbanized world and the development of urbanism as a way of life has been far more dramatic and spectacular than the much better known population explosion."[4]

---

[4] J. John Palen, *The Urban World* (New York: McGraw-Hill, 2008), p. 5.

"The spectacular growth of large cities on this planet represents an awesome challenge to the church of Jesus Christ on all six continents. . . . If we consider the impact of *urbanization* and *urbanism* in our world, we can see that city growth is even more significant. By *urbanization* we mean the development of cities as *places* where size, density and heterogeneity are measured. We might call this the *magnet* function of cities, drawing humanity into huge metroplexes. By *urbanism* we mean the development of city as *process*—that is, the *magnifier* function of cities, spinning out urban values, products and lifestyles into a world linked by media, even in rural and small-town places. . . . Sorry, you have an urban future, whether you like it or not."

Ray Bakke, *A Theology as Big as the City*, p. 12

Growth of cities in the Southern hemisphere. The original urban revolution in the nineteenth and early twentieth centuries took place in the Western nations of the world. But urban growth in the West has stabilized. And from the latter half of the twentieth century on, the growth has taken place in the poor countries of the South. In 1950 six of the largest ten cities in the world were in the Northern hemisphere; in 2012 only one of those cities, New York, was in the top ten, and the rest were in the Southern hemisphere. In 1950 New York was the biggest city in the world, but by 2012 it was eighth. Today, the United States has 73 cities over 500,000 and Western Europe 62, while China alone has 145, India 93, and the remaining countries of Asia 168. Similarly, Latin America has become increasingly urban throughout the twentieth century, with over 75% of its population living in cities, and with 114 cities of over a half million people. Africa, though it started a little later in the game, is now the most rapidly urbanizing part of the world. On that continent there are now 91 cities over 500,000, and it is projected that urban growth there will continue at a galloping rate. The only megacities in 1950 were located in the Northern Hemisphere (New York and London), but today 21 out of the 27 megacities in the world are in the Southern Hemisphere. And these rates will not slow down. According to the United Nations, the majority of population growth in the next quarter century is expected to take place in cities of the Southern hemisphere. The urban population will double in 38 years, but in the poorer countries of the South it will take 30 years to double; and 93% of all population growth will take place in the cities of the Southern hemisphere, with 80% of that growth occurring in Asia and Africa.

Enormous socioeconomic need. Earlier in the twentieth century the majority of the poor lived in rural settings. Today the poor are primarily found in cities. Throughout the cities of many countries in the Southern hemisphere appalling numbers of people live in the squalor of slums. Over a billion people live in absolute poverty, over 75% of them in urban slum conditions without water, sanitation or basic public services. In the world's richest thirty countries about 2% of the population lives in slums. By contrast, over 80% of the urban population of the world's poorest countries lives in slums. For example, perhaps as many as 90% of the citizens of Addis Ababa, Ethiopia, live in slums, some 2.5 million people. Over 15 million people in Mexico City and over 14 million in Calcutta live in wretched slum conditions. The worst statistics are found in Sub-Saharan Africa, where a staggering 72% of the urban population lives in slums, while in South Asia the number stands at about 60%. And future projections for these areas do not look good. The numbers are expected to climb dramatically in all parts of the third world, with the outlook being especially dire in Sub-Saharan Africa, where the number of people living in slums will rise from 250 million to almost 400 million.

The Importance of Cities for Mission

This brief excursion through some urban statistics begins to open up the importance of the city for the mission of the church. A number of reasons for the strategic importance of urban mission can be identified.

Sheer numbers. Quite simply, the cities are where the people are. Rapid urban growth alone demands that the church attend to the city. We are in the midst of an urban revolution or urban explosion. Today, Palen notes, "the number of people living in cities outnumbers the entire population of the world only 100 years ago."[5] As Timothy Keller, a pastor in New York

---

[5]Ibid.

City, puts it, "In cities, you have more 'image of God' per square inch than anywhere else in the world."[6] The population of the world is continuing to grow at an exponential rate. But what is important for this chapter is to recognize that the majority of this population growth is taking place and will continue to take place in cities, especially the cities of the Southern hemisphere. A 2001 press release issued by the United Nations stated, "Virtually all the population growth expected at

> IF THE CHURCH IS TO REACH THE PEOPLE OF THE WORLD, IT MUST BE IN THE CITIES WHERE THEY LIVE.

the world level during the next 30 years will be concentrated in urban areas"; moreover, "almost all of the population increase expected during 2000-2030 will be absorbed by the urban areas of the less developed regions. During that period the urban population of the less developed regions is expected to increase by 2.0 billion persons, nearly as much as will be added to the world population, 2.2 billion."[7] So if the church is to reach the people of the world, it must be in the cities where they live.

Cultural power and influence. Cities are the centers of cultural power and influence. Sociologist Manuel Castells observes that the "destiny of humanity is being played out in urban areas, in particular, the great metropolises."[8] As cities host the most powerful cultural institutions of the world, they exercise formidable influence on the rest of the country, and when networked together, they impact our global world. Cities are where we find concentrations of political power and government, institutions of higher education, business and finance, venues for leisure and entertainment, communities of the arts, and centers of media. The strategic importance of urban mission is apparent when we see that there are four kinds of people in the cities: the next generation, the unreached, the poor, the shapers of culture. About the last group Keller says, "The people who tend to make

---

[6]Timothy Keller, "Why God Loves Cities," address to the Third Lausanne Congress on World Evangelization, Cape Town, October 17-24, 2010 (www.spu.edu/depts/uc/response/new/2011-spring/features/god-loves-cities.asp).

[7]"Future World Population Growth to Be Concentrated in Urban Areas of World," United Nations press release POP/815, March 21, 2001 (www.un.org/News/Press/docs/2002/pop815.doc.htm).

[8]Manuel Castells and Jordi Borja, *Local and Global: Management of Cities in the Information Age* (London: Earthscan, 1997), p. 3.

films, write the books, do the business deals—they're here. The people that have the biggest impact on the cultures of the world are here."[9] Thus, the urban centers of great metropolitan regions are "nerve centers" that disproportionately impact the world.[10] It certainly is true that as the city goes, so goes the rest of culture.

But it is more than that. Not only are cities powerfully shaping their own cultures and nations, but also as the more influential global cities of our world go, so goes our entire world. There is ongoing debate as to the degree that globalization is weakening the nation-state. Certainly, the rise of communication, travel and information technology has changed the face of the modern world. Computers make it possible in the single push of a button to transfer millions of dollars from one place to another. Nation-states cannot control the cash flow that can make or break their economic well-being. Further, with new forms of communication technology and access to the worldwide web, the governments of nation-states cannot control information or shape the mindset of their citizens. So even if the prediction of the downfall of nation-states is premature, it certainly is true that they have lost a degree of power because of rapid and widespread technological revolution. The loss of power for the nation-state has meant a rise in power for the city as an international world of nation-states become a global web of cities connected and networked in a variety of ways. These cities, especially global cities, now have a tremendous power to influence the global affairs that affect all people in the world. The Christian church cannot turn its back on such places of power and influence.

The focal point of a global missionary encounter. In order to properly understand the cultural influence of the city, we must go beyond simply the institutions that wield power—business, finance, academic, media, political—and drive deeper to the religious core that shapes these cultural institutions as well as the urban population. In the past, our analysis of cities has relied on secular sociology and anthropology, which are blind to the foundational religious beliefs that shape our cities. We need to understand the city as a communal way and pattern of life in which religion is "made

---

[9]Keller, "Why God Loves Cities."
[10]Timothy Keller, "Our New Global Culture: Ministry in Urban Centers," p. 1 (www.copgny.org/files/Movement%20Day/Ministry_In_Urban_Centers.pdf).

visible in different ways."[11] Religious commitments create and shape the urban landscape, they integrate and unify the life of the city, and they direct the institutional powers at work in the city.

We might metaphorically describe the city as the geographical space positioned directly above major "religious" tectonic plates that are shaping our global world. As these tectonic plates shift, the cities are affected and reconfigured. Two religious tectonic plates directly beneath the city are the pluralistic coexistence of the world's religions and economic modernity and globalization with its flipside in consumerism. It is precisely in the city that the missionary encounter with pluralism and the great religions of the world—as well as with the idols of Western humanism—is primarily taking place.

> IT IS PRECISELY IN THE CITY THAT THE MISSIONARY ENCOUNTER WITH PLURALISM AND THE GREAT RELIGIONS OF THE WORLD—AS WELL AS WITH THE IDOLS OF WESTERN HUMANISM—IS PRIMARILY TAKING PLACE.

While the religions of the world once lived in comparative isolation in countries defined by that religious identity today, it is in cities that we find a meeting of all these religions. This is an important reason for the church to focus attention on the city. "The city has become the global stage," Conn says, "on which the world's religions, once isolated by place of origin or ethnicity, now increasingly dialogue."[12] If the church is to be a major dialogue partner at the roundtable of religions, holding as it does the truth of the gospel of Jesus Christ, it cannot abandon the city.

But it is in the city that perhaps an even more important missionary encounter is taking place with the most powerful global religion in our time. In a previous chapter I argued that a missiology of Western culture is a priority for our day because the beliefs of the West are now the shared culture of at least the urbanized centers of the world. The urban revolution began in Western culture as it was driven by the Industrial Revolution. Much of the urban explosion in the Southern hemisphere is propelled by

---

[11]Harvie M. Conn, "A Contextual Theology of Mission for the City," in *The Good News of the Kingdom: Mission Theology for the Third Millennium*, ed. Charles Van Engen, Dean S. Gilliland and Paul Pierson (Maryknoll, NY: Orbis Books, 1993), p. 98.

[12]Ibid., p. 97.

the dynamics of globalization. The Industrial Revolution is a part of the religious story that has shaped Western culture, and globalization is the continuing spread of this religious story around the world especially in urban centers. A missionary encounter with this post-Enlightenment culture is the reality of Christian life in the city.

<hr>

"Mission is no longer about crossing the oceans, jungles and deserts, but about crossing the streets of the world's cities. From now on, nearly all ministry will be crosscultural amid the urban pluralism caused by the greatest migration in human history from Southern hemispheres to the North, from East to West and, above all from rural to urban."

Ray Bakke, *A Theology as Big as the City*, p. 13

<hr>

We need to recognize that "what is at stake here are fundamental allegiances—loyalty to different gods."[13] Which gods will shape the patterns of life in the cities of our world? If the church is to be at the cutting edge of a missionary encounter with the most powerful global religion of our day, it must be in the cities of the world.

Poverty and socioeconomic need. We have briefly noted the statistics of growing urban poverty. In the urban centers of the world are found growing hunger, disease, unemployment and violence. Greenway and Monsma claim that the "*urban poor constitute the largest unclaimed frontier Christian missions has ever encountered.*"[14] Many have neither heard the gospel nor seen it demonstrated. They live outside the reach of most churches, and very few attempt to reach them. The causes of their poverty are rarely understood. Greenway and Monsma list ten causes of urban poverty in the Southern world: lack of employment opportunities, especially among those who lack skills and capital; scarcity of affordable, decent housing; millions of abandoned street children; gravitation of the elderly to cities without support systems; breakdown of family structures; corruption of government au-

---

[13]Brian Walsh, *Subversive Christianity: Imaging God in a Dangerous Time* (Bristol: Regius, 1992), p. 15.
[14]Greenway and Monsma, *Cities*, p. 45.

thority and callous indifference to poor; inadequate infrastructures and public services; the failure of the church both in terms of relocation at a distance from the poor and abnegation of responsibility for their needs; a mentality of self-aggrandizement among many churches in the Southern world. This list is quite helpful in identifying the various needs that churches can tackle as they become sensitized to this large unclaimed frontier.

Nevertheless, they have not addressed what the United Nations sees as the primary cause of urban poverty in the South: the unjust economic structures at a global and international level. The neoliberal economic policies of the West have become the accepted practice and international standard for a global market. And, although the implementation of this economic system at an international level has brought good, the playing field is not level.[15] Third-world countries are at a tremendous disadvantage in the global market, and it is primarily the urban poor in slums who pay the price. N. T. Wright speaks of the "massive economic imbalance of the world" as "the major task that faces us in our generation" and "the number one moral issue of our day." With prophetic indignation, he goes on to strongly denounce it:

> The present system of global debt is the real immoral scandal, the dirty little secret—or rather the dirty enormous secret—of glitzy, glossy Western capitalism. Whatever it takes, we must change this situation or stand condemned by subsequent history alongside those who supported slavery two centuries ago and those who supported the Nazis seventy years ago. It is that serious.[16]

If Wright is even close to being correct, then this constitutes an important opportunity, even a priority, for the church in mission. The church must find ways to be present with the gospel in the midst of the cities of the world, especially among the urban poor.

Decreasing presence of Christians. In the previous paragraphs we noted that the church has often relocated at a distance from the poor. In 1900 close

---

[15]I have addressed this in "Probing the Historical and Religious Roots of Economic Globalization," in *The Gospel and Globalization: Exploring the Religious Roots of a Globalized World*, ed. Michael W. Goheen and Erin G. Glanville (Vancouver: Regent, 2009), pp. 69-90. I identify five different ways that the poorer countries are excluded from full and equal participation in the market: exclusion from capital, exclusion from currency, exclusion from decision-making power, exclusion from markets, exclusion from scarcities (pp. 83-85).

[16]N. T. Wright, *Surprised by Hope: Rethinking Heaven, the Resurrection, and the Mission of the Church* (New York: HarperCollins, 2008), pp. 216-17.

to 70% of the population of the city was Christian. That has steadily decreased, until today the number stands at about 40%.[17] No doubt some of this is simply because of the growing urban poor in cities of the world where the percentage of Christians is low—Asia, for example. But

> THE CHURCH MUST FIND WAYS TO BE PRESENT WITH THE GOSPEL IN THE MIDST OF THE CITIES OF THE WORLD, ESPECIALLY AMONG THE URBAN POOR.

that does not tell the whole story. There is often Christian flight from the city, especially in the West, that is the result of the desire for a more comfortable lifestyle in the suburbs.

Negative stereotypes and terms of derision about the city abound in Christian circles: "Crime-ridden. Busy. Scary. Drug-infested. Liberal. Overcrowded. Hopeless."[18] Conn believes that in the Western church negative stereotypes and myths about the city "paralyze Christian initiative to reach cities for Christ, . . . are stumbling blocks in the way of urban church planting, . . . [and] send Christian leaven and salt running for safety on suburban kitchen shelves."[19] He proceeds to name and dispel several stereotypes that he believes are responsible for this Christian flight from the city: the rural/urban myth ("It's the city, what do you expect?"); the depersonalization misunderstanding ("In the city I'm a number, not a person"); the crime generalization ("I'm afraid of the city"); the secularization myth ("Any faith dies in the city"); the privatization generalization ("It's bigger than any of us"); the power misunderstanding ("You can't fight city hall"); the monoclass generalization ("Nobody in the city but poor folks"). He does recognize "grains of truth in the generalizations" but wants to "shovel away the accumulated snowdrifts" that have crippled urban mission.[20] Yet, even if there is more than a grain of truth in such urban myths, the church is called to be in dif-

---

[17]The graph in David G. Barrett, *World-Class Cities and World Evangelization* (Birmingham, AL: New Hope, 1986), p. 16, traces this decline. In the 2012 version of "Status of Global Mission, 2012, in the Context of AD 1800-2025," put out by the Center for the Study of Global Christianity, Gordon Conwell Theological Seminary, the percentage is 41.2% (www.gordonconwell.edu/resources/documents/StatusOfGlobalMission.pdf).

[18]Chuck DeGroat and Rachael Butler, "A Church for the City: Present Realities and Future Challenges," *Perspectives* 27, no. 2 (2012) (available at www.rca.org/Page.aspx?pid=8184).

[19]Harvie Conn, *A Clarified Vision for Urban Mission: Dispelling the Urban Stereotypes* (Grand Rapids: Zondervan, 1987), p. 9.

[20]Ibid.

ficult places where there is need for the sake of the gospel. There in the city "is precisely where the world's greatest brokenness and the world's greatest opportunity collide."[21]

◇◇

"The Bible clearly describes a God who is completely interested and involved with both the structures and the individuals that compose society. The schism in the church that has pitted social and personal ministries against each other in the city, a tragic legacy of the fundamentalist-modernist controversy early in the twentieth century, still marginalizes the church's ministry in the rapidly urbanizing developing world. The church must learn how to go up to the urban powerful and down to the urban powerless with equal integrity."

Ray Bakke, *A Theology as Big as the City*, p. 14

◇◇

AN AGENDA FOR URBAN MISSION

Conn has offered an action-reflection agenda for urban mission that helpfully highlights a number of urgent issues. Three of these are especially important: holistic mission; the calling of the church in the public sector; urban church planting.[22] These same three can be found in Keller's "ministry fronts" for urban churches: holistically serving the city, especially the poor, in word and deed; producing cultural leaders who integrate faith and work in society; routinely multiplying itself into new churches with the same vision. But Keller adds two more that are equally important: welcoming, attracting and engaging non-Christian people; transforming character and establishing a countercultural community through deep community and small groups.[23] These five items must be priorities on the agenda for the faithful urban church.

Engaging secular folk. In the Western world, where the culture is increasingly secularized, it is essential to learn how to welcome and engage secular

---

[21]DeGroat and Butler, "Church for the City."
[22]Conn, "Urban Mission," pp. 332-34. The fourth is the new missionary force that is emerging from churches in the Southern hemisphere. I will take that up in the final chapter.
[23]Keller, "New Global Culture," p. 13.

people. This will mean a number of things. It will involve learning how to welcome skeptics and address their fervent intellectual and religious questions with a respectful and humble yet intelligent apologetic. Keller lists, for example, the following "defeaters"—widely held objections to the Christian faith that remain barriers to believing the gospel—which must be continually addressed.[24]

- The Other Religions. "No one should insist their view of God is better than all the rest. All religions are equally valid."

- Evil and Suffering. "A good, all-powerful God wouldn't allow this evil and suffering. Therefore, this God doesn't exist or can't be trusted."

- The Ethical Straitjacket. "We must be free to choose for ourselves how to live—no one can impose it on us. This is the only truly authentic life."

- The Record of Christians. "If Christianity is the true religion, why would so much oppression happen in history with the support of the church?"

- The Angry God. "Christianity is built around a condemning, judgmental deity who demands blood sacrifices even to forgive."

- The Issue of Science. "As a believer in evolution, I cannot accept the Bible's prescientific accounts of the origin of life."

- The Unreliable Bible. "The Bible can't be trusted historically or scientifically, and much of its teaching is socially regressive."[25]

Defensive, self-righteous and polemical responses are sure to turn away unbelievers. Humility and respect, without sacrificing rigorously thoughtful answers, can go a long way toward dispelling unbelief. I remember lecturing in the heart of a large Asian city. A professor from a public university in that city was in attendance, and during the question time he raised the problem of the violent record of Christians in history. My response was one

> HUMILITY AND RESPECT, WITHOUT SACRIFICING RIGOROUSLY THOUGHTFUL ANSWERS, CAN GO A LONG WAY TOWARD DISPELLING UNBELIEF.

---

[24]See Timothy Keller, *The Reason for God: Belief in an Age of Skepticism* (New York: Riverhead Books, 2008).
[25]Keller, "New Global Culture," p. 14.

of repentance and pain that so often as believers we do not live up to the gospel. I was told that the next Sunday he was baptized; it was not so much the content of my response as the tone that was convincing.

Welcoming and engaging our unbelieving neighbors will also mean learning a language in our preaching and liturgy that is comprehensible to those without a Christian background without becoming gimmicky, dumbing down or abandoning history and tradition. In this regard, Chuck DeGroat and Rachael Butler comment on their own church, City Church in San Francisco:

> At City Church, you will find worship and preaching that is historically liturgical but eminently comprehensible, where significant intellectual and spiritual questions are addressed with respect. Seekers and skeptics know they are in a church, but they are made to feel welcomed and respected. Their questions are not ignored. In fact, download a few sermons and you will notice a theme—City Church expects that skeptics will come, because the table has been set for them. Members and regular attendees feel comfortable inviting their skeptical friends, not because worship is somehow "dumbed down" or made to be seeker friendly, but precisely because skeptics will encounter Christian worship in its historic forms, and have it explained in a way that is inviting and comprehensible. Gimmicks won't work, especially in the midst of crisis and difficulty.[26]

Engaging our secular friends will also mean that we make the gospel relevant as good news to their whole lives. An otherworldly gospel does not have traction with a generation rightly concerned about issues of justice, environment and peace or who want to understand what the Christian faith says about the places where these career-driven professionals spend most of their week. N. T. Wright believes that the religious yearning of people living in the West today revolves around four issues: the longing for justice, the quest for spirituality, the hunger for relationships, the delight in beauty.[27] What does the gospel say to these issues?

We just noted City Church in San Francisco as a church that works at welcoming and engaging the unbelieving folk of its city. When asked about

---

[26]DeGroat and Butler, "Church for the City."
[27]N. T. Wright, *Simply Christian: Why Christianity Makes Sense* (New York: HarperCollins, 2006), pp. 3-51.

important issues for urban ministry, senior pastor Fred Harrell provided the following list. What is intriguing is the sensitivity to the unbelieving community and to finding ways to welcome them into the community of the people of God. What are the important issues for forming a missional congregation in a highly secularized city such as San Francisco?

- Creating a community that tries to remember what it's like not to believe.

- Creating a culture that expects convinced, unconvinced, and everything in between to be present at every meeting and gathering.

- Communicating a full-fledged gospel that seeks the flourishing of all and is communicated with a commitment to be comprehensible to all.

- Normalizing brokenness and creating a culture of humility and authenticity.

- Recognizing and remembering we live in a post-Christendom world.

- Realize that you must be a strong leader that will not allow your vision to be co-opted by Christians who are hoping you will simply recreate their Christian subculture from back home (wherever home is).[28]

Harrell's list certainly raises important questions. I remember hearing Lesslie Newbigin argue for a distinctive Christian vocabulary and set of ecclesial practices based on the gospel into which the unbeliever is socialized. But these are not necessarily incompatible. The operative word here—and Harrell rightly grasps this—is "hospitality." How can the Christian community offer welcoming hospitality to our non-Christian friends and neighbors?

Establishing a countercultural identity through community. The church is called to be a preview and foretaste of the coming kingdom of God. When the word "countercultural" is used, it is important to be clear that this is not meant to be only a loud no to culture. It is not just about standing against and in contrast to our culture. There are two sides to being a countercultural or alternative community: standing in contrast to the idolatry that shapes the urban context, but also living in fulfillment of the creational currents. In other words, urban

> THE CHURCH IS CALLED TO BE A PREVIEW AND FORETASTE OF THE COMING KINGDOM OF GOD.

---

[28]Private email correspondence July 2, 2012.

life manifests currents of life that flow from an embrace of the good creational dimensions of creation as well as currents of death that emerge because human beings distort God's good gifts. A countercultural community looks for, celebrates and embraces all the good of the city; a countercultural community also looks for, laments and rejects all the idolatry.

The trouble is that every aspect of urban life will have what is creationally good and what is idolatrously twisted. For example, the sexual revolution has celebrated the goodness of human sexuality, but it has also taken it out of the bounds of lifelong commitment and a self-giving relationship. How does the church celebrate the goodness of human sexuality in a way that affirms it as God's gift as well as stand against what has distorted it? An attractive countercultural community will learn to say yes—a resounding affirmation to all that God has given in creation and has been discovered and enjoyed in the city; it will also learn to say no—an equally firm rejection of all that demeans and degrades human dignity in the way of idolatry.

Here are some questions for reflection on what such a community might be: How can we celebrate and embody the commitment to work among young professionals yet challenge the economistic or consumerist spirit and the workaholism that often attends it? How can we celebrate and embody the multiculturalism and ethnic diversity of our cities without allowing it to become an oppressive ideological power? How can we celebrate and embody the joy in consuming the things and experiences of God's good creation while opposing the consumerism that dominates city life? How can we celebrate and embody the concern of many in the city for justice and peace, joining them in their efforts while engaging this issue with the integrity of the gospel rather than the ways of humanism? How can we pursue the unity and reconciliation that our cities long for while rejecting the relativistic and pluralistic center that is offered for such a goal? How can we celebrate and embody the freedom that modern technology has given us and yet stand against the rootlessness that accompanies this freedom?

Keller points to five areas in which our countercultural identity must become a reality in the city: sexuality (neither prudish nor adapting to the idolatry of sex in our culture), money (promoting radically generous lifestyles), power (commitment to power sharing and building relationships between classes and races), unity (finding ways to express our unity with brothers and sisters in Christ by attending to the heart of the gospel rather than divisive theological details),[29] community (the need for small groups and communal life in an urbanized environment where often extended family support is lacking).

Practicing holistic mission. Two things are clear enough from the brief statistical analysis presented in this chapter: there are many people living in cities who do not know Jesus Christ, and there is enormous poverty and social need. The question of holistic mission becomes more than a theoretical issue. It is a concrete and vital problem of human need. Where should the urban church focus its financial and human resources? "Should it focus its attention narrowly on personal evangelism and wait to see urban transformation through transformed individuals? What is the relationship between evangelism and social responsibility in the city, where the vastness of need underlines such a relationship?"[30]

"These urban poor now constitute an unreached people's bloc that is the third largest in the world, the most responsive to the gospel, and one that is doubling every decade. The cries of these poor call us to devote every effort to one task—that of finding men and women who can initiate kingdom movements among these poor. But structures need creating to serve such laborers. They need to be taught a theology that will enable them to understand the patterns of such kingdom movements, and they need a demonstration of the demands of life among the poor."

Viv Grigg, *Cry of the Urban Poor*, p. 2

Perhaps nowhere is this question more urgent than in cities of the Southern hemisphere. In a setting where more than 75 percent of the people live in poverty, the evangelical Latin American Theological Fraternity

---

[29]A fine example of an initiative in unity and ecumenical life for the sake of the city is the program True City: Churches Together for the Good of the City (www.truecity.ca).

[30]Conn, "Urban Mission," p. 332. See also Ronald J. Sider, Philip N. Olson and Heidi Rolland Unruh, *Churches That Make a Difference: Reaching Your Community with Good News and Good Works* (Grand Rapids: Baker Books, 2002).

struggled with the social calling of the church. Without shirking its evangelistic mandate—there is a call for holistic mission that includes proclamation,
discipleship, worship, service—this group urges the urban church to take up
its social task in a multipronged manner that includes at least the following
seven elements: a better understanding of urban social and economic structures in the light of Scripture that equips the church to respond to the
complex reality of the city; the social and cultural incarnation of the church
in the city with a rich pilgrim ecclesiology that challenges individualism;
concrete action for the weak and oppressed in social, economic and political
programs; ecumenical cooperation among churches that shows a united
front to non-Christians and mutually strengthens churches in urban
mission; the prophetic role of the church that sensitively challenges the
centers of power; the recovery of the church as a community of compassion
that is empathetic and sensitive to human tragedy; the recovery of "universal
priesthood" of all believers, who can have a positive influence through their
various professions and trades.[31] These seven approaches repay careful
study for all churches committed to faithfully taking up their social calling.

  Training believers for their calling in the public sector. The primary way
the church can pursue justice at the structural level is not through its ministry as an institutional church but rather through individual believers
taking up their tasks in the public square. Conn says, "Can Christians, ex-
ercising their responsibility as a priesthood of believers outside the institutional structures of the church, participate in a new way in urban issues of
poverty and homelessness, unemployment and urban slums? Are there
other ways for Christians to participate in meeting the needs of the global
city without doing it through the church as an institution? The CEBs suggest
that possibility."[32] The reference to CEBs (from the Spanish *comunidades
eclesiales de base*) is to base ecclesial communities in Latin America, which
we encountered in a previous chapter. They are small ecclesial groups often
existing in the context of grinding urban poverty that put a high priority on
equipping and training their members to seek justice in the public square.

  This is an important aspect of urban mission also because so many people

---

[31]"Seeking the Peace of the City: The Valle de Bravo Affirmation," *Urban Mission* 7, no. 1 (1989):
  22-24.
[32]Conn, "Urban Mission," pp. 333-34.

have flocked to the city because of work. That is their primary context; they are living out their lives primarily in terms of their occupations. Keller observes, "Because city-center people do not have much in the way of private lives, discipleship must involve integrating one's faith and work. Discipleship must demonstrate how to be distinctively Christian within one's job, including how to handle peculiar temptations and ethical quandaries, how to produce work from a distinctly Christian worldview, and how to help other Christians in the industry do their work excellently."[33]

In terms of the mission of the church, there are two important reasons, which we noted in a previous chapter, for nurturing people for their calling in the urban marketplace. First, this is the primary place where a witness to the gospel can take place in life and in word. Second, as agents of the justice and love of the kingdom, the work of believers in the public square may be an instrument of God's common grace. Herman Bavinck comments that God, by his common grace, "powerfully opposes the destructive might of sin." It is not just in the life of individuals that God's grace is active; rather, the "entirety of the rich life of nature and society exists thanks to God's common grace. . . . The love of family and kin, societal and political life, art and science are all in themselves objects of his divine good pleasure. . . . They all together constitute . . . the original order that God called into being at creation and that he still preserves and maintains, sin notwithstanding."[34] Faithfulness to the gospel in the various occupations and professions in which believers work throughout the week may be a way in which God exercises his power and grace, not just by drawing people to himself, but also by upholding his creation order for human life and preserving human life from total injustice and alienation.

> AS AGENTS OF THE JUSTICE AND LOVE OF THE KINGDOM, THE WORK OF BELIEVERS IN THE PUBLIC SQUARE MAY BE AN INSTRUMENT OF GOD'S COMMON GRACE.

Sadly, it is rare to find churches that take this aspect of mission seriously. So it is encouraging to see urban initiatives that are tackling this task. In San Fran-

---

[33]Keller, "New Global Culture," p. 5.
[34]Herman Bavinck, "Common Grace," trans. Raymond C. Van Leeuwen, *Calvin Theological Journal* 24, no. 1 (1989): 60.

cisco the Newbigin House of Studies fellows program is training a number of young professionals across the spectrum of cultural life to live out the gospel in their various callings.[35] In Phoenix, the Surge School of Missional Training Center has gathered a number of churches to train leaders to wrestle together with how the gospel might shape the whole of their lives, including their occupations.[36] In New York City, Redeemer Presbyterian Church has established a Center for Faith and Work that is doing a variety of things to shape the urban Christian for his or her calling in the marketplace.[37] Redeemer works at this task at three levels: theoretical (theological education to equip people to think Christianly about their callings), mentoring (providing educators and mentors who enable people in various ways to fulfill their calling), community (finding ways within the congregation to support all in their work).[38]

Planting urban churches.[39] "The day of church planting for the world's cities has yet to dawn" says Conn. "The invisible, unreached peoples of the world's cities must be found—the poor, the industrial workers, the government employees, the new ethnic and tribal groups settling in urban areas. If we are to reach the world of the twenty-first century, we must reach its cities. And that will demand a new campaign of church planting."[40]

Certainly, this was the pattern of the book of Acts, as is clear from Antioch on. Paul plants churches in urban areas that are then called to be a witness to the gospel in life, word and deed in the place where they have been set. This is especially true for the slums of third-world cities. Viv Grigg describes a certain Asian megacity and says that the poor in the slums of that city "had never known a poor people's movement or their own churches. No one had ever proclaimed Jesus to them. No holy man had ever lived among them to show them Jesus in word and deed, in acts of mercy and deeds of power." And this one city is not an isolated case. "The sad news," Grigg says, "is that, after thorough research in eight cities, I found only two embryo movements. The conclusion: The greatest mission surge in history

---

[35]See www.newbiginhouse.org/Story.
[36]See missionaltraining.org/services/laity.
[37]See www.faithandwork.org/. See also Matthew Kaemingk, "Herman Bavinck, Lesslie Newbigin, and Reformed Mission in the Global Workplace," *The Bavinck Review* 3 (2012): 103-5.
[38]Keller, "New Global Culture," p. 16.
[39]For a rich collection of chapters on urban church planting, see Harvie M. Conn, ed., *Planting and Growing Urban Churches: From Dream to Reality* (Grand Rapids: Baker Books, 1997).
[40]Conn, "Urban Mission," p. 334.

has entirely missed the greatest migration in history, the migration of Third World rural peasants to great mega-cities."[41] Grigg has set out to fill this gap in the church's mission with this Urban Leadership Foundation.[42]

Viv Grigg names three spiritual movements important for changing urban squatter poverty in a third-world city:

1. "Movements of churches among the poor may transform the micro-economic and local political environment."
2. "Middle-class professionals, practicing a holistic discipleship and possessing an intimate knowledge of the poor, may effect change in the implementation and governing of the cities at an urban planning level."
3. "Christians in the international elite may change the macro-economic systems of international debt, unjust trade, and increasing monopolization by unaccountable multinational corporations."

Viv Grigg, *Cry of the Urban Poor*, p. 257

But urban church planting, whether in the Northern or the Southern hemisphere, will be serviceable to God's mission only if the churches that are planted are truly missional congregations. If we plant introverted churches that are domesticated by the idols of their culture, then our evangelistic endeavors will be like harvesting the wheat only to carry it into a burning barn. What is needed are churches planted with a missional consciousness that lives out a missional identity in the midst of the city. Churches must be planted as missional congregations that welcome and engage non-Christians,

> THE NEED IS NOT SIMPLY FOR MORE CHURCHES; THE NEED IS FOR FAITHFUL MISSIONAL CONGREGATIONS ROOTED IN JESUS CHRIST WHOSE PRESENCE, DEEDS AND WORDS MAKE THE GOSPEL KNOWN.

---

[41]Viv Grigg, "Sorry! The Frontier Moved," in Conn, *Urban Churches*, pp. 150-51.
[42]See www.urbanleaders.org/home/.

that nurture an alternative community in their gathered life, that engage in holistic mission, and that train believers for their callings in various sectors of public life. The need is not simply for more churches; the need is for faithful missional congregations rooted in Jesus Christ whose presence, deeds and words make the gospel known.

A THEOLOGY OF MISSION FOR THE CITY

If the church is to carry out this agenda, a theology of mission for the city must be developed to equip the church for its urban vocation. In various places Conn counsels us on what this should look like. He distinguishes between a theology of mission *in* the city and a theology of mission *for* the city. The first simply sees the city as the inconsequential setting or place where mission is operative. A theology of mission can proceed in isolation from the city; the city is, in fact, marginal to real theologizing. The second scenario—the one Conn calls for—sees the city as a fundamental component in designing a theology of mission, a definitive category important enough to create a new subdiscipline of urban missiology.[43] In this case an urban mission theology, for Conn, faces the challenge of integrating theology, urban studies and contextualization.

Another way of articulating the three prongs of this urban theology is to speak of reflection on the gospel, reflection on the urban context, and contextualization. These are not three separate tasks isolated or independent from each other; rather, each implies a particular focus with the whole task in view.

The need for reflection on the gospel. Too often we strategize pragmatically about how to reach the cities for Christ and so construct a missiology of the city. We discuss evangelization, church renewal and church expansion. These are not unimportant, but what we need is deeper theological reflection that accompanies the church in its urban mission—a "missiological vision *for* the city must also be a theological vision *of* the city."[44] The church, in order to be authentic, must wrestle with numerous theological matters, many of them common to the whole mission of the church: the nature of

[43]Harvie M. Conn, foreword to *God So Loves the City: Seeking a Theology for Urban Mission*, ed. Charles Van Engen and Jude Tiersma (Monrovia, CA: MARC, 1994), pp. vii-viii.
[44]Conn, "Contextual Theology of Mission," p. 101.

the gospel, the nature of the church, the nature of mission, issues of contextualization, a theology of religions to equip for an encounter with religious pluralism, apologetics and answers to the urgent questions of the urban masses, missional ecclesiology and the forms that a missional church must take (both as individual congregations and ecumenically as the church together), the relationship between evangelism and issues of justice and mercy, issues of liturgy and worship, and so on.

Other issues, though perhaps not quite so obvious, are equally important. For example, the Bible's teaching on the principalities and powers is significant. If in some way Paul, when he speaks of "principalities and powers" (Rom 8:38; Eph 3:10; 6:12; Col 2:15), is referring to the spiritual realities and forces that shape the human institutions of culture, it will be essential for an urban theology to attend to this. Or, for another example, we have reduced the power, scope and gravity of sin in many ways, yet so often in Scripture sin is understood in terms of idolatry—not simply individual idols, but communal idols that shape whole cultures (cf. Rom 1:21-23, 25). What idolatry is at work in shaping the culture of the city? How do these idols become visible in the institutions and patterns of urban life?

Reflection on the gospel must move beyond narrowly "theological" subjects and ask questions traditionally associated with worldview studies. The very nature of the gospel and Christ's salvation demands this. Herman Bavinck issues this crucial reminder:

> Christ did not come just to restore the religio-ethical life of man and leave all the rest of life undisturbed, as if the rest of life had not been corrupted by sin and had no need of restoration. No, the love of the Father, the grace of the Son, and the communion of the Holy Spirit extend even as far as sin has corrupted. . . . Therefore Christ has also a message for home and society, for art and science.[45]

And we might add for music and literature, media and entertainment, leisure and work, technology and sexuality, money and finance, business and politics, environment and sports, social work and friendship, and so on. For an urban population that wants to understand the relevance of the

---

[45]Herman Bavinck, "Common Grace," trans. Raymond C. Van Leeuwen, *Calvin Theological Journal* 24, no. 1 (1989): 61-62.

gospel and needs to be challenged with the gospel of the kingdom, this will be an important task.

But our theological reflection will not only be a matter of wrestling with Scripture to shed its light on current issues; it will also involve studying the church-in-mission throughout history to learn how it has struggled to be faithful to Scripture. We think, for example, of the early church, born into an urban environment in the Roman Empire. It was in this context that the "first urban Christians lived resistively against the culture of the Empire by meeting needs, offering hospitality, and celebrating new possibilities of community. They created alternative assemblies (*ekklēsia*) and households (*oikos*), which were a direct challenge to, and imitation of, the building blocks of Roman civic life."[46] Or, much later, we note the study of John Wesley and Methodism that established itself in the midst of industrial cities forming communities committed to holy living and identifying with the poor.[47] Many others could be mentioned, of course, but today's urban theology should not ignore the struggles of the church in the past.

The need for urban studies. We will need a study of cities that is deeply shaped by the gospel. Research into the urban context is essential, and this is a frequent theme in writing on urban mission. Understanding the history of cities, the original vision that formed them, the patterns of life characteristic of the city, the demographic layout, and the various cultural institutions within the city and much more will require a Christian analysis that draws on many of the social sciences. But the danger is that the social sciences are perhaps the most secular part of the university today. The church's use of the disciplines of social science that will equip the church must not be held captive by the secular bias of today's sociological and anthropological disciplines. Instead, faithful Christian study of the city will take seriously the category of religion as a foundational, integrating and directing power. Conn notes that research for urban mission often has been on the microlevel of urban demographics, and so now a shift must take place in which we

---

[46]A. Davey, "Urban Mission," in *Dictionary of Mission Theology: Evangelical Foundations*, ed. John Corrie (Downers Grove, IL: InterVarsity Press, 2007), p. 419. See also Wayne A. Meeks, *The First Urban Christians: The Social World of the Apostle Paul* (New Haven: Yale University Press, 1983).

[47]See Theodore W. Jennings Jr., *Good News to the Poor: John Wesley's Evangelical Economics* (Nashville: Abingdon, 199). Interestingly, this book arose out of teaching theology and equipping church leaders in the context of Mexico City.

"turn as well to the issue of urbanism, to the city as a way of life, and to the proper connection between 'religion' and urbanism."[48]

History will be an important part of our research. Four examples can illustrate how historical research is important for urban mission today. First, historical analysis will enable us to see how cities began to form in Europe and the United States during the Industrial Revolution. This will allow us to see the cultural worldview story that shaped the structuring of the city and thus to recognize the difficulties faced by the city as well as why so many Christians abandoned the urban environment.

"In the richer countries of the West, cities have survived the tumultuous end of the industrial age and are now wealthier, healthier, and more alluring than ever. In the world's poorer places, cities are expanding enormously because urban density provides the clearest path from poverty to prosperity. Despite the technological breakthroughs that have caused the death of distance, it turns out that the world isn't flat; it's paved. The city has triumphed. But as many of us know from personal experience, sometimes city roads are paved to hell. The city may win, but too often its citizens seem to lose. . . . For every Fifth Avenue, there's a Mumbai slum; for every Sorbonne, there's a D.C. high school guarded by metal detectors."

Edward Glaeser, *Triumph of the City*, pp. 1-2

Second, historical analysis will also able us to discern the differences between the growth of cities in the Southern hemisphere and urban growth in the North and the West. Urban growth in the South has taken place much more rapidly. This has left third-world cities with less time to assimilate the growth and create infrastructures needed for the increasing population. It has also occurred more recently and therefore has been impacted by the processes of globalization and its underlying religious beliefs. Both of these facts give us insight into the cities of the South. We can understand, for

---

[48]Harvie M. Conn, "Introduction to Part 1," in Conn, *Urban Churches*, p. 34.

example, why the city is such a symbol of hope for many living in the third world. Moreover, it gives us insight into the brutal poverty of these cities.

Third, historical analysis of specific cities will enable us to understand the various ways they were formed. Not all cities are given shape by the same cookie-cutter molds. Different factors and dynamics have shaped various cities in their unique histories. It is important to understand various kinds of cities. In 1982 one urbanologist distinguished seven different kinds of cities, including, for example, neighborhood cities, international cities, wired cities, regional cities and leisure cities.[49] No doubt much has changed since that time, but it does alert us to the fact that there are different kinds of cities molded by their differing histories. This kind of historical analysis is essential for a right understanding of the demographics of a particular city as well as its needs and dynamics.

And, fourth, historical analysis will enable us to see the kinds of urban shifts taking place today. There is a revitalization of American cities. "People began to reconsider the benefits of living in proximity to one another, of walking and biking instead of paying high fuel costs, of experiencing the energy that comes when vital souls cluster together with a common vision. A certain enlightened sensitivity toward global issues, a commitment to the poor and environmental concerns, among other things, brought a diverse throng of new urbanites to revitalize the city. . . . The great revival of certain cities . . . is due, in large part, to the "clustering force" of unique individuals who seem to feed off of each other's energy, creativity, and vitality."[50]

A second shift is toward megaregions or regional cities, which "produce half of the world's economic activity, two thirds of the scientific activity, and three quarters of all global inventions."[51] Neal Peirce says that these "great metropolitan regions—not cities, not states, not even nation-states—are starting to emerge as the world's most influential players."[52] These great regional cities have

---

[49]Arthur Shostak, "Seven Scenarios of Urban Change," in *Cities in the 21st Century*, ed. Gary Gappert and Richard V. Knight (Beverly Hills, CA: Sage Publications, 1982), pp. 69-93, quoted in David Barrett, *World-Class Cities and World Evangelization* (Birmingham, AL: New Hope, 1986), pp. 19-20.
[50]DeGroat and Butler, "Church for the City."
[51]Ibid.
[52]Neal Peirce, "The 'Citistates' Are on the Rise, and the Competition Is Fierce," *The Philadelphia Inquirer*, July 26, 1993, p. A11, quoted in Harvie M. Conn, *The American City and the Evangelical Church* (Grand Rapids: Baker Books, 1994), p. 182.

an urban center that is their heart and nerve center. There are gathered together professionals, major industry and financial centers, major cultural institutions. Residents in the city center are professionals as well as leaders in business, finance, academia and the arts, and they also include new immigrant families, students, and those with alternative lifestyles, such as the gay community.[53]

This kind of analysis using not only historical research but also other social sciences—all shaped by the gospel—will enable the church to understand its urban context and raise the right questions and seek the right approaches to being a church for the city.

The need for contextualization. Contextualization wrestles with the fusion of the two horizons. When we speak of urban mission, we have in view the normative biblical horizon and the contemporary urban horizon. Contextualization sets the urban world within the context of the biblical story in such a way that it both affirms and critiques that world. It requires, of course, a deepening understanding of both the biblical text and the urban context. Contextualization that attempts to relate two things—gospel and culture—is abstract. In fact, it is precisely in the church as an incarnated community called to live out the gospel in the urban-cultural context that these two stories meet. The urban congregation is the place where the gospel comes alive in its affirmation and challenge to the city.

> THE URBAN CONGREGATION IS THE PLACE WHERE THE GOSPEL COMES ALIVE IN ITS AFFIRMATION AND CHALLENGE TO THE CITY.

The desire to be a church for the city may prompt the following questions: "Where are we located? What are the men and women in this region really hungry for? What will this mean for our local ministry? What changes will we need to make?"[54] These are helpful questions for certain aspects of the church's mission. For example, understanding what men and women hunger for will be important for evangelism or ways of ministering to individuals in the local congregation. What changes do we need to make that will be important for the ministry of the local congregation in creating a welcoming environment? How do we relate the gospel to the religious hungerings and cravings of the urban population?

[53]Keller, "New Global Culture," p. 1.
[54]DeGroat and Butler, "Church for the City."

Keller's "manifesto" on urban mission also offers helpful insight into contextualization but also primarily in terms of evangelism and congregational ministry to individuals. He helpfully shows a spectrum of how various kinds of urbanites have appropriated the modern or postmodern forms of humanism that shape Western culture and lays out the implications for ministering to them. In a particularly insightful section he discusses the marks of people living in global cities—professionally driven, sexually engaged, consumer-oriented, geographically and socially rootless, pragmatic thinkers, naturally suspicious, ethnically diverse, civic minded—and the ministry implications of those characteristics.[55]

We need to recognize, however, that mission goes beyond evangelism and the ministry of the local congregation, as important as those aspects of mission are. In light of the last section, we can note at least three more things: being a countercultural community, carrying out our callings in the public life of culture, doing holistic ministry. Each of these will bring different types of questions. The gospel will be related to the urban context at different points. For example, if the church is to be a countercultural community, it will need to reflect deeply on the macroreligious beliefs that shape a city and certainly identify the idols that hold sway over it. Of course, since contextualization is always both a yes and a no to a culture, it will mean celebrating the life-giving aspects of urban life as well. This will enable God's people to embody currents of life in the city and to forsake currents of death and thus offer an attractive alternative community to become part of. If the people of God are to carry out their callings in culture, we will need to ask how the cultural worldview shapes the economic, political, artistic and technological world in which we live. What can be affirmed as creational and therefore embraced and celebrated? What does the church need to stand against?

This only touches the surface. In fact, contextualization is a constant mindset and way of life. It is a continuing struggle with how to live out the gospel in a particular cultural setting. If the church is to be faithful, it must reflect deeply on the gospel and its implications, on its urban context, and on how to live out that gospel in the urban context.

---

[55]Keller, "New Global Culture," pp. 1-7.

Theological education. In addition to a theology of mission for the city we need theological education that trains leaders and pastors for ministry in the city. "With the growing importance of cities also come new requirements for training and development of urban church leaders. However, few traditional seminaries emphasize mission in an urban context. . . . Urban ministry is the future of the church's mission in the twenty-first century."[56] Moreover, the demands and complexity of urban ministry require that education be much more than theological. A broad liberal arts education rooted in the gospel will offer urban church leaders tools for faithful ministry.

ELEMENTS OF FAITHFUL MISSIONAL CONGREGATIONS

The most powerful witness of the gospel in the city will be congregations that incarnate the gospel in the context of urban life. This has spawned not only theological reflection on what such a church might look like but also empirical studies of churches that have manifested a faithful presence in the city. Of course, theological reflection and empirical study need not be two separate things—in fact, they should not! Conn speaks of an action-reflection agenda; that is, it is in the context of an active commitment to living out God's mission in the city that we need to reflect on the light of the gospel for our witness.

> THE MOST POWERFUL WITNESS OF THE GOSPEL IN THE CITY WILL BE CONGREGATIONS THAT INCARNATE THE GOSPEL IN THE CONTEXT OF URBAN LIFE.

What do particular congregations that are working out their missional calling in the city look like? I will draw on two studies of urban congregations and briefly note the elements that they found in these churches.

A look at six congregations in three continents.[57] Greenway and Monsma examine six different urban churches on three continents: two from Asia, two from Latin America, two from Africa. By attending to Greenway and Monsma's analysis and reading more of the stories of these churches, we can compile the following list of characteristics that made these churches "great models":

---

[56]Mark Gornik, "Urban Mission," in *The Routledge Encyclopedia of Missions and Missionaries*, ed. Jonathan J. Bonk (New York: Routledge, 2007, 2010), p. 451.
[57]Greenway and Monsma, *Cities*, pp. 156-68.

- commitment to the gospel

- the attempt to understand the culture and dynamics of the city

- prayer

- identification with and concern for the poor

- high priority on fellowship, on small and cell groups

- strong emphasis on training good leaders

- contextualization

- high demand for "lay" involvement

- strong discipleship programs for new Christians

- the entire church mobilized for evangelism and mission

A study of twenty-eight congregations. From the more mainline wing of the church, Nile Harper sets out to tell the story of urban congregations that are engaged in a transforming ministry in the city. He looked for churches that believed that congregational life and social responsibility were interdependent. The churches ranged in size from 135 to 15,000 members. Harper's book covers twenty-eight churches in fifteen American cities.

After listing vital signs in urban churches, he tells the story of each church and concludes with a section called "What We Can Learn." There is much food for thought, and clearly no one pattern can be identified for faithful urban churches. Harper draws things together in the final chapter. Two sets of conclusions are worth considering. The first consists of the barriers that pastors identified as hindering church revitalization. These barriers included things such as resistance to becoming more inclusive, resistance to new worship patterns, anxiety about survival, lack of vision, holding on to worn-out traditions, and a neglect of the nurturing life of the church in favor of outreach activities.[58]

The second set of conclusions details the positive factors that pastoral leaders identified as most important in church revitalization. They are divided into internal and external factors. The internal factors deal with issues of the nurture of congregations and the strengthening of spiritual life. Pos-

---

[58]Nile Harper, *Urban Churches, Vital Signs: Beyond Charity toward Justice* (Grand Rapids: Eerdmans, 1999), p. 305.

itive internal factors include the centrality of worship, strong Christian education, community building, holistic approach to ministry, and strong pastoral leadership. The external factors treat issues of the mission of the church in the community. Positive external factors include identifying indigenous leadership, forming various kinds of partnerships, developing a culture of community, and empowering people for community redevelopment.[59]

CONCLUSION

The book of Jonah ends with God posing a rhetorical question to the prophet: "Should I not have concern for the great city of Nineveh, in which there are more than a hundred and twenty thousand people who cannot tell their right hand from their left—and also many animals?" (Jon 4:11). God wants to enlist Jonah in his mission, but the starting point is sharing in the love of God, who is "a gracious and compassionate God, slow to anger and abounding in love, a God who relents from sending calamity" (Jon 4:2). As Jonah sits in his introversion and indifference, he is meant to be a picture of Israel. The whole story is a stinging reproach to Israel's lack of concern for the nations, for whom they have been chosen.[60] God wants Jonah to share his love for the great city of Nineveh—small by today's standards but great in its day. In essence, the last verse of Jonah says to God's people, "If you love what God loves . . . you'll love the city."[61]

FURTHER READING

Bakke, Ray. *A Theology as Big as the City.* Downers Grove, IL: InterVarsity Press, 1997.

Conn, Harvie M., and Manuel Ortiz. *Urban Minisry: The Kingdom, the City, and the People of God.* Downers Grove, IL: InterVarsity Press, 2001.

Greenway, Roger S., and Timothy M. Monsma. *Cities: Mission's New Frontier.* Grand Rapids: Baker, 1989.

Grigg, Viv. *Cry of the Urban Poor: Reaching the Slums of Today's Megacities.* Monrovia, CA: MARC, 1992.

---

[59]Ibid., pp. 306-7.
[60]John H. Stek, "The Message of the Book of Jonah," *Calvin Theological Journal* 4, no. 1 (1969): 23-50; Stephen B. Chapman and Lacey C. Warner, "Jonah and the Imitation of God: Rethinking Evangelism and the Old Testament," *Journal of Theological Interpretation* 21 (2008): 43-69.
[61]Keller, "Why God Loves Cities."

Sider, Ronald J., Philip N. Olson and Heidi Rolland Unruh. *Churches That Make a Difference: Reaching Your Community with Good News and Good Works*. Grand Rapids: Baker, 2002.

DISCUSSION QUESTIONS

1. James Scherer believes that "mission in the 21st century will be won or lost in the battle for the soul of big cities." Discuss what this idea means and in what ways you agree or disagree.

2. Review the elements of a faithful missional congregation in the city. Tell some stories from your own experience that illustrate these elements. Are there any you would add to the list?

3. Of the "defeaters," or widely held objections to the Christian faith that Keller lists, which have you encountered or observed? How did you respond?

ESSAY TOPICS

1. Discuss the strategic importance of cities for the church's mission today.

2. How would you define and describe an agenda for urban mission today?

3. Harvie Conn argued that holistic mission and training believers for their task in the public square are essential issues for the missional church in the city. Do you agree? Discuss.

11

Missions

A Witness to the Gospel Where There Is None

ભ

DURING THE NINETEENTH AND EARLY twentieth centuries mission, in common parlance, was conceived exclusively in terms of the task of taking the gospel from Western culture to other parts of the world. Throughout the twentieth century the non-Western church began to grow, and a broader understanding of mission began to develop. In the middle of the century the great missionary leader Max Warren could say, "We have to be ready to see the day of missions, as we have known them, as having already come to an end."[1] The meaning of "mission" rapidly expanded and became an all-embracing term that included the whole task of the church to witness to the gospel. The cross-cultural task of taking the gospel to places or peoples where it had not been heard was in danger of being obscured.

In 1961 Lesslie Newbigin became the editor of the largest missionary journal of the time, the *International Review of Missions.* Understandably, there was a move afoot to remove the "s" from "missions" in the title to bring it into line with the current thinking of the day. Newbigin fought a battle to keep the "s." He believed that the missionary task of the church to take the gospel to places where it had not been heard was being eclipsed. He was not opposed to the broadening of mission; in fact, he believed it to be in line with the gospel. Rather, his concern was to highlight the missionary focus

---

[1]Max Warren, "Christian Mission and the Cross," in *Missions Under the Cross: Addresses Delivered at the Enlarged Meeting of the Committee of the International Missionary Council at Willingen, in Germany, 1952, with Statements Issued by the Meeting,* ed. Norman Goodall (London: Edinburgh House Press, 1953), p. 40.

within the total mission of the church. The strength with which he struggled for one letter indicates how important he believed this issue to be.

One might smile at the idea of battling over one letter. And yet we are reminded that the historian Edward Gibbon mocked the early church for fighting over a simple diphthong. He was referring, of course, to the battle between those who held that Jesus was *homoousios* with the Father and those who used the term *homoiousios*. And yet one letter maintained the truth of the gospel. Jesus was not similar or very much like the Father (*homoiousios*) but rather was God himself, sharing the same nature with the Father (*homoousios*).

Maintaining the "s" on missions is not quite so serious. However, what the "s" may protect within the total mission of the church is extremely important. Whether or not it is best to maintain this missionary focus with one letter or to find other language certainly is a topic worthy of discussion; terminology is important. For the purposes of this chapter I will maintain the language of Newbigin and discuss missions as an essential aspect of the total mission of the church.[2]

MISSION, MISSIONS AND CROSS-CULTURAL PARTNERSHIP

Making distinctions. Mission is the whole task of the church to witness to the whole gospel in the whole world. It involves the whole life of the people of God—gathered and scattered, public and private, individual and corporate, dimension and intention. "Mission" is a comprehensive term that is synonymous with the way many use the term "witness."

Missions is one aspect of the broader mission of the church. Thus, it is narrower and has a particular focus. That focus is to establish a witness to the gospel in places or among peoples where there is none or where it is very weak. While it is only one aspect of the mission of the church, it is an essential and indispensable component. The church's missionary calling is to the ends of the earth—that is, the ultimate horizon of mission. And so if

---

[2]A number of quite practical issues in missions studies need to be addressed if one is preparing for a cross-cultural missionary vocation. I will not be dealing with those topics. Thankfully, there are two fine books that do: Gailyn Van Rheenen, *Missions: Biblical Foundations and Contemporary Strategies* (Grand Rapids: Zondervan, 1996), chapters 3-8; A. Scott Moreau, Gary R. Corwin and Gary B. McGee, *Introducing World Missions: A Biblical, Historical, and Practical Survey* (Grand Rapids: Baker Academic, 2004), parts 3-5.

there are places that lack a witnessing community, it is the task of the church to create a witness in life, word and deed there until a community is established that will take responsibility for mission there. Thus, missions is finished when a church has been formed as an authentic witness to the gospel.

Missions normally will be cross-cultural, but that is not what defines it. Missions often will be outside of one's own country, but that is not always the case. For example, there are large numbers of different peoples and languages within India and China. They are bound together often by artificial national boundaries. Large numbers of these peoples do not have a church in their midst where they can see and hear the gospel. Missions may well be sending someone from South India to North India among a people where there is no witness to the gospel. What defines missions today is not exclusively the crossing of cultural or national boundaries with the gospel, but creating a gospel witness where it is absent or weak.

> WHAT DEFINES MISSIONS TODAY IS NOT EXCLUSIVELY THE CROSSING OF CULTURAL OR NATIONAL BOUNDARIES WITH THE GOSPEL, BUT CREATING A GOSPEL WITNESS WHERE IT IS ABSENT OR WEAK.

To further flesh out the nature of missions, we can note that missions is not cross-cultural partnership. Cross-cultural partnership is when churches in other cultures send people to take part in the task of mission in various ways. For example, if I were to go to Kenya to take up a post as a professor in a seminary to train African leaders, I would be involved not in missions but rather in cross-cultural partnership. I am not establishing a witnessing presence to the gospel in a place where there is none; I am crossing cultural boundaries to aid the church in Kenya. On the other hand, if I were to go to Kenya to live among Somali refugees or the Muslim tribes of the northeast—two groups within Kenya that have a negligible number of Christians—to witness to the gospel, that is missions. Thus, we define missions not by its cross-cultural nature but rather by the focus of creating a witnessing presence to the gospel in a place or among a people where it is nonexistent or weak.

This is not to diminish cross-cultural partnership, which indeed is important for a number of good reasons. It is an expression of partnership.

Each church has, on the one hand, different needs; on the other hand, each church has different gifts and resources to offer the global church in its shared missional calling. Both the gifts and needs in Africa differ from those in Asia or in North America. Moreover, whenever cross-cultural encounters occur, mutual enrichment and critique can take place. When we stand outside the culture we are able to see what others within that culture cannot see. Finally, cross-cultural partnership has the potential to demonstrate in a powerful way that the church is a people who transcend cultural and national barriers. Christianity is not a national or ethnic or continental religion; it is a gathering of the new humankind from all the nations and peoples of the earth. So missions is not cross-cultural partnership. Both may be cross-cultural in nature, but missions has a unique task in this global mission of the church.

Importance of these distinctions. To some, this might seem like splitting hairs. But it is not. There are at least two important reasons that such distinctions must be made. First, it is precisely because we have continued in a colonial mindset and not made these distinctions that we have viewed missions as anything that happens "overseas." Consequently, our missionary resources, both people and money, are absorbed into cross-cultural partnership, and the task of taking the gospel to those who have never heard is being neglected. For example, the growing interest in missional church has given rise to a vast literature. And this is good. Yet in the burgeoning missional church movement little is said about taking the gospel to places where it is unknown. Mission has swallowed up missions.

Our missions resources are primarily being used for cross-cultural partnership. Bryant Myers speaks of the disproportionate allocation of our mission resources as a "scandal."[3] Just over 1% of our financial resources and only about 10% of our personnel resources that are devoted to cross-cultural work actually serve the purpose of establishing a witnessing presence to the gospel in unevangelized areas. The large majority of our resources are being used to build up already well-established churches in other parts of the world. And sometimes those churches are stronger than the sending church. To use the example above: 90% of the worldwide

---

[3]Bryant Myers, *The New Context of World Mission* (Monrovia, CA: Mission Advanced Research and Communication Center, 1996), pp. 48, 55.

church's resources are being used to fund people such as seminary professors in Nairobi rather than church planters and evangelists in northern Kenya. And the percentage of Christians in Kenya is higher than Canada. Again, support for cross-cultural partnership or interchurch aid is not unimportant; it is a legitimate part of mission and a meaningful expression of the ecumenical church. The scandal derives from the fact that the allocation of these resources is so utterly disproportionate. Missions has been neglected, not purposely but because of the confusion caused by older assumptions about mission. And fuzzy terminology contributes to this ongoing scandal.

The second reason that the distinction is important is that missions maintains an important geographical horizon for the mission of the church. To lose that universal horizon is to affect the mission of the church negatively. Mission cannot be confined to the immediate neighborhood, although it must begin there. Mission looks to the ends of the earth and the redemption of all nations. This universal vision will be the ultimate horizon of the mission of the church.

Thus, missions is not simply another aspect of the total mission of the church, standing alongside others. Rather it is the ultimate redemptive-historical horizon of the whole missionary task that provides perspective and direction. The horizon of missions ensures that the whole life of the church is missional. Mission without missions is an emaciated and parochial concept. "The Church's mission is concerned with the ends of the earth. When that dimension is forgotten, the heart goes out of the whole business."[4]

> MISSION WITHOUT MISSIONS IS AN EMACIATED AND PAROCHIAL CONCEPT.

OUR LEGACY: REDUCTION AND RESPONSE

The legacy of modern missions. A brief look at the legacy of the modern missionary movement and our response today will put us in a better position to reevaluate our past and know how to proceed. The missionary movement of the nineteenth and twentieth centuries has been severely

---

[4]Lesslie Newbigin, *One Body, One Gospel, One World: The Christian Mission Today* (London: International Missionary Council, 1958), p. 27.

criticized by some and nobly defended by others. But what must be distinguished is faithfulness to the task of taking the gospel to places where it needed to be heard (which deserves noble defense) and the cultural framework that shaped the missionary enterprise (which sometimes deserves severe criticism).

Much of the criticism leveled against missions in the modern period must be acknowledged as true. However, it is also true that there is much to be thankful for. Much has been accomplished: the church is now alive in every part of the world, and the cross-cultural missionary enterprise of the last centuries certainly has played a role in that. And there has been much faithfulness and sacrifice on the part of so many. But we live in a different time, and we need to reflect on mission in a new context.

"Past practices cannot continue to be the model for the future of missions. Our dilemma then can be put in these terms: while our mission structures and attitudes have been formed by a particular historical and cultural situation, missions must now be carried out in a wholly different situation."

James F. Engel and William A. Dyrness,
Changing the Mind of Missions, p. 47

In the nineteenth and early twentieth centuries the majority of the church lived in the West. It was right for the church to be concerned to take the gospel to countries where a church did not exist or where it was too small and weak to offer a robust witness. This cross-cultural impulse was as it should be. In fact, for the Western church not to be concerned to take the gospel to other parts of the world would have been to neglect an essential part of its task.

However, valid critiques are to be made of the way the task was carried out. Criticism of the modern missionary enterprise comes from two sides. First, the missionary enterprise was uncritical of the Enlightenment worldview and colonial framework that shaped it. We observed in a previous chapter the way that this corrupted mission: it led confidence in the superiority of Western culture as it became a globally dominant civilization along with the correlative assumption of the inferiority of non-Western cultures; there was little awareness of the distinction between the gospel and the Western form that it took, and thus little critique of the powerful idolatrous story shaping the West; and, most distressing of all, missions was woven together with Western colonialism and imperialism that allowed the West to impose its political will, cultural ideals and commercial interests on the rest of the world.

James Engel and William Dyrness want to know where we have gone wrong in the missionary task. They analyze the way that post-Enlightenment modernity has impacted the modern missionary movement and ask, "What has gone wrong with the harvest?" They speak of the "invasion of modernity into Christianity."[5] Running through the heart of modernity is a fundamental cultural dichotomy between the sacred and secular, the private and the public. As the Christian church capitulated to this unbiblical dichotomy, the gospel was excluded from most of life. This affected mission in three ways. First, there were two omissions from the Great Commission: the omission of social action and of rigorous, holistic discipleship in favor of evangelism. Second, an optimistic and secular confidence in progress through instrumental reason, technology and specialized institutions led to a managerial missiology replete with organizational brilliance, highly centralized bureaucratic structures, and preoccupation with strategies and methods. Third, an uncritical embrace of Western individualism led missions to focus exclusively on individuals: the task of mission was to reach and evangelize individuals. In this process the church, God's chosen instrument for his mission, was displaced.

Many others have offered their version of where we have gone wrong, and there is much to be learned from this just criticism. Of course, we also need to ask what we have done right. And on that score we must be clear: the goal to take the gospel to non-Western nations was a biblical impulse. The "what" must be distinguished from the "how," the manner and methods from the task itself. We may be critical of the how, of the manner and methods, but the task of establishing a witness to the gospel in places where none existed was and remains fundamentally biblical.

---

[5]James F. Engel and William A. Dyrness, *Changing the Mind of Missions: Where Have We Gone Wrong?* (Downers Grove, IL: InterVarsity Press, 2000), pp. 55-81.

A second critique is that mission has been reduced to missions. The modern missionary enterprise narrowed the mission of the church to one aspect of the total mission of the church, namely, taking the gospel to parts of the world where there was no witness. Part of the fallout of this reduction was a church that did not critique its own culture. We may and must be critical of this reductionist view. Mission is as wide as life. But, once again, missions was the proper response of the church to a situation where most of the non-Western world had not heard the gospel. Missions surely must find a new path in this day of the global church, but taking the good news to peoples and places where there is no present witness remains integral to the church's mission.

> MISSIONS SURELY MUST FIND A NEW PATH IN THIS DAY OF THE GLOBAL CHURCH, BUT TAKING THE GOOD NEWS TO PEOPLES AND PLACES WHERE THERE IS NO PRESENT WITNESS REMAINS INTEGRAL TO THE CHURCH'S MISSION.

The response of the twentieth-century church to the legacy of modern missions. Broadly speaking, there has been a twofold contemporary response to the modern missionary movement in the Protestant church. Generally, the Ecumenical tradition has been acutely and painfully aware of the way that modern missions has been corrupted by modernity and colonialism. This has led to embarrassment and the desire to dissociate from missions as the task of taking the gospel to places where it is not yet known. Of course, other factors have played a role. But as a general statement, it can be said that the Ecumenical tradition is no longer in the missions game.

Alternatively, those in the Evangelical tradition have continued their vigorous commitment to missions, and sometimes it has been business as usual. There sometimes continues to be the uncritical adoption of assumptions from Enlightenment modernity and a continuing indebtedness to the legacy of the colonial era. If in the Ecumenical tradition there is eclipse, in the Evangelical tradition there has been entrenchment. This is changing, but there is still a ways to go.

As we look at these two responses to modern missions, we see a similar problem. The fundamentally biblical task of taking the gospel to places where it has not been heard and the Western practice of the past two centuries have not been carefully distinguished. Those who reject our missionary past can only see the corruption of the enterprise by the idols of post-Enlightenment culture; those who continue in the status quo can only see that it is biblical to establish a witness to the gospel where there is none. What is needed, of course, is to recognize the valid task but also, having learned from the past, to ask what faithfulness to the gospel might look like today.

<><><><><><><><><><><><><><><><><><><><><><><><><><><><><><><><><><><><><><><><><><><><><><>

"The missionary movement is now in its old age. . . . The conditions that produced the movement have changed, and they have been changed by the Lord of history. And the church has been changed out of all recognition by the agency of the missionary movement itself. It can be misleading to refer to this as the end of an era, for this implies some sort of historic finality. In fact the continuities are far more important. The task of world evangelization that formed the declared programme of missionary movement is not over; it never is. The essentially missionary nature of the church, the essentially missionary calling of the Christian, is where we began. . . . What is changing is not the task, but the means and the mode."

Andrew F. Walls, *The Missionary Movement in Christian History*, p. 261

<><><><><><><><><><><><><><><><><><><><><><><><><><><><><><><><><><><><><><><><><><><><><><>

A RETURN TO SCRIPTURE

A fresh approach to missions today must begin with a return to Scripture. We can briefly set out four elements of the Bible's teaching relevant for our subject. First, and quite simply, the gospel is true and therefore has universal significance. Thus, it is a message for all nations.

Second, God's mission from the beginning has had a universal horizon. One might trace this in Scripture by looking at how all nations have been in view in God's mission from the beginning. This can be seen in a phrase that reoccurs throughout Scripture: "to the ends of the earth" (Acts 1:8; cf. Ps 67:7; Is 49:6; 52:10). The ends of the earth have always been the universal and ultimate horizon of God's redemptive work, the goal toward which his mission moves. "The movement of God's purpose always starts from the particular on its way to the universal. God always singles out some for the sake of all. The early Christians embarking on their mission to Gentiles as well as Jews, were carrying forward the universal purpose God established precisely when he chose Abraham, Israel, David and Zion."[6]

Third, we must take seriously the pattern found in the book of Acts that begins with the church at Antioch (Acts 11:19-26; 13:1-3). Here we find a central New Testament pattern for missions. The church at Antioch and the following chapters in Acts give us a window into how the Holy Spirit carries out his mission to the nations. The story as narrated in Acts 13:1-3 is portrayed "as the first planned efforts of overseas missions."[7] And although this a unique and unrepeatable moment in redemptive history when the church first intentionally moves beyond its Jewish setting to the Gentiles, the church in Antioch nevertheless is portrayed with the "images of the ideal community."[8] In other words, the author wants us to view what is happening in mission here as a paradigm for the church in coming ages.[9]

Wilbert Shenk rightly observes two different modes of mission in the Antioch church. The first he calls the "organic mode" of mission (Acts 11:19-26). In the organic mode of mission the church "challenged the regnant plausibility structure of their culture on the basis of the claims of the reign of God. . . . Witness to God's reign, present and coming, was at the heart of the disciple community's life. The church grew organically." This is what I have referred to as mission. But there is a second mode, what Shenk calls the "sending mode" (Acts 13:1-3). In this mode "certain individuals were set apart for an itinerant ministry that would enable the faith to spread to key cities and regions throughout the Roman world."[10]

---

[6]Richard Bauckham, *Bible and Mission: Christian Witness in a Postmodern World* (Grand Rapids: Baker Academic, 2003), p. 47.

[7]Ben Witherington III, *The Acts of the Apostles: A Socio-Rhetorical Commentary* (Grand Rapids: Eerdmans, 1998), p. 390.

[8]Richard P. Thompson, *Keeping the Church in Its Place: The Church as Narrative Character in Acts* (New York: T & T Clark, 2006), p. 153.

[9]For a detailed analysis of Paul's mission, see Eckhard Schnabel, *Early Christian Mission*, vol. 2, *Paul and the Early Church* (Downers Grove, IL: InterVarsity Press, 2004), pp. 923-1485. He notes later that one must be careful in naively embracing historical experiences as normative. He provides a stimulating discussion (pp. 1569-88), engaging a number of contemporary missiologists, about how to "distinguish hermeneutically between what is descriptive and what is (possibly) prescriptive" (p. 1570).

[10]Wilbert Shenk, *Write the Vision: The Church Renewed* (Valley Forge, PA: Trinity Press International, 1995), pp. 92-93.

Roland Allen (1869-1947) was critical of the Western missionary practice of his day. He analyzed Paul's methods and compared them to contemporary practice. Paul spent only a few years at most in each place and left behind a church to continue the mission.[11] Allen also asked why the early church in Acts grew so quickly, something that he calls "the spontaneous expansion of the church." He concluded that the church witnessed to the gospel in each place primarily through two things: a spontaneous evangelism and the "irresistible attraction of the Christian church" that draws people to it "to discover the secret of a life which they instinctively desire to share."[12] However, he added a third to word and life: "the expansion of the Church by the addition of new churches."[13] Acts shows the pattern of planting new churches in areas where there were none. Then those churches by word and life bore witness to the gospel.

"If missions is to adapt, it must be (1) sensitive to the initiative of God, (2) motivated by a vision of the reign of Christ as refracted through the multiple cultures of the world, (3) characterized by mutual sharing from multiple centers of influence and (4) committed to partnership and collaboration. For this to happen among agencies, nothing short of a top-down, bottom-up organizational *transformation* is necessary."

James F. Engel and William A. Dyrness, *Changing the Mind*, p. 147

A fourth biblical insight to set the ground for the remainder of the chapter is that missions is the task of the local congregation first. Mission in the organic mode leads to mission in the sending mode. It is the church at Antioch, under the prompting of the Holy Spirit, that takes the initiative to send Paul and Barnabas throughout the Roman Empire. However, it does not remain the project of one local congregation but rather gives way to a partnership. As the missionary journeys continue, we see other churches becoming involved in supporting Paul both financially and in prayer. Mis-

---

[11]Roland Allen, *Missionary Methods: St. Paul's or Ours?* (Grand Rapids: Eerdmans, 1962).
[12]Roland Allen, *The Spontaneous Expansion of the Church* (Grand Rapids: Eerdmans, 1962), p. 7.
[13]Ibid.

sions is the task of every congregation and of the whole church together taking the whole gospel to the whole world.

World Need

During the days of the apostle Paul it was clear enough where the need was: anywhere beyond the boundaries of Jerusalem and Israel. And during the nineteenth and early twentieth centuries the need for missions was beyond the countries of the West. But what about today? How do we identify the world need today when the church is found throughout all the nations of the earth? Sometimes students ask me if there is still a place for the Western missionary. My answer is a resounding yes because there are still many places and peoples without a witnessing community in their midst. How might we identify those places and peoples?

Unreached people groups. One of the ways that missions advocates have tried to identify places of missionary need in the last three or four decades is with the notion of the unreached people group. Harvie Conn said in 1984 that in the "last decade especially a concept has arisen within evangelical circles to remind us in a fresh way of that unfinished task—unreached people groups. As a technical category, it has been shaped out of the need for strategy planning to reach three-fourths of the world's population who do not know Christ in a saving way. At least a billion people can be evangelized by local churches. But there are at least another two billion who can only be reached by cross-cultural missionaries. The 'unreached people' emphasis is one approach to the task."[14]

The concept gained traction when Ralph Winter used the term "unreached peoples" at the Lausanne Conference (1974) and when it was popularized from 1979 to 1987 in the MARC series entitled *Unreached Peoples*.[15] Since that time, beyond Ralph Winter, the two most important figures to participate in the discussion of unreached peoples are David Barrett, editor

---

[14]Harvie Conn, foreword to *Reaching the Unreached: The Old-New Challenge*, ed. Harvie M. Conn (Phillipsburg, NJ: Presbyterian & Reformed, 1984), p. vii.

[15]Samuel Wilson, "Peoples, People Groups," in *Evangelical Dictionary of World Missions*, ed. A. Scott Moreau (Grand Rapids: Baker Books, 2000), p. 745. Ralph Winter has also offered his version of the history as it stood in 1983 in two articles, "Unreached Peoples: The Development of the Concept" and "Unreached Peoples: What Are They and Where Are They?" in Conn, *Reaching the Unreached*, pp. 17-60.

of the *World Christian Encyclopedia*,[16] and Patrick Johnstone, who for years edited and published the helpful *Operation World* manual.[17] There have been many others, and while we can observe numerous twists and turns, new terminology and differing definitions, the idea continues to hang on within evangelical circles.[18]

A plethora of definitions have come down since that period, but all the definitions in one way or another are trying to identify two things: What is a people group? What does it mean that they are unreached? As to the first question, an early definition from the 1982 Lausanne Strategy Working Group identified a people group as a "people who perceive themselves to have a common affinity for one another. . . . From the viewpoint of evangelization, this is the largest possible group within which the Gospel can spread without encountering barriers to understanding or acceptance." This was the start of a process of defining what constituted a people group. Today four different kinds of models are offered: (1) "linguistic," a people group bound together by one language or a particular dialect; (2) "ethno-linguistic," a people group bound together by a language and a certain ethnicity; (3) "ethnic," a people group bound together not only by language and ethnicity but also by other factors such as religion, caste and culture; (4) "unimax," a people group defined as "the maximum sized group sufficiently unified to be reached by a single indigenous church planting movement. 'Unified' here refers to the fact that there are no significant barriers of either understanding or acceptance to stop the spread of the gospel."[19] This last group adds various factors such as education, politics, ideology, historical enmity, customs and behavior.[20] Clearly, each of these definitions will yield different

---

[16]David B. Barrett, George T. Kurian and Todd M. Johnson, *World Christian Encyclopedia: A Comparative Survey of Churches and Religions in the Modern World* (2nd ed.; 2 vols. Oxford: Oxford University Press, 2001).

[17]*Operation World* is now in its seventh edition (Colorado Springs, CO: Biblica Publishing, 2010) and is now edited by Jason Mandryk. The sixth edition (2001; updated and revised 2005) was authored jointly by Mandryk and Patrick Johnstone. The first five editions were the work of Patrick Johnstone.

[18]Joshua Project, "What Is a People Group?" (www.joshuaproject.net/resources/articles/what-is -a-people-group.php).

[19]Ralph D. Winter and Bruce A. Koch, "Finishing the Task: The Unreached Peoples Challenge," *International Journal of Frontier Missions* 16, no. 2 (1999): 70 (www.ijfm.org/PDFs_IJFM/16_2_ PDFs/02%20Winter_Koch10.pdf).

[20]Joshua Project, "How Many People Groups Are There?" (www.joshuaproject.net/assets/media/ assets/articles/how-many-people-groups-are-there.pdf).

numbers and offer differing advantages for analysis. But each is trying to ask what is it that binds a people together for the purpose of identifying the missions task that needs to be done.

The second question asks what it means for these people to be unreached. The various definitions are concerned to establish whether or not there is an indigenous church among that group that has sufficient resources to reach them with the gospel. This aspect of the definition is clear in the refinements within the Lausanne's definition. In March 1982 an unreached people group was defined as a "people group . . . among which there is no indigenous community of believing Christians *able* to evangelize this people group"; later, "able" was amended, and it read, a "people group among which there is no indigenous community of believing Christians *with adequate numbers and resources* to evangelize this people group without outside (cross-cultural) assistance."[21] According to this definition, missions is finished only when an indigenous church is planted that has adequate numbers and resources to evangelize its own people.

A key component of these definitions is the notion of contextualization. It is not enough simply to have churches in the midst of these people groups. These churches must be sufficiently indigenous to evangelize their neighbors in a way that is familiar. The emphasis on an indigenous church has the concern that church members be sufficiently at home in a people group so that their lives, words, and deeds effectively contextualize the gospel so that it is understood.

So what is the "unfinished task"? In 2004 a special report to Lausanne identified 4,300 ethno-linguistic people groups out of 13,330 as least evangelized (32%) and 13,000 unimax peoples out of 27,000 as unreached (48%).[22] At the time of this writing, according to the figures from the Joshua Project, which seeks to identify people groups with the least followers of Christ, there are 16,804 people groups in the world, and 7,289 of them are unreached or least reached, or 40.7% of the world's popula-

---

[21]Winter, "Unreached Peoples: The Development of a Concept," p. 37.

[22]Todd M. Johnson, Peter F. Crossing and Bobby Jangsun Ryu, "Looking Forward: An Overview of World Evangelization, 2005-2025; A Special Report for the Lausanne 2004 Forum on World Evangelization Center for the Study of Global Christianity, Gordon-Conwell Theological Seminary," p. 11 (www.gordonconwell.edu/resources/documents/Lausanneinsert.pdf).

tion.[23] These numbers are based on calculations that assume that less than 5% of the unreached or least-reached people groups are Christian, and less than 2% are evangelical.

There are concerns about the usefulness of this concept in today's urban world. Samuel Wilson comments, "Most of the definitions remain to this day more serviceable for nonurban, traditional peoples."[24] Harvie Conn and Manuel Ortiz, however, seem to be more favorable toward this concept for urban mission. They say at one point in their discussion "The Nature of People Groups" that this is "the approach we need to build strategies that can address the overlapping pluralism of urban life."[25] They are critical of a definition that limits people groups to ethnicity and therefore miss the heterogeneity and social complexity of urban life. They want to include "residence, class, caste, career, nationality, leisure, travel, clubs, societies, industrialization, and so on."[26] The emphasis of Conn and Ortiz is on understanding the common affinity that binds people together and shapes their self-understanding so that the gospel can be contextualized effectively. They are not uncritical of how this might be used to divide the church or base a strategy on the social sciences rather than Scripture. However, they are working with a view of contextualization that understands the gospel to be both at home and at odds, affirming and critical of culture. Thus, a contextualized witness to a people group need not simply affirm race or class in an exclusivist way.

The discussion of unreached peoples is long and complex. There is much to affirm and much to be cautious about. Yet it is worthwhile to look at it as a tool that is helping the church to recognize that the task of missions is not done. Conn believes that the "terms 'people groups' and 'unreached people groups' are . . . functional attempts at blocking out the job that still needs doing. . . . The value of a definitional struggle is that it serves as a pedagogical tool for stirring up interest in reaching the lost."[27]

---

[23]Joshua Project (www.joshuaproject.net).
[24]Wilson, "Peoples," p. 745.
[25]Harvie M. Conn and Manuel Ortiz, *Urban Ministry: The Kingdom, the City, and the People of God* (Downers Grove, IL: InterVarsity Press, 2001), p. 315.
[26]Harley Schreck and David Barrett, "Two Ways of Understanding Peoples and Their Evangelization," in *Unreached Peoples: Clarifying the Task*, ed. Harley Schreck and David Barrett (Monrovia, CA: MARC, 1987), pp. 16-17, quoted in Conn and Ortiz, *Urban Ministry*, p. 316.
[27]Quoted in James W. Reapsome, "Definitions and Identities: Samples from the Ongoing Discussion," in Conn, *Reaching the Unreached*, pp. 64-65.

Perhaps Conn's perspective is best: defining people groups is no more than a fallible and functional tool that might help us recognize that there is a job to be done. We need to beware that this does not turn missions into a managerial enterprise. Data-crunching and increasingly refined statistics can lead to an approach based on the technological mindset of post-Enlightenment modernity, one that sees efficiency and growth as the ultimate criteria of missional success.[28] But as one tool utilized as part of a broader understanding of missions, the concept of people groups may help to highlight peoples who have not heard the gospel and point those with gifts to the places and peoples still in need.

> DATA-CRUNCHING AND INCREASINGLY REFINED STATISTICS CAN LEAD TO AN APPROACH BASED ON THE TECHNOLOGICAL MINDSET OF POST-ENLIGHTENMENT MODERNITY, ONE THAT SEES EFFICIENCY AND GROWTH AS THE ULTIMATE CRITERIA OF MISSIONAL SUCCESS.

Three major blocs. I remember a mission class in the early 1980s in which Conn was lecturing on unreached people groups. After a rather complex discussion he threw up his hands, laughed, and said, "I still think the most helpful way for analyzing the unfinished missions task is the three major blocks—700 million Muslims, 500 million Hindus, and 1 billion Chinese." Of course, those numbers have continued to climb, and we now have 1.6 billion Muslims, close to 1 billion Hindus, and 1.3 billion Chinese. This certainly does point to the need for missions.

The question is, however, whether or not this is too blunt an instrument. Paul Hattaway has published a massive book, over seven hundred pages, titled *Operation China: Introducing All the Peoples of China.* The concern of the book is to highlight the fact that there are more than 100 million people in 450 distinct minorities in China. Although this accounts for only about 6.7% of the total population, these minorities inhabit 62.5% of China's territory. The situation in India is similarly complex. The monumental work of K. S. Singh introduces 461 tribal communities in India.[29] K. Rajendran notes

---

[28]Jacques Ellul, *The Technological Society,* trans. John Wilkinson (New York: Knopf, 1964); Engel and Dyrness, *Changing the Mind of Missions,* p. 113.

[29]K. S. Singh, *People of India: The Scheduled Tribes* (Oxford: Oxford University Press, 1994).

that there are nearly 150 mega–people groups totaling more than a million people with strategic positioning both geographically and politically.[30] The Muslim situation is equally complex, spread over many countries. Yet, again, to point to three major blocs reminds us that there are many people and peoples who need to hear and see the gospel.

The 10/40 Window. Another popular tool that has been developed to identify world need is the "10/40 Window." In a plenary session at the July 1989 Lausanne II Conference in Manila, Luis Bush stated that most of the unreached people groups "live in a belt that extends from West Africa across Asia, between ten degrees north to forty degrees north of the equator."[31] Bush calls for the church to focus missions on this part of the world for a number of reasons. Here I list five of those reasons.

First, it is where the people are. Two-thirds of the world's population lives within this window—over 4.5 billion people. Second, it is where most of the unevangelized people and countries of the world are found. About 97% of the 3 billion people who live in the 55 most unevangelized countries of the world live inside this window. The Joshua Project adds that an "estimated 2.85 billion individuals live in approximately 5,823 unreached people groups . . . in the 10/40 Window. The 10/40 Window also contains the largest unreached peoples over one million. In addition, the 10/40 Window contains the overwhelming majority of the world's least evangelized mega-cities—that is those with a population of more than one million. The top 50 least evangelized megacities are all in the 10/40 Window!"[32] Third, it is where we find the majority of the three main religious blocs of the world. Over 800 million Muslim, over 700 million Hindus, and over 200 million Buddhists are living in the 10/40 Window. The fourth reason for giving priority to this area is that it is where the majority of the world's poor live: 80% of the poorest of the poor live within this window. The 50 countries with the lowest quality of life are located in this area. And yet, fifth, only a small percentage of missionaries are working in this area. Estimates differ, but it

---

[30]K. Rajendran, "Understanding Unreached Peoples," *India Missions* (July-September 2005): 8-17.

[31]Luis Bush, *Getting to the Core of the Core: The 10/40 Window* (San Jose, CA: Partners International, 1990), p. 1.

[32]Joshua Project, "What Is the 10/40 Window?" (www.joshuaproject.net/resources/articles /10-40-window.php).

is clear that well below 10% are working within the window and likely an even lower percentage among the poor.

The same point must be made about the 10/40 Window that has been made about unreached people groups. It is a helpful tool that begins to identify world need—no more or no less than that. It highlights parts of the world that have been neglected and invites the church to consider this area in its missionary task.

Asia. Another way to indicate the continuing need for missions in the world is to simply look at the continent of Asia. Jason Mandryk highlights the unfinished task in Asia with the following statistics. Over 81% of 4.7 billion non-Christians in the world live in Asia. The three largest non-Christian religions are rooted in Asia. There are 1.1 billion Muslims, 950 million Hindus, 920 million Buddhists, as well as 680 million Asians with no formal religious affiliation. There are thirty-two Asian countries that are less than 10% Christian, and twelve that are less than 2%. In the world there are over 16,000 ethno-linguistic peoples and over 7,000 that are unreached. About 75% (over 5,000) of those unreached people groups are found in Asia.[33]

The Asian slums present an especially interesting opportunity. Viv Grigg calls attention to those living in Asia. He argues that it is in Asian slums that we find the fastest growing cultural bloc, the most responsive peoples, with the biggest social needs. And yet, surprisingly, these peoples are the least targeted by Christian missions. "The target of world evangelism, the great unreached areas, remains in Asia. Here we find the slums of the cities relatively unreached by the love of God. Nowhere in Asia, with the exception of Korea, does the church in the slums have more than four percent of all the existing churches in the city. In each city, there are only a handful of slum churches. In no city is there a movement of poor people's churches."[34]

This brief sketch is meant simply to confirm that the day of missions is not over. It is God's mission first and foremost. Yet he calls us as his covenant partners and friends to join him in his mission to all nations or people groups and to the ends of the earth.

---

[33]Jason Mandryk, *Operation World: The Definitive Prayer Guide to Every Nation* (7th ed.; Colorado Springs, CO: Biblica Publishing, 2010), p. 69.
[34]Viv Grigg, "Squatters: The Most Responsive Unreached Bloc," *Urban Mission* 6, no. 5 (1989): 45-46.

PROBLEMS HINDERING A FRESH MISSIONS INITIATIVE

In view of the needs of the world, what is hindering a fresh missions initiative?

Lack of fervor. Over one hundred years ago Andrew Murray wrote a deeply moving book in response to the report that emerged from the Ecumenical Missionary Conference held in New York in 1900. He reflects on the depleting resources for missions and the lack of will to carry out the missionary task. He searches for the root of this "missionary problem." He points to the need for pastors "to believe that the great aim of the existence of their congregations is to make Christ known to every creature"; for all of God's people to "read and take an interest in the *news of the kingdom and its extension*";[35] for theological seminaries "*to kindle missionary passion in every person who passes through the school,* that he may thereby become an able minister of Christ."[36] Yet he professes anxiety in all these areas because "behind all these needs is a deeper need: *There is a need of a great revival of spiritual life, of truly fervent devotion to our Lord Jesus, of entire consecration to His service.* It is only in a church in which this spirit of revival has at least begun, that there is any hope of any very radical change in the relation of the majority of our Christian people to mission work."[37] He analyzes in more detail the root spiritual problem that is paralyzing missions: a low spiritual state of the church, a lukewarm love for Christ, a sickly worldliness, and a lack of vital prayer. "The missionary problem is a personal one. *Seek the deepening of the spiritual life, and missionary consecration will follow.*"[38]

Is this analysis not the same that could always be made of Christ's church? Does the church not always struggle with complacency wrought by selfishness and comfort? But the reasons change in each generation and in the various families of the church. In the Ecumenical tradition relativism has eroded a conviction of the truth of the gospel, which paralyzes any missionary zeal. In the Evangelical tradition there is a self-satisfaction that comes from comfort, compromise with capitalism, and accommodation to the consumeristic spirit of our age. One mission leader finds the "triumph of a self-centered lifestyle" to be the primary reason for "missionary malaise,"

---

[35] Andrew Murray, *Key to the Missionary Problem*, contemporized by Leona F. Choy (Fort Washington, PA: Christian Literature Crusade, 1979), p. 25.
[36] Ibid., p. 13.
[37] Ibid., pp. 25-26.
[38] Ibid., p. 86.

> ONE MISSION LEADER FINDS THE "TRIUMPH OF A SELF-CENTERED LIFESTYLE" TO BE THE PRIMARY REASON FOR "MISSIONARY MALAISE."

the decline in commitment to missions, in the last few decades.[39]

Murray's remedy is the right one. He calls for prayer: confession of the sin of indifference, prayer for the missionary enterprise, prayer for spiritual renewal and a return to our first love. He calls for more sacrificial giving, for education in the missionary task, for pastors and leaders to take responsibility for leading the church in mission, for seminary professors to take their responsibility to train pastors with a missionary fervor, and for the work of the Spirit to kindle our love for Christ and for other people.

Inadequate allocation of missions resources. Over 90% of our resources are being used for cross-cultural partnership. And a very small amount, perhaps 1.2%, of those resources is allocated to reaching the 1.1 billion people in the least evangelized parts of the world. "Today half of all Christians in the world, and perhaps 70 percent of all evangelicals, live in these traditional 'mission fields,' but we continue to invest 90 percent of our recruiting, training, and funding to send Western missionaries to pretty much those same fields."[40] Todd Johnson speaks of a "massive imbalance." He says, "Over ninety percent of all Christian evangelism is aimed at other Christians and does not reach non-Christians. . . . Close examination of virtually any Christian evangelistic activity reveals this massive imbalance."[41]

An Urbana video from 2000 gives the following statistics: Christians earn $12.3 trillion, of which they give 1.7% to Christian causes; they give 5.4% of that 1.7% to foreign mission; only 1% of that 5.4% goes to people who most need to hear the gospel. Myers tells us that in the "unevangelized part of God's world . . . about 5.6% of income to Christians went to foreign missions. Only 0.36% of this went to sharing the gospel with the 1.2 billion people in

---

[39]Jim Raymo, "Reflections on the Missionary Malaise," *Evangelical Missions Quarterly* 33, no. 4 (1997): 443.
[40]Chuck Bennett, "The Problem with Success," *Evangelical Missions Quarterly* 32, no. 1 (1996): 21.
[41]Todd Johnson, "World Christian Trends, Update 2007," *Lausanne World Pulse* (August 2007) (www.lausanneworldpulse.com/766?pg=all).

the least-evangelized world."[42] Earlier he says, "Over 90% of the foreign missionaries, 87% of the mission funding and over 94% of the full-time Christian workers are directed toward those countries where 60% or more of their people identify themselves as Christians."[43]

If all these figures are correct, then this certainly is one of the problems hindering a fresh missions initiative. First, our giving for the sake of the gospel appears to be miserly. Stan Guthrie claims that evangelicals, despite all their talk of tithing, give only 2.6% of their income to charities of any kind.[44] And our giving for work beyond our own self-interested boundaries is likewise parsimonious. But even the small amount of money that finally does make it to cross-cultural work is not being channeled to the places of greatest evangelistic need. "For all the current emphasis on unreached peoples" writes Guthrie, "only 0.01 per cent of the average Christian family income is aimed at reaching the so-called 10/40 Window."[45]

Legacy of colonialism. In the nineteenth and early twentieth centuries the modern missions task of the church was carried out during a period of Western dominance along the paths constructed by colonialism. Colonialism provided the framework in which many of our mindset, practices and organizations for mission were formed. Many authors, both Western and non-Western, are helping us to see the lingering legacy of colonialism in our practices today. I have noted the problem of collapsing missions into any cross-cultural endeavor. I will briefly mention only two more.

Colonialism was dismantled during the middle part of the twentieth century, but persisting economic issues continue to cause problems. The West continues to carry financial power, and how to use that power is not clear. The one who gives must be responsible for how that money is used. Yet that can easily lead to an unhealthy dependence; after all, the one who pays the piper calls the tune. How can the church in the West use its gift of wealth responsibly without disempowering the poorer churches? Our co-

[42]Bryant L. Myers, *Exploring World Mission: Context and Challenge* (Monrovia, CA: World Vision International, 2003), p. 76.

[43]Bryant L. Myers, *The Changing Shape of World Mission* (Monrovia, CA: MARC, 1993), p. 19.

[44]Stan Guthrie, *Missions in the Third Millennium: 21 Key Trends for the 21st Century* (Milton Keynes: Paternoster, 2000), pp. 21-22.

[45]Ibid., p. 23.

lonial past, with the mindset and structures that it has produced, make this question difficult to answer.

The second problem is the relationship between mission organizations to the churches both at home and in other parts of the world. I will address this issue in the next section. But there is also the problem of Western missionary bodies relating to non-Western churches. The word "partnership" has been around for some time and rightly points to the ideal. The Bible teaches us that mission is the task of the church together, and we realize that the churches in various parts of the world

> HOW CAN THE CHURCH
> IN THE WEST USE ITS
> GIFT OF WEALTH
> RESPONSIBLY WITHOUT
> DISEMPOWERING THE
> POORER CHURCHES?

have differing gifts to offer. Yet our colonial legacy of denominational missions and one-track relations between mission societies and churches have often led to lingering financial, spiritual and strategic paternalism on the one side and infantile dependence on the other. Multilateral and adult partnerships need to emerge, but many potential problems remain. Nonetheless, the difficult questions about sharing resources, responsibilities and power must be faced if there is to be true partnership and interdependence.

STRUCTURES OF MISSIONS—WHO WILL DO THE JOB?

Who should be responsible for this fresh missions initiative? In the past it has been emperors, popes or monks. Over the past several hundred years Western denominational or independent missionary societies have taken the lead. Today we see two important changes. First, the local congregation is waking up to see that missions is its biblical responsibility. This is creating tension with past organizational structures created for missions. Second, the missionary force of the third world is increasing dramatically. Questions of partnership in both cases are important for the future missions enterprise of the church in the twenty-first century.

Local churches and mission societies. For centuries it has been denominational and independent mission societies that carried out the missionary task. In the last century there has been a recovery of the missionary nature of the church. In the story of the Bible the church is the primary organ of God's mission. So that leaves us with the problem of how to deal with our history. Who takes responsibility for missions: local congregations or missions societies? If both are to somehow play a role, how are they to fruitfully and authentically partner in this task?

Engel and Dyrness have wrestled with this problem. They start from the scriptural foundation that mission is the responsibility of the local congregation. "A central theological reality is that the church is uniquely equipped to be the locus of missions because it is essentially missionary by its very nature. This means that the church itself is the missionary reality that God

---

"The older missionary movement . . . developed a characteristic form of organization, the mission agency based on the model of the voluntary society. . . . As it developed it became a quite efficient means for achieving certain ends: sending and equipping people for the purpose of Christian proclamation and service overseas, and mustering 'home' interest and support for their work. . . . The original organs of the missionary movement were designed for one-way traffic; for sending, for giving. Perhaps there is now an obligation of Christians to 'use means' better fitted for two-way traffic, fellowship, for sharing, for receiving, than have yet been perfected."

Andrew F. Walls, *The Missionary Movement in Christian History*, p. 260

---

sends into the world—*it is far more than an institutional source from which funds and missionaries are sent or agency developed programs carried out.*"[46] The problem is that the missional nature of the church in both the West and the non-West has been diminished by the central role of mission agencies. They have been important, enabling isolated and ill-equipped churches to participate in the cross-cultural missions task. Nevertheless, this has weakened the church's missionary concern, and Engel and Dyrness call for a renewed commitment on the part of the local congregation to the global missionary task.

Newbigin shares their concern. A "true congregation of God anywhere

---

[46]Engel and Dyrness, *Changing the Mind of Missions*, p. 74; see also p. 122.

in the world is at the same time part of God's mission to the ends of the earth."[47] Therefore, "every church, however small and weak, ought to have some share in the task of taking the gospel to the ends of the earth. Every church ought to be engaged in foreign missions. This is part of the integrity of the gospel. We do not adequately confess Christ as the Lord of all men if we seek to be his witnesses only among our neighbours. We must seek at the same time to confess him to the ends of the earth. The foreign missionary enterprise belongs to the integrity of our confession."[48] Thus, "it is the duty and privilege of every part of the church everywhere to be involved not only in the missionary task at its own door, but also in some other part of the total world-wide task. . . . And every Christian has the duty and privilege to take his proportionate share, whether in intercession, in dissemination of knowledge, in giving, or in actual life-service."[49]

It will take patience and work to overcome the deeply ingrained pattern of thinking that sees mission as primarily the responsibility of denominational and independent missions organizations. But it is crucial to fostering a missions mindset in local congregations.

Tom Telford has examined a number of missions-minded churches[50] and analyzed what has made them effective. He offers nine "criteria for a top-notch missions program" within the local congregation: an outward focus and strategy; at least 30 percent of its budget for missions; an ongoing training program for missionary candidates; missions education integrated through all the programs of the church; sending its own people as missionaries; concern about and prayer for the lost; a pastor who leads in vision and outreach; interest in helping other churches in missions; a strong evangelism program in its own community.[51]

The renaissance of the local church in missions is giving rise to growing

[47]Lesslie Newbigin, "Report on the Division of World Mission and Evangelism to the Central Committee," *Ecumenical Review* 15 (1962): 89.
[48]Lesslie Newbigin, *A Word in Season: Perspectives on Christian World Missions* (Grand Rapids: Eerdmans, 1994), p. 13.
[49]Lesslie Newbigin, *One Body, One Gospel, One World: The Christian Mission Today* (London: International Missionary Council, 1958), p. 31.
[50]Tom Telford, *Today's All-Star Missions Churches: Strategies to Get Your Church into the Game* (Grand Rapids: Baker, 2001).
[51]Tom Telford with Lois Shaw, *Missions in the 21st Century: Getting Your Church into the Game* (Wheaton, IL: Harold Shaw Publishers, 1998), pp. 158-60.

tensions between congregations and mission societies. A number of local churches have grown critical of missions societies as they exist today. It begins with the biblical and theological concern: the church is the primary organ of God for mission and therefore ought to be the primary sending body of missionaries. Yet their criticism extends to the ossified, traditionalist and rigid thinking about mission and the high cost of mission societies. Congregations can be, they believe, more flexible and relevant with a lower budget. The problem is, of course, that most churches do not have the expertise, size or experience to do what missions societies have been doing for decades.

> THE RENAISSANCE OF THE LOCAL CHURCH IN MISSIONS IS GIVING RISE TO GROWING TENSIONS BETWEEN CONGREGATIONS AND MISSION SOCIETIES.

The way forward will be a partnership that finds a way to allow the local congregation to be the primary engine of missions while at the same time utilizing the vast experience and expertise of mission bodies to equip, enable and coordinate the church in its task. The role of mission societies should be to come alongside the congregations with their expertise and administrative structures to equip the church for its missionary task. For this to happen, a renaissance and institutional transformation of these missions organizations must take place.[52]

Growth of third-world missions. In 1991 Larry Pate wrote about the changing balance in global mission. He analyzed the dramatic growth in two-thirds-world missions. At the time there were about 88,000 missionaries from the Western world and about 48,000 missionaries from the non-Western world. With the estimated growth rate of 13.3% he predicted that by the year 2000 the non-Western missionary force (164,230) would surpass the West (131,720) and make up about 55% of global Protestant missionaries.[53]

---

[52]Engel and Dyrness, *Changing Mind of Missions*, pp. 143-72.
[53]Larry Pate, "The Changing Balance in Global Mission," *International Bulletin of Missionary Research* 15, no. 2 (1991): 56, 58-61. See also Lawrence E. Keyes and Larry D. Pate, "Two-Thirds World Missions: The Next 100 Years," *Missiology* 21, no. 2 (1993): 187-206; Larry D. Pate *From Every People: A Handbook of Two-Thirds World Mission Agencies* (Monrovia, CA: MARC, 1989).

"The territorial 'from-to' idea that underlay the older missionary movement has to give way to a concept much more like that of Christians
within the Roman Empires in the second and third centuries: parallel
presences in different circles and at different levels, each seeking to
penetrate within and beyond its circle. This does not prevent movement and interchange and enterprise—these things certainly marked
Christians in pre-Constantinian Roman Empire—but it forces revision
of concepts, images, attitudes, and methods that arose from the presence of a Christendom that no longer exists."

Andrew F. Walls, *The Missionary Movement
in Christian History*, pp. 258-59

Michael Jaffarian disagrees. He says that for "some years now, the idea
that there are more Four-Fifths-World missionaries than Western missionaries has been showing up in various missions presentations and publications. Unfortunately, it is just not true."[54] He cites two errors that Pate has
made: he has assumed that early growth will continue, and he has counted
domestic missionaries in the case of the non-Western missionary force.
However, definitions of missions are important here. In both China and
India there are massive numbers of missionaries who work within their own
country. Call them "domestic" if you want to, but national boundaries are
artificial. There are large numbers of peoples within both of these countries
who speak a different language and are made up of different ethnic groups,
and who have no indigenous church. These missionaries are going to peoples
and places where there is no witness, where there is no indigenous church,
even if that is within the national boundary. Such a situation is not so likely
in the West.

Exact statistics on the distribution of the missionary force are hard to
come by. The missionary force in Africa and Asia continues to grow. According to *Operation World*, four of the five largest sending nations are from
the third world (China, India, South Korea, Nigeria); only the United States

---

[54]Michael Jaffarian, "Are There More Non-Western Missionaries Than Western Missionaries?"
International Bulletin for Missionary Research 28, no. 3 (2004): 131.

is in the top five. Three more countries from the third world are sending over 2,000 missionaries.[55] MANI (Movement for Africa National Initiatives), a pan-African group that mobilizes and networks, is promoting Vision 5015—50,000 Nigerian missionaries in the next fifteen years.[56] There may be as many as 100,000 church-planting evangelists from China to parts of Asia and the Middle East, which would make it the largest sending nation in the world.[57] South Korea has sent out over 20,000 missionaries, and there are massive numbers in seminary training for missions. The fact that the missionary

> IT IS QUITE CLEAR THAT THE NON-WESTERN MISSIONARY FORCE IS GROWING AT AN EXPONENTIAL RATE, FAR ABOVE THAT OF THE WEST.

force in the West is in decline and in parts of the non-West on the rise suggests that future of missions will be African and Asian. Samuel Escobar informs us that the missionary force from Latin America has risen from just over 1,000 in 1982 to close to 10,000 today.[58] This calls for growing cooperation and partnership among groups from the West and non-West for the sake of the world.[59]

Whether or not one accepts entirely this line of argument or all these statistics, it is quite clear that the non-Western missionary force is growing at an exponential rate, far above that of the West. Even Jaffarian offers statistics using his criterion (actually Barrett and Johnson's) that show that between 1990 and 2000 the increasing numbers of non-Western missionaries was almost double the Western missionaries.[60]

Partnership. Partnership is an important goal that has been discussed in missionary circles for more than half a century since the church in the non-

[55]Mandryk, *Operation World*, p. 951.
[56]Ibid., p. 33.
[57]Ibid., pp. 68, 951. Obviously, the problem is that there can be no statistics on missionaries in China. Mandryk writes, "According to some reliable sources, China's population of missionaries (those who go and are sent out as such from their churches) exceeds even the USA, although the large majority remain within China itself" (p. 7).
[58]Samuel Escobar, "Christianity in Latin America: Changing Churches in a Changing Culture," in *Introducing World Christianity*, ed. Charles E. Farhadian (Malden, MA: Wiley-Blackwell, 2012), p. 180.
[59]See Enoch Wan and Michael Pocock, eds., *Missions from the Majority World: Progress, Challenges, and Case Studies* (Pasadena, CA: William Carey Library, 2009).
[60]Jaffarian, "More Non-Western Missionaries?" p. 132.

Western world began to grow. But the issue has become more popular in missiology only in the last several decades. The question is how to forge partnerships between various mission agencies, between the various churches, between mission agencies and churches, and between Western and the non-Western bodies. If mission is in, from, and to all six continents, then partnership is a necessity.

The drive for partnership is driven by both theological and "practical" considerations. Theologically, the nature of the church and the importance of unity as essential to the church, the recognition that the church is one body with many parts, drive partnership. Practically speaking, partnership is more efficient and cheaper. Some tasks simply cannot be tackled effectively without collaboration in ecumenical partnership.

A number of problems are remnants of our colonial past. The financial dependence of the younger churches on missionary boards has led to a one-track relationship that shaped the ongoing relationship in terms of paternalism on the one side and continuing infantile dependence on the other. The goal is interdependence, neither dependence nor independence. This can happen only as multilateral adult relationships between many churches and "parachurch" organizations are formed. Wrestling with the stewardship of Western wealth in a way that is enabling and responsible continues to be an issue as well. However, despite the numerous problems that exist, continuing struggle and reflection in the area of partnership must continue. Truly, in spite of many tensions and difficulties, this kind of partnership is "a goal worth fighting for and expending huge amounts of energy to achieve because it is so much more effective, it enables the world to see 'how much these Christians love one another,' and because God smiles on it."[61] Indeed, the very nature of the church as a sign of the kingdom compels us to carry on in partnerships despite the thorny issues that accompany them.

> THE VERY NATURE OF THE CHURCH AS A SIGN OF THE KINGDOM COMPELS US TO CARRY ON IN PARTNERSHIPS DESPITE THE THORNY ISSUES THAT ACCOMPANY THEM.

---

[61]Moreau, Corwin and McGee, *Introducing World Missions*, p. 282.

NEW INITIATIVES TODAY

Many, but not all, of the older patterns and ways of carrying out the missionary task are obsolete. The career missionary is still an important part of the picture. However, new initiatives are emerging that may be important for the future of missions.

Supporting national missionaries. With the growth and maturity of the non-Western church, questions arise as to the ongoing relationship between Western missions organizations and the non-Western churches. There are four possibilities for Western missionaries: to leave but possibly send money for national workers; to work under the national leaders; to work alongside the indigenous church in a complementary way but with a degree of autonomy; to forge partnerships and work together. These are not necessarily mutually exclusive. The two main strategies that have been most popular are departure in tandem with supporting national workers and partnerships.

"Our basic concerns with the prevailing practice of world missions today fall broadly into two categories, one historical and the other biblical. . . . Western missions theology and practice has fallen captive to modernity. . . . Equally critical as its captivity to modernity was that missions strategy lost sight of the breadth and depth of biblical thinking about God's purposes for his creation. . . . These historical and theological concerns are compounded by the reality at the dawn of the third millennium that God has raised up a mighty body of believers in the younger churches who are eagerly carrying the message of salvation around the world—even back to our Western nations."

James F. Engel and William A. Dyrness,
Changing the Mind of Missions, pp. 174-76

The move toward the support of national workers picked up after World War II. Western churches sent money to support indigenous missionaries and workers. Groups such as the Coalition on the Support of Indigenous Ministries emerged to support indigenous church planting, evangelism, relief and development, leadership training and theological education.[62] Gospel for Asia supports over eleven thousand native missionaries mainly in the 10/40 Window.[63] Founder and president K. P. Yohannan's book *Revolution in World Missions*, which argues for supporting national workers, has 1.5 million copies in print.

National missionaries provide several advantages. The cost for a missionary is cheaper. For example, a missionary working for Gospel for Asia costs $7,200 to $14,400 per year, while the cost for a Western missionary is $75,000 per year. The national missionaries carry no Western baggage, are often more effective at evangelism, and know the culture and language of the people they are trying to reach. But there are disadvantages as well. Money in poor countries raises the ugly head of corruption and greed and can create division that arises from envy. Sending money can also create an unhealthy dependence of non-Western missionaries on Western funds. Robertson McQuilken believes, "Sharing financial resources in a way that is spiritually empowering and Great Commission–completing for both donor and recipient is our greatest unsolved problem."[64]

Tentmaking. Tetsunao Yamamori says, "We will need many kinds of missionaries and Christian workers in the coming decades. The task ahead of us is enormous. . . . If we want to make a difference in our efforts to fulfill the Great Commission, we need to be willing to try new things. I believe kingdom business will be a strategy of choice for the twenty-first century."[65] The term usually given to efforts such as this is "tentmaking." The term arises from the apostle Paul, a missionary who supported himself with the skill or profession of making tents (Acts 18:2-3). Ruth Siemens believes that in this new millennium "far more Paul-type tentmakers are needed than ever before in history."[66] Perhaps it is true that before long

---

[62]See www.cosim.info.

[63]See www.gfa.org/about/the-missionaries.

[64]Robertson McQuilkin, "Stop Sending Money! Breaking the Cycle of Missions Dependency," *Christianity Today* 43, no. 3 (March 1, 1999): 59.

[65]Tetsunao Yamamori, preface to *On Kingdom Business: Transforming Missions through Entrepreneurial Strategies*, ed. Tetsunao Yamamori and Kenneth Eldred (Wheaton, IL: Crossway Books, 2003), p. 10.

[66]Ruth E. Siemens, "The Vital Role of Tentmaking in Paul's Mission Strategy," *International Journal of Frontier Missions* 14, no. 3 (1997): 121.

AAAA

"the greatest percentage of people will be going out in this way."[67]

Why are tentmakers such an attractive option today?[68] First, tentmakers often are able to get into resistant countries. The missionary who puts "missionary" on his or her visa may be rejected, while the Christian who is an engineer or in business or healthcare is more likely to be granted access. Second, tentmakers do not have to raise support, since their work salary covers their expenses. This conserves scarce funds for other kinds of missionaries who require it. Some criticize this approach, but it seems to be good stewardship of scarce resources. Third, tentmakers have everyday, natural contacts with unbelievers. In fact, if evangelism is best done in an organic way, then tentmaking provides the best way to connect in a natural way.

Many professions lend themselves to this type of mission work, but certainly education, healthcare, agriculture, science, engineering, technology, architecture, urban planning, business and finance, and computer science are careers that can bless a nation as well as provide a Christian presence.

Various concerns arise as to the legitimacy and effectiveness of tentmaking. For example, a major question involves the main task of the tentmaker. Is this person an evangelist or an engineer? A church planter or an educator? There is no easy answer to this question. It will vary according to the situation and person. Dangers arise for the person who sees himself or herself primarily as an evangelist or a church planter who wears a professional cloak that facilitates that primary task. This can be seen as a covertly dishonest way to enter a country. And certainly, working at a full-time job can leave one with little energy to devote to church planting. Because of this, Gary Ginter wants to speak of "kingdom professionals" or "kingdom entrepreneurs" instead of "tentmakers." A kingdom professional really is a businessperson, an engineer, a teacher, or whatever else first. That is their calling; they are in the country to bless that country with their work. But they establish a Christian presence as a professional and a witness to the gospel in life and word, which should be the reality of all Christians. But then do they have the energy and time and expertise to do evangelism and church planting? Or is their job only to witness in word, deed and life to those who have never heard? Ralph Eckhardt answers, "Tentmakers are usually not

[67]Carol Davis, quoted in Guthrie, *Missions in the Third Millennium*, p. 140.
[68]For a list of nine benefits of tentmaking, see Siemens, "Vital Role of Tentmaking," p. 121.

going to build churches and equip other saints for ministry, but that is not necessarily their task in the overall scheme. Their responsibility is simply to witness, by word and deed, to people who have never been introduced to the gospel message before."[69] Doing the job well and benefiting the country with one's gifts is essential for the task. A tentmaker "better make, and sell, some tents."[70]

Those who hold an understanding of mission that refuses dualistic categories and instead embraces a good doctrine of creation and vocation will not be as vexed as others about this. There is the important issue of determining one's calling: is it to be a professional or a church planter? But anyone who chooses to be a kingdom professional does so following God's call and will find that by simply being a Christianly faithful professional, they can both bless the receiving country through their work and bear faithful witness to the gospel in life, word and deed where such witness is lacking or weak.

Short-term "missions." Short-term missions began just after World War II with Operation Mobilization and Youth with a Mission and has grown dramatically over the last two or three decades. According to Mission Advanced Research Centre, 22,000 people were on short-term missions in 1979, and that rose to 120,000 in 1989, 250,000 in 1995, and 450,000 in 1998.

There has been a passionate debate about the benefits and drawbacks.[71] However, before we can summarize those, we have an important question to face: "Is this really missions?" This is not an unimportant or a nitpicking question! Earlier in this chapter I addressed the issue of the problems that arise when we simply call anything done overseas "missions." In fact, most of short-term work is not missions at all; it is cross-cultural partnership or serve-projects. (This is why I have placed "missions" in quotation marks in the title of this subsection.) This is not to diminish the importance and significance of this work. Once again: cross-cultural partnership is an important part of the mission of the church. Nevertheless, it is important to underscore the task of missions as the establishment of a witness to the gospel in life, deed and word where there is none or where it is weak.

---

[69]Quoted in Guthrie, *Missions in the Third Millennium*, p. 142.
[70]Ibid., p. 143.
[71]Two good resources for reading about the benefits and drawbacks of short-term missions are www.mislinks.org/practicing/short-term-missions and www.soe.org/explore/resources/short-term-mission-resources.

As one reads the vast literature detailing the benefits of short-term work, the following elements emerge: the worker personally benefits from becoming better aware of his or her own ethnocentrism, of the existence of the world church, and of cross-cultural practice; it may spark a lifelong commitment to missions or cross-cultural partnership that leads to vision, giving and prayer; there may be genuine benefits for the place and location where short-termers go in the form of service, gifts, resources for tasks; short-termers may encourage and aid long-term missionaries, cross-cultural workers and the national church if the project fits into long-term goals.

The drawbacks are equally evident: the time is brief, not allowing acquisition of effective knowledge of the language, culture, dynamics, needs, and so on, and thus long-term results are unlikely; it fits the quick-fix, task-oriented pattern of Western culture rather than the incarnational model of Jesus' mission; it is very expensive, draining money that could be used for long-term missions; it can sap the resources of missionaries or national church because the inability to speak the language or understand the culture requires the missionary's or local church's help; it reflects a culture in which a new generation seeks easy and immediate gratification, eschewing sacrifice and a long obedience in the same direction; it may actually do some damage if workers are culturally insensitive; sometimes such projects bypass national churches or missions.

But it is safe to say that short-term trips are here to stay, and so we need to use this mode in the most faithful way in God's mission. In 2003 the Fellowship of Short-Term Mission Leaders established some excellent standards, titled "U.S. Standards of Excellence in Short-Term Mission."[72] These standards, as they are fleshed out and used well, could be a tremendous benefit for churches involved in short-term work projects. The seven standards are:

- God-Centeredness: An excellent short-term mission seeks first God's glory and his kingdom.

- Empowering Partnerships: An excellent short-term mission establishes healthy, interdependent, on-going relationships between sending and receiving partners.

---

[72]Stands of Excellence in Short-Term Missions, "The 7 Standards" (www.soe.org/explore/the-7-standards).

- Mutual Design: An excellent short-term mission collaboratively plans each specific outreach for the benefit of all participants.

- Comprehensive Administration: An excellent short-term mission exhibits integrity through reliable set-up and thorough administration for all participants.

- Qualified Leadership: An excellent short-term mission screens, trains, and develops capable leadership for all participants.

- Appropriate Training: An excellent short-term mission prepares and equips all participants for the mutually designed outreach.

- Thorough Follow-Through: An excellent short-term mission assures debriefing and appropriate follow-through for all participants.

The skeptic will ask, "Is it possible to establish these standards on a short-term project, or does the very nature of such a project make it unrealistic or even impossible?" It is a legitimate question, but if short-term trips and projects are here for the long haul, then it is important to aim for these ideals.

CONCLUSION

The day of missions is not over. A certain era has passed, and we can both thank God for what was accomplished and assess critically the fruit of two centuries of labor with the criterion of the gospel. We still need to identify places and peoples where there is no church to reach them and then forge ahead in seeking new ways to carry out the task before us. But in all that we do, we remember that it is God's mission, and we simply offer our paltry gifts to witness to his salvation, to the ends of the earth, for his glory.

FURTHER READING

Engel, James F., and William A. Dyrness. *Changing the Mind of Missions: Where Have We Gone Wrong?* Downers Grove, IL: InterVarsity Press, 2000.

Guthrie, Stan. *Missions in the Third Millennium: 21 Key Trends for the 21st Century*. Milton Keynes, UK: Paternoster, 2000.

Moreau, A. Scott, Gary R. Corwin and Gary B. McGee. *Introducing World Missions: A Biblical, Historical, and Practical Survey*. Grand Rapids: Baker, 2004.

Steffen, Tom, and Lois McKinney Douglas. *Encountering Missionary Life and Work: Preparing for Intercultural Ministry.* Grand Rapids: Baker, 2008.

Van Rheenen, Gailyn. *Missions: Biblical Foundations and Contemporary Strategies.* Grand Rapids: Zondervan, 1996.

DISCUSSION QUESTIONS

1. Do you know where the money given for crosscultural missions in your church is going? What is the ratio of those sent to do missions and those engaged in crosscultural partnership? Do the statistics surprise you?

2. Discuss and weigh the value and pitfalls of short-term missions.

3. What new initiatives in missions today seem most promising? Why?

ESSAY TOPICS

1. Discuss the importance of making a distinction between mission and missions, between missions and crosscultural partnership.

2. Discuss how our legacy in crosscultural missions has handicapped us in rightly understanding missions today.

3. Evaluate the issue of mission societies today in both historical and theological terms. What is a way forward?

Sidebar Sources

CB

Anderson, Gerald. "Christian Mission in Our Pluralistic World." In *Practicing Truth: Confident Witness in Our Pluralistic World*, edited by Linford Stutzman. Scottdale, PA: Herald Press, 1999.

Bakke, Ray. *A Theology as Big as the City*. Downers Grove, IL: InterVarsity Press, 1997.

Bauckham, Richard. *Bible and Mission: Christian Witness in a Postmodern World*. Grand Rapids: Baker Academic, 2003.

Bavinck, J. H. *The Church Between Temple and Mosque*. Grand Rapids: Eerdmans, 1961.

———. *Impact of Christianity on Non-Christian World*. Grand Rapids: Eerdmans, 1949.

———. *An Introduction to the Science of Missions*. Grand Rapids: Baker, 1961.

Bevans, Stephen B., and Roger P. Schroeder. *Constants in Context: A Theology of Mission for Today*. Maryknoll, NY: Orbis, 2004.

Bosch, David J. *Believing in the Future: Toward a Missiology of Western Culture*. Valley Forge, PA: Trinity Press International, 1998.

———. *Transforming Mission: Paradigm Shifts in Theology of Mission*. Maryknoll, NY: Orbis, 1991.

———. *Witness to the World: The Christian Mission in Theological Perspective*. Atlanta: John Knox, 1980.

Conn, Harvie. "Do Other Religions Save?" In *Through No Fault of Their Own? The Fate of Those Who Have Never Heard*, edited by William V. Crockett and James G. Sigountos, pp. 195-208. Grand Rapids: Baker, 1991.

———. "The Missionary Task of Theology: A Love/Hate Relationship?" *Westminster Theological Journal* 45, no. 1 (1983): 1-21.

Engel, James F., and William A. Dyrness. *Changing the Mind of Missions: Where Have We Gone Wrong?* Downers Grove, IL: InterVarsity Press, 2000.

Flemming, Dean. *Recovering the Full Mission of God: A Biblical Perspective on Being, Doing and Telling*. Downers Grove, IL: IVP Academic, 2013.

Glaeser, Edward. *Triumph of the City*. New York: Penguin, 2011.

Grigg, Viv. *Cry of the Urban Poor*. Rev. ed. Waynesboro, GA: Authentic Media, 2004.

Hastings, Ross. *Missional God, Missional Church*. Downers Grove, IL: IVP Academic, 2012.

Hauerwas, Stanley, and William Willimon. *Resident Aliens*. Nashville: Abingdon, 1989.

International Congress on World Evangelization. "The Lausanne Covenant." 1974. www.lausanne.org/en/documents/lausanne-covenant.html.

Jenkins, Philip. *The Next Christendom: The Coming of Global Christianity*. New York: Oxford University Press, 2002.

Johnstone, Patrick. *The Future of the Global Church*. Downers Grove, IL: InterVarsity Press, 2011.

Kirk, J. Andrew. *What Is Mission? Theological Explorations*. Minneapolis: Fortress, 2000.

Kraemer, Hendrik. *Religion and the Christian Faith*. Cambridge, UK: James Clarke, 2002.

Marshall, I. Howard. *New Testament Theology: Many Witnesses, One Gospel*. Downers Grove, IL: IVP Academic, 2004.

Neill, Stephen. *Colonialism and Christian Missions*. New York: McGraw Hill, 1966.

Noll, Mark A. *The New Shape of World Christianity*. Downers Grove, IL: IVP Academic, 2009.

Noll, Mark A., and Carolyn Nystrom. *Clouds of Witnesses*. Downers Grove, IL: InterVarsity Press, 2011.

Mbiti, John. "Theological Impotence and the Universality of Church." In *Mission Trends 3*, edited by Gerald H. Anderson and Thomas F. Stransky, pp. 6-18. Mahwah, NJ: Paulist Press, 1976.

Netland, Harold. *Encountering Religious Pluralism*. Downers Grove, IL: InterVarsity Press, 2001.

Newbigin, Lesslie. "Baptism, the Church and Koinonia: Three Letters and a Comment." In *Religion and Society* 19, no. 1: 66-90.

———. *The Good Shepherd: Meditations on Christian Ministry in Today's World*. Grand Rapids: Eerdmans, 1977.

———. *The Gospel in a Pluralist Society*. Grand Rapids: Eerdmans, 1989.

———. *Mission and the Crisis of Western Culture*. Haddington, UK: Handsel Press, 1989.

———. *The Open Secret: An Introduction to the Theology of Mission*. Grand Rapids: Eerdmans, 1995.

———. *The Other Side of 1984: Questions for the Churches*. Geneva: World Council of Churches, 1983.

———. "Stewardship, Mission, and Development." Unpublished address given at the Annual Stewardship Conference of the British Council of Churches, Stanwick, June 1970.

———. *Trinitarian Faith and Today's Mission*. Atlanta: John Knox, 1964.

———. *A Word in Season: Perspectives on Christian World Missions*. Grand Rapids: Eerdmans, 1994.

Packer, J. I. "The Gospel: Its Content and Communication." In *Down to Earth: Studies in Christianity and Culture*, edited by J. R. W. Stott and R. Coote, pp. 100-103. Grand Rapids: Eerdmans, 1980.

Sanneh, Lamin. *Translating the Message*. Revised and expanded. Maryknoll, NY: Orbis, 2009.

———. *Whose Religion Is Christianity?* Grand Rapids: Eerdmans, 2003.

Schnabel, Eckhard. *Paul the Missionary*. Downers Grove, IL: InterVarsity Press, 2008.

"A Statement on the Missionary Calling of the Church." In *Missions Under the Cross: Addresses Delivered at the Enlarged Meeting of the Committee of the International Missionary Council at Willingen, in Germany, 1952; with Statements Issued by the Meeting*, ed. Norman Goodall, pp. 188-92. London: Edinburgh, 1953.

Verkuyl, Johannes. "The Biblical Notion of the Kingdom." In *The Good News of the Kingdom: Mission Theology for the Third Millennium*, edited by Charles Van Engen, Dean Gilliland and Paul Pierson, pp. 71-81. Maryknoll, NY: Orbis, 1993.

Walls, Andrew F. "Mission History as the Substructure of Mission Theology." *Swedish Missiological Themes* 93 (2005): 367-78.

———. *The Missionary Movement in Christian History*. Maryknoll, NY: Orbis, 1996.

Wright, Christopher J. H. *The Mission of God*. Downers Grove, IL: InterVarsity Press, 2006.

Wright, N. T. *The Challenge of Jesus*. Downers Grove, IL: InterVarsity Press, 1999.

Subject Index

Name Index

Scripture Index

Finding the Textbook You Need

The IVP Academic Textbook Selector
is an online tool for instantly finding the IVP books
suitable for over 250 courses across 24 disciplines.

_____

ivpacademic.com
_____